SECOND EDITION

MICROCOMPUTERS: CONCEPTS

LARRY LONG / NANCY LONG

PRENTICE HALL, Englewood Cliffs, New Jersey 07632

Library of Congress Cataloging-in-Publication Data

Long, Larry E.
    Microcomputers. Concepts / Larry Long, Nancy Long.—2nd ed.
       p.   cm.
    Includes index.
    ISBN 0-13-584525-4
    1. Microcomputers.   I. Long, Nancy.   II. Title.
QA76.5.L6557   1992
004.16—dc20   91-38150
                                       CIP

Acquisition Editor: P. J. McCue
Editor-in-Chief: Garret White
Production Editor: Nancy DeWolfe
Marketing Manager: Patti Arneson
Copy Editor: Nancy DeWolfe
Designer: David Levy
Cover Designer: Jerry Votta
Prepress Buyer: Trudy Pisciotti
Manufacturing Buyer: Bob Anderson
Page Layout: Diane Koromhas

MS-DOS® is a registered trademark of Microsoft Corporation;
Windows® is a trademark of Microsoft Corporation.

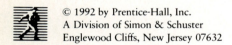

© 1992 by Prentice-Hall, Inc.
A Division of Simon & Schuster
Englewood Cliffs, New Jersey 07632

All rights reserved. No part of this book may be
reproduced, in any form or by any means,
without permission in writing from the publisher.

Printed in the United States of America
10 9 8 7 6 5 4 3 2 1

ISBN 0-13-584525-4 01

Prentice-Hall International (UK) Limited, *London*
Prentice-Hall of Australia Pty. Limited, *Sydney*
Prentice-Hall Canada Inc., *Toronto*
Prentice-Hall Hispanoamericana, S.A., *Mexico*
Prentice-Hall of India Private Limited, *New Delhi*
Prentice-Hall of Japan, Inc., *Tokyo*
Simon & Schuster Asia Pte. Ltd., *Singapore*
Editora Prentice-Hall do Brasil, Ltda., *Rio de Janeiro*

TO TROY AND BRADY, OUR SONS

OVERVIEW

Chapter 1	**MICROS AND PERSONAL COMPUTING**	3
Chapter 2	**INTERACTING WITH MICROS**	37
Chapter 3	**PROCESSORS AND PLATFORMS**	63
Chapter 4	**MICRO PERIPHERAL DEVICES: I/O AND DATA STORAGE**	91
Chapter 5	**TEXT AND IMAGE PROCESSING: WORD PROCESSING, DESKTOP PUBLISHING, AND GRAPHICS**	125
Chapter 6	**DATA MANAGEMENT: SPREADSHEET AND DATABASE**	165
Chapter 7	**DATA COMMUNICATIONS AND NETWORKS**	199

Chapter 8 MICROCOMPUTER SYSTEMS	233
Chapter 9 MICROCOMPUTERS AND SOCIETY	265
Appendix A MS-DOS TUTORIAL AND EXERCISES	282
Appendix B WINDOWS OVERVIEW	311
Appendix C BUYING MICROCOMPUTERS AND THEIR PERIPHERAL DEVICES	336
GLOSSARY	349
INDEX	369

CONTENTS

PREFACE TO STUDENT   xv

PREFACE TO INSTRUCTOR   xvii

Chapter 1 MICROS AND PERSONAL COMPUTING   3

1–1 The Information Society   4
     The Computer Revolution   4
     The Personal Computer Boom   5
     Why Are Micros So Popular?   5

1–2 Learning About Microcomputers   6
     Cyberphobia   6
     Computer Competency   6

1–3 Personal Computing   7
     Business and Domestic Applications for Personal Computing   7
     The Microcomputer Family of Productivity Software   8
     Information Services   14
     Expert Systems   16

1–4 Computers: Big, Small, and Very Small   17
     Micros versus Minis, Mainframes, and Supercomputers   17
     Microcomputers: Small but Powerful   19

1–5 Uncovering the "Mystery" of Computers   22
     What Is a Computer?   22
     How a Computer System Works   23

The Hardware 24
What Can a Computer Do? 25
Computer System Capabilities 25

1–6 Historical Perspective 26
Personal Computer Milestones 26
PC Software Milestones 28

SUMMARY OUTLINE AND IMPORTANT TERMS 31
REVIEW EXERCISES 33
SELF-TEST 34

▶ *Shareware: Affordable Software 10*

Chapter 2 INTERACTING WITH MICROS 37

2–1 Interacting with the System 38
2–2 The Disk Operating System (DOS) 39
PC Operating Systems 39
DOS Is the Boss 39

2–3 Microcomputer Operation 40
Installation of Hardware and Software 40
Power Up/Power Down 41
Entering Commands and Data 43
Levels of Command Interaction 49

2–4 User-Friendly Software 52
Help Commands 52
Windows 53
Graphical User Interfaces 54

2–5 Care and Maintenance of a Micro 54
2–6 Backup: Better Safe Than Sorry 56

SUMMARY OUTLINE AND IMPORTANT TERMS 58
REVIEW EXERCISES 60
SELF-TEST 60

Chapter 3 PROCESSORS AND PLATFORMS 63

3–1 A Bit About the Bit 64
3–2 Encoding Systems: Combining Bits to Form Bytes 65
3–3 Components of a Computer System: A Closer Look at the Processor and Primary Storage 66
Primary Storage 67
The Control Unit 69
The Arithmetic and Logic Unit 72
The Machine Cycle 72

3-4 Describing the Processor: Distinguishing Characteristics   73
   Word Length   74
   Processor Speed   74
   Capacity of RAM   74
   Running Several Programs Concurrently   75

3-5 Configuring a Microcomputer System   78
   A Typical Microcomputer Configuration   78
   Linking Micro Components   79
   Expansion Slots and Add-on Boards   81

3-6 Platforms   82
   The Single-User Environment   82
   The Multiuser Environment   84
   MCA versus EISA   84

SUMMARY OUTLINE AND IMPORTANT TERMS   85
REVIEW EXERCISES   88
SELF-TEST   88

▶ *The Computer on a Chip   70*

Chapter 4 MICRO PERIPHERAL DEVICES: I/O AND DATA STORAGE   91

4-1 I/O Devices: Our Interface with the Computer   92
   Input Devices: Getting Data into the System   92
   Output Devices: Computers Communicate with Us   100

4-2 Secondary Storage: Permanent Data Storage   108
   Primary and Secondary Storage   108
   Sequential and Direct Access: New Terms for Old Concepts   110
   Magnetic Disks: Rotating Storage Media   110
   Magnetic Tape: Ribbons of Data   116

4-3 Optical Laser Disks: High-Density Storage   117

SUMMARY OUTLINE AND IMPORTANT TERMS   120
REVIEW EXERCISES   122
SELF-TEST   122

Chapter 5 TEXT AND IMAGE PROCESSING: WORD PROCESSING, DESKTOP PUBLISHING, AND GRAPHICS   125

5-1 Word Processing   126
   Function   126
   Concepts   127
   Use   139

5-2 Desktop Publishing   142
    Function   142
    Concepts   142
    Use   148

5-3 Graphics   148
    Displaying and Printing Graphic Images   149
    Paint Software   150
    Draw Software   153
    Presentation Graphics   154
    Computer-Aided Design   158
    Screen Capture and Graphics Conversion   159

SUMMARY OUTLINE AND IMPORTANT TERMS   159
REVIEW EXERCISES   162
SELF-TEST   162

Chapter 6 DATA MANAGEMENT: SPREADSHEET AND DATABASE   165

6-1 Spreadsheet: The Magic Matrix   166
    Function   166
    Concepts   166
    Use   176

6-2 Database: Dynamic Data Tool   181
    Function   181
    Concepts   182
    Use   193

SUMMARY OUTLINE AND IMPORTANT TERMS   194
REVIEW EXERCISES   196
SELF-TEST   196

Chapter 7 DATA COMMUNICATIONS AND NETWORKS   199

7-1 Data Communications   200
    From One Room to the World   200
    Communications Software versus Other Micro Software   201

7-2 The Beginning of an Era: Cooperative Computing   202
    Intracompany Networking   202
    Intercompany Networking   202
    External Computing Support: Service via Computer   203
    Connectivity: Linking Hardware, Software, and Data Bases   204

7-3 Data Communications Hardware   204
    The Modem   205
    The Down-Line Processor   207
    The Front-End Processor   208

7-4 The Data Communications Channel: Data Highways   209
   Transmission Media   209
   Data Transmission in Practice   213

7-5 Data Transmission Services   213
   Common Carriers   213
   Specialized Common Carriers   214

7-6 Networks: Linking Computers and People   214
   Network Topologies   214
   The Micro/Mainframe Link   216

7-7 Local Area Networks   216
   LAN Defined   216
   LAN Hardware and Software   218
   Bridges and Gateways   221

7-8 Line Control: Communications Protocols   221
   Asynchronous Transmission   222
   Synchronous Transmission   223

7-9 Using Micro-Based Communications Software   223
   The Function of Communications Software   223
   Preparing for an Interactive Session with a Remote Computer   224
   Communications Software in Practice   226

SUMMARY OUTLINE AND IMPORTANT TERMS   228
REVIEW EXERCISES   230
SELF-TEST   231

Chapter 8 MICROCOMPUTER SYSTEMS   233

8-1 Types of Micro Systems   234
   Information Systems   234
   Decision Support Systems   237
   Expert Systems   238

8-2 The Systems Development Process   239
   Systems Analysis: Understanding the System   239
   Systems Design: A Science or an Art?   241
   Programming: Ideas Become Reality   246
   System Conversion and Implementation   251
   Post-Implementation Activities   253

8-3 Prototyping: Creating a Model of the Target System   254
   The Prototype System   255
   Creating the Prototype System   256

8-4 Computer and System Security   256
   Points of Vulnerability in the Micro Computing Environment   257
   Information Systems Security   259
   Level of Risk   259

SUMMARY OUTLINE AND IMPORTANT TERMS 259
REVIEW EXERCISES 261
SELF-TEST 262

Chapter 9 MICROCOMPUTERS AND SOCIETY 265

9–1 Computers: Can We Live Without Them? 266

9–2 Microcomputer Trends and Issues 268
    PC Trends 268
    PC Issues 272

9–3 Your Challenge 279

SUMMARY OUTLINE AND IMPORTANT TERMS 280
REVIEW EXERCISES 281
SELF-TEST 281

▶ *Computer Crimes: Categories and Techniques* 275

Appendix A MS-DOS TUTORIAL AND EXERCISES 282

A–1 Introduction 283

A–2 Files, Directories, and Paths 284
    Naming Files 284
    Referencing Files 284
    Directories and Subdirectories 284
    DOS, Directories, and Local Area Networks 286
    Wildcards 286

A–3 Booting the System 288

A–4 DOS Commands 289
    Internal and External Commands 289
    Changing the Active Disk Drive 289
    FORMAT: Preparing the Disk for Use 292
    Creating, Changing, and Removing a Directory 293
    Working with DOS Files and Directories 296

A–5 DOS Keyboard Functions 298
    Output Control Keys 298
    DOS Function Keys 299
    System Control Keys 301

A–6 Backup 301
    DISKCOPY: Copy an Diskette 301
    CHKDSK: Check the Disk 303

A–7 Batch Files 303
   The AUTOEXEC.BAT File 303
   Other Batch Files 304
   Creating and Executing Batch Files 304
   Modifying Batch Files 307

REVIEW EXERCISES 307
STEP-BY-STEP TUTORIAL EXERCISES 308
PRACTICE 308

▸ *Performing MS-DOS Tutorials on Diskette-Based Personal Computers* 283
▸ *Keystroke Conventions Used in the Step-by-StepTutorials* 287
▸ *DOS Command-Key Summary* 306

Appendix B WINDOWS OVERVIEW   311

B–1 About Windows 312
   What Is Windows? 312
   Non-Windows versus Windows Applications 313

B–2 Windows Concepts 314
   The Desktop 314

B–3 Windows Applications 323
   Program Manager 323
   File Manager 324

B–4 Windows Accessory Applications 328
   Write 328
   Paintbrush 328
   Terminal 329
   Desktop Software 330
   Games 331

B–5 Using Windows 331
   The Help Feature 332
   Switching Between Windows 332
   Transferring Information Between Applications 333
   Terminating an Application and a Windows Session 334
   Summary 334

REVIEW EXERCISES 335

Appendix C BUYING MICROCOMPUTERS AND THEIR PERIPHERAL DEVICES   336

C–1 Where to Buy PCs 337
   PC Retailers 337
   The "Perks" of Employment 338

C–2 Steps in Buying a Microcomputer   338
C–3 Factors to Consider When Buying a Micro   342
C–4 PC Buyer's Worksheet   345
REVIEW EXERCISES   348

GLOSSARY   349

INDEX   369

PREFACE TO STUDENT

In the past five years, microcomputers have experienced one giant leap in technology after another. The capabilities of these miniature miracles has blossomed to encompass everything from the routine to the exotic. The greatest change, however, is not in their technology but in their acceptance by potential users. People in every line of work and of every interest are now convinced that micros are a major force in society—a force to reckon with and therefore a force to be understood. This book and its supplements are designed to help you make effective use of micros and micro software in your academic pursuits, at home, and in your career.

Nine chapters offer a detailed look at microcomputer technology, operation, and applications. Three appendices provide a hands-on tutorial for MS-DOS (a micro operating system), a Windows (a graphical user interface) overview, and a microcomputer buyer's guide. The optional software skills modules enable you to learn to use and operate such popular microcomputer software packages as word processing, spreadsheet, and database.

Getting the Most from This Text

The layout and organization of the text, the skills modules, and their contents are designed to be interesting; to present concepts in a logical and informative manner; to provide a reference for the reinforcement of classroom lectures; and to provide you with an opportunity to get plenty of hands-on experience.

Reading a Chapter. A good way to approach each chapter is to

1. Look over the Student Learning Objectives.
2. Read the Summary and Important Terms.
3. Read over the major headings and subheadings and think about how they are related.
4. Read the chapter and note the important terms in **boldface** type and in *italic* type.
5. Relate photos and photo captions to the text. (A picture is worth a thousand words.)
6. Go over the Summary Outline and Important Terms again, paying particular attention to the boldface terms.
7. Take the Self-Test. Reread those sections that you do not fully understand.
8. Answer the questions in the Review Exercises.

Reading the Skills Modules and Completing the Step-by-Step Tutorials.
A good way to approach Appendix A, on MS-DOS, and each skills module is to

1. Review the skills module by thumbing through all the pages. Pay particular attention to the input/output examples to get a feel for software's function and what it looks like.
2. Read over the major headings and subheadings and think about how they are related.
3. Read the module and relate the text to the boxed step-by-step keystroke tutorials.
4. Review the module again. Reread those sections you do not fully understand.
5. Do the step-by-step keystroke tutorials. Check your progress frequently by referring to sample outputs in the book. (The hands-on exercises direct you to do the keystroke tutorials.)
6. Do the problem-solving exercises.

You, Computers, and the Future

Learning about micros and micro software is more than just education—it's an adventure! However, the microcomputer field is so dynamic that you have to run pretty fast just to stand still. When you complete this course, you will have acquired a base of knowledge that will enable you to race ahead of the pack.

Keep your course notes and this book because they will provide valuable reference material in other courses and in your career. The material addresses a broad range of microcomputer concepts and skills that frequently arise in other classes, at work, and even at home.

PREFACE TO INSTRUCTOR

WYNIWYG

Traditionally, when you examine a text, *w*hat *y*ou *s*ee *i*s *w*hat *y*ou *g*et—it's WYSIWYG. We are proud to offer a WYNIWYG (*w*hat *y*ou *n*eed *i*s *w*hat *y*ou *g*et) alternative:

***Microcomputers: Concepts*, Second Edition.**

- Covers microcomputer technology, operation, applications, and issues
- Includes an MS-DOS skills module, a Windows overview, and a micro buyer's guide

***Microcomputers: Concepts and Software*, Second Edition,** consists of two parts.

- Part I—*Microcomputers: Concepts*, Second Edition
- Part II—WordPerfect 5.1, Lotus 1-2-3 2.2, and dBASE III PLUS skills modules.

A Custom Lab Manual. You select those skills modules that meet your lab requirements then, if appropriate, you can add your personal touch.

We have designed a flexible text support package that, through custom publishing, can be tailored to meet your curriculum needs.

Microcomputers: Concepts, Second Edition, is the core text. It is designed to make the reader a knowledgeable consumer and user of microcomputers. Nine chapters contain a comprehensive coverage of microcomputer technology, operation, applications, and issues. Three appendices consist of an MS-DOS skills module, a Windows overview, and a microcomputer buyer's guide.

Microcomputers: Concepts and Software, Second Edition, combines the complete contents of *Microcomputers: Concepts* with hands-on skills modules for the three most widely used software packages in the academic environment—WordPerfect 5.1, Lotus 1-2-3 2.2, and dBASE III PLUS. Each skills module includes an *application description*, *step-by-step keystroke tutorials*, and *hands-on practice exercises*.

Upon successful completion of the tutorials and practice exercises, most students will have a solid intermediate-level foundation of skills adequate to meet their short- and long-term application needs. Those who wish to learn a software package's more exotic features will be ready to do so with ease. *Microcomputers: Concepts and Software* is spiral-bound to better accommodate the laboratory environment.

The custom lab manual is designed by you for your curriculum. Skills modules are available for MS-DOS, Windows, and a variety of popular word processing, spreadsheet, and database packages. Each skills module includes an *application description, step-by-step keystroke tutorials*, and *hands-on exercises*. **You** select the ones you need. Through custom publishing, Prentice Hall binds the applications software skills modules you selected. (Your Prentice Hall representative can provide details on publication deadlines.)

The initial skills modules offering reflects the need at this point in time. We and Prentice hall are committed to responding to your curriculum requirements and to the ever-changing software marketplace. If your lab needs are not met by the following initial skills modules offering, contact your local Prentice Hall representative to check on the status of the constantly evolving offering. If you need one or more skills modules that are not yet available, we will work with you to fulfill your lab requirements.

Initial Skills Modules Offering

MS-DOS

Word Processing	*Spreadsheet*	*Database*
WordPerfect 4.2	Lotus 1-2-3 2.2	dBASE III PLUS
WordPerfect 5.1	Quattro	dBASE IV
	Quattro Pro	

WINDOWS

Word Processing
WordPerfect for Windows

PREFACE TO INSTRUCTOR

Target Course

The target course for the *Microcomputers* books

- Provides comprehensive conceptual coverage of three or more of the following areas:
  Microcomputer technology
  Microcomputer operation
  Microcomputer applications
  Microcomputer issues
- Accommodates students from a broad spectrum of disciplines, interests, and career orientations.
- Provides hands-on laboratory instruction and practice in two or more of the following skills:
  MS-DOS
  Windows
  Word processing
  Spreadsheet
  Database
  BASIC programming

Computer Competency Today

Fifteen years ago we challenged our noncomputer students and professionals to acquire a *passive computer competency*; that is, we taught them enough about computers to enable them to articulate their automation and information processing requirements to computer specialists. Today passive computer competency is inadequate. Micros are everywhere. Graduates in computer *and* noncomputer fields are encouraged to exploit the potential of microcomputers; therefore, both must pursue an *active computer competency*. The material in this book and the accompanying applications software skills modules are designed to provide readers with an active computer competency. The student who successfully completes the course that uses components of the *Microcomputers* books is ready to use the power of micros and make informed decisions when faced with such micro-related situations as configuration, purchasing, and so on.

Features

Conceptual Coverage

- *Readability*. All elements are integrated with the text to create a reading and study rhythm that complements and reinforces learning.
- *Presentation style*. The text and all supplements are written in a style that remains pedagogically sound while communicating the energy and excitement of microcomputers to the student.

- *Currency-plus.* The material is more than current, it's "current-plus"—anticipating the emergence and implementation of computer technology.
- *Chapter pedagogy.* Chapter pedagogy is designed to facilitate learning (Student Learning Objectives, numbered section heads, highlighted terms, informative boxed features, Memory Bits, Summary Outline and Important Terms, Review Exercises, and a Self-Test).

Skills Modules

- *Flexibility.* Through custom publishing, you select the skills modules you need.
- *Practicality.* The material is designed to provide students with the understanding and skills they need to become productive users of micros and micro software.
- *Step-by-step tutorials.* Students learn applications software by working through carefully designed tutorials, one step at a time.
- *Guided learning.* The guided learning approach to step-by-step tutorials enables students to progress naturally from keystroke-by-keystroke demonstrations to problem solving.
- *Practice Exercises.* Each skills module contains a wide variety of problem-solving exercises.

The Skills Modules

Microcomputers: Concepts, Second Edition, contains the MS-DOS skills module. *Microcomputers: Concepts and Software,* Second Edition, contains MS-DOS plus skills modules for popular software packages. The custom lab manual contains as many skills modules as you need to meet your lab requirements. All skills modules follow the same pedagogical philosophy.

Pedagogical Philosophy

Learning effectiveness was a key consideration in the design of the skills modules, the premise being: *Students learn by doing.* We designed the modules to get the student on the microcomputer and enable him or her to see results as soon as possible. We do this at three levels of instruction.

1. *Step-by-step keystroke sequences.* Interspersed throughout the application description are *step-by-step* tutorial boxes that lead students, *keystroke-by-keystroke,* through demonstrations of features and procedures being discussed. We have developed a keystroke convention that enables users to progress rapidly through commands while focusing on the task at hand. This is in contrast to tutorials that force the user to extract keystrokes from wordy descriptions.

   Keystroke sequences, the first level of instruction, enable the reader to become familiar with the fundamentals of the operation and use of a particular package. The keystroke sequences expose the reader to the menu/command structure, and they demonstrate features,

functions, and common operations (word processing block moves, database queries, and so on).
2. *Guided completion.* Step-by-step keystroke sequences, the first level of instruction, can provide some much-needed assistance to a user who is learning new skills, but they can be (and often are) overused. A reader who sees only detailed keystroke sequences tends to rely on them rather than make the commitment to learn the software package. To foster learning and long-term understanding, we feel that the reader needs to be weaned away from keystroke sequences. We do this through guided completion, the second level of instruction.

   Guided completion is a pedagogical concept that works in tandem with the keystroke sequences. At this level instruction, students are presented with a combination of *keystroke sequences* and *task descriptions* in the step-by-step keystroke tutorials. The task descriptions address capabilities previously presented as keystroke sequences. They tell the student *what to do*, not *how to do it*. For example, prior to a demonstration of the List Files options, the reader might be asked, "Make A:WP the current directory and display its files (see Step 3.1)." At this point in the skills module, it is assumed that the student knows how to perform this task. Those who do not must refer again to the original discussion and the accompanying keystroke-by-keystroke presentation.
3. *Problem solving.* At the problem-solving level of instruction, the reader is given carefully constructed software-related problems that complement recent step-by-step tutorials. Except for occasional hints, the reader uses his or her own understanding of the software and imagination to solve the problem. These problems/exercises are placed at the end of the lab sessions.

The Teaching/Learning System

The *Microcomputers* books are the cornerstone of a comprehensive teaching/learning system. Other components of the system are described in the paragraphs that follow.

Instructor's Manual and Test Item File (IM&TIF). The IM&TIF contains lecture outlines for each chapter and appendix in the text, solutions to exercises, and the test item file.

Example Files Diskette. The example files diskette contains text and graphics that facilitate learning. The files are in two directories—one for the student and one for the instructor. The availability of student files shifts the focus away from time-consuming text entry to practice and learning the functional aspect of the software. For example, the text for a newsletter tutorial can be loaded from the example files diskette. The files on the instructor's directory reflect the end result of a particular series of step-by-step tutorials (for example, a fully formatted newsletter).

Test Item File Diskettes. The test item file diskettes are used in conjunction with Prentice Hall DataManager software and the hard copy in the IM&TIF.

Prentice Hall DataManager. The PH DataManager is an integrated IBM-PC–compatible test-generation and classroom-management software package. The package permits instructors to design and create tests, to maintain student records, and to provide practice testing for students.

Computerized Testing Service. This call-in service provides customized exams by return mail.

Color Transparency Acetates. Fifty color transparency acetates, which support material in the text, are offered to facilitate in-class explanation.

Educational Software. A variety of educational versions of commercial software packages are available through Prentice Hall. The list includes WordPerfect 4.2, Quattro, dBASE III PLUS, and Paradox 3.0. This list is dynamic and changes with the software marketplace. Your Prentice Hall representative has up-to-date information on the availability of software through Prentice Hall.

Video Software Tutorials—*The Video Professor*. This series includes video tutorials for MS-DOS, WordPerfect, Lotus 1-2-3, dBASE III PLUS, Microsoft Word, and others.

ABC News/Prentice Hall Video Library. This series offers documentary and feature-style stories on computers and computer technology from such award-winning news shows as *Nightline*.

SuperSoftware (IBM PC and Apple IIe). SuperSoftware is a dual-purpose educational software package. It is equally effective as a stand-alone interactive software package for students or as a teaching tool to demonstrate interactively a myriad of computer-related concepts, such as computers (configuring a micro), information processing (airline reservations), software (mail merge with word processing), and programming (sorting). SuperSoftware, which contains 60 hands-on lab activities, is designed to instruct, intrigue, and motivate.

BASIC for Introductory Computing. This booklet (90 pages) by Larry and Nancy Long can be purchased from Prentice Hall with the main text at nominal extra cost.

The New York Times/Prentice Hall Contemporary View Program. *The New York Times* and Prentice Hall are sponsoring A CONTEMPORARY VIEW: a program designed to enhance student access to current information of relevance in the classroom.

Through this program, the core subject matter provided in the text is supplemented by a collection of time-sensitive articles from one of the world's most distinguished newspapers, *The New York Times*. These articles demonstrate the vital, ongoing connection between what is learned in the classroom and what is happening in the world around us.

To enjoy the wealth of information of *The New York Times* daily, a reduced subscription rate is available in deliverable areas. For information, call toll-free: 1-800-631-1222.

Prentice Hall and *The New York Times* are proud to co-sponsor A CONTEMPORARY VIEW. We hope it will make the reading of both textbooks and newspapers a more dynamic, involving process.

This once-per-year compilation of approximately 20 pertinent and timely articles on computers and automation is available to students, and instructors get a free subscription to *The New York Times* for classroom use.

Author Hotline. If you have questions about the *Microcomputers* books, its package, or course planning, call us on the hotline. The telephone number is in the Instructor's Manual.

Acknowledgments

We talked personally with literally hundreds of professors about the evolution of microcomputer education and what they wanted for a text and as support material. Their collective comments have guided our thinking about content, organization, depth of coverage, and orientation. We would like to extend our deepest gratitude to these dedicated professionals. In addition, we wish to thank the many students who classroom-tested our approach to keystroke tutorials.

Microcomputers: Concepts, Second Edition, was signed, designed, and produced by our friends and colleagues at Prentice Hall. The key players in this process are respectively Ted Werthman, P. J. McCue, Nancy DeWolfe, Leah Jewell, and Patti Arneson. We are forever indebted to our Prentice Hall family for its contribution and its ongoing commitment to quality.

Literally hundreds of companies have in some way participated in the compilation of this book and its support package. A grateful academic community would like to thank them, one and all, for their ongoing commitment to education.

NANCY LONG, Ph.D.
LARRY LONG, Ph.D.

ABOUT THE AUTHORS

Dr. Larry Long, of Long and Associates, is a lecturer, author, consultant, and educator in the computer and information services fields. He has written over 25 books on a broad spectrum of computer/MIS-related topics from introductory computing, to programming, to MIS strategic planning. Dr. Long addresses a breadth of management, computer, and MIS issues in his executive seminars.

Dr. Long has served as a consultant to all levels of management in virtually every major type of industry. He has over 20 years of classroom experience at the University of Oklahoma, Lehigh University, and the University of Arkansas, where he continues to be an active lecturer. He received his Ph.D., M.S., and B.S. degrees in Industrial Engineering from the University of Oklahoma and holds certification as a C.D.P. and a Professional Engineer.

Dr. Nancy Long, also of Long and Associates, has coauthored a number of books with her husband. She has a decade of teaching and administrative experience at all levels of education: elementary, secondary, college, and continuing education. Dr. Long received a Ph.D in Reading Education and Educational Psychology, an M.S. in Personnel Services, and a B.S. in Elementary Education from the University of Oklahoma. Her wealth of knowledge in the areas of pedagogy and reading education is evident throughout the text and the supplements.

CHAPTER 1

MICROS AND PERSONAL COMPUTING

STUDENT LEARNING OBJECTIVES

▶ To grasp the scope of microcomputer understanding that a person would need to become an active participant in the computer revolution.
▶ To describe common applications of personal computing.
▶ To summarize the services available through commercial information services.
▶ To describe different types of microcomputers.
▶ To understand the fundamental components and operational capabilities of a microcomputer system.
▶ To put the technological development of personal computers into historical perspective.

1-1 THE INFORMATION SOCIETY

We are rapidly becoming an **information society**, a society in which workers focus their energies on providing a myriad of information services. Today every other person in the nation's work force is a **knowledge worker.** A knowledge worker's job revolves around the use, manipulation, and dissemination of information. By the turn of the century it is estimated that two out of three workers will be knowledge workers. The driving force behind our transition into an information society is the **computer**.

The Computer Revolution

In only four decades, computer technology has come a very long way. The first commercial computer was big enough to fill a gymnasium and was considered too expensive for all but the largest companies. Today we use small computers, called **microcomputers,** for all kinds of domestic and business applications. They are thousands of times faster and

Today we are rapidly becoming an information society where "knowledge workers" depend on computer-generated information to accomplish their jobs. These insurance adjusters use their personal computers to compile claims information.

more powerful than the first commercial computers. If the automobile industry had experienced similar progress, a new car would now cost less than a gallon of gas!

The *computer revolution* is upon us. The emergence of the small, powerful, and affordable microcomputer has brought computing to the personal level. To people in virtually every area of endeavor, microcomputers are becoming a *part of life*. With the rapid growth in the number and variety of computer applications, they are rapidly becoming a *way of life*. This book and its accompanying learning system will enable you to experience the adventure of computers *as you* learn skills that will make you an active participant in the computer revolution, both at work and at home.

The Personal Computer Boom

For the most part, a microcomputer is used by one person at a time. Therefore, the **micro** is also called a **personal computer**, or **PC** for short. The attention given by the media to these desktop miracles of technology was intense during their infant years—the late 1970s and early 1980s. Fear of falling behind the competition motivated businesses to purchase personal computers by the truckload. Parents hurried to buy a personal computer so little Johnny or Mary could march to the head of the class.

Unfortunately, businesses, parents, and others bought PCs with very little knowledge of what they do or what to do with them. In fact, the first personal-computer boom was actually a bust! A great many PCs were sold, but relatively few made significant contributions to businesses, homes, or educational institutions. Because they were misunderstood and did not live up to their fanfare, the buying public cooled toward PCs.

A decade later, these miniature marvels have vastly expanded capabilities, they are easier to use, and we have more realistic and informed expectations of them. Now people are educating themselves about the use and application of micros, and they are buying them with purpose and direction. The result is millions of micro enthusiasts.

Personal computers are everywhere, from kindergartens to corporate boardrooms. You can see them at work, at school, and possibly in your own home. The most recent boom has made it possible for people in every walk of life to see firsthand the usefulness of personal computers. Each passing month brings more power at less expense and an expansion of the seemingly endless array of microcomputer **software**. *Software* is a collective reference to internal instructions, called **programs**, that cause the computer to perform desired functions (for example, word processing).

Why Are Micros So Popular?

The relatively low cost and almost unlimited applications for the microcomputer have made it the darling of the business community. Fifteen years ago very few people had heard of a microcomputer. Now the num-

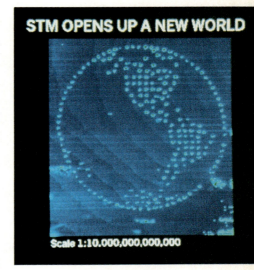

This is the world's smallest map. The image, which is magnified 13 million times, demonstrates that individual atoms can be moved across a surface and positioned with great accuracy. The scanning microscope used to draw this map was controlled by a computer similar to the ones you see on desktops in almost every office.

ber of microcomputers sold in one month exceeds the total number of computers in existence in the United States 15 years ago.

When you use a micro or personal computer, the capabilities of a complete computer system are at the your fingertips. Some are more powerful than computers that once handled the data processing requirements of large banks. Modern PCs and their support software are designed to be easy to use and understand. The wide variety of software available for microcomputers offers something for almost everyone, from video games to word processing, to education, to home finances, to inventory control.

A personal computer can be an electronic version of a scratch pad, a file cabinet, a drawing board, a teacher, a typewriter, a musical instrument, and even a friend. It can help you think logically, improve your spelling, select the right word, expand your memory, organize data, add numbers, and much more.

These reasons for the micro's popularity pale when we talk of the *real* reason for its unparalleled success—it is just plain fun to use, whether for personal, business, or scientific computing.

1-2 LEARNING ABOUT MICROCOMPUTERS

Cyberphobia

Computers are synonymous with change, and any type of change is usually met with some resistance. We can attribute much of this resistance to a lack of knowledge about computers and perhaps to a fear of the unknown. People seem to perceive computers as mystical, and it is human nature to fear what we do not understand, be it extraterrestrial beings or computers. Fear of the computer is so widespread that psychologists have created a name for it: **cyberphobia**. Cyberphobia is the irrational fear of, and aversion to, computers. In truth, computers are merely machines and do not merit being the focus of such fear. If you are a cyberphobic, you will soon see that your fears are unfounded.

Computer Competency

A decade ago most people were content to leave computers to computer professionals. At that time, the term **computer competency** had little meaning. Well, things have changed. Computers, especially personal computers, are becoming an integral part of our learning experience. By the time you complete this course, you should

1. Feel comfortable using a microcomputer.
2. Be able to make the computer work for you through judicious application of microcomputer software.
3. Be an intelligent consumer of microcomputer-related products and services.
4. Understand how microcomputers are changing society and how they will do so in the future.

Twenty years ago college curricula in architecture included little or no study of computers. Today architects rely on computers for everything from design to cost analysis. The computer has dramatically changed the way architects do their jobs. The same is true of hundreds of other professions.

You are about to embark on an emotional and intellectual *journey* that will stimulate your imagination, challenge your every resource from physical dexterity to intellect, and, perhaps, alter your sense of perspective. Learning about personal computers is more than just education—it's an adventure.

1-3 PERSONAL COMPUTING

A microcomputer sits easily on a desktop and can be controlled by *one person*. The growth of this kind of computing, called **personal computing**, has altered forever the way we approach our jobs, our education, and our domestic affairs. In a few years, personal computers will be as commonplace as telephones are now, both at home and at work.

Business and Domestic Applications for Personal Computing

Inexpensive microcomputers have made automation financially feasible for virtually any business environment. As a result, microcomputer software is available to support thousands of common and not-so-common business applications. There is, of course, an established need for applications such as payroll, accounting, sales analysis, project management, and inventory control. There are also hundreds of industry-specific software packages for thoroughbred breeding, for medical laboratories, for professional football teams, for pre-owned car dealers, and for just about any other area of business.

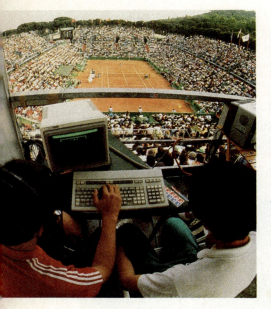

In professional tennis matches, a scorer familiar with tennis uses a microcomputer to enter data on each point played. After or during the match, information is summarized and displayed for coaches or television commentators. The statistics highlight each player's strengths, weaknesses, and patterns of play.

Domestic applications include some of the following: maintaining an up-to-date asset inventory of household items; storing names and addresses for a personal mailing list; maintaining records for, preparing, and sending income tax returns; creating and monitoring a household budget; keeping an appointment and social calendar; maintaining a prioritized things-to-do list; handling household finances (such as checkbook balancing, bill paying, and coupon refunding); letter writing; self-paced education; and, of course, entertainment. You can purchase software for all these applications, and you can probably obtain software for your special interest, whether it be astrology, charting biorhythms, composing music, or dieting.

The Microcomputer Family of Productivity Software

Thousands of commercially available software packages run on microcomputers, but the most popular is the family of productivity software packages (see Figure 1–1). The most widely used productivity packages include *word processing, desktop publishing, spreadsheet, graphics, database,* and *communications software.* In contrast to software designed for a *specific* application, these software packages are *general-purpose* and provide the framework for a great number of business and personal applications.

These software packages are often characterized as *productivity tools* because they help relieve the tedium of many time-consuming manual tasks. Thanks to *word processing software*, retyping is a thing of the past. *Desktop publishing software* makes it possible to produce near-typeset-quality copy for restaurant menus, newsletters, brochures, and a thousand other items without the expense of a commercial printer. *Spreadsheet software* permits us to perform certain arithmetic and logic operations without writing programs. Say goodbye to grid paper, plastic

Computers are revolutionizing legal practices. Rather than spending days researching any related cases in legal casebooks, this attorney uses key words to search a massive full-text data base containing more cases than any law office's library. A search of applicable "computer negligence" cases was completed in 20 minutes.

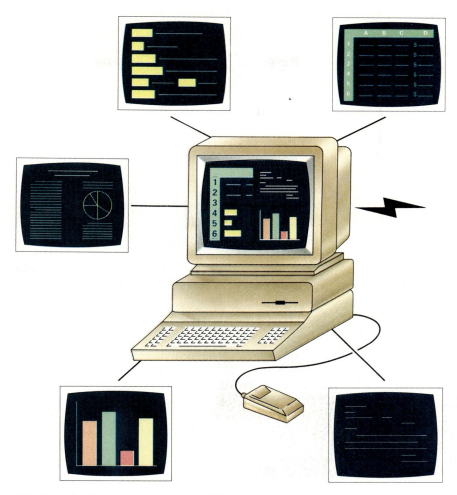

FIGURE 1–1 Microcomputer Productivity Software
Popular microcomputer productivity software packages include (clockwise from top left) database, electronic spreadsheet, communications, word processing, graphics, and desktop publishing.

templates, and the manual plotting of data: *Graphics software* prepares appealing images as well as pie and bar graphs without our drawing a single line. With *database software* we can format and create a data base in minutes. And *communications software* enables micro users to establish a communications link with other micros or with larger computers.

The functions, concepts, and uses of each of these micro software tools are discussed in some detail in Chapters 5, 6, and 7. The purpose of each of the micro productivity software packages is described briefly here.

Word Processing Software. **Word processing** is using the computer to enter text, to store it on magnetic storage media, to manipulate it in preparation for output, and to produce a **hard copy** (printed output).

Many applications involve written communications: letters, reports, memos, and so on. In addition to being one of the microcomputer productivity tools, word processing is also part of a set of applications collectively referred to as **office automation**. Office automation encompasses those computer-based applications associated with general office work.

If you use word processing to prepare your reports, you will have to key in the full draft only once. Revisions and corrections are made to a computer-based file before the report is printed in final form. If you forget a word or need to add a paragraph, you do not have to retype a page or, in the worst case, the whole report. For example, the original text for this book was keyed in only once on a microcomputer. Editorial changes were then entered by the authors on a keyboard before the final manuscript was submitted to the publisher. See Chapter 5, "Text and Image Processing: Word Processing, Desktop Publishing, and Graphics," for examples that illustrate the use of word processing software.

▶ SHAREWARE: AFFORDABLE SOFTWARE

Thousands of software authors have written a wide variety of excellent programs, from business graphics to trivia games. However, most of these authors do not have the funds to launch their creations in the commercial software marketplace. (A million-dollar marketing campaign would be considered minimal.) The alternative is to make their software available as *shareware*. Shareware is software that is readily available to PC users via electronic bulletin boards and other low-cost distribution channels.

Here is how shareware works. A PC user logs on (establishes a data communications link) to an electronic bulletin board, then downloads copies of the desired software to his or her system. Or, he or she can order shareware diskettes from any of the approximately 200 companies that specialize in its distribution. The user pays the same nominal amount for a diskette (from $1.75 to $5.00), whether it contains a spreadsheet program or clip art.

When you download or order shareware, it is implied that you register the software with the developer if you like it and intend to use it. The registration fees vary from $10 for utility programs to $100 for full-feature word processing packages. Software developers use several methods to encourage the registration of their software. At a minimum, the developers provide technical support and update information to registered users. Some shareware is distributed with only start-up documentation: Complete documentation is sent to registered users. Some shareware developers make enhancements available to registered users.

A relatively small amount of the software available through electronic bulletin boards and software distribution companies is *public-domain software*. Public-domain software need not be registered.

The Software Labs, one of the largest distributors of shareware, offers almost 2000 diskettes full of shareware and public-domain software. Software authors submit their creations to a shareware distributor such as The Software Labs and are compensated when they receive fees from users who register their software.

The wide variety of shareware now available includes programs that print signs and banners, help you with your taxes, teach you to speak Japanese, help you manage projects, provide access to many delicious recipes, and suggest lottery numbers. You also can get complete systems for church accounting, stamp collection, billing and invoicing, and investment management. Full-featured packages for word processing, spreadsheet, database, and graphics, along with scores of games from golf to martial arts, are available at a relatively low cost.

Desktop Publishing Software. The ultimate extension of word processing is **desktop publishing (DTP)**. In fact, some are calling desktop publishing software the next generation of word processing software. Desktop publishing refers to the capability of producing *near-typeset-quality copy* from equipment that sits on a desktop. Desktop publishing is changing the way companies, government agencies, and individuals print newsletters, brochures, user manuals, pamphlets, periodicals, greeting cards, and thousands of other items.

Traditionally, drafts of documents to be printed are delivered to commercial printers to be typeset. Desktop publishing has made it possible to eliminate this expensive typesetting process for those documents that require only near-typeset quality. In practice, near-typeset-quality copy is acceptable for most printed documents. The output of the desktop publishing process is called *camera-ready copy.* Duplicates of the camera-ready copy are reproduced by a variety of means, from copy machines to commercial processing.

The primary focus of desktop publishing software is page composition. DTP users integrate text, graphics, photos, and other elements into a visually appealing *page layout.* Generally, the text and graphics used by DTP during the page composition process are generated with the help of word processing and graphics software. See Chapter 5 for examples that illustrate the use of desktop publishing software.

Spreadsheet Software. **Spreadsheet software** provides a computer-based version of the traditional accountant's spreadsheet. Both enable the user to work with a tabular structure of rows and columns. But instead of writing the entries manually in the rows and columns on a paper spreadsheet, the user has them stored in an electronic version that can contain thousands of entries.

The applications of spreadsheet software are endless: Think of anything that has rows and columns. For example, spreadsheet software is used frequently for income statement analysis, home budgeting, sales forecasting, and grade reporting.

The intersection of a row and column is called a **cell** and is referred to by its position within the matrix. In an income statement, for example, the entry in Cell A1 (the first, or A, column, Row 1) might be "Net sales," and the entry in Cell B1 might be "$183,600."

	A	B	C
1	Net sales	$183,600	
2	Cost of goods sold	$116,413	

Notice that columns are lettered and rows numbered. Cell entries can be either words or numbers. See Chapter 6, "Data Management: Spreadsheet and Database," for examples that illustrate the use of spreadsheet software.

Once the data are entered for an income statement, spreadsheet software permits the user to manipulate and analyze the data. For example, an accountant can use spreadsheet capabilities to forecast profit for the coming year by electronically revising the current income statement to reflect anticipated growth.

Graphics Software. **Graphics software** enables you to create line drawings, art, and presentation graphics. Simple black-and-white drawings or elaborate multicolor drawings can be produced with graphics software and an input device called a **mouse**. Among other things, the mouse permits the entry of curved lines. Graphics software is the paintbrush of computer art, now a well-accepted form of artistic expression.

Presentation graphics usually take the form of *bar*, *pie*, and *line* graphs. Often the graphs are based on data in a data base or a spreadsheet. A pie graph is easily produced from a spreadsheet containing regional sales data. Each slice of the pie might depict the sales for each region as a percentage of total sales. The slices are in proportion. For example, if sales in the northeast region are $10 million and sales in the southwest region, $5 million, the northeast region's slice is twice the size of the southwest region's. See Chapters 5 and 6 for examples that illustrate the use of graphics software.

Database Software. **Database software** permits the user to create and maintain a data base and to extract information from the data base. *Database* as one word is commonly used to refer to database software. *Data base* as two words refers to the highest level of the hierarchy of data organization. Data organization is discussed in Chapter 6.

With database software, the user first identifies the format of the data, then designs a display-screen format that permits interactive entry and revision of the data. Once a record (for each salesperson, for example) is part of the data base, it can be displayed, revised, added, or deleted. The user also can retrieve and summarize data based on certain criteria. For example, a sales manager might request a display of all salespeople over quota for July. In addition, data can be sorted for display in a variety of formats. For example, the sales manager might request a printed list of salespeople by total sales, highest sales first, and another listing alphabetically by last name. See Chapter 6 for examples that illustrate the use of database software.

Communications Software. **Communications software** transforms a micro into an "intelligent" **video display terminal**, or **VDT**. A VDT, or **terminal**, is a televisionlike video screen, called a **monitor**, with a typewriterlike **keyboard** that enables remote communication with a computer. A micro, however, can do more than a VDT. Not only can a micro transmit to and receive data from a remote computer, it can process and store data as well. A terminal with processing capability is said to be *intelligent*.

Communications software automatically *dials up* the desired remote computer (perhaps your company's central computer system) and logs on; that is, the software establishes a communications link with the remote computer, usually via a telephone line. Once on-line, you can communicate with the remote computer or request that certain data be

Microcomputers and productivity software have become fixtures in every business environment. At this bank, staffers use their micros in combination with word processing, graphics, and desktop publishing software to turn out better looking sales proposals in less time.

transmitted to your micro so you can work with the data using the micro as a *stand-alone computer*.

Communications software enables you to log onto a commercial information service and make an airline reservation, pay a bill, send a note to a friend, or play a game. These are just a few of the many services provided by an information service. See Chapter 7, "Data Communications and Networks," for examples that illustrate the use of communications software.

Productivity Software Summary. In each productivity software category there are dozens of commercially available software packages from which to choose. The software packages within each category accomplish essentially the same functions. They differ primarily in the scope and variety of the special features they have to offer and in their "user-friendliness."

One of the advantages of micro productivity software packages is that they can work together to provide users with an even greater processing capability. For example, a manager might use several micro productivity software packages to handle a variety of administrative duties. To track product sales by region, a manager might use electronic spreadsheet software. At the end of each week the manager might summarize and plot sales data in a bar graph. Based on the results of the bar graph, the manager might write a memo recommending that the top field sales representatives be considered for special recognition. Using communications software, the manager can transmit both the graph and the memo of

Computers can help us read and understand poetry. Robert Browning's poem "Meeting at Night" can be highlighted to demonstrate the concept of parenthetical rhyme. An aspiring poet can examine this and other attributes of Browning's classic as well, such as metrical accent.

The functions of many traditional office fixtures can be performed by a desktop PC, such as typewriters and opaquing fluid, calculators, notepads and worksheets, drawing equipment, telephone indices, calendars, tickler files, filing cabinets, important reports and memos, and reference books such as a dictionary or thesaurus. The beverage glass and coffee cup, however, will continue to occupy their place on the desktop.

> **MEMORY BITS**
>
> *Microcomputer Productivity Packages*
> - Word processing
> - Desktop publishing
> - Spreadsheet
> - Graphics
> - Database
> - Communications

commendation to the company's central computer system for distribution to appropriate vice presidents. (This type of transmission—micro to another computer—is called **uploading**. The reverse is called **downloading**.) This example illustrates how the capabilities of the individual software packages complement the capabilities of the others.

Many commercial software vendors offer packages that integrate two or more of the major productivity tools. These packages are referred to as **integrated software**. A popular combination includes electronic spreadsheet, database, and graphics capabilities. Several integrated packages include all but desktop publishing. Integrated software permits us to work as we always have, on several projects at a time, but with the assistance of a computer.

Information Services

Personal computers normally are used as *stand-alone computer systems* but, as we have seen from earlier discussions, they also can double as *remote terminals*. This *dual-function* capability provides you with the flexibility to work with the PC as a stand-alone system or to link with a larger computer and take advantage of its increased capability. With a PC, you have a world of information at your fingertips. In addition, the personal computer can be used in conjunction with the telephone system to transmit data to and receive data from a commercial **information service** (also called an *information network*).

A growing trend among personal computer enthusiasts is to subscribe to a commercial information service, such as CompuServe, The Source, Prodigy, Dow Jones News/Retrieval Service, Western Union, and NewsNet. The largest information service, CompuServe, now has over 200,000 subscribers. Next is The Source. These information services have one or several large computer systems that offer a variety of information services, from hotel reservations to daily horoscopes. In addition to a micro, all you need to take advantage of these information services is a **modem** (the interface between the telephone line and a micro), a telephone line, and a few dollars. You normally pay a one-time fee. For the fee, you get a **password** and **personal identification number** (**PIN**) that permit you to establish a communications link with the service. You also are given a booklet that lists the telephone numbers you would dial to establish a link with the information service. If you live in a medium-to-large city, the telephone number you would dial is usually local. Your bill is based on how much you use the information service.

The following list summarizes the types of services available commercially.

- *Home banking.* Check your account balances, transfer money, and pay bills in the comfort of your home or office.
- *News, weather, sports.* Get the latest releases directly from the wire services.
- *Entertainment.* Read reviews of the most recently released movies, videos, and records. Chart your biorhythms or ask the advice of an astrologer.

- *Games.* Hundreds of single-player games, such as digital football, and multiplayer games, such as MegaWars, are available. You can even play a game of chess with a friend in another state! Or you might prefer to match wits with another trivia buff.
- *Financial information.* Get up-to-the-minute quotes on stocks, securities, bonds, options, and commodities. You also can use this service to help you manage a securities portfolio and to keep tax records.
- *Brokerage services.* Purchase and sell securities 24 hours a day from your microcomputer.
- *Bulletin boards.* Use special-interest electronic bulletin boards as a forum for the exchange of ideas and information. Information services have hundreds of **bulletin-board systems** (**BBS**s) to choose from on topics ranging from gardening, to astrology, to IBM personal computers, to wine, to human sexuality, to computer art, to aviation, to graphics showing the FBI's most wanted fugitives.

    There are thousands of privately sponsored bulletin-board systems. The Clean Air BBS focuses on health and smoking topics. The U.S. Census Bureau sponsors several BBSs. People looking for jobs might scan the listings on the Employ-Net BBS. Catch up on which fish are biting and which are not by tapping into the Fly-Fishers Forum BBS. The do-it-yourselfer might want to log onto the Popular Mechanics Online BBS. Enter your own movie review on the Take 3 BBS. Lawyers talk with one another on the Ye Olde Bailey BBS. A Denver BBS is devoted to parapsychology. Some senators and members of Congress sponsor BBSs to facilitate communication with their constituents. A number of BBSs are devoted to religious topics.
- *Electronic mail.* Send **electronic mail** to and receive it from other users of the information service. Each subscriber is assigned an ID and an electronic mailbox. **E-mail**, another name for electronic mail, sent to a particular subscriber can be "opened" and read only by that subscriber.
- *Shop at home.* Select what you want from a list of thousands of items offered at discount prices. Unless you plan on ordering an automobile or a truck, your order is delivered to your doorstep. Payment may be made via **electronic funds transfer** (**EFT**); that is, money is exchanged electronically between your account and that of the shopping service.
- *Reference.* Look up items of interest in an electronic encyclopedia. Scan through various government publications. Recall articles on a particular subject from dozens of newspapers, trade periodicals, and newsletters. Students seeking a college might want to query the service for information about certain schools.
- *Education.* Choose from a variety of educational packages, from learning arithmetic to preparing for the Scholastic Aptitude Test (SAT). You can even determine your IQ!
- *Real estate.* Moving? Check out available real estate by scanning the listings for the city to which you are moving.
- *Home.* Use your micro to access thousands of culinary delights. For

An information network includes such services as electronic mail, electronic shopping, and news.

The microcomputer has made it possible for millions of people to work at home. This real estate agent is using her microcomputer and an on-line multilist service to plan tomorrow's showings for her clients.

example, if you're hungry for a particular type of cuisine, enter appropriate descriptors to obtain a recipe (for example: entree, Spanish, rice, crab).

- *Health.* Address medical questions to a team of top physicians. Diagnose your own illness while interacting with an on-line expert system. Plan and monitor your next diet.
- *Travel.* Plan your own vacation or business trip. You can check airline, train, and cruise schedules and make your own reservations. You can even charter a yacht in the Caribbean, locate the nearest bed-and-breakfast inn, or rent a lodge in the Rockies.

These and many other time-saving applications eventually should make personal computers a "must-have" item in every home and office.

Expert Systems

One of the fastest-growing applications for microcomputers is the **expert system.** Expert systems are part of the general area of research known as **artificial intelligence** (**AI**). Expert systems provide "expert" advice and guidance on a wide range of topics, from locomotive maintenance to surgery. An expert system is interactive—it responds to questions, asks for clarification, makes recommendations, and generally helps in the decision-making process. In effect, interacting with an expert system is like talking to a well-informed partner.

At the heart of an expert system is a **knowledge base**. A knowledge base is created by **knowledge engineers**, who translate the knowledge of human experts into rules and strategies. A knowledge base is heuristic; that is, it provides the expert system with the capability of recommending directions for user inquiry. It also encourages further investigation

This financial analyst relies on historical and predictive data as well as up-to-the-second stock trading information. He sometimes requests a second opinion from an expert system before advising his clients.

into areas that may be important to a certain line of questioning but not apparent to the user.

A knowledge base grows because it "learns" from user feedback. An expert system learns by "remembering": It stores past occurrences in its knowledge base. For example, a recommendation that sends a user on a "wild goose chase" is thereafter deleted as a workable strategy for similar future inquiries. Expert systems simulate the human thought process. To varying degrees, they can reason, draw inferences, and make judgments.

Microcomputer-based expert systems have fared well against expert human physicians in the accuracy of their diagnoses of illnesses. Other expert systems help crews repair telephone lines, financial analysts counsel their clients, computer vendors configure computer systems, and geologists explore for minerals. Look for expert systems to play a major role in the integration of microcomputers into the workplace.

> ▶ MEMORY BITS
>
> *Personal Computing*
> - Business and domestic applications
> - Productivity software
> - Information services
> - Expert systems

1-4 COMPUTERS: BIG, SMALL, AND VERY SMALL

Micros versus Minis, Mainframes, and Supercomputers

All computers, no matter how small or large, have the same fundamental capabilities—*processing*, *storage*, *input*, and *output*. The four basic categories of computers are listed here in ascending order of their processing capabilities:

- Microcomputer system
- Minicomputer system
- Mainframe computer system
- Supercomputer system

This supercomputer, which is one of the world's fastest computers, has the processing power of thousands of microcomputers. If computer technology continues to advance at the same pace, we may well see this power on a desktop within the next 10 to 15 years.

It should be emphasized that these are relative categories, and what people call a minicomputer system today may be called a microcomputer system at some time in the future.

Micros are computer systems. **Minicomputers**, **mainframes**, and **supercomputers** are computer systems. Each offers many **input** and **output** alternatives; that is, ways to enter data to the system and present information generated by the system. In addition, each is supported by a wide variety of packaged software. There are, of course, obvious differences in size and capabilities. Everything associated with minicomputers, mainframes, and supercomputers is larger in scope than that associated with microcomputers: Execution of programs is faster; disk storage has more capacity; printer speeds are faster. Computers in these three categories can service many terminals and, of course, they cost more. (Interestingly, the execution of a million instructions costs more on a mainframe computer than on a microcomputer!)

Besides size and capability, the single most distinguishing characteristic of minicomputers, mainframe computers, and supercomputers is the manner in which each type is used. The three larger computers, with their expanded processing capabilities, provide a computing resource that can be shared by many people. In contrast, most microcomputers are used by one user at a time. It is common in a company for the finance, personnel, and accounting departments to share the resources of a mini, mainframe, or supercomputer, possibly all at the same time.

Microcomputers: Small but Powerful

Microprocessors. Here is a tough one. What is smaller than a dime and found in wristwatches, sewing machines, and jukeboxes? The answer: a **microprocessor**. Microprocessors play a very important role in our lives. You probably have a dozen or more of them at home and may not know it. They are used in telephones, ovens, televisions, thermostats, greeting cards, automobiles, and, of course, personal computers.

The microprocessor is a product of the microminiaturization of electronic circuitry; it is literally a "computer on a chip." **Chip** refers to any self-contained integrated circuit. The size of chips, which are about 30 thousandths of an inch thick, vary in area from fingernail size (about ¼-inch square) to postage-stamp size (about 1-inch square). The first fully operational microprocessor was demonstrated in March 1971. Since that time, these relatively inexpensive microprocessors have been integrated into thousands of mechanical and electronic devices—even elevators, band saws, and ski-boot bindings. In a few years virtually everything mechanical or electronic will incorporate microprocessor technology into its design.

Microcomputers. There is no commonly accepted definition of a microcomputer or, for that matter, of a minicomputer or a supercomputer. A microcomputer is just a small computer. However, it is a safe bet that any computer you can pick up and carry is probably a micro. But do not be misled by the *micro* prefix. You can pick up and carry some very powerful computers!

> ▶ **MEMORY BITS**
> *Categories of Computer Systems*
> - Microcomputer system
> - Minicomputer system
> - Mainframe computer system
> - Supercomputer system

The component that houses the processing and storage capabilities of this high-end microcomputer is designed to rest on the floor. It is sometimes difficult to distinguish the appearance and functionality of this system from some low-end minicomputers.

The microprocessor is sometimes confused with its famous offspring, the microcomputer. A keyboard, video monitor, and memory were attached to the microprocessor; power was added and the microcomputer was born! Suddenly, owning a computer became an economic reality for individuals and small businesses.

The system board. In a microcomputer, the microprocessor, the electronic circuitry for handling input/output signals from the **peripheral devices** (keyboard, printer, and so on), and the memory chips are mounted on a single circuit board called a **system board**, or **motherboard**. Before being attached to the system board, the microprocessor and other chips are mounted onto a **carrier**. Carriers have standard-sized pin connectors that allow the chips to be attached to the system board.

The system board, the "guts" of a microcomputer, is what distinguishes one microcomputer from another. The central component of the system board, the microprocessor, is not made by the manufacturers of micros but by companies, such as Motorola and Intel, that specialize in the development and manufacture of microprocessors. All of Apple's Macintosh-series micros use Motorola chips: the Motorola 68000 in earlier models, the Motorola 68020 in the Macintosh II, and the Motorola 68030 in recent models.

The system board for the original IBM PC, the IBM PC/XT, and most of the IBM-PC compatibles manufactured through 1984 used the Intel 8088 microprocessor chip. The Intel 8088 chip is a slower version of the Intel 8086, which was developed in 1979. At the time of the introduction of the IBM PC (1981), the Intel 8086 was thought to be too advanced for the emerging PC market. Ironically, the more powerful Intel 8086 chip was not used in micros until the introduction of the low-end models of the IBM PS/2 series in 1987. The 8086 is considered the

The system board (in the man's hand) controls all activity within a microcomputer. This system board contains an Intel 486 microprocessor.

base technology for all microprocessors used in IBM-PC–compatible and PS/2 series computers. The IBM PC/AT (Advanced Technology), which was introduced in 1984, employed an Intel 80286 microprocessor. As much as six times faster than 8088, the 80286 provided a substantial increase in PC performance. High-end IBM-PC–compatible micros and PS/2s use the more advanced Intel 80386 and 80486 chips. When someone talks about a "286," "86," or "486" machine, he or she is referring to a micro that uses an Intel 80286, 80386, or 80486 chip.

The *SX* versions of Intel chips, such as the 386SX and 486SX, are less expensive and less powerful than the processors upon which they are based. Intel plans to introduce the 80586 and the 80686 during the first half of the 1990s. The performance of the 586 chip is expected to be double that of the 486. The 686 chip is being designed to accommodate multimedia applications that involve sound and motion video.

After the microprocessor and other chips have been mounted on the system board, it is simply inserted in the slot designed for the system board. The processing components of most micros are sold with several empty **expansion slots** so you can purchase and plug in optional capabilities in the form of **add-on boards**. Add-on boards are discussed in more detail in Chapter 3, "Processors and Platforms."

Pocket, laptop, and desktop PCs. Personal computers come in four different physical sizes: **pocket PCs**, **laptop PCs**, **desktop PCs**, and **tower PCs**. The pocket and laptop PCs are light (a few ounces to about 15 pounds), compact, and can operate without an external power source, so they earn the "portable" label as well. There are also some "transportable" desktop PCs on the market, but they are more cumbersome. They fold up to about the size of a small suitcase, weigh about 25 pounds, and require an external power source. Desktop PCs and tower PCs are not designed for frequent movement and therefore are not considered portable. Typically, the monitor is positioned on top of the processing component of a desktop PC. The processing component of the tower PC is designed to rest on the floor, usually beside or under a desk. The tower PC resembles the processing component of a desktop PC that has been placed on end.

The power of a PC is not necessarily directly related to its size. A few laptop PCs can run circles around some of the desktop PCs. Some user conveniences, however, must be sacrificed to achieve portability. For instance, the miniature keyboards on pocket PCs, sometimes called **palmtop PCs**, make data entry and interaction with the computer difficult and slow. The only display screen available on most laptop PCs is monochrome (as opposed to color). Portable computers take up less space and, therefore, have a smaller capacity for permanent storage of data and programs.

Multiuser micros. In the early 1960s mainframe computer systems could service only one user at a time. By the mid-1960s technological improvements had made it possible for computers to service several users simultaneously. Now, a quarter century later, some mainframes service thousands of users at the same time!

Some people take their computers with them wherever they go. This high-performance palmtop computer can run the same applications as its desktop cousin.

▶ **MEMORY BITS**

Types of Personal Computers
- Pocket PC or palmtop PC
- Laptop PC
- Desktop PC (transportable)
- Desktop PC (stationary)
- Tower PC

When searching for a personal computer, this medical sales representative identified portability as her primary criterion. She purchased a laptop PC because it gave her the flexibility to carry her files and the power of a computer wherever she goes. During a flight to Chicago, she decided to review physician profiles before making sales calls.

This insurance agent frequently visits the homes of prospective clients. He uses his transportable PC to give them on-the-spot analysis of the risk posture. To prepare the computer for movement, he fastens the keyboard in position to cover the monitor and attaches a handle to the top of the micro.

We can draw a parallel between what happened to the mainframe in the 1960s and what is happening to microcomputers today. Until recently micros were "personal" computers—for individual use only. But technological improvements have been so rapid that it has become difficult for a single user to tap the full potential of state-of-the-art micros. To tap this unused potential, hardware and software vendors are marketing products that permit several people to use the system at once.

These **multiuser micros** are configured with as many as a dozen VDTs. These terminals, often located in the same office, share the microcomputer's resources and its peripheral devices. With a multiuser micro, a secretary can transcribe dictation at one terminal while a manager does financial analysis at another terminal and a clerk enters data to a data base at yet another. All this can take place at the same time on the same multiuser micro. Multiuser microcomputer systems are installed in thousands of small businesses, from hardware stores to veterinarians' offices.

1–5 UNCOVERING THE "MYSTERY" OF COMPUTERS

What Is a Computer?

The word *computer* is an integral part of just about everyone's daily-use vocabulary. But to many people it is some kind of miraculous black box. Technically speaking, the computer is any counting device. But in the

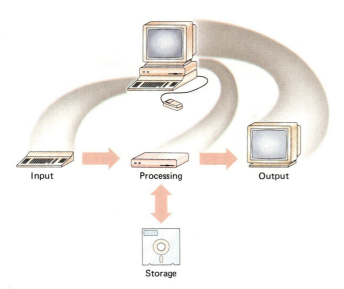

FIGURE 1-2 The Four Fundamental Components of a Microcomputer System
In a microcomputer system, the storage and processing components often are contained in the same physical unit. In the illustration, the diskette storage medium is inserted into the unit that contains the processor.

context of modern technology, we define the computer as *an electronic device capable of interpreting and executing programmed commands for input, output, computation, and logic operations.*

Computers may be technically complex, but they are conceptually simple. The microprocessor is the "intelligence" of a **computer system**. A computer system—any computer system—has only four fundamental components: *input, processing, output,* and *storage*. Note that a *computer system*, not a computer, has four components. The actual computer is the processing component and is combined with the other three to form a computer system (see Figure 1-2).

How a Computer System Works

A computer system can be compared to the biological system of the human body. Your brain, which is the processing component, is linked to the other components of the body by the central nervous system. Your eyes and ears are input components that send signals to the brain. If you see someone approaching, your brain matches the visual image of this person with others in your memory (storage component). If the visual image is matched in memory with that of a friend, your brain sends signals to your vocal chords and right arm (output components) to greet your friend with a hello and a handshake. Computer system components interact in a similar way.

The payroll system in Figure 1-3 illustrates how data are entered and how the four computer system components interact to produce information (such as a "year-to-date overtime report") and the payroll checks.

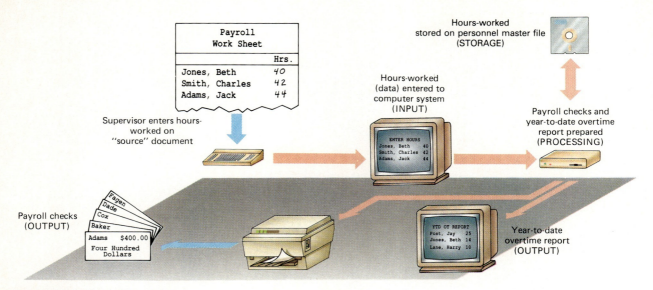

FIGURE 1-3 Payroll System
This microcomputer-based payroll system illustrates input, storage, processing, and output.

The hours-worked data are *input* to the system and are *stored* on the personnel **master file**. The payroll master file is a collection of **records**, each of which contains data about a particular employee. Note that the storage component of a computer system stores data, not information! **Data** (the plural of *datum*) are the raw material from which information is derived. **Information** is data that have been collected and processed into a meaningful form.

The payroll checks are produced when the *processing* component executes a program. In this example, the employee record is recalled from storage, and the pay amount is calculated. The *output* consists of the printed payroll checks. Other programs extract data from the personnel master file to produce a year-to-date overtime report and any other information that might help in the decision-making process.

The Hardware

In the microcomputer-based payroll example (see Figure 1-3), data are entered (input) on a *keyboard* and displayed (output) on a *monitor*. The payroll checks are then printed on a device called a **printer.** Data are stored for later recall on **magnetic disk**. Normally a microcomputer's magnetic disk storage and processing capabilities are housed in the same physical unit. There are a wide variety of **input/output (I/O)** and storage devices. The variety of hardware devices that make up a microcomputer system are discussed in detail in Chapter 4, "Micro Peripheral Devices: I/O and Data Storage."

CHAPTER 1 Micros and Personal Computing

What Can a Computer Do?

The previous section discussed how the *input/output* and *data-storage* hardware components are configured with the *processing* component to make up a computer system (see Figure 1–2). The focus of this section is on the operational capabilities of a microcomputer system.

Input/Output Operations. The computer *reads* data from input and storage devices. The computer *writes* information to output devices and data to storage devices. Before data can be processed, they must be "read" from an input device or data storage device. Input data are usually entered by a user via a keyboard or some other input device or retrieved from a data storage device, such as a magnetic disk drive. Once data have been processed into information, the information is "written" to an output device, such as a printer, and updated data are written to a data storage device.

Input/output (I/O) operations are illustrated in the payroll system example in Figure 1–3. Hours-worked data are entered and read into the computer system. These data are written to magnetic disk storage for recall at a later date.

Processing Operations. The computer is totally objective. That is, any two computers instructed to perform the same operation will arrive at the same result. This is because the computer can perform only *computation* and *logic operations*.

The computational capabilities of the computer include adding, subtracting, multiplying, and dividing. Logic capability permits the computer to make comparisons between numbers and between words and then, based on the result of the comparison, perform appropriate functions. In the payroll-system example of Figure 1–3, the computer calculates the gross pay in a computation operation (for example, 40 hours at $15/hour = $600). In a logic operation, the computer compares the number of hours worked to 40 to determine the number of overtime hours an employee has worked during a given week. If the hours-worked figure is greater than or equal to 40 (42, for example), the difference (2 hours) is credited as overtime and paid at time and a half.

> ▶ **MEMORY BITS**
>
> *Computer Operations*
> - Input/output
>   Read
>   Write
> - Processing
>   Computation
>   Logic

Computer System Capabilities

In a nutshell, computers are fast, accurate, and reliable; they do not forget anything; and they do not complain.

Speed. The smallest unit of time in the human experience is, realistically, the second. Computer operations (such as the execution of an instruction or adding two numbers) are measured in **milliseconds**, **microseconds, nanoseconds,** and **picoseconds** (one thousandth, one millionth, one billionth, and one trillionth of a second, respectively). A beam of light travels down the length of this page in about one nanosecond!

> **MEMORY BITS**
>
> *Fractions of a Second*
>   Millisecond = .001 second (one thousandth of a second)
>   Microsecond = .000001 second (one millionth of a second)
>   Nanosecond = .000000001 second (one billionth of a second)
>   Picosecond = .000000000001 second (one trillionth of a second)

Accuracy. Errors do occur in computer-based systems, but precious few can be directly attributed to the computer system itself. The vast majority can be traced to a program logic error, a procedural error, or erroneous data. These are *human errors*.

Reliability. Computer systems are particularly adept at repetitive tasks. They don't take sick days and coffee breaks, and they seldom complain. Moreover, it is not unusual for the **mean time between failure (MTBF)** for a microcomputer to be five or more years, depending on the manufacturer and the environment in which it is used. Many micros have been retired without ever visiting a computer repair shop.

Memory Capability. Computer systems have total and instant recall of data and they have an almost unlimited capacity to store these data. A typical microcomputer system will have many millions of characters stored and available for instant recall. To give you a benchmark for comparison, this book contains approximately one million characters.

1–6 HISTORICAL PERSPECTIVE

Personal Computer Milestones

The First PCs. The history of microcomputers is of special significance to us because their entire history has occurred within our lifetimes. In terms of the way people live and work, John V. Atanasoff's invention of the electronic digital computer (1942) can be considered one of the most significant events in history. But not until 1975 and the introduction of the **Altair 8800** personal computer, a product of the microminiaturization of electronic circuitry, was computing made available to individuals and very small companies. This event has forever changed how we as society perceive computers.

The Altair 8800, which sold for $650 ($395 as a kit), was marketed by a small electronics company called Micro Instrumentation and Telemetry Systems (MITS). After *Popular Electronics* featured the Altair 8800 on its cover, MITS received thousands of orders and eventually sold about 10,000. People wanted their own personal computers. Within two years, 30 other companies would be manufacturing and selling personal computers.

Perhaps the most prominent entrepreneurial venture during the early years of PCs was the **Apple II** computer. It all began in 1976 when two

Not until 1975 and the introduction of the Altair 8800 personal computer was computing made available to individuals and very small companies. This event has forever changed how society perceives computers. Certainly the most prominent entrepreneurial venture during the early years of personal computers was the Apple II computer.

young computer enthusiasts, Steven Jobs and Steve Wozniak (then 21 and 26 years of age, respectively), collaborated to create and build their Apple II computer. Raising $1300 by selling Jobs' Volkswagen and Wozniak's programmable calculator, they opened a makeshift production line in Jobs' garage. Seven years later, Apple Computer, Inc., earned a spot on the Fortune 500, a list of the 500 largest corporations in the United States.

IBM Becomes a Player. In 1981 International Business Machines (IBM), the giant of the computer industry, tossed its hat into the PC ring with the announcement of the **IBM PC**. In the first year, 35,000 were sold. In 1982 (the first complete sales year), 800,000 were sold and the IBM PC was well on its way to becoming the standard for the micro industry. When software vendors began to orient their products to the IBM PC, many microcomputer manufacturers created and sold **clones** of it. These clones, called *IBM-PC compatibles*, run most or all the software designed for the IBM PC.

Some industry analysts argue that IBM's dominance has helped stabilize the growth of the micro industry in its infancy. Others argue that the overwhelming influence of the IBM personal computers tends to stifle the efforts of those entrepreneurs who want to push the limits of modern technology. In any case, whatever IBM does in the personal computer arena has immediate and far-reaching effects on the PC

In 1981 IBM tossed its hat into the personal computer ring with the announcement of the IBM PC. In the first year, 35,000 were sold. In 1982, 800,000 were sold, and the IBM PC was well on its way to becoming the standard for the micro industry. When software vendors began to orient their products to the IBM PC, many microcomputer manufacturers created and sold clones of the IBM PC. These clones, called IBM-PC–compatibles, run most or all the software designed for the IBM PC.

marketplace. The successor to the IBM PC, the **IBM Personal System/2**, or **IBM PS/2** (introduced in 1987), will almost certainly become a milestone in PC history.

Other Significant Contributions. Several other personal computers have established their place in PC history. Introduced in 1982, the **Commodore-64** was significant because it signaled the buying public that powerful micros could be manufactured and sold at a reasonable cost—$599. In the same year, Compaq Computer Corporation bundled the equivalent of an IBM PC in a transportable case and named it the **Compaq Portable:** Thus began the era of the portable computer. In 1984 Apple Computer introduced the **Macintosh** with a very "friendly" graphical user interface—proof that computers can be easy and fun to use.

PC Software Milestones

The Programming Era. In the early years you had to be a programmer if you wanted to use a micro to address a particular application. The first commercially successful micro, the Altair 8800, was packaged with MBASIC from the fledgling Microsoft Corporation, now a giant in the software industry. MBASIC was based on **BASIC**, a "beginner's" programming language created during the early 1960s at Dartmouth College. Although many programming languages are available for PCs, BASIC continues to dominate in the PC environment.

During its first few years, the personal computer industry was waiting for the software industry to catch up. Today it is the other way around. The software industry continues to grow at a fever pitch.

Operating Systems. A micro's **operating system** provides the interface between the hardware and the applications software. During the late 1970s, Digital Research's **CP/M** (Control Program for Microcomputers) was the dominant non-Apple operating system. As an already established micro operating system, CP/M seemed to be the most obvious selection as the operating system for the soon-to-be-announced IBM PC. However, when IBM approached them, the people at Digital Research responded with too many demands. The people at Microsoft were more accommodating. When IBM chose **MS-DOS** from Microsoft Corporation, it, like the IBM PC, eventually became the standard for the industry. The IBM version of MS-DOS is called **PC-DOS**. (Both are discussed in Chapter 2, "Interacting with Micros.")

CP/M and MS-DOS are single-user operating systems. Until the mid-1980s micros were not fast enough to support more than one user. In 1985, AT&T introduced a powerful multiuser desktop PC based on the **UNIX** operating system. (Ironically, UNIX was created in 1969 for the single-user environment. The prefix *un* means one.) Now UNIX or versions of UNIX are the mainstay of IBM-PC–compatible computers that operate in a multiuser environment.

Applications Software. Several software packages are assured prominent places in PC history. With the introduction of **VisiCalc**, the first spreadsheet software program, in 1979, micros became a viable business tool. Before that, micros were used primarily in the educational environment and by hobbyists. VisiCalc blazed the trail for **Lotus 1-2-3** (1982), another spreadsheet software program. The success of Lotus Development Corporation's 1-2-3 is now legendary. Ashton-Tate's **dBASE II**, a database software package introduced in 1979, made it possible for micro users to create their own information systems without the aid of a professional programmer. In 1979 MicroPro International Corporation introduced **WordStar**, a word processing package that to this day enjoys an almost cultlike following. A Borland International product called **SideKick** deserves honorable mention because it introduced the concept of *memory-resident programs* to the buying public during the early 1980s. SideKick remains operational while other applications programs are running; that is, you can call up a notepad, calculator, calendar, or other application program during a word processing or electronic spreadsheet session.

Graphical User Interfaces. In the modern era, Microsoft has introduced **Windows**, a **graphical user interface**. Graphical user interfaces, which are discussed in more detail in Chapter 2, enable the user to select processing options by simply positioning an arrow over a graphic representation of the desired function or program. (For example, a drawing of a

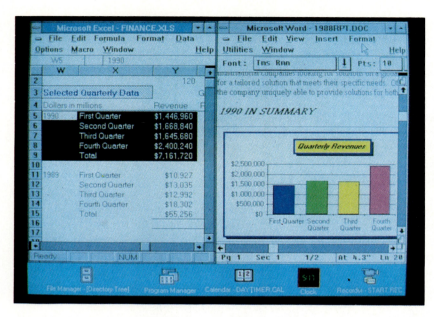

Microsoft's Windows provides users with an easy-to-use graphical user interface.

file cabinet represents files.) Windows is significant in that software vendors and users are embracing it as the foundational single-user interface software for the foreseeable future.

Summary. During this quick stroll through the short history of personal computers, we were able to highlight only a few of the many significant innovations and events that have occurred since the introduction of the Altair 8800. As an active participant in the microcomputer revolution, you will be a part of all the history-making events of the future.

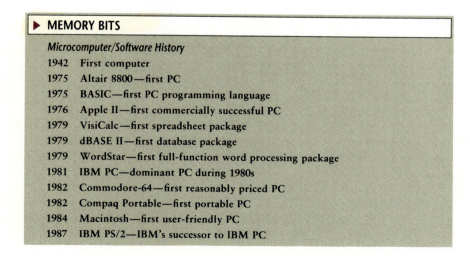

▶ MEMORY BITS

Microcomputer/Software History
- 1942 First computer
- 1975 Altair 8800—first PC
- 1975 BASIC—first PC programming language
- 1976 Apple II—first commercially successful PC
- 1979 VisiCalc—first spreadsheet package
- 1979 dBASE II—first database package
- 1979 WordStar—first full-function word processing package
- 1981 IBM PC—dominant PC during 1980s
- 1982 Commodore-64—first reasonably priced PC
- 1982 Compaq Portable—first portable PC
- 1984 Macintosh—first user-friendly PC
- 1987 IBM PS/2—IBM's successor to IBM PC

SUMMARY OUTLINE AND IMPORTANT TERMS (STUDY)

1-1 THE INFORMATION SOCIETY. In an **information society**, **knowledge workers** use, manipulate, and disseminate information. The **computer**, especially the **microcomputer**, is paving the way for our transition into an information society.

The **micro** is also called a **personal computer**, or **PC** for short, because it is used by one person at a time.

1-2 LEARNING ABOUT MICROCOMPUTERS. To overcome **cyberphobia** and gain **computer competency**, you should learn how to use a microcomputer and microcomputer software.

1-3 PERSONAL COMPUTING. Personal computing has altered forever the way we approach our jobs, our education, and our domestic affairs. Microcomputer software is available to support thousands of business and domestic applications.

The most popular productivity software packages include *word processing*, *desktop publishing*, *spreadsheet*, *graphics*, *database*, and *communications software*. These general-purpose packages provide the framework for a great number of business and personal applications.

- **Word processing software** allows users to enter, store, manipulate, and print text.
- **Desktop publishing software** permits users to produce *near-typeset-quality copy* from the confines of a desktop.
- **Spreadsheet software** enables users to work with the rows and columns of a spreadsheet of data.
- **Graphics software** allows users to create images and presentation graphics, such as pie and bar graphs.
- **Database software** permits users to create and maintain a data base and to extract information from the data base.
- **Communications software** enables users to send and receive transmissions of data to and from remote computers via a **modem** and a telephone line, and to process and store the data as well. It transforms a micro into an "intelligent" **video display terminal** (**VDT**) with a **monitor** and a **keyboard**.

Packages that integrate two or more of these productivity tools are referred to as **integrated software**.

The dual-function capability of personal computers enables them to be used in conjunction with the telephone system to transmit data to and receive data from a commercial **information service**. Some of the services available commercially are home banking, news, weather, sports, entertainment, games, financial information, brokerage services, bulletin boards, electronic mail, shop at home, reference, education, real estate, home and health, and travel. Log onto an information service by entering a **password** and **personal identification number** (**PIN**).

Expert systems, an area of **artificial intelligence** (**AI**) research, provide "expert" advice and guidance on a wide range of activities. An expert system is an interactive system that responds to questions, asks for clarification, makes recommendations, and generally helps in the decision-making process. The expert system's **knowledge base** is created by **knowledge engineers** who translate the knowledge of human experts into rules and strategies.

1-4 COMPUTERS: BIG, SMALL, AND VERY SMALL. Micros, **minicomputers, mainframes,** and **supercomputers** all have the same fundamental capabilities—*processing, storage,* **input,** and **output**. There are, of course, obvious differences in size and capabilities. Everything associated with minicomputers, mainframes, and supercomputers is larger in scope than that associated with microcomputers. The resources of the three larger computers are shared by many people, whereas microcomputers are used primarily by one user at a time.

The **microprocessor**, a product of the microminiaturization of electronic circuitry, is literally a "computer on a chip." **Chip** refers to any self-contained integrated circuit. In a microcomputer, the microprocessor, the electronic circuitry for handling input/output signals from the **peripheral devices** (keyboard, printer, and so on), and the memory chips are mounted on a single circuit board called a **system board**, or **motherboard**. The processing components of most micros are sold with several empty **expansion slots** so you can purchase and plug in optional capabilities in the form of **add-on boards**.

Personal computers come in four different physical sizes: **pocket PCs, laptop PCs, desktop PCs,** and **tower PCs**. Pocket and laptop PCs are considered portable. **Multiuser micros**, which are configured with as many as a dozen VDTs, permit several people to use the system at once.

1-5 UNCOVERING THE "MYSTERY" OF COMPUTERS. A computer is an electronic device capable of interpreting and executing programmed commands for input, output, computation, and logic operations. All computer systems have only four fundamental components: input (for example, via the keyboard), processing (executing a program), output (via a monitor or a **printer**), and storage. (For example, **master files** and **records** can be stored on **magnetic disk**.)

Data are the raw material from which information is derived. **Information** is data that have been collected and processed into a meaningful form. The computer *reads* data from input and storage devices. The computer *writes* information to output devices and data to storage devices.

The computer's processing capabilities are limited to *computation* and *logic operations*.

The computer is fast, accurate, reliable, and has an enormous memory. Computer operations are measured in **milliseconds, microseconds, nanoseconds,** and **picoseconds**.

1-6 HISTORICAL PERSPECTIVE. The first personal computer, the **Altair 8800**, was introduced in 1975. The commercial success of the Altair (about 10,000 units) paved the way for the **Apple II** computer, one of the most successful new products in business history.

Computer giant International Business Machines Corporation (IBM) introduced the **IBM PC** in 1981. Many microcomputer manufacturers create and sell **clones** of the IBM PC, called *IBM-PC compatibles*. The successor to the IBM PC, the **IBM Personal System/2**, or **IBM PS/2**, was introduced in 1987.

Introduced in 1982, the **Commodore-64** demonstrated that powerful micros could be manufactured and sold at a reasonable cost. That same year, the **Compaq Portable** began the era of the portable computer. In 1984 Apple Computer introduced the **Macintosh** and its very "friendly" graphical user interface.

The Altair 8800 was packaged with Microsoft Corporation's MBASIC, a "beginner's" programming language. **BASIC** remains the dominant programming language in the micro environment.

A micro's **operating system** provides the interface between the hardware and the applications software. In the beginning, Digital Research's **CP/M** was the main non-Apple operating system. However, **MS-DOS** from Microsoft Corporation was chosen for the IBM PC and eventually became the standard for the industry. In 1985, AT&T introduced a powerful multiuser desktop PC that was based on the **UNIX** operating system.

With the introduction in 1979 of **VisiCalc**, the first spreadsheet software program, micros became a viable business tool. **Lotus 1-2-3** (1982), another spreadsheet software program, followed with amazing success. Ashton-Tate's **dBASE II**, a database software package introduced in 1979, made it possible for micro users to create their own information systems. Also in 1979, MicroPro International Corporation introduced **WordStar**, and it quickly became an enormously popular word processing package. Borland International's **SideKick** introduced the concept of *memory-resident programs*.

Recently, Microsoft introduced **Windows,** a **graphical user interface** that enables users to select processing options by simply positioning an arrow over a graphic representation of the desired function or program.

REVIEW EXERCISES

1. What are the four fundamental components of a microcomputer system?
2. Which component of a microcomputer system executes the program?
3. Light travels at 186,000 miles per second. How many milliseconds does it take for a beam of light to travel across the United States, a distance of about 3000 miles?
4. Compare the information-processing capabilities of human beings to those of computers with respect to speed, accuracy, reliability, and memory.
5. Describe the relationship between data and information.
6. In computerese, what is meant by *read* and *write*?
7. Name at least four popular microcomputer software tools that are collectively referred to as *productivity software*.
8. Which microcomputer productivity tool would be most helpful in writing a term paper?
9. List at least six services that might be provided by a commercial information service.
10. What device provides the interface between the telephone system and a micro?

11. List at least five domestic applications for personal computers.
12. In spreadsheet software, what is the intersection of a row and a column called?
13. What is an integrated software package?
14. How much time elapsed between the invention of the electronic digital computer and the introduction of the first commercially available personal computer?
15. Which software package made the most significant contribution to the emergence of the personal computer as a viable business tool?
16. Describe the capabilities of a multiuser micro.
17. What is the relationship between a microprocessor, a system board, and a microcomputer?
18. In terms of physical size, how are PCs categorized?
19. What is the name given to printed output?
20. Give two examples each of input hardware and output hardware.

SELF-TEST (by section)

1-1 a. A person whose job revolves around the use, manipulation, and dissemination of information is called: (a) a computerphobe, (b) a knowledge worker, or (c) a data expert?
   b. For the most part, a microcomputer is used by one person at a time. (T/F)

1-2 a. To be computer-competent, you must be able to write computer programs. (T/F)
   b. The irrational fear of, or aversion to, computers is called _cyberphobia_.

1-3 a. The microcomputer productivity tool that manipulates data organized in a tabular structure of rows and columns is called _spreadsheet_ software.
   b. Desktop publishing refers to the capability of producing _near-typeset-quality_ copy from the confines of a desktop.
   c. A terminal with processing capability is said to be: (a) astute, (b) clever, or (c) intelligent? (smart)
   d. What type of microcomputer-based system relies on a knowledge base to provide users with expert advice: (a) expert system, (b) master system, or (c) intelligent system? (~~smart~~)

1-4 a. The most distinguishing characteristic of any computer system is physical size. (T/F)
   b. The processing component of a system board is a _microprocessor_.
   c. The smallest of the four types of personal computers is the laptop PC. (T/F)

1-5 a. A printer is an example of a microcomputer-system output component. (T/F)
   b. The two types of processing operations performed by computers are _computation_ and _logic_.
   c. A microsecond is 1000 times longer than a nanosecond. (T)/F
   d. _Data_ are the raw material from which _info_ is derived.

1-6 a. The first PC to be introduced to the marketplace was the Apple II. (T/F)
   b. The company responsible for the creation of MS-DOS is: (a) Digital Research, (b) Microsoft, or (c) Apple?

Self-test answers.   1-1 **(a)** b; **(b)** T.   1-2 **(a)** F; **(b)** cyberphobia.   1-3 **(a)** spreadsheet; **(b)** near-typeset-quality; **(c)** c; **(d)** a.   1-4 **(a)** F; **(b)** microprocessor; **(c)** F.   1-5 **(a)** T; **(b)** computation, logic; **(c)** F; **(d)** Data, information.   1-6 **(a)** F; **(b)** b.

CHAPTER 2
INTERACTING WITH MICROS

STUDENT LEARNING OBJECTIVES

▶ To describe the function and purpose of a microcomputer's disk operating system (DOS).
▶ To understand the scope of knowledge needed to interact effectively with a personal computer.
▶ To describe various keyboard, mouse, and data entry conventions.
▶ To grasp concepts related to the effective use of micros and micro software.
▶ To describe the proper care and maintenance of personal computers and disk storage media.
▶ To demonstrate file backup procedures.

2-1 INTERACTING WITH THE SYSTEM

To interact effectively with a personal computer you need to be knowledgeable in four areas.

1. General microcomputer software concepts (for example, windows, viruses, macros, uploading, and menus).
2. The operation and use of microcomputer hardware (such as magnetic disk, printers).
3. The function and use of **DOS**, the disk operating system, and/or a **graphical user interface**, both of which provide a link between the you, the microcomputer system, and the various applications programs (for example, Lotus 1-2-3, PC Paintbrush).
4. The specific applications programs you are using.

The first three areas are prerequisites to the fourth; that is, you will need a working knowledge of micro software concepts, hardware, and DOS and/or a **GUI** (graphical user interface) before you can make effective use of applications programs like Quicken (accounting), Harvard Graphics (presentation graphics), WordPerfect (word processing), or any of the thousands of micro software packages on the market today. The first three topics are addressed in the chapters and appendices of this book. The tutorials and exercises in this book's companion modules address the fourth.

Although some personal computers can service several workstations, the operating systems for most are oriented to servicing a single user. This city planner has arranged his computer system so all components are within arm's reach.

2-2 THE DISK OPERATING SYSTEM (DOS)

The nucleus of a microcomputer system is its **operating system.** The operating system monitors and controls all input/output and processing activities within a computer system. All hardware and software, including micro productivity software, are under the control of the operating system. Micro users need a working knowledge of their micro's operating system because they must use it to interface, or link, their applications programs with microcomputer hardware.

PC Operating Systems

The four most popular micro operating systems based on number of installations are:

- *MS-DOS* *(Microsoft Corporation)*. MS-DOS is the operating system used with IBM-PC–compatible computers. The version of MS-DOS used with the IBM PC is called *PC-DOS*. Appendix A, "MS-DOS Tutorial and Exercises," contains details on the use and application of this popular operating system.
- *Macintosh DOS* *(Apple Computer, Inc.)*. **Macintosh DOS** is the operating system for the Macintosh line of computers.
- *Operating System/2 or OS/2 (Microsoft/IBM)*. **OS/2** is the successor to MS-DOS. It is more sophisticated and offers greater capabilities, but it also requires more sophisticated and expensive hardware. Millions of users of IBM and IBM-compatible computers know and feel comfortable with MS-DOS. Most of them are reluctant to upgrade their hardware to accommodate OS/2 and learn another operating system. In addition, relatively little software is available to run under OS/2. The net result of these drawbacks is that MS-DOS remains the preferred operating system for both end users and developers of micro software, at least for the present.
- *UNIX (AT&T)*. Originally a mainframe operating system, **UNIX** and its spinoffs, such as **XENIX**, are used frequently with multiuser microcomputers.

The logic, structure, and nomenclature of the different operating systems vary considerably. Our emphasis will be on PC-DOS, the operating system used with the IBM-PC series of computers and the IBM Personal System/2 series of computers, and on MS-DOS, the operating system used with IBM-PC–compatible computers. In practice, these operating systems, which are essentially the same, are referred to simply as DOS (rhymes with *boss*), an acronym for *disk operating system*. DOS is a "disk" operating system because the operating system is stored on disk.

DOS Is the Boss

Just as the processor is the center of all hardware activity, DOS is the center of all software activity. The operating system is a family of **systems software** programs that must be installed on a microcomputer sys-

For occasional users, operating system commands can be difficult to learn and use. Designers of the OS/2 operating system address this concern by providing a graphical user interface between the operating system, applications software, and user files. The photo shows how the user can view several applications at the same time.

tem before it can be used. Systems software is independent of any applications software. Because all hardware, software, and input/output are controlled by DOS, you might even call DOS "the boss."

One of the DOS family of programs is always *resident* in RAM during processing. This program, called COMMAND.COM, loads other operating system and applications programs into RAM as they are needed or as directed by you, the user. COMMAND.COM is usually referred to as COMMAND "dot" COM (rhymes with *mom*).

Besides controlling the ongoing operation of microcomputer systems, DOS has two other important functions.

- *Input/output control.* DOS facilitates the movement of data between peripheral devices, the processor, programs, and **RAM**. (**Random-access memory** provides temporary storage of data and programs during processing.)
- *File and disk management.* DOS and its file and disk management utility programs enable users to perform such tasks as making backup copies of work disks, erasing disk files that are no longer needed, making inquiries about the number and type of files on a particular disk, and preparing new disks for use. DOS also handles many file- and disk-oriented tasks that are *transparent* to the end user. For example, DOS keeps track of the physical location of disk files so that we, as users, need only refer to them by name (for example, *myfile*) when loading them from disk to RAM.

The DOS commands needed to perform user-oriented input/output tasks and file and disk management tasks are discussed in Appendix A, "MS-DOS Tutorial and Exercises."

2-3 MICROCOMPUTER OPERATION

Installing Hardware and Software

When you purchase a microcomputer system, typically you will receive several boxes containing the various components of the system. Unless yours is a portable PC, the system will come in several pieces: probably a keyboard, a monitor, a printer, and a processor unit that houses the disk drives. Normally all that must be done to complete the installation of the hardware is to link the pieces of the system with the various types of cables. (See Chapter 3, "Processors and Platforms," for more on cables.) A computer, however, does nothing without software.

Now you must install the software—first DOS, then any other software that you intend to run. Software installation is a three-step process for DOS and all applications software packages.

1. *Make a backup copy.* Rather than risk the possibility of accidental loss of data or programs on their master diskettes during installation, most users elect to duplicate the vendor-supplied diskettes prior to beginning the installation procedure. In this way, if they make an installation error that results in the loss of data or programs, they can

CHAPTER 2 Interacting with Micros   41

This personnel manager has just received a new microcomputer system and is preparing to install it. Once all the devices have been connected, she will install the operating system.

repeat the procedure with their backup diskettes. Be sure to store the master diskettes in a safe place.

2. *Copy files.* Copy the program and data files from the vendor-distributed diskettes to the permanently installed hard disk. The first step usually is accomplished by entering "install" or "setup" at the DOS prompt for the disk drive containing the applications diskette.

3. *Set system information.* An applications software package is designed to accommodate a variety of microcomputer systems, so you must describe your system to the package. The software assumes you have a "typical" PC. If your system deviates from what is defined as "typical" in the software package, you will need to revise these **defaults** (standard settings) to fit the specifications of your system (for example, type of computer, monitor, keyboard layout, printer, and so on).

Power Up/Power Down

Booting the System. Micros are similar to copy machines, toasters, and other electrical devices—you must turn them on by applying electrical power. The power-on procedure on a micro is straightforward—flip the on/off switch on the processor unit to *on*. On some micros, the monitor may have a separate on/off switch. Turn on the printer only when you need to produce a hard copy of your work.

When you **power up,** or add electrical power to a micro system, you also **boot** the system. The booting procedure is so named because the computer "pulls itself up by its own bootstraps" (without the assistance of humans). When you boot the system, several significant events take place (see Figure 2-1).

1. A program that is permanently stored in **read-only memory**, or **ROM** (rhymes with *mom*), is executed. ROM is discussed in Chapter 3, "Processors and Platforms." The program verifies that the electronic components are operational and readies the computer for processing. After a short period, a beep signals the end of the **system check** and the program searches for the disk containing DOS, the operating system.
2. Upon finding DOS, the ROM program loads DOS from disk storage to RAM (internal memory) then passes control of the system to DOS.
3. DOS executes predefined user instructions, then usually—but not always—presents the user with a **system prompt** (C:\>, or A> when DOS is loaded from diskette) and awaits a user command.

On micros with a permanently installed hard disk, the booting procedure takes place automatically when you flip the power on. On other micros, you must insert the interchangeable disk containing the operating system into the disk drive, close the disk-drive door, and flip the switch to *on*. All new micros sold after 1988 are configured with a hard disk and at least one interchangeable disk drive.

FIGURE 2-1 The Boot Procedure

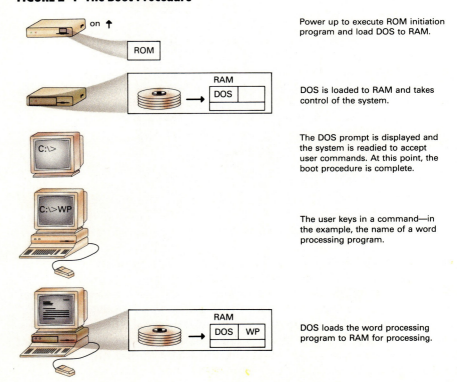

The Graceful Exit. Unlike electrical appliances, you do not simply flip the switch to *off*; you must **power down** in an orderly manner. This involves a **graceful exit** from all active applications programs prior to shutting off the power. All applications programs have an exit routine that, when activated, returns you to DOS or a higher level applications program. For example, if you are running a grammar checker program within a word processing program, you must exit the grammar checker program, store your documents, and initiate the word processing exit routine. When all applications are *closed* (no longer active) and the DOS prompt is visible, it is safe to shut off the power.

It is not "graceful" to power down when an application is still active (for example, a spreadsheet is still being displayed). Exit routines perform some administrative processing that, if bypassed, can result in loss of user data and problems during subsequent sessions.

Entering Commands and Data

Micros Can Be Very Picky. A personal computer is responsive to your commands, but it does *exactly* what you tell it to do—no more, no less. If you do something wrong, it tells you and then gives you another chance.

Whether entering a DOS command or an applications program command, you must be explicit. For example, if you wish to copy a word processing document file from one disk to another, you cannot just enter "copy" or even "copy MYFILE". You must enter the command that tells the micro to copy MYFILE from Disk A to Disk C (for example, in MS-DOS, "copy a:myfile c:"). If you omit necessary information in a command or the format of the command is incorrect, an error message is displayed and/or an on-screen prompt will request that you reenter the command correctly. DOS, in particular, demands strict adherence to command **syntax**, the rules for entering commands, such as word spacing, punctuation, and so on.

Micros are not always so picky. You can enter DOS commands and filenames as either uppercase or lowercase characters. For example, the system interprets the command "copy a:myfile c:" and "COPY A:MYFILE C:" the same way. Some software packages do not distinguish between uppercase and lowercase commands; however, all software packages do make the distinction between uppercase and lowercase entries for *keyed-in data* (for example, an employee's last name in a document you are producing).

The Keyboard. A microcomputer's *keyboard* is normally its primary input and control device. You enter data and issue commands via the keyboard. Besides the standard typewriter keyboard, most micro keyboards have **function keys**, also called **soft keys** (see Figure 2–2). When tapped, these function keys trigger the execution of software, thus the name "soft key." For example, tapping one function key might call up a list of possible activities that can be performed—a displayed list of user options commonly referred to as a menu. Another function key might

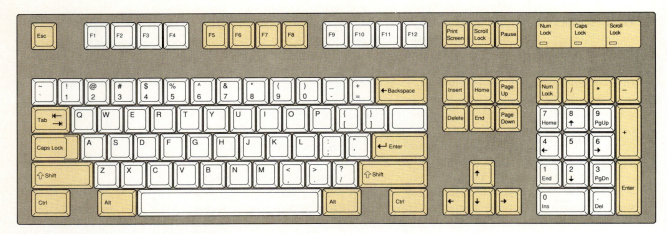

FIGURE 2–2 Microcomputer Keyboard
This is representative of the microcomputer keyboard being configured with the latest IBM-compatible micros. In the figure, the alphanumeric characters follow the commonly used QWERTY layout. The positioning of the function keys, the cursor-control keys, and the keypad may vary substantially from keyboard to keyboard. On earlier versions of IBM-PC–compatible keyboards, the 10 function keys were aligned in two columns on the left end.

cause a word processing document to be printed. Function keys are numbered and assigned different functions in different software packages. The software packages are usually distributed with **keyboard templates** that designate which commands are assigned to which function keys. For example, HELP (on-line user assistance) is often assigned to F1, or Function Key 1. The templates usually are designed to fit over the keyboard or to be attached with an adhesive.

Most keyboards are equipped with **a key pad** and **cursor-control keys** (see Figure 2–2). The key pad permits rapid numeric data entry. It is normally positioned to the right of the standard alphanumeric keyboard. The cursor-control keys, or "arrow" keys, allow you to move the text cursor *up* and *down* (usually a line at a time) and *left* and *right* (usually a character at a time). The text cursor always indicates the location of the next keyed-in character on the screen. To move the cursor rapidly about the screen, simply hold down the appropriate cursor-control key.

For many software packages, you can use the cursor-control keys to view parts of a document or worksheet that extend past the bottom, top, or sides of the screen. This is known as **scrolling.** Use the up and down cursor-control keys to *scroll vertically* and the left and right keys to *scroll horizontally*. For example, if you wish to scroll vertically through a word processing document, move the up or down cursor-control key to the edge of the current screen and continue to press the key to view more of the document, one line a time. Figure 2–3 illustrates vertical and horizontal scrolling.

In summary, there are three basic ways to enter a command on the keyboard:

CHAPTER 2 Interacting with Micros

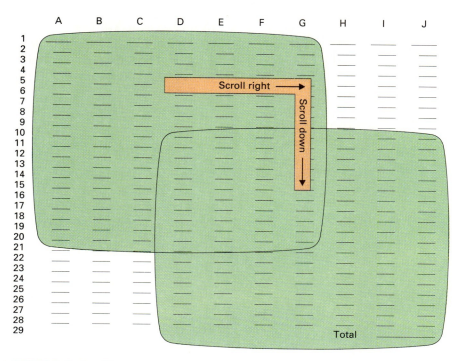

FIGURE 2–3 Scrolling
When an electronic spreadsheet does not fit on a single screen, you can scroll horizontally (to the right as shown in the figure) and vertically (down in the figure) to view other portions of the electronic spreadsheet.

- *Key in* the command using the alphanumeric portion of the keyboard.
- Press a *function key*.
- Use the *cursor-control keys* to select a *menu option* from the displayed menu. (Menus are discussed in detail in the next section.)

Recently, PCs have introduced two new dimensions in communication—stereo sound and full-motion video. This multimedia capability enables the creation of more effective and stimulating presentations, training programs, and demonstrations. Multimedia presentations can combine full-motion video, slides, photographs, illustrations, text, graphics, animations, and narration. Multimedia hardware and software enable you to capture sounds and images from disks, tapes, video cameras, and audio players. Once stored, the sounds and images can be manipulated to meet presentation needs.

Other important keys common to most keyboards are the *ENTER*, *HOME*, *END*, *Page up* and *Page down* (abbreviated as PGUP and PGDN), *Delete* (DEL), *Insert-overstrike toggle* (INS), *Backspace* (BKSP), *Escape* (ESC), *SPACEBAR*, *Shift*, *Control* (CTRL), *Alternate* (ALT), and *TAB* keys (see Figure 2–2).

ENTER Traditionally the ENTER key is used to send keyed-in data or a selected command to RAM for processing. For example, when you want to enter data into an electronic spreadsheet, the characters you enter are displayed in an edit area until you press ENTER, also called the *carriage return*. When you press ENTER, the data are displayed in the appropriate area in the spreadsheet. Like most of the special keys, ENTER has other meanings, depending on the type of software package you are using. In word processing, for example, you would designate the end of a paragraph by pressing the ENTER key.

When you highlight a menu option in a software package with a cursor-control key, you press ENTER to select that option. More often than not, ENTER can be interpreted as "Do."

In graphical user interfaces, the trend is away from using the ENTER key after each entry. In place of the ENTER key, the user clicks the mouse or taps TAB or a function key. Often ENTER is reserved to signal the system that all user options are set and processing can continue.

HOME Pressing the HOME key results in different actions for different packages, but often the cursor is moved to the beginning of a work area (the beginning of the screen or document in word processing, the upper left-hand corner of the spreadsheet, or the first record in a data base).

END With most software packages, press END to move the cursor to the end of the work area (the end of the screen or document in word processing, the lower right corner of the spreadsheet, or the last record in a data base).

PGUP, PGDN Press PGUP (*page up*) and PGDN (*page down*) to vertically scroll *a page (or screen) at a time* to see parts of the document or spreadsheet that extend past the top or bottom of the screen, respectively. PGUP and PGDN are also used to position the cursor at the previous and next record when using database software.

DEL   Press DEL to *delete* the character at the cursor position.

INS   Press INS to **toggle** (switch) between the two modes of entering data and text—*insert* and *typeover*. Both modes are described and illustrated in the word processing discussion in Chapter 5, "Text and Image Processing: Word Processing, Desktop Publishing, and Graphics." The term *toggle* is used to describe the action of pressing a single key to alternate between two or more modes of operation (insert and replace), functions (underline *on* and underline *off*), or operational specifications (for type of data base field: character, numeric, date, memo).

BKSP   Press the BKSP, or *backspace*, key to move the cursor one position to the left and delete the character in that position.

ESC   The ESC, or *escape*, key may have many functions, depending on the software package, but in most situations you can press the ESC key to negate the current command.

SPACEBAR   Press the SPACEBAR at the bottom of the keyboard to key in a space at the cursor position. *Note:* On a computer, a space is recorded internally like any other character, even though it is not displayed or printed.

SHIFT, CTRL, ALT   The SHIFT, CTRL (*control*), and ALT (*alternate*) keys are used in conjunction with another key to expand the functionality of the keyboard. Just as you depress the SHIFT key to enter a capital letter or one of the special characters above the numbers, you hold down a CTRL or ALT key to give another key new meaning. For example, on some word processing systems you press HOME to move the cursor to the top left corner of the screen. When you press CTRL and HOME together, the cursor is positioned at the beginning of the document. When used in conjunction with the SHIFT, CTRL, and ALT, each function key can be assigned four meanings (F1, SHIFT+F1, CTRL+F1, and ALT+F1).

TAB   In word processing, the TAB key retains its traditional meaning in that it advances the text cursor to the next user-defined tab stop. In most other programs, it advances the text cursor to the next logical area into which data can be entered. For example, a program might position the cursor at the first of three data entry areas.

After entering the required data in the first area, sometimes called a field, the user taps the TAB key to advance to the next. Tapping the TAB key with the text cursor in the last field positions the cursor at the first field again. Tap SHIFT+TAB (hold down SHIFT and tap TAB) to move to the previous field. Typically, you would tap the ENTER key to enter the data in all fields simultaneously.

Each keystroke you enter is sent first to an intermediate **keystroke buffer** that can save from 15 to hundreds of keystrokes. Under normal processing conditions, the keystroke is sent immediately from the buffer to the processor. In many instances, however, you may have to wait for processing to finish (such as during a disk read operation). When this happens, you can key ahead. For example, if you know that the next prompt to be displayed is "Enter filename:" you can enter the desired filename in anticipation of the prompt. When the prompt appears, the filename you entered is loaded from the keystroke buffer and displayed after the prompt. Judicious use of the keystroke buffer can make your interaction with micro software packages much more efficient.

The Mouse. Another device used for input and control is the **mouse**. The hand-held mouse, sometimes called the "pet peripheral," is rapidly becoming a must-have item on micros. Attached to the computer by a cable (the mouse's "tail"), the mouse is a small device that, when moved across a desktop, moves the **graphics cursor** accordingly. The graphics cursor, which can be positioned anywhere on the screen, is often displayed as a small arrow or crosshair. Depending on the application, the text and graphics cursors may be displayed on the screen at the same time. The graphics cursor is used to *point* and *draw*.

All movements of the mouse are reproduced by the graphics cursor on the screen. For example, when a mouse positioned to the right of the keyboard is moved up and away from its user, the graphics cursor moves toward the top right corner of the screen. Use the mouse for quick positioning of the graphics cursor over the desired menu item or a graphic image, called **an icon** (a graphic rendering of a file cabinet or a diskette, for example). When positioned at a menu item or an icon, the graphics cursor is said to "point" to that item or icon.

Most mice have two buttons—left and right (Figure 2–4). Typically, you would tap, **or click, the left button to select a menu item or execute the program represented by an icon**. The function of the right button varies between software packages, but often it is used to call up a menu of options. A *double-click*, which is tapping a button twice in rapid succession, gives each button a different meaning. Some software packages permit a *simultaneous click*, or tapping both buttons simultaneously, to give the mouse added functionality.

Press and hold a button to **drag** the graphics cursor across the screen. When using a graphics software program, you drag the graphics cursor across the screen to create the image. When using a word processing

The laptop being placed in an attaché case includes a keyboard, our primary means of entering data into a computer system. This man is also taking a mouse (upper left corner of briefcase). The mouse is rolled across the desktop to move the graphics cursor quickly about the screen.

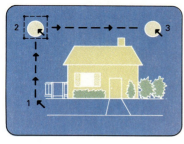
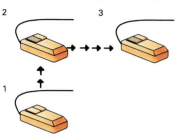

FIGURE 2–4 The Mouse and the Graphics Cursor
In the example, the user moved the sun image from the left to the right side of the screen. The graphics cursor, or pointer, was initially at Position 1 on the display screen. The user moved the mouse up (toward monitor) to position the pointer over the image to be moved (Position 2). The image, which includes the sun, is temporarily enclosed within a rectangular box. To reposition the sun image to the right of the display (Position 3), the image within the box was dragged (by pressing and holding the mouse's left button) to the desired location. The drag operation was completed when the mouse button was released.

program, you highlight a block of text to be deleted by dragging the graphics cursor from the beginning to the end of a block.

Levels of Command Interaction

You can interact with software packages, such as spreadsheet and database, at three different levels of sophistication: the *menu level*, the *macro level*, and the *programming level*. These three levels of command interaction are discussed in the following sections.

Menus. When using micro applications software, you issue commands and initiate operations by selecting activities to be performed from a *hierarchy of menus*.

Menu trees. Menu hierarchies are sometimes called **menu trees** (see Figure 2–5). When you select an item from the **main menu**, you are often presented with another menu of activities, and so on. Depending on the items you select, you may progress through as few as one and as many as eight levels of menus before processing is started for the desired activity.

Let's use presentation graphics software to illustrate how you might use a hierarchy of menus. One of the options on the main menu of a graphics software package might be "Create New Chart." If you select this option, you are presented with another menu and an opportunity to choose one of five types of charts.

    Text   Bar   Pie   Line   Organization

If you select the *text* option, another menu asks you to choose from three available types of text charts.

    Tile Chart   Simple List   Bullet List

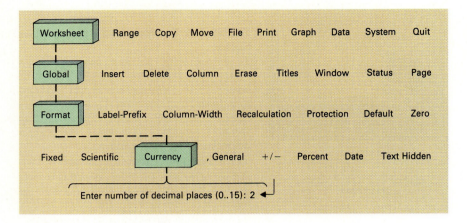

FIGURE 2–5 A Hierarchy of Menus
This figure illustrates how a user of Lotus 1-2-3, a popular electronic spreadsheet program, progresses through a hierarchy of menus to format all numeric entries in a currency format with two decimal places. (For example, the entry 1234.56 would be displayed as $1,234.56.) Selecting the Worksheet *option causes a display of the second-level menu. The* Global *option indicates that further menu options apply to all relevant spreadsheet entries. At the third and fourth levels of menu options, the user selects the* Format *and* Currency *options. Upon selecting the* Currency *option, the user is prompted to enter the desired number of decimal places.*

If you select the *bullet list* option, you are presented with the bullet list work screen.

Types of menus. A menu can appear as a **bar menu** in the **user interface** portion of the display, a **pull-down menu**, a **pop-up menu**, or a **pop-out menu**. The user interface is from one to six lines at the bottom and/or top of the screen.

The bar menu provides a *horizontal list* of menu options. The result of a menu selection from a bar menu at the top of the screen may be a subordinate bar menu (see Figure 2–5) or a pull-down menu (see Figure 2–6). The subordinate menu is "pulled down" from the selected bar menu option and displayed as a *vertical list* of menu options. The entire pull-down menu is shown in a box directly under the selected bar menu option and over whatever is currently on the screen.

Like the pull-down menu, the pop-up menu is superimposed on the current screen in a window. Pop-up menus are displayed as the result of a selection from a higher level menu or via a function key.

The pop-out menu is displayed next to the menu option selected in a higher level pop-up or pull-down menu. The pop-out menu becomes the active menu, but the higher level menu continues to be displayed.

Menu item selection. Micro software packages provide users with three ways to select an item from a menu.

1. Use the left/right or up/down cursor-control keys to highlight the desired menu option and tap ENTER.

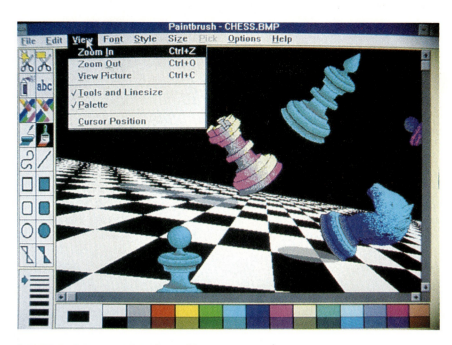

FIGURE 2–6 Bar and Pull-Down Menus
The Paintbrush (a graphics paint program) main menu is presented in a bar menu above the user work area. In the example, the View *option in the bar menu is selected and the* View *menu is presented as a pull-down menu.*

2. Enter the **mnemonic** (pronounced *neh MON ik*) of the desired item. A letter or number within the text of the menu item is noted as its mnemonic, which means memory aid. The mnemonic is usually the first letter in the first word unless there is another option with the same first letter. For example, to work through the hierarchy of spreadsheet menus shown in Figure 2–5, the user would enter *W*, *G*, *F*, and *C*, for *W*orksheet, *G*lobal, *F*ormat, and *C*urrency.
3. Use the mouse to position the graphics cursor at the desired option and click the left button.

Defaults. As you progress through a series of menus, eventually you are asked to enter the specifications for data to be graphed (graphics software), the size of the output paper (word processing software), and so on. As a convenience to the user, many of the specification options are already filled in for common situations. For example, word processing packages set output document size at 8½ by 11 inches. If the user is satisfied with these **default options**, no further specifications are required. The user can easily revise the default options to accommodate less common situations. So, to print a document on legal-sized paper, the default paper length of 11 inches would have to be revised to 14 inches.

Menu summary. During any given point in a work session, the options available to the user of a micro productivity tool normally are displayed somewhere on the screen. For example, in spreadsheets, the active menu is displayed in the user interface. If you are ever confused

> **MEMORY BITS**
>
> *Types of Menus*
> - Bar menu (horizontal list)
> - Pull-down menu (vertical list)
> - Pop-up menu
> - Pop-out menu

about what to do next, the options usually are displayed on the current screen.

Macros and Programming. At the menu level of command interaction, you are initiating individual commands. At the macro and programming levels of interaction, you can string together commands and even introduce logic operations.

A handy feature available with most micro software packages is the **macro**. A macro is a sequence of frequently used operations or keystrokes that can be recalled as you need it. You create a macro by recording a sequence of operations or keystrokes and storing them on disk for later recall. To **invoke**, or execute, the macro, you either refer to it by name (perhaps in the text of a word processing file) or enter the series of keystrokes that identify it (for example, ALT+D, CTRL+F4). Three common user-supplied macros in word processing could be the commands necessary to format the first-, second-, and third-level headings in a report. For example, the user might want the first-level heading to be centered, boldface, in a large typeface, and followed by two line spaces; the second level to be flush left, boldface, in a normal-sized typeface, and followed by an indented paragraph; and the third level to be flush left, underlined, italic, and followed on the same line by the beginning of the first paragraph. In electronic spreadsheets, macros are commonly used to produce graphs automatically from spreadsheet data.

Some software packages allow users the flexibility to do their own **programming**—that is, create logical sequences of instructions. For example, a database software program can be written that will retrieve records from a particular data base, depending on preset criteria; process the data according to programmed instructions; and print a report. The programming capability enables users to create microcomputer-based information systems for an endless number of applications, from payroll processing to tennis league scheduling.

2–4 USER-FRIENDLY SOFTWARE

Virtually all vendors of micro software tout their product as being **user-friendly**. Software is said to be user-friendly when someone with limited computer experience has little difficulty using the system. User-friendly software communicates easily understood words, phrases, and icons to the end user, thus simplifying his or her interaction with the computer system. A user-friendly environment facilitates **navigation** between the elements of the software package. Navigation refers to movement within and between an application's work areas. A central focus of the design of any modern micro software package is user-friendliness.

Help Commands

A handy feature available on most software packages is the **help command**. When you find yourself in a corner, so to speak, you can press the HELP key, often assigned to Function Key 1 (F1), to get a more

---

▶ **MEMORY BITS**

Levels of Command Interaction
- Menu level
- Macro level
- Programming level

detailed explanation or instructions on how to proceed. In most micro software packages, the help commands are context sensitive—the explanation relates to what you were doing when you issued the help command. (For example, if you were entering data into a data base, the explanation would address how to enter data.) When you are finished reading the help information, the system returns you to your work at the same point you left it.

Windows

Windows have become symbolic of the user-friendly environment. A window is a rectangular display temporarily superimposed over whatever is currently on the screen. You can "look through" several windows on a single display screen; however, you can manipulate text, data, or graphics in only one window at a time. This is called the **current window**. Generally, each window contains a separate application.

Windows can overlap one another on the display screen. For example, some integrated software packages allow users to view a spreadsheet in one window, a bar graph in another window, and a word processing document in a third window. With windows, you can work the way you think and think the way you work. Several projects are at your finger tips, and you can switch between them with relative ease.

You can perform work in one of several windows on a display screen, or you can **zoom** in on a particular window—that is, the window you select expands to fill the entire screen. Tapping a program-specific key combination normally will return the screen to a multiwindow display.

To work on the computer the way we think, we need access to several resources at once. The use of windows enables this auditor to see a tabular report, a letter, and a menu of system options on the same screen.

A multiwindow display permits you to see how a change in one window affects another window. For example, as you change the data in a spreadsheet, you can see how an accompanying pie graph is revised to reflect the new data.

You can even create **window panes!** As you might expect, a window is divided into panes so you can view several parts of the same window subarea at a time. For example, if you are writing a long report in a word processing window, you might wish to write the conclusions of the report in one window pane while viewing other portions of the report in another window pane.

Graphical User Interfaces

DOS is text-based, command-driven software. That is, we issue commands to DOS by entering them on the keyboard, one character at a time. For example, to copy a word processing document from one disk to another, we might enter "copy c:myfile a:" via the keyboard at the DOS prompt, "C:\>".

    C:\> **copy c:myfile a:**

DOS commands are syntax-sensitive, so we must follow the rules for constructing the command, otherwise an error message is displayed. The trend, however, is away from command-driven interfaces to a user-friendly, graphics-oriented environment called a *graphical user interface*, or *GUI*.

GUIs provide an alternative to often cryptic text commands. With a GUI, you can interact with DOS and other software packages by selecting options from menus that are temporarily superimposed over whatever is currently on the screen or by using a mouse to position the graphics cursor over the appropriate icon.

Graphical user interfaces have effectively eliminated the need for users to memorize and enter cumbersome commands. In Windows, a GUI marketed by Microsoft Corporation, a file is copied from one disk to another disk by dragging the files icon from one window to another.

The universal acceptance of GUIs has prompted software entrepreneurs to create GUI alternatives for DOS and several popular command-driven software packages. The software that provides a GUI alternative to a command-driven interface is called a shell. In effect, a shell is another layer of software between the user and a command-driven interface. Many people prefer using a DOS shell to entering text-based DOS commands.

2–5 CARE AND MAINTENANCE OF A MICRO

Micros, peripheral devices, and storage media are very reliable. Apply the dictates of common sense to their care and maintenance, and they will give you months, even years, of maintenance-free operation. A few helpful hints are listed here.

Computers are interactive—that is, in their own special way they can communicate with human beings. This capability makes them excellent educational tools. This child is learning about the concept of association. Computers also help adults learn about everything from auto mechanics to zoology.

- Avoid excessive dust and extremes in temperature and humidity.
- Avoid frequent movement of desktop and tower micros.
- Install a *surge protector* between the power source and the micro. Micros as well as other electronic devices can be seriously damaged by a sudden surge of power caused by such things as a bolt of lightning striking a power line.

A blank diskette, costing only a dollar or so, has a very modest value. But once you begin to use the diskette, its value, at least to you, increases greatly. Its value includes the many hours you have spent entering data, preparing spreadsheets, or writing programs. Such a valuable piece of property should be handled with care. The following are a few guidelines for handling 5¼-inch diskettes and 3½-inch microdisks.

Do

- *Do* label each diskette and use a felt-tipped pen on the label.
- *Do* cover the *write-protect notch* on all important diskettes intended for read-only use, such as the program diskettes for micro software packages. On microdisks, slide the *write-protect tab* to its open position.

- *Do* store diskettes in their envelopes so the exposed surface is covered.
- *Do* store diskettes vertically or, if stored flat, place no more than 10 in a stack.
- *Do* store diskettes and microdisks at temperatures between 50 to 125 degrees Fahrenheit.
- *Do* keep a backup of diskettes and microdisks containing important data and programs.
- *Do* remove diskettes and microdisks from disk drives before you turn off the computer.

Don't

- *Don't* fold, spindle, or mutilate diskettes.
- *Don't* force a diskette or microdisk into the disk drive. It should slip in with little or no resistance.
- *Don't* touch the diskette or microdisk surface.
- *Don't* place diskettes or microdisks near a magnetic field, such as magnetic paper-clip holders, tape demagnetizers, or electric motors.
- *Don't* expose diskettes or microdisks to direct sunlight for a prolonged period.
- *Don't* insert or remove a diskette or microdisk from a disk drive if the "drive active" light is on.

2-6 BACKUP: BETTER SAFE THAN SORRY

Safeguarding software and your data may be more important than safeguarding micro hardware. The first commandment in personal computing is

𝕭𝖆𝖈𝖐 𝖚𝖕 𝖞𝖔𝖚𝖗 𝖋𝖎𝖑𝖊𝖘.

If data and program files are destroyed, it may be impossible for them to be re-created within a reasonable period of time. If, on the other hand, the hardware is destroyed, it can be replaced fairly quickly. The impact of losing critical software or files makes **backup** a major concern.

When you create a document, a spreadsheet, or a graph and you wish to recall it at a later time, you *store* the file on disk. You can, of course, store many files on a single disk. If the disk is in some way destroyed (scratched, demagnetized, and so on), you have lost your files unless you have a backup disk. To minimize the possibility of losing valuable files, you should periodically back up (make a copy of) your work disk.

The frequency with which a work disk is backed up depends on its *volatility*, or how often you use the files on the disk. If you spend time every day working with files on a work disk, you should back it up each day. Others are backed up no more often than they are used. Because some updating will occur between backup runs, the re-creation of lost files means that subsequent updates and changes must be redone from the point of the last backup.

Figure 2–7 illustrates the backup procedure for a work diskette that is used daily. Two *generations* of backup are maintained on backup disks A and B. After each day's processing, the contents of the work disk are copied (or dumped) alternately to Disk A or B. In this manner, one backup is always current within a day's processing. If the work disk and the most recent backup are accidentally destroyed, a third backup is current within two days' processing. Disks A and B are alternated as the most current backup.

At one time or another, just about every computer specialist has experienced the trauma of losing work for which there was no backup. It is no fun seeing several days (or weeks) of work disappear, but it does emphasize the point that it is well worth the effort to make backup copies of your work.

FIGURE 2–7 Backup Procedure for Diskette-Based User Files
The diskette containing user files is backed up alternately to Diskette A or B at the end of each day so that one backup file is always current within one day's processing.

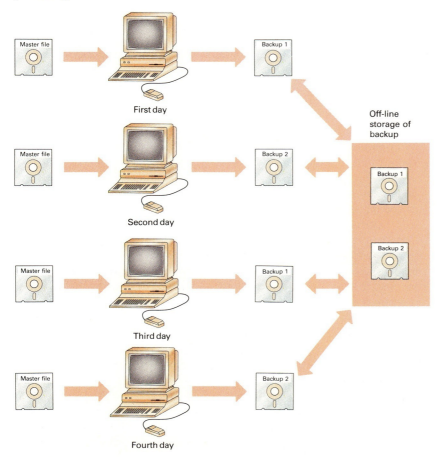

SUMMARY OUTLINE AND IMPORTANT TERMS

2-1 INTERACTING WITH THE SYSTEM. The effective micro user will understand general micro software concepts, how to operate the hardware, **DOS** and/or a **graphical user interface** (**GUI**), and one or more applications programs.

2-2 THE DISK OPERATING SYSTEM (DOS). The **operating system** monitors and controls all input/output and processing activities within a computer system. The four most popular micro operating systems based on number of installations are **MS-DOS** (or **PC-DOS**), **Macintosh DOS**, **OS/2**, and **UNIX** (and spinoffs, such as **XENIX**).

DOS, the center of all software activity, is a family of systems software programs that must be installed on a microcomputer system before it can be used. Systems software is independent of any applications software. The DOS COMMAND.COM program loads other operating system and applications programs into RAM as needed.

DOS has two primary functions. The DOS input/output control function facilitates the movement of data between peripheral devices, the processor, programs, and **RAM** (**random-access memory**). The DOS file- and disk-management function permits users to perform a variety of file maintenance tasks, such as copying files.

2-3 MICROCOMPUTER OPERATION. When you purchase a microcomputer system, you must install the software in a three-step process: make a backup copy; copy files to the permanently installed hard disk; and set system information, revising **defaults** (standard settings) as needed.

When you **power up** a micro, you **boot** the system. First, a program in **read-only memory**, or **ROM**, initializes the system and runs a **system check**. Next, DOS is loaded to RAM, takes control of the system, and presents the user with a **system prompt**.

To **power down** in an orderly manner, **gracefully exit** from all active applications programs prior to shutting off the power.

Whether entering a DOS command or an applications program command, you must be explicit. DOS, in particular, demands strict adherence to command **syntax**.

A microcomputer's keyboard is normally its primary input and control device. In addition to the standard typewriter keyboard, most micro keyboards have **function keys**, also called **soft keys**. Tapping a function key might present the user with a **menu**, which is a displayed list of user options. The software packages are usually distributed with **keyboard templates** that designate which commands are assigned to which function keys. Most keyboards are equipped with a **key pad** and **cursor-control keys**. Use the cursor-control keys for **scrolling**.

Other important keys common to most keyboards are the *ENTER*, *HOME*, *END*, *Page up* and *Page down* (abbreviated as PGUP and PGDN), *Delete* (DEL), *Insert-overstrike* **toggle** (INS), *Backspace* (BKSP), *Escape* (ESC), *SPACEBAR*, *Shift*, *Control* (CTRL), *Alternate* (ALT), and *TAB* keys. In addition to its traditional function, the TAB key facilitates movement between data entry areas, sometimes called **fields**. Each keystroke you enter is sent first to an intermediate **keystroke buffer**.

CHAPTER 2 Interacting with Micros

The hand-held **mouse,** when moved across a desktop, moves the **graphics cursor** accordingly. The graphics cursor is used to *point* and *draw*. Use the mouse for quick positioning of the graphics cursor over the desired menu item, called an **icon.** Typically, you would **click** the mouse's left button to select a menu item. You would press and hold a button to **drag** the graphics cursor across the screen.

You can interact with software packages, such as spreadsheet and database, at three different levels of sophistication: the *menu level*, the *macro level*, and the *programming level*. At the menu level you are initiating individual commands. At the macro and programming levels of interaction you can string together commands and even introduce logic operations.

Menu hierarchies are sometimes called **menu trees.** When you select an item from the **main menu,** you are often presented with another menu of activities, and so on. A menu can appear as a **bar menu** in the **user interface** portion of the display, a **pull-down menu,** a **pop-up menu,** or a **pop-out menu.**

Micro software packages provide users with three ways to select an item from a menu: use the left/right or up/down cursor-control keys; enter the **mnemonic;** or use the mouse to position the graphics cursor at the desired option. Most menus present users with **default options.**

A **macro** is a sequence of frequently used operations or keystrokes that can be recalled as you need it. To **invoke** the macro, you can either refer to it by name or you can enter the series of keystrokes that identify it. Micro software users can create logical sequences of instructions called *programs*.

2–4 **USER-FRIENDLY SOFTWARE. User-friendly** software communicates easily understood words, phrases, and icons to the end user, thus simplifying his or her interaction with the computer system. A user-friendly environment facilitates **navigation** between the elements of the software package. The on-line **help command** provides **context-sensitive** explanations or instructions on how to proceed.

Windows are rectangular displays temporarily superimposed over whatever is currently on the screen. You can manipulate text, data, or graphics in only one window at a time, the **current window. Zoom** in on a particular window to fill the entire screen. **Window panes** enable users to view several parts of the same window subarea at a time.

The trend is away from command-driven interfaces, like DOS, to a user-friendly, graphics-oriented environment called a *graphical user interface*, or *GUI*. The software that provides a GUI alternative to a command-driven interface is called a **shell.**

2–5 **CARE AND MAINTENANCE OF A MICRO.** Apply the dictates of common sense to the care and maintenance of micros, peripheral devices, and storage media. For example, avoid excessive dust, extremes in temperature and humidity, and don't fold, spindle, or mutilate the disks.

2–6 **BACKUP: BETTER SAFE THAN SORRY.** Safeguarding software and your data may be more important than safeguarding micro hardware. The impact of losing critical software or files makes **backup** a major concern. The frequency with which a work disk is backed up depends on its volatility. It is common practice to maintain two generations of backup.

REVIEW EXERCISES

1. What is the purpose of soft keys? Of cursor-control keys?
2. Describe the attributes of user-friendly software.
3. Contrast a bar menu with a pull-down menu.
4. Most word processing packages have a default document size. What other defaults would a word processing package have?
5. Briefly describe two ways you can use a keyboard to enter commands to a microcomputer software package.
6. During a micro software session, what key would you commonly press to move to the beginning of the work area? To negate the current command?
7. Name three microcomputer operating systems.
8. When would you use the zoom feature of a microcomputer software package?
9. How is a pop-up menu displayed?
10. What is a macro and how can using macros save time?
11. What does "booting the system" mean?
12. What must be accomplished to power down in an orderly manner?
13. What key is tapped to toggle between insert and typeover modes?
14. The help command is often assigned to which function key?
15. What is software called that provides a graphical-user-interface alternative to a software package's command-driven interface?
16. When multiple windows are open, the user manipulates text, data, or graphics in which window?
17. Why would you use the mouse to drag the graphics cursor over text in a word processing document?
18. Which two cursor-control keys are used to scroll horizontally?

SELF-TEST (by section)

2-1 Both DOS and/or a _user interface_ (Graphical GUI) provide a link between the user, the microcomputer system, and the applications programs.

2-2 a. DOS is an acronym for disk operating system. (T)/F)
   b. The name of the DOS program that is always resident in RAM during microcomputer operations is _COMMAND.COM_.

2-3 a. A micro user must "kick the system" to load DOS to RAM prior to processing. (T/F)
   b. DOS displays a system _Prompt_ to signal the user that it is ready to accept a user _Command_.
   c. Use the _keypad_ for rapid numeric data entry.
   d. When interacting with a microcomputer via a keyboard, you must wait until the execution of one command is finished before issuing another. (T/F)
   e. Press and hold a mouse button to _drag_ the graphics cursor across the screen.

f. A sequence of frequently used operations or keystrokes that can be activated by the user is called a: (a) menu, (b) <u>macro</u>, or (c) program?

g. Pictographs, called <u>icons</u>, are often associated with user-friendly software.

2-4 a. When software makes it easy for someone with limited computer experience to use it, the software is said to be: (a) <u>user-friendly</u>; (b) a programming pal; or (c) simple software?

b. <u>Zoom</u> in on a particular window to fill the entire screen.

2-5 Always label diskettes with a ballpoint pen. (T/(F))

2-6 The frequency with which a work disk is backed up depends on its volatility. ((T)/F)

Self-test answers. **2-1** graphical user interface (GUI). **2-2 (a)** T; **(b)** COMMAND.COM. **2-3 (a)** F; **(b)** prompt, command; **(c)** keypad; **(d)** F; **(e)** drag; **(f)** b; **(g)** icons. **2-4 (a)** a; **(b)** Zoom. **2-5** F. **2-6** T.

CHAPTER 3
PROCESSORS AND PLATFORMS

STUDENT LEARNING OBJECTIVES

▶ To describe how data are stored in a computer system.
▶ To demonstrate the relationships between bits, bytes, characters, and encoding systems.
▶ To understand the translation of alphanumeric data into a format for internal computer representation.
▶ To explain and illustrate the principles of computer operations.
▶ To identify and describe the relationships between the internal components of a computer.
▶ To distinguish microprocessors by their speed, memory capacity, and word length.
▶ To identify the different types of random-access memory on an MS-DOS microcomputer.
▶ To describe approaches to configuring microcomputer systems.
▶ To distinguish between the various platforms available to microcomputer users.

3-1 A BIT ABOUT THE BIT

Data are stored *temporarily* during processing in a section of the computer system called **primary storage**, or random-access memory (RAM). If you will remember, RAM was introduced and discussed briefly in Chapter 2, "Interacting with Micros." Data are stored *permanently* on **secondary storage** devices such as magnetic tape and disk drives. We discuss primary storage in detail later in this chapter. Secondary storage is covered in Chapter 4, "Micro Peripheral Devices: I/O and Data Storage." Data are stored in both primary and secondary storage as combinations of the two digits in the base-2 **binary** numbering system—1 and 0.

The computer's seemingly endless potential is, in fact, based on only two electronic states—*on* and *off*. The physical characteristics of the computer make it possible to combine these two electronic states in various ways to represent letters and numbers. An "on" or "off" electronic state is represented by a **bit**. (*Bit* is short for *bi*nary dig*it*.) The presence or absence of a bit is referred to as *on-bit* (a binary 1) and *off-bit* (a binary 0), respectively. Physically, these states are achieved in many different ways. In primary storage the two electronic states are represented by the direction of current flow. Another approach is to turn the circuit itself on or off. In secondary storage the two states are made possible by the magnetic arrangement of the surface coating on magnetic tapes and disks (see Chapter 4).

Bits may be fine for computers, but human beings are more comfortable with letters and decimal numbers (the base-10 numerals 0 through 9). Therefore, the letters and decimal numbers that we input to a com-

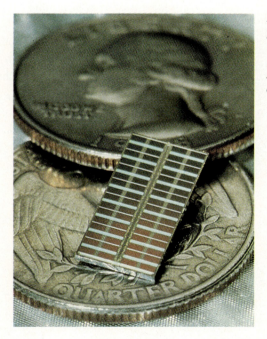

In the first generation of computers (1951–59), each bit was represented by a vacuum tube. Today computers use fingernail-sized chips that can store over one million bits each.

puter system must be translated into 1s and 0s for processing and storage. The computer translates the bits back into letters and decimal numbers on output. This translation is performed so we can recognize and understand the output. It is made possible by encoding systems.

3-2 ENCODING SYSTEMS: COMBINING BITS TO FORM BYTES

Computers do not talk to each other in English, Spanish, or French. They have their own languages, which are better suited to electronic communication. In these languages, bits are combined according to an **encoding system** to represent letters (**alpha** characters), numbers (**numeric** characters), and special characters (such as *, $, +, and &). For example, in the seven-bit **ASCII** encoding system (American Standard Code for Information Interchange—pronounced AS key), which is used primarily in micros and data communications, a B and a 3 are represented by 1000010 and 0110011, respectively.

Letters, numbers, and special characters are referred to collectively as **alphanumeric** characters. Alphanumeric characters are *encoded* into a bit configuration on input so the computer can interpret them. When you press the letter B on a PC keyboard, the B is transmitted to the processor as a coded string of binary digits (for example, 1000010 in ASCII). The characters are *decoded* on output so we can interpret them. For example, a monitor's *device controller* will interpret an ASCII 0110011 as a 3 and display a 3 on the screen. This coding, which is based on a particular encoding system, equates a unique series of bits (1s) and no-bits (0s) with a specific character. Just as the words *mother* and *father* are arbitrary English-language character strings that refer to our parents, 1000011 is an arbitrary ASCII code that refers to the letter C. The combination of bits used to represent a character is called a **byte** (pronounced *bite*). Figure 3–1 shows the binary value (the actual bit configuration) and the decimal equivalent of all 128 of the standard ASCII characters.

The seven-bit ASCII code can represent up to 128 characters (2^7). Although the English language has considerably fewer than 128 *printable* characters, the extra bit configurations are needed to represent a variety of common and not-so-common special characters (such as: - [hyphen]; @ [at]; | [a broken vertical bar]; and ~ [tilde]) and to signal a variety of activities to the computer (such as ringing a bell or telling the computer to accept a piece of datum).

ASCII is a seven-bit code, but the microcomputer byte can store eight bits. There are 256 (2^8) possible bit configurations in an eight-bit byte. Hardware and software vendors use the extra 128 bit configurations to represent control characters or noncharacter images to complement their hardware or software product. For example, the IBM-PC version of extended ASCII contains the characters of many foreign languages (such as Ä [umlaut] and é [acute]) and a wide variety of graphic images that can be combined on a text screen to produce larger images (for example, the box around a window on a display screen).

Character	ASCII Code Binary Value	Decimal Value
A	100 0001	65
B	100 0010	66
C	100 0011	67
D	100 0100	68
E	100 0101	69
F	100 0110	70
G	100 0111	71
H	100 1000	72
I	100 1001	73
J	100 1010	74
K	100 1011	75
L	100 1100	76
M	100 1101	77
N	100 1110	78
O	100 1111	79
P	101 0000	80
Q	101 0001	81
R	101 0010	82
S	101 0011	83
T	101 0100	84
U	101 0101	85
V	101 0110	86
W	101 0111	87
X	101 1000	88
Y	101 1001	89
Z	101 1010	90
a	110 0001	97
b	110 0010	98
c	110 0011	99
d	110 0100	100
e	110 0101	101
f	110 0110	102
g	110 0111	103
h	110 1000	104
i	110 1001	105
j	110 1010	106
k	110 1011	107
l	110 1100	108
m	110 1101	109
n	110 1110	110
o	110 1111	111
p	111 0000	112
q	111 0001	113
r	111 0010	114
s	111 0011	115
t	111 0100	116
u	111 0101	117
v	111 0110	118
w	111 0111	119
x	111 1000	120
y	111 1001	121
z	111 1010	122

Character	ASCII Code Binary Value	Decimal Value
0	011 0000	48
1	011 0001	49
2	011 0010	50
3	011 0011	51
4	011 0100	52
5	011 0101	53
6	011 0110	54
7	011 0111	55
8	011 1000	56
9	011 1001	57
Space	010 0000	32
.	010 1110	46
<	011 1100	60
(	010 1000	40
+	010 1011	43
&	010 0110	38
!	010 0001	33
$	010 0100	36
*	010 1010	42
)	010 1001	41
;	011 1011	59
,	010 1100	44
%	010 0101	37
—	101 1111	95
>	011 1110	62
?	011 1111	63
:	011 1010	58
#	010 0011	35
@	100 0000	64
'	010 0111	39
=	011 1101	61
"	010 0010	34
½	1010 1011	171
¼	1010 1100	172
▒	1011 0010	178
■	1101 1011	219
	1101 1100	220
	1101 1101	221
	1101 1110	222
■	1101 1111	223
√	1111 1011	251
n	1111 1100	252
2	1111 1101	253
■	1111 1110	254
(blank)	1111 1111	255

FIGURE 3–1 ASCII Codes
This figure contains the binary and decimal values for commonly used ASCII characters.

3-3 COMPONENTS OF A COMPUTER SYSTEM: A CLOSER LOOK AT THE PROCESSOR AND RAM

Let's review. We have learned that a computer system has input, output, storage, and processing components and that the *processor* is the "intelligence" of a computer system. We have discussed how data are represented inside a computer system in electronic states called bits. We are now ready to expose the inner workings of the nucleus of the computer

CHAPTER 3 Processors and Platforms

system—the processor. We call the processor in a microcomputer a *microprocessor*.

The internal operation of a personal computer is interesting, but there really is no mystery to it. The mystery is in the minds of those who listen to hearsay and believe science fiction writers. The computer is a non-thinking electronic device that has to be plugged into an electrical power source, just like a toaster or a lamp.

Literally hundreds of different types of computers are marketed by scores of manufacturers. The complexity of each type may vary considerably, but in the end each processor, sometimes called the **central processing unit** or **CPU**, has only two fundamental sections: the *control unit* and the *arithmetic and logic unit*. RAM also plays an integral part in the internal operation of a processor. These three—RAM, the control unit, and the arithmetic and logic unit—work together. Let's look at their functions and the relationships between them.

Primary Storage

The Technology. Unlike magnetic secondary storage devices, such as tape and disk, primary storage, or RAM, has no moving parts. With no mechanical movement, data can be accessed from RAM at electronic speeds—close to the speed of light. Most of today's PCs use CMOS (Complementary Metal-Oxide Semiconductor) technology for RAM. A state-of-the-art CMOS memory chip, which is about one eighth the size of a postage stamp, can store about 4,000,000 bits, or over 400,000 characters of data!

But there is one major problem with semiconductor storage. It's *volatile*. That is, when the electrical current is turned off or interrupted, the data are lost. Researchers are working to perfect a nonvolatile primary storage that will retain its contents after an electrical interruption. Several nonvolatile technologies, such as **bubble memory**, have emerged, but none has exhibited the qualities necessary for widespread application. However, bubble memory is superior to CMOS for use in certain computers. It is highly reliable, it is not susceptible to environmental fluctuations, and it can operate on battery power for a considerable length of time. These qualities make bubble memory well suited for use with laptop PCs.

Function. RAM provides the processor with *temporary* storage for programs and data. *All programs and data must be transferred to RAM from an input device* (such as a keyboard) *or from secondary storage* (such as a disk) *before programs can be executed or data can be processed*. RAM space is always at a premium; therefore, after a program has been executed, the storage space it occupied is reallocated to another program awaiting execution. Figure 3–2 illustrates how all input/output (I/O) is "read to" or "written from" RAM (primary storage). In the figure, an inquiry (input) is made on a keyboard. The inquiry, in the form of a message, is routed to processor. The message is interpreted, and the processor initiates action to retrieve the appropriate program and data from secondary storage. The program and data are "loaded," or moved,

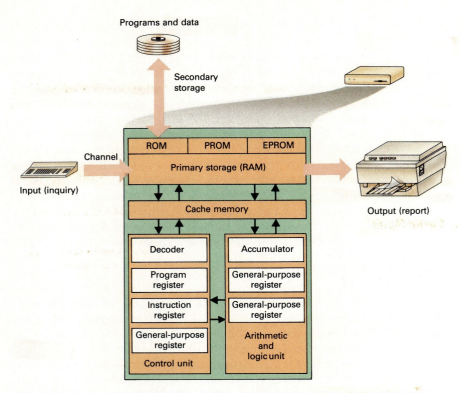

FIGURE 3–2 Interaction Between Primary Storage and Microcomputer System Components
All programs and data must be transferred from an input device or from secondary storage before programs can be executed and data can be processed. During processing, instructions and data are passed between the various types of internal memories, the control unit, and the arithmetic and logic unit. Output is transferred to the printer from RAM.

to RAM from secondary storage. This is a *nondestructive read* process. That is, the program and data that are read reside in both RAM (temporarily) and secondary storage (permanently). The data are manipulated according to program instructions and a report is written from RAM to a printer.

A program instruction or a piece of data is stored in a specific RAM location called an **address**. Addresses permit program instructions and data to be located, accessed, and processed. The content of each address is constantly changing as different programs are executed and new data are processed.

ROM, PROM, and EPROM. A special type of RAM, called *read-only memory (ROM)*, cannot be altered by the end user. The contents of ROM are "hard-wired" (designed into the logic of the memory chip) by the manufacturer and can be "read only." ROM programs are sometimes referred to as **firmware**. When you turn on a microcomputer system, a program in ROM automatically readies the computer system for use, loads DOS, and produces the initial display screen prompt. This procedure, which is referred to as booting the system, is discussed in Chapter 2, "Interacting with Micros."

A variation of ROM is **programmable read-only memory** (**PROM**). PROM is ROM into which you, the user, can load "read-only" programs and data. However, to do so you must have some sophisticated equipment. Some microcomputer software packages, such as spreadsheets, are available as PROM units as well as on diskette. Once a program is loaded to PROM, it is seldom if ever changed. However, if you need to be able to revise the contents of PROM, there is **EPROM**, erasable PROM.

Cache Memory. Programs and data are loaded to RAM from secondary storage because the time required to access a program instruction or piece of data from RAM is significantly less than from secondary storage. Thousands of instructions or pieces of data can be accessed from RAM in the time it would take to access a single piece of data from disk storage. RAM is essentially a high-speed holding area for data and programs. In fact, nothing really happens in a computer system until the program instructions and data are moved to the processor. This transfer of instructions and data to the processor can be time-consuming, even at RAM's microsecond speeds. To facilitate an even faster transfer of instructions and data to the processor, some computers are designed with **cache memory** (see Figure 3–2). Cache memory is employed by computer designers to increase the computer system **throughput** (the rate at which work is performed).

Like RAM, cache is a high-speed holding area for program instructions and data. However, cache memory uses a technology that is about 10 times faster than RAM and about 100 times more expensive. With only a fraction of the capacity of RAM, cache memory holds only those instructions and data that are likely to be needed next by the processor.

The Control Unit

Just as the processor is the nucleus of a computer system, the **control unit** is the nucleus of the processor. If you will recall from an earlier discussion, the control unit and the arithmetic and logic unit are the two fundamental sections of a processor. The control unit has three primary functions:

1. To read and interpret program instructions
2. To direct the operation of internal processor components
3. To control the flow of programs and data in and out of RAM

A program must be loaded to RAM before it can be executed. During execution, the first in a sequence of program instructions is moved from RAM to the control unit, where it is decoded and interpreted by the **decoder**. The control unit then directs other processor components to carry out the operations necessary to execute the instruction.

▶ MEMORY BITS

Internal Storage
- Primary storage (main memory, RAM)
- ROM, PROM, and EPROM
- Cache
- Registers

▶ THE COMPUTER ON A CHIP

1.

2.

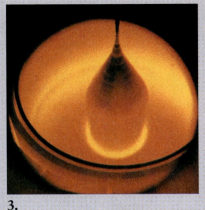

3.

4.

5.

6.

The 1879 invention of the light bulb symbolized the beginning of electronics. Electronics then evolved into the use of vacuum tubes, then into transistors, and now integrated circuits. Today's microminiaturization of electronic circuitry is continuing to have a profound effect on the way we live and work.

These relatively inexpensive "computers on a chip" have thousands of uses, many of which we now take for granted. They are found in almost every type of modern machine, from computers to robots, from "smart" home appliances to "talking" cash registers, from automobile dashboards to high-flying spaceships.

Current technology permits the placement of hundreds of thousands of transistors and electronic switches on a single chip. Chips already fit into wristwatches and credit cards, but electrical and computer engineers want them even smaller. In electronics, smaller is better. The ENIAC, the first full-scale digital electronic computer, weighed 50 tons and occupied an entire room. Today a complete computer is fabricated within a single piece of silicon the size of a child's fingernail.

Chip designers think in terms of nanoseconds (1/1,000,000,000 of a second) and microns (1/1,000,000 of a meter). They want to pack as many circuit elements as they can into the structure of a chip. High-density packing reduces the time required for an electrical signal to travel from one circuit element to the next—resulting in faster computers. Current research indicates that chips eventually will be produced that contain millions of circuit elements!

The fabrication of integrated circuits involves a multistep process using various photochemical etching and metallurgical techniques. This complex and interesting process is illustrated here with photos, from silicon to the finished product.

Design

1. Chips are designed and manufactured to perform a particular function. One chip might be a microprocessor for a personal computer. Another might be primary storage. Another might be the logic for a talking vending machine. Chip designers use computer-aided design (CAD) systems to create the logic for individual circuits. A chip contains from one to 30 layers of circuits. In this multilayer circuit design, each layer is color-coded so the designer can distinguish between the various layers.

2. An electron-beam exposure system etches the circuitry into a glass stencil called a *mask*. A mask such as this one is produced for each circuit layer. The number of layers depends on the complexity of the chip's logic.

Fabrication

3. Molten silicon is spun into cylindrical ingots. Because silicon, the second most abundant

7.

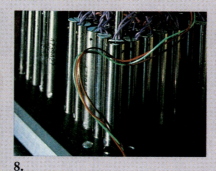
8.

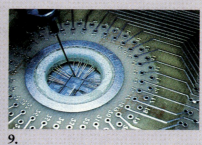
9.

10.

11.

12.

substance, is used in the fabrication of integrated circuits, chips are sometimes referred to as "intelligent grains of sand."

4. The ingot is shaped and prepared prior to being cut into silicon wafers. Once the wafers are cut, they are polished to a perfect finish.

5. Silicon wafers that eventually will contain several hundred chips are placed in an oxygen furnace at 1200 degrees Centigrade. In the furnace the wafer is coated with other minerals to create the physical properties needed to produce transistors and electronic switches on the surface of the wafer.

6. The mask is placed over the wafer and both are exposed to ultraviolet light. In this way the circuit pattern is transferred onto the wafer. Plasma (superhot gases) technology is used to etch the circuit pattern permanently into the wafer. This is one of several techniques used in the etching process. The wafer is returned to the furnace and given another coating on which to etch another circuit layer. The procedure is repeated for each circuit layer until the wafer is complete.

7. The result of the coating/etching process is a silicon wafer that contains from 100 to 400 integrated circuits.

8. It takes only a second for this instrument to drill 1440 tiny holes in a wafer. The holes enable the interconnection of the layers of circuits. Each layer must be perfectly aligned (within a millionth of a meter) with the others.

Testing

9. The chips are tested while they are still part of the wafer. Each integrated circuit on the wafer is powered up and given a series of tests. Fine needles make the connection for these computer-controlled tests. The precision demands are so great that as many as half the chips are found to be defective. A drop of ink is deposited on defective chips.

Packaging

10. A diamond saw separates the wafer into individual chips in a process called *dicing*.

11. The chips are packaged in protective ceramic or metal carriers. The carriers have standard-sized electrical pin connectors that allow the chip to be plugged conveniently into circuit boards. Because the pins tend to corrode, the pin connectors are the most vulnerable part of a computer system. To avoid corrosion and a bad connection, the pins on some carriers are made of gold.

12. The completed circuit boards are installed in computers and thousands of other computer-controlled devices.

The control unit contains high-speed working storage areas called **registers** that can store no more than a few bytes (see Figure 3–2). The speed at which registers handle instructions and data is about 10 times faster than that of cache memory. They are used for a variety of processing functions. One register, called the **instruction register**, contains the instruction being executed. Other general-purpose registers store data needed for immediate processing. Registers also store status information. For example, the **program register** contains the address of the next instruction to be executed. Registers facilitate the movement of data and instructions between RAM, the control unit, and the arithmetic and logic unit.

The Arithmetic and Logic Unit

The **arithmetic and logic unit** performs all computations (addition, subtraction, multiplication, and division) and all logic operations (comparisons).

Examples of *computations* include the payroll deduction for social security, the day-end inventory, the balance on a bank statement, and the like. A *logic* operation compares two pieces of data. Then, based on the result of the comparison, the program "branches" to one of several alternative sets of program instructions. Let's use an inventory system to illustrate the logic operation. At the end of each day the inventory level of each item in stock is compared to a reorder point. For each comparison indicating an inventory level that falls below (<) the reorder point, a sequence of program instructions is executed that produces a purchase order. For each comparison indicating an inventory level at or above (= or >) the reorder point, another sequence of instructions is executed.

The arithmetic and logic unit also does alphabetic comparisons. For example, when comparing Smyth and Smith, Smyth is evaluated as being greater alphabetically, so it is positioned after Smith.

The Machine Cycle

You have probably heard of computer programming languages such as COBOL, BASIC, and RPG. There are dozens of programming languages in common usage. However, in the end COBOL, BASIC, and the other languages are translated into the only language that a computer understands—machine language. Machine language instructions are represented inside the computer as strings of binary digits up to 32 digits in length.

Every machine language has a predefined format for each type of instruction. The relative position within the instruction designates whether a sequence of characters is an **operation code**, an **operand**, or irrelevant. The typical machine language will have from 50 to 200 separate operation codes. The operation code, or **op-code**, is that portion of the fundamental computer instruction that designates the operation to be performed (add, compare, retrieve data from RAM, and so on). The operand is that portion of the instruction that designates data or refers

> ▶ **MEMORY BITS**
>
> *The Processor*
> - The control unit
>   Decodes instructions
>   Controls processor operation
>   Interacts with RAM
> - The arithmetic and logic unit
>   Performs computation operations
>   Performs logic operations

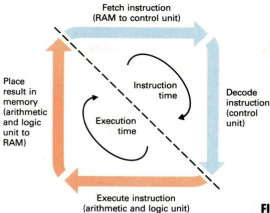

FIGURE 3-3 The Machine Cycle

to one or more addresses in RAM in which data can be found or placed. The op-code determines whether the operand contains data, addresses, or both.

Every computer has **a machine cycle.** The following actions take place during the machine cycle (see Figure 3-3):

- *Fetch instruction.* The next instruction to be executed (op-code and operand) is retrieved, or "fetched," from RAM or cache memory and loaded to the instruction register in the control unit (see Figure 3-2).
- *Decode instruction.* The instruction is decoded and interpreted.
- *Execute instruction.* Using whatever processor resources are needed (primarily the arithmetic and logic unit), the instruction is executed.
- *Place result in memory.* The results are placed in the appropriate memory position (usually RAM or a register in the arithmetic and logic unit called the **accumulator**). (See Figure 3-2.)

The speed of a processor is sometimes measured by how long it takes to complete a machine cycle. The timed interval that comprises the machine cycle is the total of the **instruction time,** or **I-time,** and the **execution time,** or **E-time** (see Figure 3-3). The I-time is made up of the first two activities of the machine cycle—fetch and decode the instruction. The E-time comprises the last two activities of the machine cycle—execute the instruction and store the results.

3-4 DESCRIBING THE PROCESSOR: DISTINGUISHING CHARACTERISTICS

People are people, and micros are micros, but how do we distinguish one micro from another? We describe people in terms of height, build, age, and so on. We describe computers or processors in terms of *word length*, *speed*, and the *capacity* of their RAM. For example, a computer might be described as a 32-bit, 25-MHz, 4-Mb micro. Let's see what this means.

Word Length

A **word** is the number of bits that are handled as a unit for a particular processor. The **word length** of the first generation of PCs was eight bits. Most of the PCs made during the 1980s had 16-bit processors. (This is another way of saying the processor has a word length of 16 bits.) State-of-the-art microcomputers, such as the Intel 386 and 486, have 32-bit processors, which can process four 8-bit bytes at a time.

Processor Speed

A *crystal oscillator* paces the execution of instructions within the processor of a microcomputer. A micro's processor speed is rated by its frequency of oscillation, or the number of clock cycles per second. Most personal computers are rated between 5 and 50 **megahertz**, or **MHz** (millions of clock cycles). The elapsed time for one clock cycle is 1/frequency (1 divided by the frequency). For example, the time it takes to complete one cycle on a 20-MHz processor is 1/20,000,000, or 0.00000005 seconds, or 50 nanoseconds. Normally several clock cycles are required to retrieve, decode, and execute a single program instruction. The shorter the clock cycle, the faster the processor.

To properly evaluate the processing capability of a micro, you must consider both the processor speed and the word length. A 32-bit micro with a 25-MHz processor has more processing capability than a 16-bit micro with a 25-MHz processor.

We seldom think in time units of less than a second; consequently, it is almost impossible for us to think in terms of computer speeds. Imagine, today's microcomputers can execute more instructions in a minute than the number of times your heart has beat since the day you were born!

Capacity of RAM

The capacity of RAM is stated in terms of the number of bytes it can store. As we learned in this chapter, a byte, or eight bits, is roughly equivalent to a character (such as A, 1, &).

Memory capacity usually is stated in terms of **kilobytes** (**KB**), a convenient designation for 1024 (2^{10}) bytes of storage, and in terms of **megabytes** (**MB**), which is 1,048,576 (2^{20}) bytes. Notice that 1 KB is about 1000 and 2 MB is about 1,000,000, thus the origin of the prefixes *kilo* and *mega*. Memory capacities of modern micros range from 640 KB to 16 MB. Occasionally you will see memory capacities of individual chips stated in terms of **kilobits** (**Kb**) and **megabits** (**Mb**).

▶ **MEMORY BITS**

Processor Description (Micros)
- *Word length:* Bits handled as a unit (8, 16, or 32)
- *Speed:* Megahertz (5 to 50 MHz)
- *RAM Capacity:* Kilobytes or megabytes (640 KB to 16 MB)

The microcomputer being used by these retail consultants is based on the Intel 80386 chip. It has a processor speed of 25 MHz, a RAM capacity of 10 megabytes, and a word length of 32 bits.

Now if anyone ever asks you what a 32-bit, 20-MHz, 4-Mb micro is, you've got the answer! This describes the processor of what is emerging as the entry-level PC.

Running Several Programs Concurrently

Multitasking. All modern micros have **multitasking** capabilities. Multitasking is the *concurrent* execution of more than one program at a time. Actually, a computer can execute only one program at a time. But its internal processing speed is so fast that several programs can be allocated "slices" of computer time in rotation; this makes it appear that several programs are being executed at once.

The great difference between processor speed and the speeds of the peripheral devices makes multitasking possible. An eight-page-per-minute printer cannot even challenge the speed of a high-performance PC. The processor is continually waiting for the peripheral devices to complete such tasks as retrieving a record from disk storage or printing a report. During these waiting periods, the processor just continues processing other programs. In this way, computer system resources are used efficiently.

In a multitasking environment, it is not unusual for several programs to require the same I/O device. For example, two or more programs may be competing for the printer. Rather than hold up the processing of a program by waiting for the printer to become available, both programs are executed and the printer output for one is temporarily loaded to magnetic disk. As the printer becomes available, the output is called from magnetic disk and printed. This process is called **spooling**.

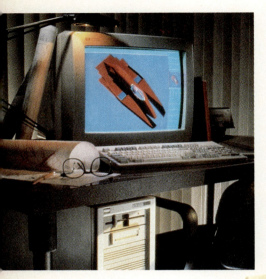

This multitasking micro can run several programs concurrently. As one example, the user can manipulate the on-screen image with a design program while another image is being printed.

Foreground and Background Processing. In a multitasking environment, programs running concurrently are controlled and assigned priorities by the operating system. On a micro the **current program**, or the one with which the user is currently interacting, is given the highest priority and is run in the **foreground**. The foreground is that part of RAM that contains the highest priority program. Other lower priority programs are run in the **background** part of RAM. The operating system rotates allocation of the processor resource between foreground and background programs, with the foreground program receiving the lion's share of time. For example, the foreground program might get 15 milliseconds of processor time out of each 20-millisecond time slice.

Memory-Resident Programs. One class of programs can be loaded to RAM and left there for later recall, even during an interactive session with word processing or spreadsheet software. Once loaded, the user can *terminate* the program *and* it will *stay resident* in memory. These RAM-resident programs are called, appropriately, **terminate-and-stay-resident**, or **TSR**, programs. A TSR in RAM can be activated instantly while running another program by tapping the TSR's **hotkey**, typically a seldom used key combination such as SHIFT+CTRL. When you are finished with the TSR, you are returned to the program you left when you tapped the hotkey—but the TSR remains in RAM.

There are a variety of helpful TSRs, including an on-line calendar, dictionary, grammar checker, scratch pad, calculator, clock, and many more.

MS-DOS and Multitasking. This discussion addresses multitasking in the MS-DOS environment. To fully understand the multitasking of MS-DOS applications, you need to be familiar with the kinds of RAM available to the user in the MS-DOS environment. Your micro always has some **conventional memory** and possibly **extended memory** and/or **expanded memory**.

- *Conventional memory (user area).* The microprocessors used in the early versions of the IBM PC were designed to address up to 1 MB of RAM (see Figure 3-4). The memory between Position 0 and the 1-MB limit is called *conventional memory*. With MS-DOS, *all* programs must run in conventional memory. When you turn on the computer, DOS and related software are loaded to the first 640 KB of conventional memory—the user area. Whatever memory is left in the user area is available for use by other programs. For example, if DOS and related software occupy 60 KB of memory, then any program you run must fit into the remaining 580 KB of conventional memory (640 KB less 60 KB). Virtually all micros sold after 1988 are configured with at least 640 KB of conventional memory; however, some earlier micros have only 512 KB or less. DOS checks memory and displays RAM capacity during the booting procedure.
- *Conventional memory (system area).* Conventional memory between 640 KB and 1024 KB (1 MB) is referred to as **reserved memory** because it is reserved for exclusive use by system programs, such as

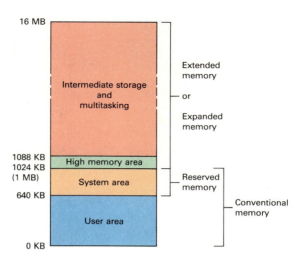

FIGURE 3–4 DOS Memory
Depending on the technology of a particular MS-DOS–based PC, the PC will be configured with up to 1024 KB (1 MB) of conventional memory and up to 15 MB of additional extended and/or expanded memory.

those that control the input to and output from the processor (see Figure 3–4). Until recently, having the extra 384 KB of reserved memory (1024 KB less 640 KB) on a PC was a luxury; however, it is now considered standard with the newer micros.

- *Extended memory.* Many of today's micros have up to an additional 15 MB of extended memory. Extended memory is just that—an extension of conventional memory. However, with one 64-KB exception, MS-DOS programs cannot run in extended memory. The exception is the **high memory area (HMA)**, the 64-KB area just above 1 megabyte (1024 KB to 1088 KB). Special software is needed to access the HMA. In general, extended memory is used as an intermediate storage area for print jobs and to optimize the transfer of data and programs between disk and RAM.

- *Expanded memory.* Micros can be equipped with up to 15 MB of expanded memory. Expanded memory is used in conjunction with special software and an add-on expanded-memory board (or an Intel 386 or higher microprocessor) to run DOS programs. As far as DOS, the operating system, is concerned, there is still only 1 MB of conventional memory in which to run all programs. However, an expanded-memory management program, which runs in conventional memory, links conventional and expanded memory in a manner that permits the concurrent execution of user programs that exceed the 1-MB barrier. *This same software can enable extended memory to work like expanded memory and run DOS programs.*

A variety of programs permit the use of expanded and extended memory for multitasking. Programs such as Windows (Microsoft Corporation) and DESQview (Quarterdeck Office Systems) interface with DOS to permit the running of as many programs as will fit in your RAM. For example, a micro with 1 MB of conventional memory and 3 MB of extended/expanded memory running under Windows can easily run WordPerfect, Lotus 1-2-3, dBASE IV, and several TSRs concurrently.

> **MEMORY BITS**
>
> *MS-DOS Memory*
> - Conventional memory (0 to 1 MB)
>   User area (0 to 640 KB)
>   System area or reserved memory (640 KB to 1 MB)
> - Extended memory (up to 15 MB)
>   An extension of conventional memory
>   Includes 64 KB of High Memory Area
> - Expanded memory (up to 15 MB)

The exact mix of RAM needed to do multitasking would depend on the technology of your PC. The IBM PC evolved to the PC-XT to the PC-AT to the Intel 386- and 486-based PCs. The way you would equip these PCs with RAM varies with the technology. Generally, the new 386- and 486-based PCs are equipped with 1 MB of conventional memory and at least 1 MB of expanded memory.

3-5 CONFIGURING A MICROCOMPUTER SYSTEM

Normally, computer professionals are called upon to select, configure, and install the hardware associated with minicomputers and mainframe computers. But for micros, the user typically selects, configures, and installs his or her own system; therefore, it is important that you know what makes up a microcomputer system and how it fits together.

A Typical Microcomputer Configuration

The computer and its peripheral devices are called the computer system **configuration**. The configuration of a microcomputer can vary. The most typical micro configuration consists of the following:

1. A microcomputer
2. A 101-key keyboard and a mouse for input
3. A color monitor for **soft-copy** (temporary) output
4. A printer for *hard-copy* (printed) output
5. Two disk drives for permanent storage of data and programs (one for a permanently installed disk and one to accommodate interchangeable diskettes)

In most microcomputer systems these components are purchased as separate physical units then linked together. Micros that give users the flexibility to configure the system with a variety of peripheral devices (input/output and storage) are said to have an **open architecture**. We use the term *architecture* to refer to a computer system's design. A component stereo system provides a good analogy with which to illustrate the concept of open architecture. In a stereo system, the tuner is the central component to which equalizers, tape decks, compact disk play-

CHAPTER 3 Processors and Platforms

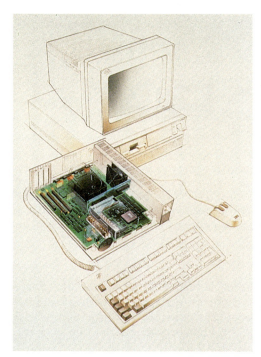

The inside of this IBM PS/2 Model 70 486 is representative of what you might see when you remove the cover of a desktop micro. The keyboard rests in front of the PC. Looking across the front from left to right, there is a speaker for audible output, a 3½-inch microdisk drive, space for another microdisk drive, and the on/off switch. The system board, located to the right of the 3½-inch microdisk drive, contains an Intel 80486 microprocessor (the square chip). The black box in the right rear is a 3½-inch fixed disk that can store over 100 million characters of data. Three expansion slots are positioned at the left rear of the micro. Serial and parallel ports (not shown) are positioned at the back of the unit.

ers, speakers, and so on can be attached. An open-architecture microcomputer system is configured by linking any of a wide variety of peripheral devices to the processor component. As a rule of thumb, if there is a need for a special type of input/output or storage device, then someone markets it. The IBM family of computers, their compatibles, and most modern micros have open-architecture systems. In a **closed architecture**, the system is fully configured when it is sold.

In keeping with conversational computerese, we will drop the *system* from *microcomputer system*. Therefore, all future references to a personal computer or a microcomputer imply a microcomputer *system*.

Linking Micro Components

An open architecture, also called a **bus architecture**, is possible because all micro components are linked via a common electrical **bus**. In Chapter 1 we compared the processing component of a microcomputer to the human brain. Just as the brain sends and receives signals through the central nervous system, the processor sends and receives electrical signals through the bus. The bus is the path through which the processor sends data and commands to RAM and all peripheral devices. It sends the data and commands in the form of electronic signals—bits. In short, the bus is the vehicle by which the processor communicates with its peripherals and vice versa. The processor, RAM, and disk-storage devices usually are connected directly to the bus—that is, without cables.

A 16-bit bus uses its data pathways to transfer 16 bits, or 2 bytes of data in parallel, between the various components. A 32-bit bus, which is

A portable micro can be configured with a variety of input and output devices. (Input/output devices are discussed in Chapter 4.) Cables from each device are connected to the input/output ports at the back of the processor unit. This IBM Model L40 SX has a 25-pin parallel and a nine-pin serial port. The micro also is configured to accommodate an external keyboard (round connector) and an external monitor (nine-pin connector).

state of the art in micros, can transfer 32 bits, or 4 bytes in parallel. Early PCs had only eight-bit buses. The capacity of the bus directly affects the throughput of the computer system. For example, the processing capability of a 20-MHz micro with a 32-bit bus is twice that of one with the same processor and a 16-bit bus.

In an open architecture, external input/output devices (that is, devices external to the processor cabinet) and some storage devices are plugged into the bus in much the same way that you plug a lamp into an electrical outlet. The receptacle, called a **port**, provides a direct link to the micro's common electrical bus.

External peripheral devices are linked to, or *interfaced* with, the processor via cables through either a **serial port** or a **parallel port**.

- *Serial ports*. Serial ports facilitate the *serial transmission* of data, *one bit at a time*. Serial ports provide an interface for low-speed printers and modems. The de facto standard for micro serial ports is the 9-pin or 25-pin (male or female) **RS-232C connector**.
- *Parallel ports*. Parallel ports facilitate the *parallel transmission* of data, *usually one byte (eight bits) at a time*. Parallel ports use the same 25-pin RS-232C connector or the 36-pin **Centronics connector**. Parallel ports provide the interface for such devices as high-speed printers, magnetic-tape backup units, and other computers.

▶ **MEMORY BITS**

Ports
- Serial
   Serial transmission (a bit at a time)
   Connectors: 9-pin or 25-pin RS-232C
- Parallel
   Parallel transmission (a byte at a time)
   Connectors: RS-232C or 36-pin Centronics

Expansion Slots and Add-on Boards

Also connected to the common electrical bus are *expansion slots*, which usually are housed in the processor cabinet. These slots enable a micro owner to enhance the functionality of a basic micro configuration with a wide variety of special-function *add-on boards*, also called **add-on cards**. These "add-ons" contain the electronic circuitry for a wide variety of computer-related functions. The number of available expansion slots varies from computer to computer. Some of the more popular add-on boards are listed below.

- *RAM.* Expands memory, usually in increments of 64 KB, 256 KB, or 1 MB.
- *Color and graphics adapter.* Permits interfacing with video monitors that have graphics and/or color capabilities. The EGA (enhanced graphic adapter) and the VGA (video graphics array) boards enable the interfacing of high-resolution monitors with the processor. (The VGA monitor has emerged as the standard for contemporary micros.) These add-on boards usually come with at least 256 KB of *dedicated RAM*, RAM that is not available to the user. Monitors are discussed more in Chapter 4, "Micro Peripheral Devices: I/O and Data Storage."
- *Modem.* A modem permits communication with remote computers via a telephone-line link. Modems are discussed more in Chapter 7, "Data Communications and Networks."
- *Internal battery-powered clock/calendar.* This board provides continuous and/or on-demand display of or access to the current date and time (e.g., Friday, March 12, 1993, 9:35 A.M.). The system board on all late-model micros includes this capability.
- *Serial port.* Installation of this board provides access to the bus via another serial port. Most micros are sold with one serial and one parallel port.
- *Parallel port.* Installation of this board provides access to the bus via another parallel port.
- *Printer spooler.* This add-on board enables data to be printed while the user continues with other processing activities. Data are transferred (spooled) at a high speed from RAM to a *print buffer* (an intermediate storage area) and then routed to the printer from the buffer.
- *Hard disk.* Hard disks with capacities of as much as 40 MB can be installed in expansion slots.
- *Coprocessor.* These "extra" processors, which are under the control of the main processor, help relieve the main processor of certain tasks, such as arithmetic functions. This sharing of duties helps increase system throughput, the rate at which work can be performed by the microcomputer system.
- *Accelerator.* The accelerator board gives the user the flexibility to upgrade a micro's processor. In effect, the higher speed processor on the accelerator board replaces the existing processor.
- *Network interface.* The network interface card (NIC) facilitates and controls the exchange of data between the micros in a PC *network*

Personal computers are everywhere and, as such, are particularly vulnerable to unauthorized use or malicious tampering. As an added layer of security, many companies are opting to use a magnetic card reader as part of the user sign-on procedure. The card reader comes with an add-on board that is inserted in one of the micro's expansion slots. The reader reads commonly carried credit cards, door-opener cards, telephone cards, and so on. When used in conjunction with authorization codes, a PC can have the same level of security as an automatic teller machine.

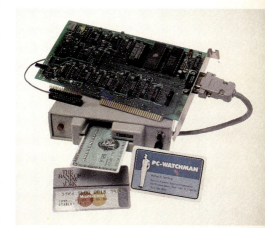

(several micros linked together). Each PC in a network must be equipped with an NIC. The cables that link the PCs are physically connected to the NICs.

- *Motion video.* This card enables full-motion color video with audio to be integrated with other output on the monitor's screen. Because the card accepts multiple inputs, videos can be shown full-screen (one video input) or in windows (multiple video inputs).
- *VCR backup.* This board enables an ordinary VHS or Beta videocassette recorder to be used as a tape backup device. One ordinary videocassette tape can hold up to 80 MB.

Most of the add-on boards are *multifunction*: They include two or more of these capabilities. For example, one popular **multifunction add-on board** comes with a serial port, a modem, and an internal battery-powered clock/calendar.

Expansion slots are at a premium. To make the most efficient use of these slots, circuit-board manufacturers have created **half-size expansion boards** that fit in a "short slot" (half an expansion slot). These half-size boards effectively double the number of expansion slots available for a given microcomputer.

3–6 PLATFORMS

Microcomputer software is written to run under a specific **platform**. A platform defines the standards followed by those who create proprietary software packages, such as word processing. Specifically, the platform is defined by the processor's design architecture and the operating system being used. The term **operating environment** is used interchangeably with *platform*.

The Single-User Environment

MS-DOS and Windows. Through 1990 the platform of choice for the vast majority of PC users was defined by micros that are functionally compatible with the 1984 IBM PC-AT architecture and run under MS-DOS. This platform dominated because

1. Most users operated in the single-user environment.
2. Thousands of software packages have been created for this platform.
3. Millions of people are familiar with this platform and are reluctant to change.
4. Users have a tremendous financial investment in software and hardware that run under this platform.

However, by itself, this platform permits relatively little multitasking capability, and users want multitasking capabilities.

Responding to this need, Microsoft Corporation introduced software that expanded this platform to include multitasking. Microsoft's Windows, by virtue of its warm acceptance in the marketplace, defines a new

At the Apple "Mac Fac" (Macintosh Factory), microcomputers are turned on and "burned in" for several days before shipment to lower the probability that a system will fail on delivery.

platform. Windows runs under MS-DOS, but programs written to take full advantage of its potential must conform to Windows standards.

Windows provides a GUI (graphical user interface) with the system and enables multitasking. Several programs are displayed in overlapping windows and data can be passed between them. Software packages that conform to Windows standards employ a GUI that looks and feels like the Windows GUI. Most popular micro programs that gained their popularity as MS-DOS programs have been converted or they are being converted to run under the Windows platform. Moreover, most software packages that run under MS-DOS and do not conform to Windows standards can be run within Windows. These programs, which are called non-Windows programs, are no less effective when run within Windows, but they cannot take full advantage of the Windows GUI.

OS/2. OS/2 is the next generation of MS-DOS. It is a single-user multitasking operating system that requires an Intel 286 or better microprocessor. In addition to multitasking, the great advantage of the OS/2 platform is that it enables up to 16 MB of RAM to be addressed (as opposed to 1 MB for MS-DOS). On the down side, OS/2 is a very sophisticated environment that requires up to 4 MB of dedicated RAM. OS/2 users interact with the system via a GUI called *Presentation Manager*.

Even though OS/2 breaks the MS-DOS 1-MB barrier, it has been slow to catch on. Software vendors are reluctant to devote resources to creating OS/2-based software for a market dominated by MS-DOS. As you might expect, users are reluctant to switch to OS/2 because of the lack of software that runs under the OS/2 platform.

The Multiuser Environment

Each of the multiuser operating systems defines a different platform for which software is created, the most popular being UNIX and its spinoffs. Many of the popular software packages have been retrofitted to run under UNIX. For example, WordPerfect, a word processing package, has a product that runs under the UNIX platform. Much of the software written for this platform addresses office or department information systems. For example, a doctor's clinic might have three terminals for administration and three for inquiry.

MCA versus EISA

Since the emergence of microcomputers in the mid-1970s, the dominant PCs have been the Apple II series, the Apple Macintosh series, the IBM-PC series (and its compatibles), and the IBM-PS/2 series. Dozens of manufacturers make clones of the IBM PC and the low-end PS/2 micros; however, the cloning may decrease or come to an end as we move into the next generation of micros.

In 1988 a group of prominent manufacturers of IBM-PC–compatible computers, known as the Gang of Nine (Compaq Computer Corpora-

Several workstations are connected to this multiuser microcomputer.

tion, Hewlett-Packard Company, AST Research Inc., Zenith Data Systems, Tandy Corporation, and others), decided to break away from IBM design architectures. The Gang of Nine and other manufacturers are banking on their collective strength being great enough to offset the market dominance that IBM has enjoyed for decades. Now we as users are being asked to make a choice that may affect our computing environment for years. For the overwhelming majority of micro users, the choice used to be between IBM and Apple. Now a large group of micro manufacturers is offering a third choice.

The concurrent processing environment being pursued by IBM is called **Micro Channel Architecture**, or **MCA** for short. MCA is found on the high-end PS/2 line of computers. Apple's state-of-the-art architecture, called **Nubus**, is being installed on high-end Macintosh computers. The Gang of Nine created and adopted the **Extended Industry Standard Architecture**, or **EISA** (rhymes with *visa*). These maverick manufacturers are using EISA architecture as the basis for micros powered by the Intel 486 microprocessors. These micros use 32-bit buses.

The MCA and EISA architectures enable processors to take greater advantage of computing resources, especially random-access memory (RAM). The RAM limit for applications software on MCA- and EISA-based micros is 16 MB. When used to its full potential, MCA and EISA define new platforms for which software must be created. Of the two, MCA exhibits a more radical departure from the PCs of the 1980s and early 1990s. EISA is compatible with the millions of 8-bit and 16-bit add-on boards currently being used in IBM-PC and compatible computers—MCA is not.

Many power users of IBM-PC–compatible microcomputers are ready to make the transition to the next generation of micros. Corporate decision makers also are aware that a transition to the next level is inevitable. The question remains: "Which architecture will emerge as the de facto industry standard—MCA, EISA, or Nubus?" Most will agree that Apple has an established niche in the marketplace and enough loyal followers to maintain its position. The real question is whether IBM with MCA or the Gang of Nine (and others) with EISA will emerge as the dominant architecture for the next generation of micros.

The vast majority of the IBM-PC–compatible users has yet to exploit the potential of the Intel 8088, 8086, 80286, and 80386 microprocessors. These people will not be directly affected by the resolution of the MCA versus EISA debate until well into the 1990s. However, anyone needing the power of the Intel 80486 microprocessor (roughly equivalent to an average minicomputer), may have to make a decision.

> **MEMORY BITS**
>
> *Platforms*
>
> Single-user environment
> - MS-DOS (PC-DOS)
> - MS-DOS/Windows
> - OS/2/Presentation Manager
>
> Multiuser environment
> - UNIX
>
> Concurrent processing technologies
> - MCA
> - EISA

SUMMARY OUTLINE AND IMPORTANT TERMS

3–1 A BIT ABOUT THE BIT. Data are stored temporarily during processing in RAM, or **primary storage**, and permanently on **secondary storage** devices, such as magnetic tape and disk drives.

The two electronic states of the computer are represented by a **bit**, short for *binary digit*. These electronic states are compatible with the **binary** numbering system. Letters and decimal numbers are translated into bits for storage and processing on computer systems.

3–2 ENCODING SYSTEMS: COMBINING BITS TO FORM BYTES. **Alphanumeric** characters are represented in computer storage by combining strings of bits to form unique bit configurations for each character. Characters are translated into these bit configurations, also called **bytes**, according to a particular coding scheme, called an **encoding system**. ASCII is the dominant encoding system in the microcomputer environment.

3–3 COMPONENTS OF A COMPUTER SYSTEM: A CLOSER LOOK AT THE PROCESSOR AND RAM. The processor is the "intelligence" of a computer system. A processor, which is also called the **central processing unit** or **CPU**, has only two fundamental sections, the **control unit** and the **arithmetic and logic unit**, which work together with RAM to execute programs. The control unit interprets instructions and directs the arithmetic and logic unit to perform computation and logic operations.

RAM (random-access memory) provides the processor with temporary storage for programs and data. Most of today's computers use CMOS technology for RAM. However, with CMOS, the data are lost when the electrical current is turned off or interrupted. In contrast, **bubble memory** provides nonvolatile memory. All input/output, including programs, must enter and exit RAM. Other variations of internal storage are **ROM**, **PROM**, and **EPROM**.

Some computers employ **cache memory** to increase **throughput**. Like RAM, cache is a high-speed holding area for program instructions and data. However, cache memory holds only those instructions and data likely to be needed next by the processor. During execution, instructions and data are passed between very high-speed **registers** (for example, the **instruction register** and the **accumulator**) in the control unit and the arithmetic and logic unit.

Every machine language has a predefined format for each type of instruction. Each instruction has an **operation code** and an **operand**. During one **machine cycle**, an instruction is *fetched* from RAM, decoded in the control unit, executed, and the results are placed in memory. The machine-cycle time is the total of the **instruction time** and the **execution time**.

3–4 DESCRIBING THE PROCESSOR: DISTINGUISHING CHARACTERISTICS. A processor is described in terms of its word length, speed, and RAM capacity. The **word length** (the number of bits handled as a unit) of microcomputers ranges from 8 bits for the early micros to 32 bits. Microcomputer speed is measured in **megahertz** (**MHz**). Memory capacity is measured in **kilobytes** (**KB**) or **megabytes** (**MB**).

Once a **terminate-and-stay-resident**, or **TSR**, program has been loaded to RAM, the user can *terminate* the program *and* it will *stay resident* in memory. TSRs can be instantly activated while running another program by tapping the TSR's **hotkey**.

CHAPTER 3 Processors and Platforms

The MS-DOS micro always has **conventional memory** and possibly **extended memory** and/or **expanded memory**.

- *Conventional memory* is memory between Memory Position 0 and the 1-MB limit, the area in which all programs must run. DOS and user programs run in the first 640 KB, and systems programs run in the remainder, called **reserved memory**.
- *Extended memory* (up to 15 MB) is an extension of conventional memory; however, DOS programs can run only in the 64-KB **high memory area** (**HMA**).
- *Expanded memory* (up to 15 MB) is used in conjunction with special software and hardware. DOS programs can run in expanded memory.

3-5 CONFIGURING A MICROCOMPUTER SYSTEM. The computer and its peripheral devices are called the computer system **configuration**, typically a microcomputer, keyboard, mouse, monitor (for **soft-copy** output), printer, and two disk drives. Micros with **open architectures** are configured with a variety of peripherals. In a **closed architecture**, the system is fully configured when it is sold.

An open architecture, also called a **bus architecture**, is possible because all micro components are linked via a common electrical **bus**. The connection to the bus is made at a **port**. External peripheral devices are linked to, or *interfaced* with, the processor via cables through either a **serial port** or a **parallel port**.

Expansion slots enable the addition of special-function **add-on cards**. Popular add-on boards include RAM, color and graphics adapter, modem, internal battery-powered clock/calendar, serial port, parallel port, printer spooler, hard disk, coprocessor, accelerator, network interface, motion video, and VCR backup. Most are **multifunction add-on boards. Half-size expansion boards** fit in a "short slot."

3-6 PLATFORMS. Microcomputer software is written to run under a specific **platform** (or **operating environment**), which is defined by the processor's design architecture and the operating system being used. Through 1990, the IBM PC-AT architecture and MS-DOS dominated. Responding to a need for multitasking, Microsoft Corporation introduced a GUI-based multitasking platform called Windows.

OS/2 is a single-user, multitasking operating system that enables up to 16 MB of RAM to be addressed. OS/2's GUI is called *Presentation Manager*.

Each of the multiuser operating systems defines a different platform, the most popular being UNIX and its spinoffs.

Since the mid-1970s the dominant PCs have been the Apple II, the Apple Macintosh, the IBM PC and its compatibles, and the IBM PS/2. The concurrent processing environment being developed by IBM for its next generation of PCs is called **Micro Channel Architecture**, or **MCA**. Apple's state-of-the-art architecture is called **Nubus**. The Gang of Nine created and adopted the **Extended Industry Standard Architecture**, or **EISA**. IBM's MCA and the alternative EISA architectures enable processors to take greater advantage of computing resources, especially RAM.

REVIEW EXERCISES

1. Distinguish between RAM, ROM, PROM, and EPROM.
2. How many ASCII bytes can be stored in a 32-bit word?
3. Which two functions are performed by the arithmetic and logic unit?
4. Does the current program run in RAM's foreground or background?
5. List examples of alpha, numeric, and alphanumeric characters.
6. Write your first name as an ASCII bit configuration.
7. What are the functions of the control unit?
8. We describe computers in terms of what three characteristics?
9. What is the basic difference between CMOS technology and nonvolatile technology, such as bubble memory?
10. Name three kinds of RAM that might be encountered in the MS-DOS environment.
11. For a given computer, which type of memory would have the greatest capacity to store data and programs: Cache or RAM? RAM or registers? Registers or cache?
12. Name two types of registers.
13. Which single-user, multitasking operating system enables up to 16 MB of RAM to be addressed?
14. Which portion of the fundamental computer instruction designates the operation to be performed?
15. What is the name of the microcomputer concurrent processing environment being pursued by IBM?

SELF-TEST (by section)

3-1 a. Data are stored permanently on secondary storage devices, such as magnetic disk. (T/F)
   b. *Bit* is the singular of *byte*. (T/F)
   c. The base of the binary number system is: (a) 2, (b) 8, or (c) 16?

3-2 The combination of bits used to represent a character is called a __byte__.

3-3 a. Data are loaded from secondary storage to RAM in a nondestructive read process. (T/F)
   b. The __control unit__ is that part of the processor that reads and interprets program instructions.
   c. The arithmetic and logic unit controls the flow of programs and data in and out of main memory. (T/F)
   d. Put the following memories in order based on speed: cache, registers, and RAM.
   e. The timed interval that comprises the machine cycle is the total of the __instruction__ time and the __execution__ time.
   f. Which of the following memory positions is located in the high memory area: (a) 64 KB, (b) 1064 KB, or (c) 64 MB?

CHAPTER 3 Processors and Platforms 89

    g. Multitasking is the <u>concurrent</u> execution of more than one program at a time.
3-4 a. The word length of most microcomputers is 64 bits. (T/**F**)
    b. The time it takes to complete one cycle on a 10-MHz processor is <u>100</u> nanoseconds.
3-5 a. The computer and its peripheral devices are called the computer system <u>configuration</u>
    b. The RS-232C connector provides the interface to a port. (**T**/F)
3-6 a. Windows provides a: (a) GUI, (b) UGI, or (c) GIU?
    b. Which of the following companies was not a member of the Gang of Nine: (a) Compaq, (b) Hewlett-Packard, or (c) IBM?

Self-test answers.   3–1 **(a)** T; **(b)** F; **(c)** a.   3–2 byte.   3–3 **(a)** T; **(b)** control unit; **(c)** F; **(d)** from the slowest memory: RAM, cache, registers; **(e)** instruction, execution; **(f)** b; **(g)** concurrent.   3–4 **(a)** F; **(b)** 100.   3–5 **(a)** configuration; **(b)** T.   3–6 **(a)** a; **(b)** c.

CHAPTER 4

MICRO PERIPHERAL DEVICES: I/O AND DATA STORAGE

STUDENT LEARNING OBJECTIVES

▶ To explain alternative approaches to and devices for data entry.
▶ To describe the operation and application of common output devices.
▶ To distinguish between primary and secondary storage.
▶ To distinguish between secondary storage devices and secondary storage media.
▶ To describe the principles of operation, methods of data storage, and use of magnetic disk drives.
▶ To describe the principles of operation, methods of data storage, and use of magnetic tape drives.
▶ To discuss the applications and use of optical laser disk storage.

4–1 I/O DEVICES: OUR INTERFACE WITH THE COMPUTER

Data are created in many places and in many ways. Before data can be processed and stored, they must be translated into a form the processor can interpret. For this, we need *input* devices. Once the data have been processed, they must be translated back into a form that *we* can understand. For this, we need *output* devices. These input/output (I/O) devices enable communication between us and the computer.

The diversity of microcomputer applications has encouraged manufacturers to develop and market a variety of I/O methods and hardware. Innovative I/O devices are being introduced continuously into the marketplace. For example, voice-recognition devices accept data (input) from human speech. Speech synthesizers produce simulated human speech as output.

Input Devices: Getting Data into the System

The Keyboard. All PCs are configured with a keyboard. The keyboard is the mainstay device for user input to a PC. The 101-key keyboard with the *QWERTY* key layout, 12 function keys, a keypad, a variety of special function keys, and dedicated cursor-control keys has emerged as the

This system is configured with two keyboards: a 101-key alphanumeric keyboard and a synthesizer keyboard. Each note the composer plays on the synthesizer keyboard is recorded and displayed in musical notation. The notes are stored on disk and can be replayed or modified.

standard. The 101-key keyboard and its important keys are discussed in some detail in Chapter 2, "Interacting with Micros," (see Figure 2–2). The original 83-key IBM-PC keyboard, which has only 10 function keys, is still in use on millions of PCs.

The QWERTY keyboard design, which derived its name from the first six letters on the top row of letters, was created in 1890 to slow down typists. This intentionally inefficient design kept fast typists from entangling the slow-moving type bars of nineteenth-century typewriters. The alternative is the *Dvorak* keyboard layout, which places the most frequently used characters on the home row (the vowels plus *d*, *h*, *t*, *n*, and *s*). You can enter nearly 4000 different words from the home row on the Dvorak keyboard, as opposed to 100 with the traditional QWERTY layout. Word processing operators who have switched to Dvorak are experiencing as much as a 75% improvement in productivity. The 101-key keyboard is available in both QWERTY and Dvorak layouts.

The Mouse. The keyboard is too cumbersome for some applications, especially those that rely on a graphical user interface (GUI) and those that require the user to point or draw. The effectiveness of GUIs depends on the user's ability to make a rapid selection from a screen full of graphic icons. The mouse can be used to position the pointer (graphics cursor) over an icon in less than a second. Computer artists use mice to enter curved lines to create images. Engineers use them to "draw" lines that connect points on a graph. The operation of the mouse is discussed in some detail in Chapter 2, "Interacting with Micros."

Other Point-and-Draw Devices. The mouse is one of several devices that move the graphics cursor to point and draw. The joystick, track ball,

This law enforcement officer is using a portable computer with handwriting recognition capability to record pertinent data at the scene of an accident. The 9-by-12-by-1¼-inch GRiDPad, made by GRiD Systems Corporation, can also accept and store a detailed drawing that shows how the accident happened. The violator uses the tethered electronic pen to sign the "ticket."

digitizer tablet and pen, and **light pen** are also input devices that move the graphics cursor.

Video arcade wizards are no doubt familiar with the *joystick* and *track ball*. The joystick is a vertical stick that moves the graphics cursor in the direction the stick is pushed. The track ball is a ball inset in a small external box or adjacent to and in the same unit as the keyboard of some portable computers. The ball is "rolled" to move the graphics cursor. Some people find it helpful to think of a track ball as an upside-down mouse.

The *digitizer tablet and pen* are a pen and a pressure-sensitive tablet with the same X–Y coordinates as the screen. The digitizing tablet is also used in conjunction with a *crosshair* device in lieu of a pen. The outline of an image drawn on a digitizer tablet is reproduced simultaneously on the display screen.

When it is moved close to the screen, the *light pen* detects light being emitted from the monitor's cathode-ray tube. The graphics cursor automatically locks onto the position of the pen and tracks its movement over the screen. An engineer may create or modify images directly on the screen with a light pen. A city planner can select from a menu of possible computer functions by simply pointing the light pen to a display of the desired function.

An engineer uses a crosshair device along with a digitizing tablet to design the intricate circuitry for a special-purpose computer.

OCR Scanners. Until recently, data entry has been synonymous with *keystrokes*. The keystroke will continue to be the basic mode of data entry for the foreseeable future, but recent innovations have eliminated the need for key-driven data entry in many applications. For example, you have probably noticed the preprinted **bar codes** on consumer items and envelopes containing utility bills and other bulk mail. **Optical character recognition (OCR)** is a way to encode (write) certain data in machine-readable format on the original source document. For example, the International Standard Book Number (ISBN) on the back cover of this book is printed in machine-readable OCR. This eliminates the need for publishers and bookstore clerks to key these data manually.

OCR characters and bar codes (see Figure 4–1) are identified by light-sensitive devices called **OCR scanners**. OCR scanners bounce a beam of light off an image, then measure the reflected light to determine the value of the image. Hand-held wand scanners, which often are used with PCs, make contact as they are brushed over the printed matter.

OCR devices can "learn" to read almost any typeface, including the one used for this book! The "learning" takes place when the structure of the character set is described to the OCR device. Special OCR devices can even read hand-printed letters if they are recorded on a standard form and written according to specific rules.

OCR scanners can be classified into the following five categories:

- *Label scanners.* These devices read data on price tags, shipping labels, and the like. A hand-held wand scanner is a label scanner.
- *Page scanners.* These devices scan and interpret the alphanumeric characters on regular typewritten pages. All scanned characters are coded in ASCII (see Chapter 3, "Processors and Platforms") and stored in an **ASCII file**. All word processing packages can read ASCII files.

This hand-held industrial computer is designed for remote data collection in manufacturing environments. The stock clerk is using a keyboard and an OCR wand scanner to enter data to the device. At the end of the day, he transmits the data to the company's main computer via a telephone hookup.

FIGURE 4–1 Various Codes That Can Be Interpreted by OCR Scanners

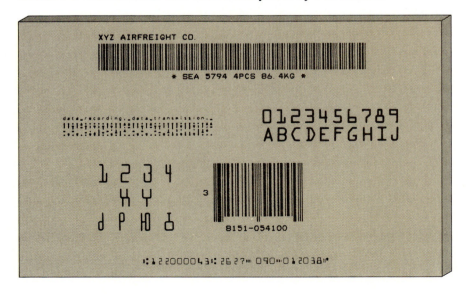

- *Document scanners.* Document scanners are capable of scanning documents of varying sizes (for example, utility-bill invoice stubs and sales slips from credit-card transactions).
- *Continuous-form scanners.* These devices read data printed on continuous forms, such as cash register tapes.
- *Optical-mark scanners.* Optical mark scanners scan preprinted forms, such as multiple-choice test answer forms. The position of the "sense mark" indicates a particular response or character.

Image Scanners. In recent years, input technology has expanded to allow the direct entry of pictorial information. An **image scanner** employs laser technology to scan and **digitize** an image. That is, the hard-copy image is translated into an electronic format that can be interpreted by and stored on computers. The image to be scanned can be handwritten notes, a photograph, a drawing, an insurance form—anything that can be digitized. Once an image has been digitized and entered to the computer system, it can be stored, retrieved, displayed, altered, merged with text, and sent via data communications to one or several remote locations.

The two types of image scanners are *flatbed* and *hand-held*.

- *Flatbed image scanner.* The flatbed image scanner works much like a copy machine. Place the image to be scanned on the glass scan area, close the lid, and start the scanning process. An 8½-by-11-inch image is scanned in a couple of seconds.

This personal reader allows visually impaired people to "hear" books and typewritten material. An optical scanner reads the words into the computer system, where they are converted into English speech using a speech synthesizer (a device that produces electronic speech). Users can request any of nine different voices (including male, female, and child's).

- *Hand-held image scanner.* The hand-held image scanner is rolled down or across the image to be scanned.

Most image scanners result in gray-scale images (images portrayed in lighter shades), whether the image is black on white or in color. However, there are both flatbed and hand-held image scanners available that can produce digitized gray-scale and color images. The flatbed produces higher resolution images and scans larger images on a single pass than the hand-held image scanner.

An image scanner can be purchased with optional hardware and software that provide it with the capability of an OCR page scanner. That is, the image scanner can read and interpret the characters on most printed or typeset documents, such as a business letter or a page from this book.

Voice Data Entry. Computers are great talkers, but they are not very good listeners. It is not uncommon for a **speech recognition** device to misinterpret a slamming door for a spoken word. Nevertheless, speech-recognition systems can be used to enter limited kinds and quantities of information. Despite its limitations, speech recognition has a number of applications. For example, some people find that speech recognition facilitates their interaction with spreadsheet programs. Instead of using the cursor-control keys to position the cursor, they simply say "Left," "Right," "Up," or "Down." Quality-control personnel who must use their hands can call out defects as they are detected. Physicians in the operating room can request certain information about a patient during the operation. A computer-based audio-response unit or a speech synthesizer makes the conversation two-way.

Figure 4–2 illustrates how it works. When you speak into a microphone, each sound is broken down and examined in several frequencies. The sounds in each frequency are digitized and matched against similarly formed *templates* in the computer's electronic dictionary. The digitized template is a form that can be stored and interpreted by computers (in 1s and 0s). When a match is found, the word (*Move* in Figure 4–2) is displayed on a VDT or, in some cases, repeated by a speech synthesizer for confirmation. If no match is found, the speaker is asked to repeat the word.

In speech recognition, the creation of the data base is called *training*. Most speech-recognition systems are *speaker-dependent*; that is, they respond to the speech of a particular individual. Therefore, a data base of words must be created for each person using the system. To create this data base, each person using the system must repeat—as many as 20 times—each word to be interpreted by the system. This "training" is necessary because we seldom say a word the same way each time. Even if we say the word twice in succession, it probably will have a different inflection or nasal quality.

State-of-the-art *speaker-independent* systems have a limited vocabulary: perhaps *yes*, *no*, and the 10 numeric digits. Although the vocabulary is limited, speaker-independent systems do not require training and can be used by anyone. However, they do require a very large data base to accommodate anyone's voice pattern.

To expedite interaction with the PC, this administrative assistant issues all word processing menu commands vocally.

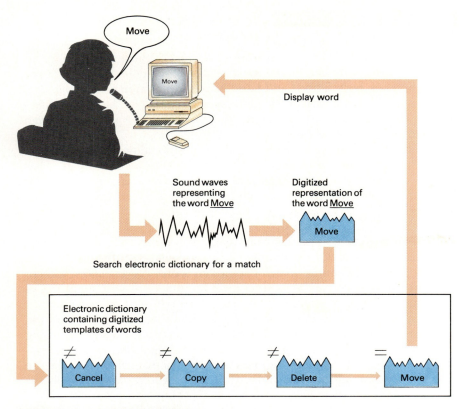

FIGURE 4–2 Speech Recognition
The sound waves created by the spoken word Move *are digitized by the computer. The digitized template is matched against templates of other words in the electronic dictionary. When the computer finds a match, it displays a written version of the word.*

Today, for the most part, we interact with our PCs by touching and seeing. In a few years we may be talking with computers as we move about our offices and homes.

Vision-Input Systems. The simulation of human senses, especially vision, is extremely complex. A computer does not actually see and interpret an image the way a human being does. A *digital camera* is needed to give computers "eyesight." To create the data base, a vision system, via a digital camera, digitizes the images of all objects to be identified, then stores the digitized form of each image in the data base. When the system is placed in operation, the camera digitizes the image being viewed. The system then compares the digitized image to be interpreted to the prerecorded digitized images in the computer's data base. The computer identifies the image by matching the structure of the input image with those images in the data base. This process is illustrated by the digital vision-inspection system in Figure 4–3.

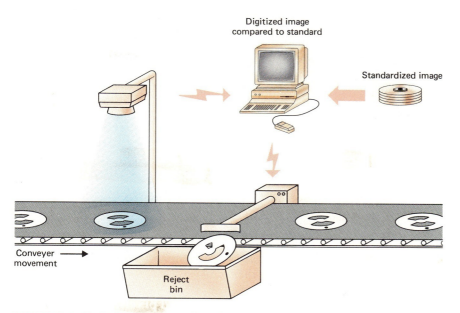

FIGURE 4–3 Digital Vision-Inspection System
In this digital vision-inspection system, the system examines parts for defects. If the digitized image of the part does not match a standard digital image, the defective part is placed in a reject bin.

Vision input requires powerful computers. Until recently vision input was limited to minicomputers and mainframes. However, today's micros have the power of yesterday's minicomputers and can easily handle vision-input tasks.

As you can imagine, **vision-input systems** are best suited for very specialized tasks in which only a few images will be encountered. These tasks are usually simple, monotonous ones, such as inspection. For example, in Figure 4–3 a digital vision-inspection system on an assembly line rejects those parts that do not meet certain quality-control specifications. The vision system performs rudimentary gauging inspections, and then signals the computer to take appropriate action.

▶ **MEMORY BITS**

Input Devices
- Keyboard (*alphanumeric keys, function keys, keypad, special function keys,* and *cursor-control keys*)
- Point-and-draw devices (*mouse, joystick, track ball, digitizing tablet and pen or crosshair,* and *light pen*)
- OCR scanners (*label, page, document, continuous-form,* and *optical mark*)
- Image scanners (*flatbed* and *hand-held*)
- Speech recognition (*speaker-dependent* and *speaker-independent*)
- Vision-input system

Output Devices: Computers Communicate with Us

Output devices translate bits and bytes into a form we can understand. The most common "output only" devices are discussed in this section. These include monitors, printers, plotters, desktop film recorders, screen-image projectors, and voice-response units.

Monitors. Alphanumeric and graphic output are displayed on the microcomputer's televisionlike monitor. The three primary attributes of monitors are the *size* of the display screen; the *resolution*, or detail, of the display; and whether the display is in *color* or *monochrome*. The diagonal dimension of the display screen varies from 5 to 25 inches. Output on a monitor is *soft copy*; that is, it is temporary and is available to the end user only until another display is requested, as opposed to the permanent *hard-copy* output of printers.

Resolution. Some monitors have a much higher **resolution**, or quality of output. Resolution refers to the number of addressable points on the screen—the number of points to which light can be directed under program control. These points are sometimes called **pixels**, short for picture elements. Each pixel can be assigned a shade of gray or a color. A low-resolution monitor has about 64,000 (320 by 200) addressable points. A monitor used primarily for computer graphics and computer-aided design may have over 16 million addressable points. The high-resolution monitors project extremely clear images that almost look like photographs.

Monochrome monitors. Monitors are either monochrome or color. Monochrome monitors display images in a single color, usually white, green, blue, red, or amber. A monochrome monitor can, however, display shades of its one color. The industry uses the term **gray scales** to refer to the number of shades of a color that can be shown on a monochrome monitor's screen. Color monitors add another dimension to the display. Their use of colors can focus attention on different aspects of the output. For example, an engineer designing pipelines for an oil refinery can use colors to highlight such things as the direction and type of fluid flow, the size of the pipes, and so on.

Some space-saving monitors are flat. Most **flat-panel monitors** are used in conjunction with portable microcomputers. Flat-panel monitors use three basic types of technology: *LCD* (liquid crystal display), the technology commonly used in digital wristwatches; *gas plasma*; and *EL* (electroluminescent). Each has its advantages. For example, LCD displays use relatively little power and EL displays provide a wider viewing angle. Up until the late 1980s all flat-panel monitors were monochrome. With the recent introduction of color LCD monitors, portable-PC buyers now have a choice.

Color monitors. IBM-PC displays are either in *text mode* or *graphics mode*. Some word processing and spreadsheet programs operate in text mode, with 25 rows of up to 80 characters in length. All GUIs and draw-and-design programs operate in graphics mode. The trend in software

This laptop PC has a flat-panel LCD monitor with 16 gray scales.

development is toward the exclusive use of the graphics mode, even in word processing and spreadsheet software.

Several color video display standards have evolved since the introduction of the IBM PC in 1981. Each is implemented by installing an add-on board and connecting it to the appropriate monitor. The four most popular monitors are listed below.

- *CGA.* The initial *c*olor/*g*raphics *a*dapter standard was low resolution (320 by 200 pixels). CGA monitors do an adequate job of presenting graphics, but their text mode displays are hard on the eyes. During the era of CGA, higher resolution monochrome monitors (720 by 350) were preferred for text mode displays.
- *EGA.* The *e*nhanced *g*raphics *a*dapter provided higher resolution (640 by 350), greater variety in the selection of colors (from 4 to 16), and a substantially improved presentation of text. The EGA monitor started the era of the all-purpose color monitor.
- *VGA.* The *v*ideo *g*raphics *a*rray standard provides a slightly improved resolution to 640 by 480 and uses up to 256 colors. (The original standard called for 16 colors, but vendors have enhanced this specification to 256.)
- *Super VGA.* The Super VGA provides resolutions from 800 by 600 to 1280 by 1024.

Interactive PC-based in-store information systems help take the frustration out of grocery shopping. This color monitor is sensitive to the touch. Suppose you can't find the nachos at your favorite supermarket. You go to the monitor and touch the letter N *on a display of the alphabet to view a list of all products that begin with* N. *Then you would scroll through the alphabetical list and touch the* nacho chips *entry. A screen of the store's layout appears with a flashing signal showing the product's precise location (green rectangle on left side of store).*

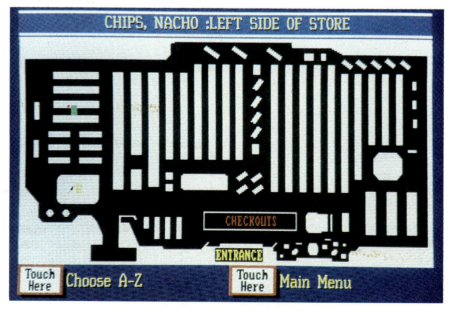

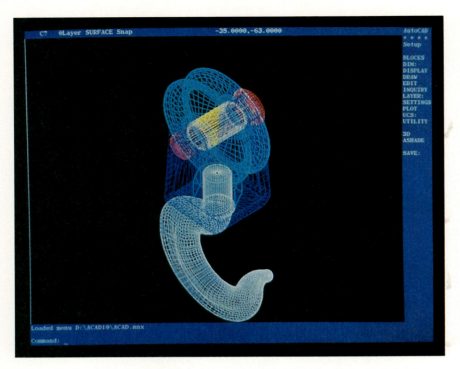

CAD (computer-aided design) applications demand large-screen high-resolution monitors.

All four—CGA, EGA, VGA, and Super VGA—are in widespread use today. Add-on graphics boards and monitors are available that enable very high resolution; however, these can be more expensive than the computer.

Printers. Printers produce hard-copy output, such as management reports, memos, payroll checks, and program listings. Microcomputer printers are generally classified as **serial printers** or **page printers**. Printers are rated by their print speed. Print speeds are measured in *characters per second* (*cps*), for serial printers, and in *pages per minute* (*ppm*) for page printers. The print-speed ranges for the these printers are 40–450 cps and 4–22 ppm, respectively.

Printers are further categorized as *impact* or *nonimpact.* An impact printer uses some type of hammer or hammers to hit the ribbon and the paper, much as a typewriter does. Nonimpact printers use chemicals, lasers, and heat to form the images on the paper. All page printers are nonimpact printers.

Serial printers. Impact serial printers rely on **dot-matrix** and **daisy-wheel** technology. Nonimpact serial printers employ **ink-jet** and **thermal** technology. Regardless of the technology, the images are formed *one character at a time* as the print head moves across the paper. Virtually all serial printers are *bidirectional*; that is, they print whether the print head is moving left to right or right to left.

CHAPTER 4 Micro Peripheral Devices: I/O and Data Storage   103

Small businesses, such as this retail sporting goods store, need the flexibility of dot matrix printers (foreground). This woman routinely adjusts the feed mechanism on the printer to accommodate a variety of print jobs. The mailing labels are printed on 4-inch-wide peel-off paper, and inventory reports (shown here) are printed on 15-inch continuous-feed stock paper.

Most serial printers can accommodate both *single-sheet paper* and *continuous-form paper*, sometimes called fan-fold paper. If you expect that much of the output will be single sheet (for example, letters and envelopes), you may need to purchase an *automatic sheet feeder*. The *tractor-feed* that handles fan-fold paper is standard with most serial printers.

- *The impact dot-matrix printer.* The impact dot-matrix printer arranges printed dots to form characters and all kinds of images in much the same way as lights display time and temperature on bank signs. One or several vertical columns of small print hammers, referred to as *pins*, are contained in a rectangular print head. The hammers are activated independently to form a dotted character image as the print head moves horizontally across the paper. The characters in Figure 4–4 are formed by a nine-pin print head within a matrix that is nine dots high and five dots wide (9×5). The number of dots within the matrix varies from one printer to the next.

  The quality of the printed output is directly proportional to the density of the dots in the matrix. The 18-pin and 24-pin dot-matrix printers form characters that appear solid, and they can be used for business letters as well as for routine data processing output. Figure

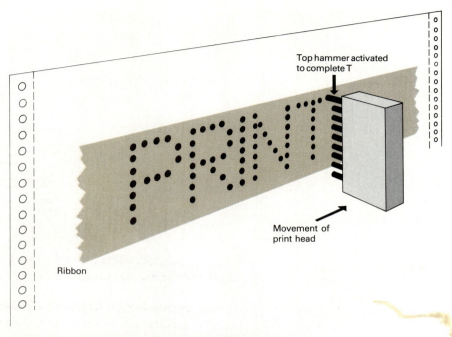

FIGURE 4–4 Dot-Matrix-Printer Character Formation
Each character is formed in a 7 by 5 matrix as the nine-pin print head moves across the paper. The two bottom pins are used for lowercase letters that extend below the line (for example, g and p).

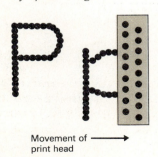

FIGURE 4–5 Near-Letter-Quality Dot-Matrix Character Formation
The 18-pin print head permits dots to overlap to increase the density and, therefore, the quality of the image.

4–5 illustrates how the dots can be overlapped with an 18-pin print head to create a *near-letter-quality* (*NLQ*) appearance. These printers are called *dual-mode* because of their dual-function capabilities (draft and NLQ).

Dot-matrix printers are further categorized as *monochrome* and *color*. The monochrome printer prints in the color of the ribbon, usually black. Color dot-matrix printers can select and print any of the colors on a multicolored ribbon (usually bands of black, yellow, red, and blue), or the printer can mix these colors via multiple passes and overstrikes to create the appearance of other colors in the rainbow. As you might imagine, you have to wait a little longer for a color graph than you would a monochrome graph.

Dot-matrix printers are more flexible than serial printers of fully formed characters (printers that use an embossed rendering of a character to reproduce the image on paper). Depending on the model, dot-matrix printers can print a variety of sizes and types of characters (even old English and script characters), graphics, and bar codes.

Features common to most dot-matrix printers include boldface, underline, subscript and superscript, and compressed print (narrower letters). Optional features include proportional spacing (using more or less space, depending on the width of the character) and italics.

- *The daisy-wheel printer.* The daisy-wheel printer produces *letter-quality* (*LQ*) output for word processing applications. An interchangeable daisy wheel containing a set of fully formed characters spins to the desired character. A print hammer strikes the character embossed on the print wheel to form the image on the paper. Although daisy-wheel printers have the highest quality text output of serial printers, they are the slowest and cannot produce graphic output. These disadvantages and the emergence of high-quality dot-matrix printers have driven the once-popular daisy-wheel printer from the market during the past few years. However, they are still found in the office.

- *The ink-jet printer.* Monochrome and color ink-jet printers employ several independently controlled injection chambers to squirt ink droplets on the paper. The droplets, which dry instantly as dots, form the images. The big advantage that nonimpact ink-jet printers have over impact dot-matrix printers is the quality of the output, especially color output. Sales of color ink-jet printers are expected to increase substantially as users, accustomed to color output on their video monitors, come to want hard-copy output in color.

- *The thermal printer.* The thermal printer is an alternative to the other serial printers. Heat elements produce dot-matrix images on heat-sensitive paper. The major disadvantage is the cost of the heat-sensitive paper. The advantages include compact size, limited noise, and low purchase price.

This color ink-jet printer produces high-quality color graphics output.

Page printers. **Desktop page printers** are of the nonimpact type and use a variety of technologies to achieve high-speed hard-copy output by printing *a page at a time.* Page printers have the capability of printing graphs and charts, and they offer considerable flexibility in the size and style of print. They can also print in portrait or landscape format. **Portrait** and **landscape** refer to the orientation of the print on the page. The familiar portrait output is like the page on this book—the lines run parallel to the shorter side of the page. In contrast, landscape output runs parallel to the longer sides of the page. Landscape is frequently the orientation of choice for spreadsheet outputs with many columns.

Most page printers employ laser technology; however, other technologies are used: ink-jet, thermal-transfer, LED (light-emitting diode), and LCS (liquid crystal shutter). Automatic sheet feeders, which hold from 100 to 200 blank pages, are standard equipment on desktop page printers. Operating at peak capacity during an eight-hour shift, the fastest desktop page printer can produce almost 10,000 pages—that's about two miles of printed pages.

Until the mid-1980s, virtually all printers configured with microcomputers were serial printers. Now economically priced desktop page printers are becoming the standard for office microcomputer systems. These printers, capable of print speeds up to 22 pages per minute, have redefined the hard-copy output potential of micros.

Desktop page printers are capable of producing *near-typeset-quality* (*NTQ*) text and graphics. The resolution (quality of output) of the typical desktop page printer is *300 dpi* (dots per inch). High-end desktop page printers, which are sometimes called *desktop typesetters*, are capable of 1000 dpi. The dpi qualifier refers to the number of dots that can

Desktop page printers are fast and versatile. This printer services the printing needs of 15 microcomputers. A page printer can produce hard copies of graphic images just as easily as it prints letters and reports.

> **MEMORY BITS**
>
> *Printer Output Quality*
> - Near-letter-quality (NLQ)
> - Dual mode (draft and NLQ)
> - Letter-quality (LQ)
> - Near-typeset-quality (NTQ)

be printed per linear inch, horizontally or vertically. That is, a 300-dpi printer is capable of printing 90,000 (300 times 300) dots per square inch.

Commercial typesetting quality is a minimum of 1200 dpi and is usually in excess of 2000 dpi. Contrast the desktop page-printer output (300 dpi) in Figure 4–6 with the typeset print in this book. Desktop page printers are also quiet (an important consideration in an office setting), and they can combine type styles and sizes with graphics on the same page. The emergence of desktop page printers has fueled the explosion of *desktop publishing* (discussed in detail in Chapter 5, "Text and Image Processing: Word Processing, Desktop Publishing, and Graphics.")

Figure 4–6 contrasts the output of a dot-matrix printer, in both draft and near-letter-quality (NLQ) modes; a daisy-wheel printer (letter quality); and a desktop page printer (near-typeset-quality).

Printer summary. Hundreds of printers are produced by dozens of manufacturers. There is a printer manufactured to meet the hard-copy output requirements of any individual or company, and almost any combination of features can be obtained. You can specify its size (some weigh only a couple of pounds), speed, quality of output, color requirements, flexibility requirements, and even noise level. Micro printers sell for as little as a good pair of shoes or for as much as a small automobile.

Plotters. Dot-matrix, ink-jet, thermal, and page printers are capable of producing page-size graphic output, but they are limited in their ability to generate high-quality graphic output that is perfectly proportioned. Engineers, architects, city planners, and others who routinely generate high-precision, hard-copy graphic output of widely varying sizes use the other hard-copy alternative—**pen plotters.**

The two basic types of pen plotters are the *drum plotter* and the *flatbed plotter.* Both have one or more pens that move over the paper under computer control to produce an image. Several pens are required to vary the width and color of the line, and the computer selects and manipulates them. On the drum plotter, the pens and the drum move concurrently in different axes to produce the image. Drum plotters are used to produce continuous output, such as plotting earthquake activity, or for long graphic output, such as the structural view of a skyscraper. On some flatbed plotters, the pen moves in both axes while the paper remains stationary. However, on most desktop plotters, both paper and pen move concurrently in much the same way as drum plotters.

FIGURE 4–6 Printer Output Comparison

```
This sentence was printed in draft mode on a 24-pin dot matrix printer.
This sentence was printed in NLQ mode on a 24-pin dot matrix printer.
This sentence was printed on a daisy-wheel printer.
This sentence was printed on a desktop page printer.
```

Presentation Graphics: Desktop Film Recorders and Screen-Image Projectors. Businesspeople have found that sophisticated and colorful graphics add an aura of professionalism to any report or presentation. This demand for *presentation graphics* has created a need for corresponding output devices. Computer-generated graphic images can be re-created on paper and transparency acetates with printers and plotters. Graphic images also can be captured on 35-mm slides, or they can be displayed on a monitor or projected onto a large screen.

Desktop film recorders reproduce a high-resolution graphic image on 35-mm film in either black and white or color. Some models allow users to process and mount their own slides. Others require outside processing. Screen-image projectors project the graphic image onto a large screen, similar to the way television programs are projected onto a large TV screen. Another type of screen-image projector transfers the graphic image displayed on the monitor onto a large screen with the use of an ordinary overhead projector.

A market research analyst uses a pen plotter to portray the results of surveys in the form of bar and line graphs.

Voice-Response Units. If you have ever called directory assistance, you probably have heard something like: "The number is five-seven-five-six-one-three-one." You may have driven a car that advised you to "fasten your seat belt." These are examples of talking machines, output from voice-response units. There are two types of voice-response units: One uses a *reproduction* of a human voice and other sounds, and the other uses a speech synthesizer. Like monitors, voice-response units provide a temporary, soft-copy output.

The first type of voice-response unit selects output from user-recorded words, phrases, music, alarms, or anything you might record on audio tape, just as a printer would select characters. In these recorded voice-response units, the actual analog recordings of sounds are converted into digital data, then permanently stored on a memory chip. When output, a particular sound is converted back into analog before being routed to a speaker. These chips are mass-produced for specific applications, such as output for automatic teller machines, microwave ovens, smoke detectors, elevators, alarm clocks, automobile warning systems, video games, and vending machines, to mention only a few.

Speech synthesizers, which convert raw data into electronically produced speech, are more popular in the microcomputer environment. To produce speech, these devices combine sounds resembling the *phonemes* (basic sound units) that make up speech. A speech synthesizer is capable of producing at least 64 unique sounds. The existing technology produces synthesized speech with only limited vocal inflections and phrasing, however.

Even with its limitations, the number of speech synthesizer applications is growing. In one application, an optical character reader scans books to retrieve the raw data. The speech synthesizer then translates the printed matter into spoken words for blind people. In another application, the use of speech synthesizers is opening a new world to speech-impaired children who were once placed in institutions because they could not communicate verbally. Speech synthesizers are also used in

These young men are using a hand-held speaking dictionary to "look up" the spelling of a word. First they enter a phonetic spelling of the word, then the computer-based dictionary interprets the input and finds the word in its memory. The speaking dictionary, made by Franklin Electronic Publishers, uses a speech synthesizer to actually pronounce the word in English and display the definition.

▶ **MEMORY BITS**

Output
- Monitor
  Described by size and resolution
  Display is:
    Text or graphics mode
    Monochrome or color
- Printers
  Serial (40–450 cps)
    Impact
      Dot-matrix (color option)
      Daisy-wheel
    Nonimpact
      Ink-jet (color option)
      Thermal
  Page (4–22 ppm)
    Desktop page
    Desktop typesetter
- Plotters
  Pen
  Flatbed
- Presentation graphics
  Desktop film recorder
  Screen-image projector
- Voice-response units
  Recorded voice
  Speech synthesizer

domestic alarm systems and computer-based training. As the quality of the output improves, speech synthesizers will enjoy a broader base of applications. They are relatively inexpensive and are becoming increasingly popular with many personal computer owners.

4–2 SECONDARY STORAGE: PERMANENT DATA STORAGE

Primary and Secondary Storage

Let's review. Within a microcomputer system, programs and data are stored in *primary storage* and in *secondary storage* (see Figure 4–7). Programs and data are stored *permanently* for periodic retrieval in secondary storage, also called **auxiliary storage**. Programs and data are retrieved from secondary storage and stored *temporarily* in high-speed primary storage (RAM) for processing (see Chapter 3, "Processors and Platforms.")

"Why two types of storage?" you might ask. Remember from Chapter 3 that most primary storage is semiconductor memory, and the data are lost when the electricity is interrupted. Primary storage is also expensive and has a limited capacity. The RAM capacity of a large mainframe computer would not come close to meeting the data and program storage needs of the typical micro user. Secondary storage, however, is relatively inexpensive and has an enormous capacity.

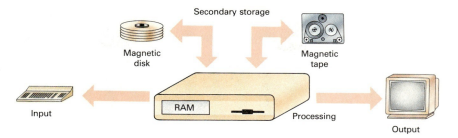

FIGURE 4–7 Primary and Secondary Storage
Programs and data are stored permanently in secondary storage and temporarily in primary storage.

Over the years, manufacturers have developed a variety of devices and media for the permanent storage of data and programs. Today the various types of **magnetic disk drives** and their respective storage media are the state of the art for storing programs and data. **Magnetic tape drives** complement magnetic disk storage by providing inexpensive backup capability and archival storage. In this section we focus on the terminology, principles, operation, and trade-offs of these secondary storage devices. We will also discuss the potential and applications of **optical laser disk** technology, a rapidly emerging alternative to magnetic disk and magnetic tape storage.

Data are stored temporarily in primary storage (chips in front middle of laptop circuit board) during processing and permanently on secondary storage, such as magnetic disk (right).

Sequential and Direct Access: New Terms for Old Concepts

An important consideration both in the design of an information system and the purchase of a computer system is the way data are accessed. Magnetic tape can be used for **sequential access** only. Magnetic disks have **random-,** or **direct-access,** capabilities as well as sequential-access capabilities. You are quite familiar with these concepts, but you may not realize it. Operationally, the magnetic tape is the same as the one in home and automobile tape decks. The magnetic disk can be compared to a phonograph record.

Suppose you have the Beatles' classic record album *Sgt. Pepper's Lonely Hearts Club Band*. The first four songs on this album are: (1) "Sgt. Pepper's Lonely Hearts Club Band," (2) "With a Little Help from My Friends," (3) "Lucy in the Sky with Diamonds," and (4) "Getting Better." Now suppose you also have this Beatles album on a tape cassette. To play the third song on the cassette, "Lucy in the Sky with Diamonds," you would have to wind the tape forward and search for it sequentially. To play "Lucy in the Sky with Diamonds" on the phonograph record, all you would have to do is move the needle directly to the track containing the third song. This simple analogy demonstrates the two fundamental methods of storing and accessing data—*sequential* and *random*.

Magnetic Disks: Rotating Storage Media

Magnetic disk drives are secondary storage devices that provide a computer system with **random-** *and* **sequential-processing** capabilities. In random processing, the desired programs and data are accessed *directly* from the storage medium. In sequential processing, the computer system must search the storage medium to find the desired programs or data. Because magnetic disk storage is used almost exclusively for direct access, random processing is discussed with magnetic disks. Sequential processing is discussed with magnetic tapes.

Because of its random- and sequential-processing capabilities, magnetic disk storage is the overwhelming choice of microcomputer users.

Hardware and Storage Media. A variety of magnetic disk drives (the hardware device) and magnetic disks (the media) are manufactured for different information processing requirements. There are two fundamental types of magnetic disks: those that are interchangeable, and those that are permanently installed, or fixed. **Interchangeable magnetic disks** can be stored **off-line** (that is, not accessible to the computer system) and loaded to the magnetic disk drives as they are needed. Once inserted in the disk drives, the disks are said to be **on-line;** that is, the data and programs on the disks are accessible to the computer system.

The trend in magnetic storage media is to **fixed disks,** also called **hard disks.** All fixed disks are rigid and usually are made of aluminum with a surface coating of easily magnetized elements, such as iron, cobalt, chromium, and nickel. In the past, interchangeable disks containing certain files and programs were taken from the shelf and loaded to

CHAPTER 4 Micro Peripheral Devices: I/O and Data Storage

the disk drives as needed. This is still true today, but to a much lesser extent. High-capacity hard-disk storage has made it possible for today's micro user to enjoy the convenience of having all data and programs readily accessible at all times.

The different types of interchangeable magnetic disks and fixed disks are shown in the accompanying photographs. As you can see, magnetic disks are available in a wide variety of shapes and storage capacities. The type used would depend on the volume of data you have and the frequency with which those data are accessed.

The diskette and microdisk. The two most popular types of interchangeable magnetic disks for micros are the **diskette** and the **microdisk**.

- *Diskette.* The diskette is a thin, flexible disk that is permanently enclosed in a soft, 5¼-inch-square jacket. Because the magnetic-coated mylar diskette and its jacket are flexible like a page in this book, the diskette is also called a **flexible disk** or a **floppy disk**.

  Early diskettes recorded data on only one side of the disk. These were *single-sided* (SS) diskettes. Today all common-usage diskettes and microdisks are *double-sided* and are labeled "DS" or simply "2." Similarly, the technological evolution of the early diskettes are classified as *double-density* (DD), as opposed to *single-density*. **Density** refers to the number of bits that can be stored per unit of area on the disk-face surface.

  The *360-KB DS/DD* (double-sided, double-density) diskette dominated during the 1980s and is still the only 5¼-inch diskette that can be used on many PCs. However, the new 5¼-inch disk drives support both the popular 360-KB diskette and the *1.2-MB DS/HD* (double-sided, high-density) diskette. The 1.2-MB diskette can store more programs and data than three 360-KB diskettes.

- *Microdisk.* The 3½-inch microdisk, also called a **microfloppy**, is enclosed in a rigid plastic jacket. Like its 5¼-inch cousin, the 3½-inch microdisk comes in two capacities, the 720-KB DS/DD and the 1.44-KB DS/HD microdisks. The microdisk is slowly displacing the 5¼-inch diskette because of its durability, convenient size, and higher capacity.

The Winchester disk. The microcomputer hard disk is called the **Winchester disk**. The Winchester disk got its nickname from the 30-30 Winchester rifle. Early disk drives had two 30-MB disks—thus the nickname "Winchester." Most of the newer personal computers are configured with at least one diskette or microdisk drive and one fixed Winchester disk. Having two disks increases system throughput. The storage capacity of these 3½- and 5¼-inch hard disks ranges from about 20 MB to 760 MB. The 760-MB hard disk has over 2000 times the capacity of a 360-KB diskette.

A Winchester hard disk contains several disk platters stacked on a single rotating spindle. Data are stored on all *recording surfaces*. For a disk with four platters, there are eight recording surfaces on which data can be stored (see Figure 4–8). The disks spin continuously at a high

The trend in interchangeable storage media for microcomputers is to the 3½-inch microdisk. This 3½-inch disk can hold up to 1.44 MB.

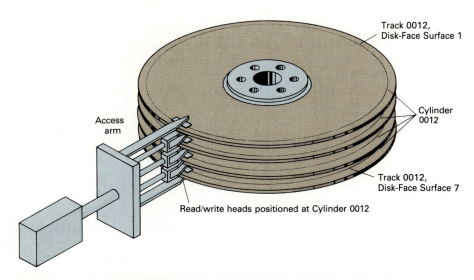

FIGURE 4–8 Fixed Hard Disk with Four Platters and Eight Recording Surfaces
A cylinder refers to similarly numbered concentric tracks on the disk-face surfaces. In the illustration, the read/write heads are positioned over Cylinder 0012. At this position, the data on any one of the eight tracks numbered 0012 are accessible to the computer on each revolution of the disk. The read/write heads must be moved to access data on other cylinders.

speed (usually 3600 revolutions per minute) within a sealed enclosure. The enclosure keeps the disk-face surfaces free from contaminants such as dust and cigarette smoke. This contaminant-free environment allows Winchester disks to have greater density of data storage than the interchangeable diskettes. In contrast to the Winchester disk, the diskettes and microdisks are set in motion only when a command is issued to read from or write to the disk. An indicator light near the disk drive is illuminated only when the diskette is spinning.

The rotational movement of a magnetic disk passes all data under or over a **read/write head**, thereby making all data available for access on each revolution of the disk (see Figure 4–8). A fixed disk will have at least one read/write head for each recording surface. The heads are mounted on **access arms** that move together and literally float on a cushion of air over (or under) the spinning recording surfaces. The tolerance is so close that a particle of smoke from a cigarette will not fit between these "flying" heads and the recording surface.

▶ **MEMORY BITS**

Disk Capacities

	DS/DD	DS/HD	Hard Disk
5¼-inch diskette	360 KB	1.2 MB	
3½-inch microdisk	720 KB	1.44 MB	
Winchester disk			20 MB to 760 MB

Winchester disks normally are permanently installed in the same physical unit as the processor and diskette drives. There are, however, interchangeable hard disks on the market. These interchangeable Winchester modules are inserted and removed in a manner that is similar to the way you insert and remove tapes on a VCR. Only a small percentage of PCs are configured to accept interchangeable Winchester disks.

The capacity of Winchester disks is increasing steadily. Already, very high-density fixed disks can store over 30 million characters on one square inch of recording surface. That's the text of this and 29 other books in a space the size of a postage stamp!

Micro Disk Organization. The way in which data and programs are stored and accessed is similar for both hard and interchangeable floppy disks. The disk-storage medium has a thin film coating of one of the easily magnetized elements (cobalt, for example). The thin film coating on the disk can be magnetized electronically by the read/write head to represent the absence or presence of a bit (0 or 1).

Data are stored in concentric circles called **tracks** by magnetizing the surface to represent bit configurations (see Figure 4–9). Bits are recorded using **serial representation**; that is, the bits are aligned in a row, one after another, in tracks. The number of tracks varies greatly between disks, from as few as 40 on some 5¼-inch diskettes to several thousand

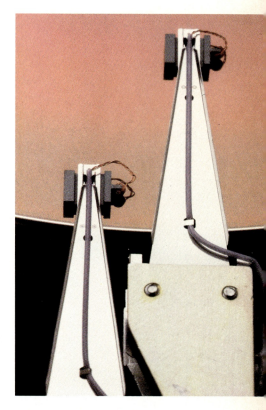

This Winchester disk contains two read/write heads for each recording surface. The access arms move the read/write heads to the appropriate track to retrieve the data. Having two access arms saves precious milliseconds because a head will never have to transverse more than half the width of the disk's recording surface.

FIGURE 4–9 Cutaway of a 5¼-Inch Diskette
Photoelectric cells sense light as it passes through the index hole. This feedback enables the computer to monitor which sector is under or over the read/write head at any given time. Data are read or written serially in tracks within a given sector.

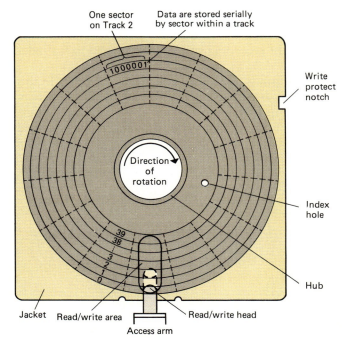

on high-capacity Winchester disks. The spacing of tracks is measured in **tracks per inch**, or **TPI**. The 5¼-inch diskettes are rated at 48 and 96 TPI and the 3½-inch microdisks are rated at 135 TPI. The TPI for Winchester disks can be in the thousands.

The *track density* (TPI) tells only part of the story. The *recording density* tells the rest. Recording density, which is measured in **bits per inch**, or **bpi**, refers to the number of bits (1s and 0s) that can be stored per inch of track. Both the 720-KB and 1.44-MB microdisks have a track density of 135 TPI, but the recording density of the high-density disk is twice that of the double-density disk.

Microcomputer disks use **sector organization** to store and retrieve data. In sector organization, the recording surface is divided into from 9 to 33 pie-shaped **sectors**. The surface of the diskette in Figure 4–9 is logically divided into 15 sectors. Typically, the storage capacity of each sector on a particular track is 512 bytes, regardless of the number of sectors per track. Each sector is assigned a unique number; therefore, the *sector number* and *track number* are all that are needed for a **disk address** on a particular disk-face surface. The disk address represents the physical location of a particular set of data or a program. To read from or write to a disk, an access arm containing the read/write head is moved, under program control, to the appropriate *track* (see Figures 4–8 and 4–9). When the sector containing the desired data passes under or over the read/write head, the data are read or written.

Each of the high-density disk-face surfaces of a Winchester disk may have several thousand tracks, numbered consecutively from outside to inside. A particular **cylinder** refers to every track with the same number on all recording surfaces (see Figure 4–8). When reading from or writing to a Winchester disk, all access arms are moved to the appropriate *cylinder*. For example, each recording surface has a track numbered 0012, so the disk has a cylinder numbered 0012. If the data to be accessed are on Recording Surface 01, Track 0012, then the access arms and the read/write heads for all eight recording surfaces are moved to Cylinder 0012.

In Figure 4–8 the access arm is positioned over Cylinder 0012. In this position, data on any of the sectors on the tracks in Cylinder 0012 can be accessed without further movement of the access arm. If data on Surface 5, Track 0145, are to be read, the access arm must be positioned over Cylinder 0145 until the desired record passes under the read/write head.

▶ **MEMORY BITS**

Characteristics of Magnetic Disks

Interchangeable media	Diskette and microdisk
Permanent media	Fixed or hard disk
Type of access	Sequential and random
Data representation	Serial
Storage scheme	Sector

Fortunately, software automatically monitors the location, or address, of our files and programs. We need only enter someone's name to retrieve his or her personnel record. The computer system locates the record and loads it to primary storage for processing. Although the addressing schemes vary considerably between disks, the address normally will include the *cylinder* (or *track*), the *recording surface*, and the *sector number*.

Disk Access Time. Access time is the interval between the instant a computer makes a request for transfer of data from a disk-storage device to RAM and the instant this operation is completed. The access of data from RAM is performed at electronic speeds—approximately the speed of light. But the access of data from disk storage depends on mechanical apparatus. Any mechanical movement significantly increases the access time. The access time for hard disks is significantly less than for floppy disks because the hard disk is in continuous motion.

The *seek time*, the largest portion of the total access time, consists of how long it takes the mechanical access arm to move the read/write head to the desired track or cylinder. Some Winchester disk drives have two sets of access arms, one for reading and writing on the inside tracks and another for the outside tracks. Two independent sets of access arms significantly reduce the average seek time because they have a shorter distance to move and one can move while the other is reading or writing.

The *rotational delay time* is the time it takes for the appropriate data to be positioned under the read/write head. On the average, it would be half the time it takes for one revolution of the disk, or about 8 milliseconds for a hard disk spinning at 3600 rpm. The rotational delay time for a diskette spinning at 400 rpm is 75 milliseconds, almost 10 times that of a hard disk. The *transmission time*, or the time it takes to transmit the data to primary storage, is negligible. The average access time for most hard-disk drives is less than 20 milliseconds—still very slow when compared with the microsecond-to-nanosecond processing speeds of computers.

> ▶ **MEMORY BITS**
>
> *Disk Access Time =*
> - Seek time +
> - Rotational delay time +
> - Transmission time

This highly magnified area of a magnetic disk-face surface shows elongated information bits recorded serially along eight of the disk's 1774 concentric tracks. One square inch of this disk's surface can hold 22 million bits of information.

Disk Caching. Even though the data **transfer rate** from magnetic disk to RAM may be millions of bytes per second, the rate of transfer between one part of RAM to another is much faster. **Disk caching** (pronounced *cashing*) enhances system performance by placing programs and data that are likely to be called into RAM for processing from a disk into an area of RAM that simulates disk storage. When an applications program issues a call for the data or programs in the disk cache area, called the **RAM disk**, the request is serviced directly from RAM rather than magnetic disk. Data or programs in the RAM disk eventually must be transferred to a disk for permanent storage.

All state-of-the-art PCs come with software that takes full advantage of the potential of RAM disks.

Magnetic Tape: Ribbons of Data

Magnetic tape storage is used primarily as a backup medium for magnetic disk storage. Occasionally, magnetic tape is used in applications that involve only *sequential processing*. A magnetic tape medium, such as the **data cartridge**, can be mounted conveniently onto a tape drive (the hardware device) for processing, then removed for off-line storage. For backup, a tape is taken from off-line storage, mounted onto a tape drive, and the contents of a disk file are copied, or "dumped," from the disk to the tape. The tape is removed and placed in off-line storage as a backup to the content of the operational magnetic disk.

Disk content can be selectively dumped to tape for backup. For example, you can request that all files altered since 5:00 P.M., July 14 be dumped to tape. Or, you can back up only those files associated with a particular application (for example, spreadsheet and word processing).

Hardware and Storage Media. The mechanical operation of a magnetic tape drive is similar to that of an audiocassette tape deck. The tape, a thin polyester ribbon coated with a magnetic material on one side, passes under a *read/write head*, and the data are either (1) read and transmitted to primary storage or (2) transmitted from primary storage and written to the tape.

The ¼-inch data cartridge is self-contained and is inserted into and removed from the tape drive in much the same way that you would load or remove an audiocassette. Like the audiocassette, the supply and the take-up reels for the ¼-inch cartridges are encased in a plastic shell.

A tape drive is rated by the **density** at which the data can be stored on a magnetic tape as well as by the speed of the tape as it passes under the read/write head. Combined, these determine the *transfer rate*, or the number of bytes per second that can be transmitted to primary storage. Like disk, tape density is measured in *bytes per inch* (*bpi*), or the number of bytes (characters) that can be stored per linear inch of tape. The density at which data are stored is often made a user option, up to about 16,000 bpi. The tape passes over the read/write head at up to 300 inches per second. Magnetic tape cartridges are available in a variety of lengths, from 150 to 600 feet, and are capable of storing up to 150 MB.

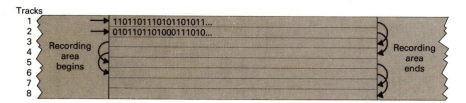

FIGURE 4–10 Cross-Section of a Magnetic Tape: Serial Representation
Data are recorded serially on this eight-track tape in a serpentine manner, two tracks at a time.

Principles of Operation. In the micro environment, the ¼-inch tape cartridge is used exclusively for backup. During backup or recovery runs, backup tapes are processed continuously from beginning to end. Most ¼-inch tape cartridges record data in a continuous stream. Drives for ¼-inch tape cartridges, often called **streamer tape drives**, store data in a **serpentine** manner (Figure 4–10). That is, data are recorded serially in **tracks**, as they are on mag disks. A data cartridge can have from 4 to 15 tracks, depending on the tape drive. The read/write head reads or writes data to one, two, or four tracks at a time. Figure 4–10 illustrates how data are written two tracks at a time. Data are written serially on the top two tracks for the entire length of the tape or until the data are exhausted. The tape is reversed, the read/write head is positioned over the next two tracks, and writing continues in a similar manner. If more backup capacity is needed, the computer operator is informed. He or she inserts a clean tape and writing continues.

4–3 OPTICAL LASER DISKS: HIGH-DENSITY STORAGE

Some industry analysts have predicted that **optical laser disk** technology, now in its infant stage of use and development, eventually may make magnetic disk and tape storage obsolete. With this technology, two lasers replace the read/write head used in magnetic storage. One laser beam writes to the recording surface by scoring microscopic pits in the disk, and another laser reads the data from the light-sensitive recording surface. A light beam is easily deflected to the desired place on the optical disk, so an access arm is not needed.

> **MEMORY BITS**

Characteristics of Data Cartridges

Medium	¼-inch magnetic tape cartridge
Tracks	4 to 15
Type access	Sequential
Data representation	Serial
Storage scheme	Serpentine

Optical laser disks are becoming a very inviting option for users. They are less sensitive to environmental fluctuations, and they provide more direct-access storage at a cost that is much less per megabyte of storage than the magnetic disk alternative. Optical laser disk technology is still emerging and has yet to stabilize; however, the read-only **CD-ROM** (pronounced *cee dee rom*) is becoming increasingly popular among micro users.

Introduced in 1980 for stereo buffs, the extraordinarily successful CD, or compact disk, is an optical laser disk designed to enhance the reproduction of recorded music. To make a CD recording, the analog sounds of music are translated into their digital equivalents and stored on a 4.72-inch optical laser disk. Seventy-four minutes of music can be recorded on each disk in digital format by 2 billion digital bits. With its tremendous storage capacity, computer industry entrepreneurs immediately recognized the potential of optical laser disk technology. In effect, anything that can be digitized can be stored on optical laser disk: data, text, voice, still pictures, music, graphics, and video.

CD-ROM, a spinoff of audio CD technology, stands for *compact disk–read only memory*. The name implies its application. CD-ROM disks, like long-playing record albums, are "pressed" at the factory and distributed with their prerecorded contents (for example, the complete works

This furniture retailer can recall the images of thousands of items from optical laser disk storage. The images are then displayed on high-resolution color monitors. This capability enables his company to maintain a lower inventory and to offer better service to all its customers. This company has gained a distinct competitive advantage by being able to show the same chair in a wide variety of fabrics.

In multimedia applications that involve full motion, the audio-video is frequently stored on CD-ROM. In this training program, sounds and full-motion video are combined to demonstrate proper technique to beginning violinists.

of Shakespeare or the first 30 minutes of *Gone with the Wind*). Once inserted into the disk drive the text, video images, and so on can be read into primary storage for processing or display; however, the data on the disk are fixed—they cannot be altered. This is in contrast, of course, to the read/write capability of magnetic disks.

The capacity of a single CD-ROM is over 550 MB—about that of 400 DS/HD 3½-inch microdisks. To put the density of CD-ROM into perspective, the words in every book ever written could be stored on a hypothetical CD-ROM that is seven feet in diameter.

The tremendous amount of low-cost direct-access storage made possible by optical laser disks has opened the door to many new applications. Currently, most of the 100 or so commercially produced CD-ROM disks contain reference material. A sampling of these disks follows: *The Groliers Electronic Encyclopedia*; *The Oxford English Dictionary*; the 1990 U.S. Census (county level); maps at the national, state, regional, and metropolitan levels; a world history tutorial; the text of 450 titles (including *Moby Dick*, the King James version of the Bible, *Beowolf*, *The Odyssey*, and many more); multilingual dictionaries (one disk contains translation dictionaries for 12 languages); scientific writings for the Apple Macintosh; and *The Daily Oklahoman* (1981–86). The cost of commercially produced CD-ROMs varies considerably from as little as $50 to several thousand dollars.

As optical laser disk technology matures to reliable, cost-effective read/write operation, it eventually may dominate secondary storage in the future as magnetic disks do today.

SUMMARY OUTLINE AND IMPORTANT TERMS

4–1 I/O DEVICES: OUR INTERFACE WITH THE COMPUTER. A variety of input/output peripheral devices provide the interface between us and the computer system.

All PCs are configured with a keyboard, usually the QWERTY 101-key version. The mouse, which is now standard on most PCs, is one of several devices that move the graphics cursor to point and draw. The **joystick**, **track ball**, **digitizer tablet and pen**, and **light pen** are also input devices that move the graphics cursor.

Optical character recognition reduces the need for manual data entry by encoding certain data in machine-readable format. **OCR scanners** (label, page, document, continuous-form, and optical-mark) recognize printed characters and certain coded symbols, such as **bar codes**. An **image scanner** enables **digitized** images of photos, drawings, and other items to be stored on magnetic disk.

Speech-recognition devices can be used to enter limited kinds and quantities of data. They do this by comparing digitized representations of words to similarly formed templates in the computer's electronic dictionary. **Vision-input systems** are best suited for tasks that involve only a few images.

Output devices translate data stored in binary into a form that can be interpreted by the end user. A soft copy of alphanumeric and graphic output is displayed on a monitor. The three attributes of monitors are size (diagonal dimension 5 to 25 inches), color (monochrome or color), and **resolution**. A monochrome monitor can display shades of one color, called **gray scales**. A monitor's resolution is determined by the number of **pixels** it has. Space-saving monochrome and color **flat-panel monitors** use LCD, gas plasma, and EL technologies.

Several color video display standards have evolved since the introduction of the IBM PC in 1981: CGA, EGA, VGA, and super VGA. IBM-PC displays are either in text mode or graphics mode.

Microcomputer printers prepare hard-copy output at speeds of 40 characters per second to 22 pages per minute. **Serial printers** are both impact (**dot-matrix** and **daisy-wheel**) and nonimpact (**ink-jet** and **thermal**). **Desktop page printers** print text and graphic images in **portrait** or **landscape** format. The resolution of the typical desktop page printer is 300 dpi (dots per inch). The emergence of desktop page printers has fueled the explosion of desktop publishing.

Desktop film recorders reproduce a high-resolution graphic image on 35-mm film in either black and white or color. **Screen-image projectors** project the graphic image onto a large screen. **Voice-response units** provide recorded or synthesized voice output.

4–2 SECONDARY STORAGE: PERMANENT DATA STORAGE. Data and programs are stored on **secondary,** or **auxiliary, storage** for permanent storage. **Magnetic disk drives** and **magnetic tape drives** are the state of the art for microcomputer data storage. Data are stored sequentially on magnetic tape; they are stored randomly on magnetic disks. **Sequential access** requires that the medium be searched from the beginning until the desired data are found. **Random,** or **direct, access** enables the desired data to be retrieved directly from its storage location.

Magnetic disk drives provide the computer system with **sequential-** and **random-processing** capabilities. Magnetic disks also support **sequential processing. Interchangeable magnetic disks** can be removed from the drive and stored **off-line; fixed disks** are installed permanently in the drive. When spinning in the drive, the disks are said to be **on-line.**

In the microcomputer environment, the two most popular types of interchangeable magnetic disks are the **diskette** (also called a **flexible disk** or a **floppy disk**) and the **microdisk** (also called a **microfloppy**). The microcomputer **hard disk** is called the **Winchester disk.**

In **sector organization,** the recording surface is divided into pie-shaped **sectors,** and each sector is assigned a number. Data are stored via **serial representation** within **tracks** on each recording surface. The spacing of tracks is measured in **tracks per inch,** or **TPI.** A particular set of data stored on a disk is assigned a **disk address** that designates its physical location (disk-face surface, track, sector). An **access arm** is moved to the appropriate track to retrieve the data.

The **access time** for a magnetic disk is the sum of the seek time, the rotational delay time, and the transmission time.

The data **transfer rate** from magnetic disk to RAM is measured in bytes per second. **Disk caching** enhances system performance by placing programs and data that are likely to be called into RAM for processing from the disk into an area of RAM that simulates disk storage, called the **RAM disk.**

Magnetic tape storage is used primarily as a backup medium for magnetic disk storage. The tape passes under a **read/write head** to read data into RAM or write data to tape. The ¼-inch **data cartridge** is the standard for microcomputers.

A tape drive is rated by the **density** at which the data can be stored on a magnetic tape as well as by its transfer rate. Tape density is measured in **bytes per inch** (**bpi**). Drives for ¼-inch data cartridges, often called **streamer tape drives,** store data in a **serpentine** manner. That is, data are recorded serially in **tracks.** A data cartridge can have from 4 to 15 tracks.

4–3 OPTICAL LASER DISKS: HIGH-DENSITY STORAGE. Optical laser disk technology is emerging as an alternative to magnetic disks and magnetic tapes. The read-only **CD-ROM** is becoming increasingly popular among micro users. In effect, anything that can be digitized can be stored on high-density optical laser disk: data, text, voice, still pictures, music, graphics, and video. The capacity of a single CD-ROM is over 550 MB. Most of the commercially produced read-only CD-ROM disks contain reference material.

REVIEW EXERCISES

1. Which output device generates graphs with the greatest precision, a pen plotter or a dot-matrix printer?
2. What is meant when someone says that speech-recognition devices are "speaker-dependent"?
3. List devices, other than key-driven, that are used to input data into a computer system.
4. Name an impact printer that prints fully formed characters.
5. What is the relationship between a joystick and a graphics cursor?
6. What output device reproduces high-resolution graphic images on 35-mm film?
7. Name a device other than a monitor that produces soft-copy output.
8. What kind of printer can produce near-typeset-quality output?
9. What are other names for flexible disks, auxiliary storage, and direct processing?
10. CD-ROM is a spinoff of what technology?
11. What is the nickname of the hard disk used with microcomputers?
12. Which type of OCR scanner is designed to read documents of varying sizes?
13. Name the types of image scanners.
14. What are the two modes of IBM-PC display?
15. List the following in order of increasing resolution: VGA, CGA, and EGA.
16. Contrast off-line and on-line storage.
17. Which has the greatest storage capacity, an HD or DD microdisk?
18. Microcomputer disks use what type of organization to store and retrieve data?
19. What comprises the largest portion of total disk access time?
20. What technique enables disk storage to be simulated in RAM?
21. People refer to drives for ¼-inch data cartridges by what name?

SELF-TEST (by section)

4–1 a. Input devices translate data into a form that can be interpreted by a computer. (T/F)
   b. The primary function of I/O peripherals is to facilitate computer-to-computer data transmission. (T/F)
   c. The quality of output on a micro's monitor is determined by its _____.
   d. Most flat-panel monitors are used in conjunction with desktop PCs. (T/F)
   e. Optical character recognition provides a way to write certain data in machine-readable format on the original source document. (T/F)
   f. In speech recognition, words are _____ and matched against similarly formed _____ in the computer's electronic dictionary.

CHAPTER 4 Micro Peripheral Devices: I/O and Data Storage

    g. Vision-input systems are best suited to generalized tasks in which a wide variety of images will be encountered. (T/F)
    h. Ink-jet printers are classified as impact printers. (T/F)
    i. What type of printers are becoming the standard for office microcomputer systems: (a) desktop page printers, (b) daisy-wheel printers, or (c) thermal printers?
    j. _____ convert raw data into electronically produced speech.

4-2 a. Data are retrieved from temporary auxiliary storage and stored permanently in RAM. (T/F)
    b. Magnetic disk drives have both _____- and _____-access capabilities.
    c. In a disk drive, the read/write heads are mounted on an access arm. (T/F)
    d. The diskette is _____ inches in diameter, and the microfloppy is _____ inches in diameter.
    e. What percentage of the data on a magnetic disk is available to the system with each complete revolution of the disk: (a) 10%, (b) 50%, or (c) 100%?
    f. The _____ denotes the physical location of a particular set of data or a program on a magnetic disk.
    g. Tape density is measured in TPI. (T/F)
    h. Streamer tape drives store data in a _____ manner.

4-3 a. _____ technology permits on-line direct access of still pictures, voice, text, and video.
    b. CD-ROM is read-only. (T/F)

Self-test answers.   4-1 (a) T; (b) F; (c) resolution; (d) F; (e) T; (f) digitized, templates; (g) F; (h) F; (i) a; (j) Speech synthesizers. 4-2 (a) F; (b) direct *or* random, sequential; (c) T; (d) 5¼, 3½; (e) c; (f) disk address; (g) F; (h) serpentine. 4-3 (a) Optical laser disk; (b) T.

CHAPTER 5

TEXT AND IMAGE PROCESSING: WORD PROCESSING, DESKTOP PUBLISHING, AND GRAPHICS

STUDENT LEARNING OBJECTIVES

- ▶ To describe the function and applications of word processing software.
- ▶ To understand word processing concepts.
- ▶ To identify and describe add-on capabilities of word processing software packages.
- ▶ To describe the function and applications of desktop publishing software.
- ▶ To understand desktop publishing concepts.
- ▶ To describe the functions of different types of graphics software.
- ▶ To understand graphics software concepts.

5-1 WORD PROCESSING

Function

Word processing is using the computer to enter, store, manipulate, and print text in letters, reports, books, and so on. Once you have used word processing software, you will probably wonder (like a million others before you) how in the world you ever survived without it!

Word processing has virtually eliminated the need for opaque correction fluid and the need to rekey revised letters and reports. Revising a hard copy is time-consuming and cumbersome, but revising the same text in electronic format is quick and easy. You simply make corrections and revisions on the computer before the document is displayed or printed in final form.

At many companies all office workers, including executives, are trained to use word processing. Workers at this company save time and money by using word processing to edit their reports. They find this approach more effective than having a secretary key in their red-pencil revisions from a hard copy.

Concepts

Creating a Document

Formatting a document. Before you begin keying in the text of a word processing document, you may need to *format* the document to meet your application needs. However, if you are satisfied with the software's preset format specifications, you can begin keying in text right away. Typically, the preset format, or *default settings*, fit most word processing applications. For example, the size of the output document is set at 8½ by 11 inches; the left, right, top, and bottom margins are set at 1 inch; tabs are set every ½ inch; and line spacing is set at 6 lines per inch. However, if you are planning to print your document on legal-size paper, then you would need to reset the size of the output document to 8½ by 14 inches.

Depending on the software package, some or all of these specifications are made in a *layout line*. You can have as many layout lines as you want in a single document. Text is printed according to specifications in the most recent layout line in the running text of the document.

Entering text. Text is entered in either **typeover mode** or **insert mode**. On most word processing systems you *toggle*, or switch, between typeover and insert modes by tapping a key, often the insert (or INS) key.

Let's use the draft copy of a memo written by Pat Kline (see Figure 5–1), the national sales manager for a manufacturer of high-tech products, to illustrate the two modes of data entry. When in typeover mode, the character you enter *types over* the character at the cursor position. For example, in the last sentence of the memo, Pat began with *The* and realized that *Our* is a better word. To make the correction in typeover

FIGURE 5–1 Word Processing: Memorandum
This first-draft memo is revised for illustrative purposes in Figures 5–2 through 5–6.

```
To:       Field Sales Staff
From:     Pat Kline, National Sales Manager
Subject:  June Sales Summary

   Good job! Sales for the month are up 21% over the same month
last year. Our top performer for the month, Phyllis Hill, set a new
one-month record--$78,167! Congratulations Phyllis.
   I've included a bar graph and a "Statistical Sales Summary."
The bar graph shows sales activity by region by product for the
month. The summary should help you place your performance into
perspective.
   Plan your schedule accordingly. The annual sales meeting is
tentatively scheduled at the Bayside Hotel in San Diego during the
first week in January.

cc: P. Powell, President; V. Grant, VP Marketing
```

mode, Pat positioned the cursor at the *T* and typed *O-u-r*, thereby replacing *The* with *Our*. When in insert mode, any text entered is *additional* text. Pat forgot to enter the full name of the hotel in the last sentence. To complete the name, Pat selected the insert mode, placed the cursor at the *i* in the word *in*, and entered *and Marina* followed by a space (see Figure 5–2).

On most word processing packages, text that extends past the defined margins is automatically *wrapped* to the next line. That is, the words that extend past the right margin are automatically moved down to the next line, and so on, to the end of the paragraph. In Figures 5–1 and 5–2, notice how the word *during* (in the last sentence) is wrapped to the next line when *and Marina* is inserted.

Word processing permits **full-screen editing**. In other words, you can move the text cursor to any position in the document to insert or type over text. You can browse through a multiscreen document by *scrolling* a line at a time, a screen at a time, or a page at a time. You can edit any part of any screen.

When you enter text, *tap the ENTER key only when you wish to begin a new line of text*. In the memo of Figure 5–1, Pat tapped ENTER after each of the three information lines, after each paragraph in the body of the memo, and after the "copy to" (cc) line. Pat also tapped ENTER to insert each of the blank lines. The TAB key was tapped at the beginning of each paragraph to indent the first line of the paragraph.

As you enter text in typeover mode, the cursor automatically moves to the next line when you reach the right-hand margin. In insert mode, the computer manipulates the text so it wraps around. This type of text movement is called **word wrap**.

FIGURE 5–2 Word Processing: Typeover and Insert Mode
This memo is the result of two revisions of the first sentence of the last paragraph. The is replaced with Our *in typeover mode. The phrase* and Marina *and a space are added in insert mode. Notice how the text wraps around to make room for the additional words.*

```
To:       Field Sales Staff
From:     K. Kline, National Sales Manager
Subject:  June Sales Summary

    Good job! Sales for the month are up 21% over the same month
last year. Our top performer for the month, Phyllis Hill, set a new
one-month record--$78,167! Congratulations Phyllis.
    I've included a bar graph and a "Statistical Sales Summary."
The bar graph shows sales activity by region by product for the
month. The summary should help you place your performance into
perspective.
    Plan your schedule accordingly. Our annual sales meeting is
tentatively scheduled at the Bayside Hotel and Marina in San Diego
during the first week in January.

cc: P. Powell, President; V. Grant, VP Marketing
```

Block Operations. Features common to most word processing software packages are mentioned and discussed briefly in this section. *Block operations* are among the handiest word processing features. They are the block-*move*, the block-*copy*, and the block-*delete* commands. These commands are the electronic equivalent of a "cut and paste job."

Let's discuss the move command first. With this feature you can select a block of text (for example, a word, a sentence, a paragraph, a section of a report, or as much contiguous text as you desire) and move it to another portion of the document. To do this, follow these steps:

1. Indicate the start and ending positions of the block of text to be moved (*mark* the text).
2. Issue the move command (a main-menu option or a function key).
3. Move the text cursor to the beginning of the destination location (where you wish the text to be moved).
4. Tap ENTER (or the appropriate function key) to complete the move operation.

At the end of the move procedure, the entire block of text you selected is moved to the location you designated, and the text is adjusted accordingly (wrapped).

The following example demonstrates the procedure for marking and moving a block of text. After reading over the memo to the field staff (Figure 5–2), Pat decided to edit the memo to make it more readable. This is done by moving the first sentence in the last paragraph to the end of the memo. To perform this operation, Pat marked the beginning

With a line of over 500 products, this clothing sales representative keeps product information handy in the form of word processing documents. He uses on-screen displays of product information during customer presentations.

(P in *Plan*) and end (the position following the period at the end of the sentence) of the block. On most word processing systems, the portions of text marked for a block operation are usually displayed in **reverse video** (see Figure 5–3a). To complete the operation (see Figure 5–3b), Pat selected the move option, then positioned the cursor at the destination location (after a space following the end of the paragraph) and tapped the appropriate key. Notice that the text in the last paragraph is wrapped to accommodate the move operation.

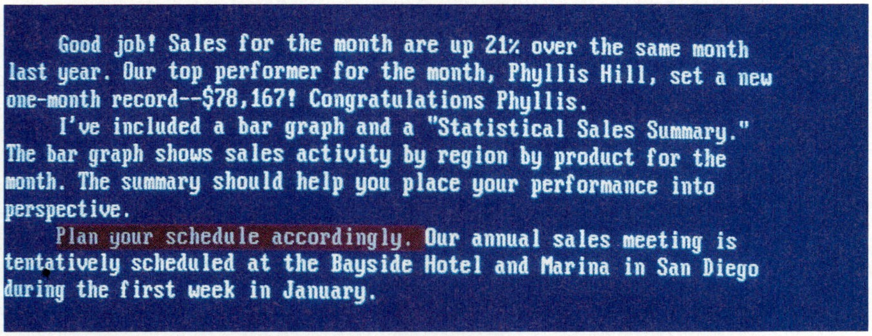

The copy command works in a similar manner, except that the text block you select is copied to the location you designate. When the operation is completed, the text block in question appears twice in the document. To delete a block of text, you mark the block in the same manner, then select the delete-block option. The meeting at the Bayside Hotel and Marina was confirmed while Pat was composing the memo in Figure 5–1. To reflect the confirmation, Pat used the block-delete command to drop the phrase *tentatively scheduled*, then inserted the word *set*. This operation is illustrated in sequence in Figure 5–4.

The Search Feature. While looking over the memo, Pat Kline decided that it would read better if all generic references to *the month* were

FIGURE 5–3 Word Processing: Marking and Moving Text
(a) The first sentence of the last paragraph of the memo is marked to be moved.
(b) The marked sentence is moved to the end of the paragraph.

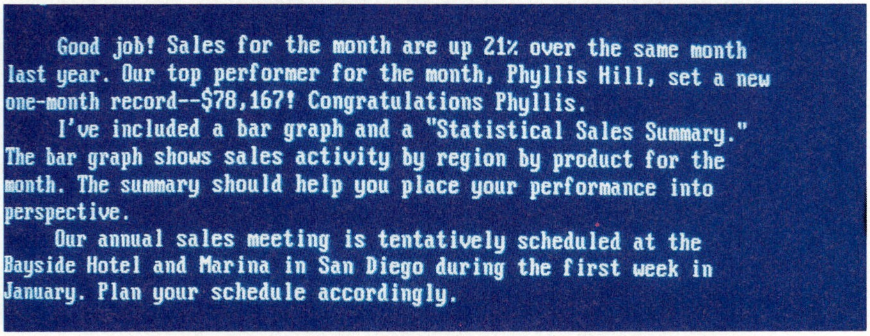

(a)

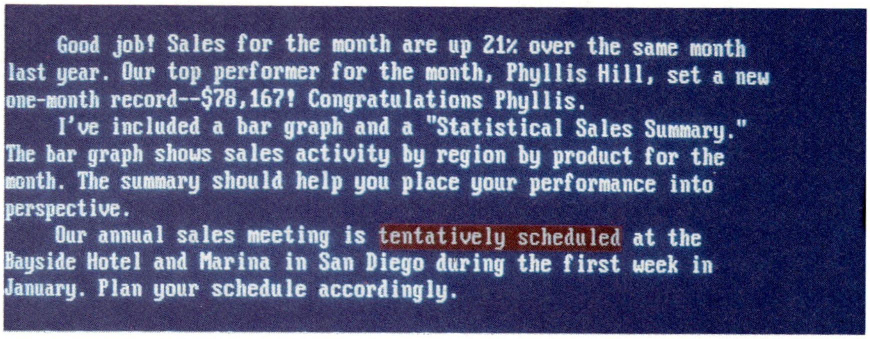

> Good job! Sales for the month are up 21% over the same month last year. Our top performer for the month, Phyllis Hill, set a new one-month record--$78,167! Congratulations Phyllis.
>   I've included a bar graph and a "Statistical Sales Summary." The bar graph shows sales activity by region by product for the month. The summary should help you place your performance into perspective.
>   Our annual sales meeting is ==tentatively scheduled== at the Bayside Hotel and Marina in San Diego during the first week in January. Plan your schedule accordingly.

(b)

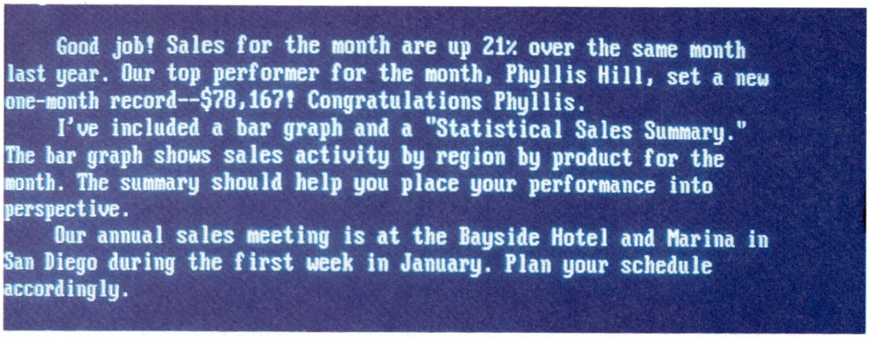

> Good job! Sales for the month are up 21% over the same month last year. Our top performer for the month, Phyllis Hill, set a new one-month record--$78,167! Congratulations Phyllis.
>   I've included a bar graph and a "Statistical Sales Summary." The bar graph shows sales activity by region by product for the month. The summary should help you place your performance into perspective.
>   Our annual sales meeting is at the Bayside Hotel and Marina in San Diego during the first week in January. Plan your schedule accordingly.

(c)

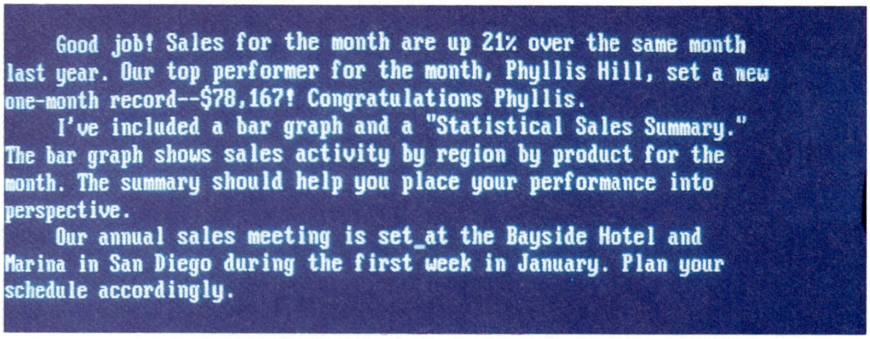

> Good job! Sales for the month are up 21% over the same month last year. Our top performer for the month, Phyllis Hill, set a new one-month record--$78,167! Congratulations Phyllis.
>   I've included a bar graph and a "Statistical Sales Summary." The bar graph shows sales activity by region by product for the month. The summary should help you place your performance into perspective.
>   Our annual sales meeting is set_at the Bayside Hotel and Marina in San Diego during the first week in January. Plan your schedule accordingly.

FIGURE 5–4 Word Processing: Marking and Deleting Text
(a) The phrase tentatively scheduled *in the first sentence of the last paragraph is marked to be deleted. (b) The phrase is deleted. (c) The word* set *is inserted at the cursor position.*

replaced by the name of the month, *June.* The necessary revisions in the memo can be made by using any of several word processing features. One option is to use the *search,* or *find,* feature. This feature allows Pat to search the entire document and identify all occurrences of a particular character string. For example, if Pat wanted to search for all occurrences of *the month* in the memo, the manager simply would initiate the search command and type in the desired *search string*—*the month*, in this example. Immediately, the cursor is positioned at the first occurrence of the character string *the month* so Pat can easily edit the text to reflect the new meeting day. From there, other occurrences of *the month* can be located by tapping the appropriate search key.

An alternative to changing each occurrence of *the month* to *June* involves using the *search-and-replace* feature. This feature enables *selective* replacement of *the month* with *June*. Issuing the *global search-and-replace* command causes *all* occurrences of *the month* to be replaced with *June*. Opting for the global search-and-replace command, Pat replaced all three occurrences of *the month* with *June* (see Figure 5–5).

Features That Enhance Appearance and Readability. Pat used several other valuable word processing features to enhance the appearance and readability of the memo before distributing it to the field sales staff. First,

FIGURE 5–5 Word Processing: Search and Replace
(a) The memo contains three occurrences of the string the month. *(b) The search-and-replace command replaces all occurrences of* the month *with* June.

(a)

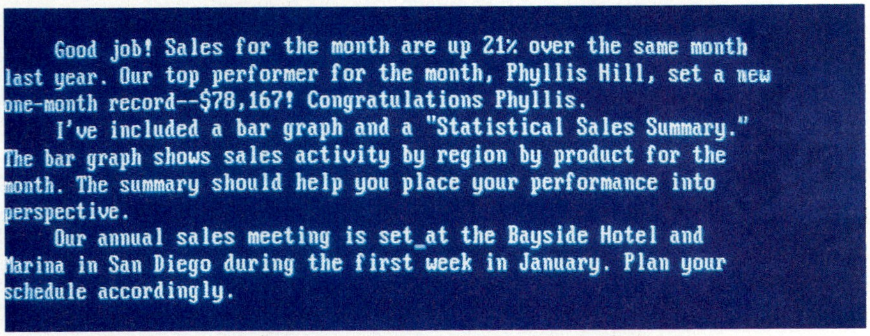

```
    Good job! Sales for the month are up 21% over the same month
last year. Our top performer for the month, Phyllis Hill, set a new
one-month record--$78,167! Congratulations Phyllis.
    I've included a bar graph and a "Statistical Sales Summary."
The bar graph shows sales activity by region by product for the
month. The summary should help you place your performance into
perspective.
    Our annual sales meeting is set at the Bayside Hotel and
Marina in San Diego during the first week in January. Plan your
schedule accordingly.
```

(b)

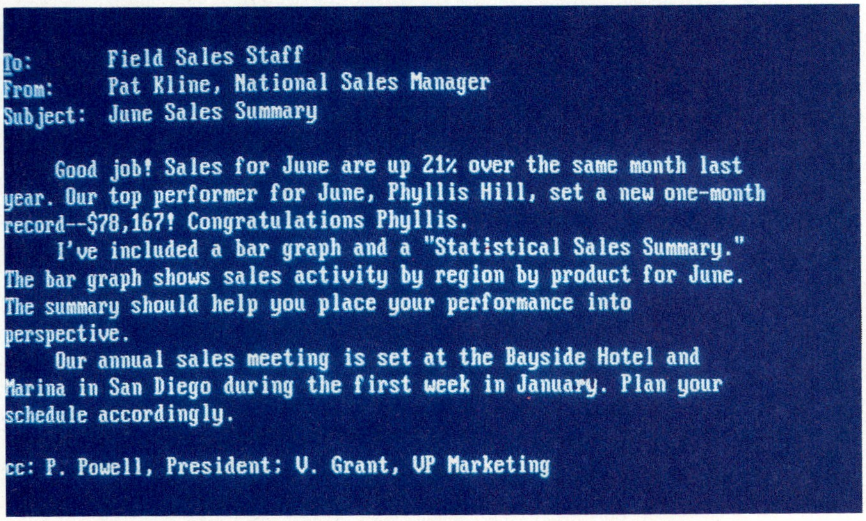

```
To:       Field Sales Staff
From:     Pat Kline, National Sales Manager
Subject:  June Sales Summary

    Good job! Sales for June are up 21% over the same month last
year. Our top performer for June, Phyllis Hill, set a new one-month
record--$78,167! Congratulations Phyllis.
    I've included a bar graph and a "Statistical Sales Summary."
The bar graph shows sales activity by region by product for June.
The summary should help you place your performance into
perspective.
    Our annual sales meeting is set at the Bayside Hotel and
Marina in San Diego during the first week in January. Plan your
schedule accordingly.

cc: P. Powell, President; V. Grant, VP Marketing
```

the manager decided to enter the current date at the top of the memo and use the automatic *centering* feature to position it at the center of the page. On most word processing systems, centering a particular line is as easy as moving the text cursor to the desired line and tapping the *center* function key. The rest is automatic (see Figure 5–6a).

Word processing provides the facility to *boldface* and/or *underline* parts of the text for emphasis. In the memo, Pat decided to highlight the remarkable 21% increase in sales by requesting that it be printed in boldface type (see Figure 5–6b). To do so, the manager marked *21%* and

FIGURE 5–6 Word Processing: Center, Boldface, and Underline
(a) The date is centered at the top of the memo. On a color monitor, text to be in printed in boldface type or underlined is displayed in different colors. (b) The memo is printed on a desktop page printer.

(a)

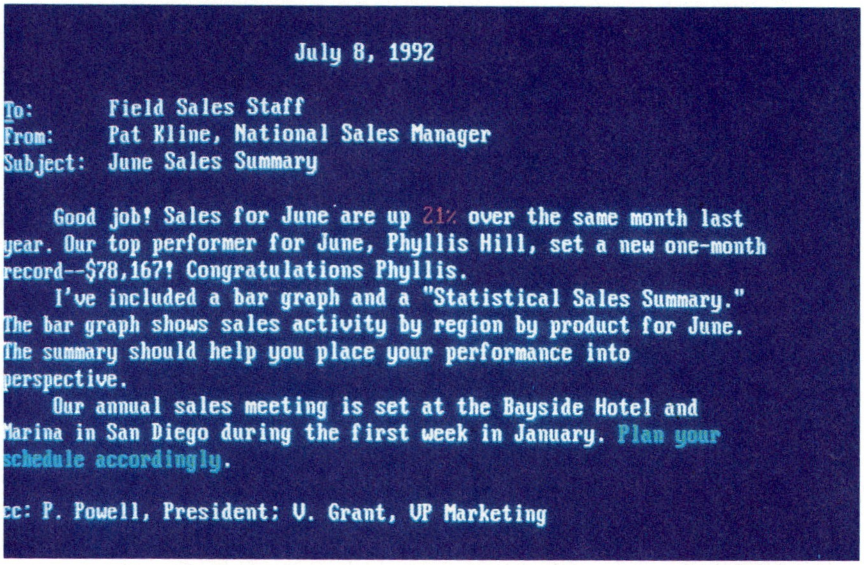

```
                        July 8, 1992

To:        Field Sales Staff
From:      Pat Kline, National Sales Manager
Subject:   June Sales Summary

    Good job! Sales for June are up 21% over the same month last
year. Our top performer for June, Phyllis Hill, set a new one-month
record--$78,167! Congratulations Phyllis.
    I've included a bar graph and a "Statistical Sales Summary."
The bar graph shows sales activity by region by product for June.
The summary should help you place your performance into
perspective.
    Our annual sales meeting is set at the Bayside Hotel and
Marina in San Diego during the first week in January. Plan your
schedule accordingly.

cc: P. Powell, President; V. Grant, VP Marketing
```

(b)

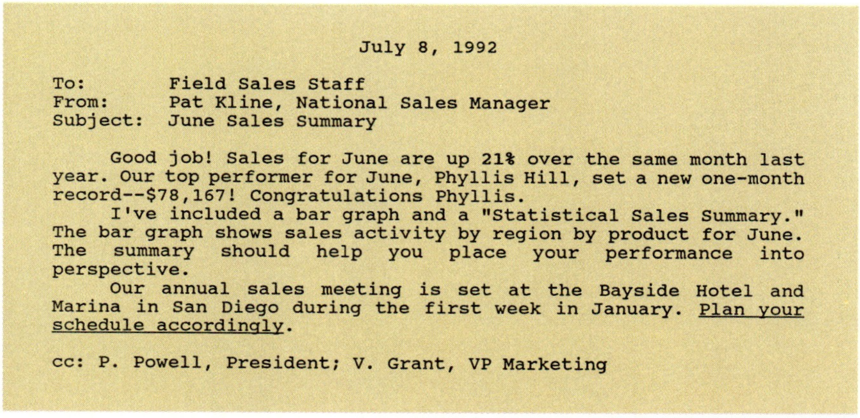

```
                        July 8, 1992

To:        Field Sales Staff
From:      Pat Kline, National Sales Manager
Subject:   June Sales Summary

    Good job! Sales for June are up 21% over the same month last
year. Our top performer for June, Phyllis Hill, set a new one-month
record--$78,167! Congratulations Phyllis.
    I've included a bar graph and a "Statistical Sales Summary."
The bar graph shows sales activity by region by product for June.
The  summary  should  help  you  place  your  performance  into
perspective.
    Our annual sales meeting is set at the Bayside Hotel and
Marina in San Diego during the first week in January. Plan your
schedule accordingly.

cc: P. Powell, President; V. Grant, VP Marketing
```

issued the boldface command. To make the point that sales representatives should plan now for the January meeting, Pat followed a similar procedure to make sure the last sentence is underlined on output (see Figure 5–6b).

On color monitors, highlighted (boldface, underline) words usually appear on the screen in a different color (Figure 5–6a). Some word processing systems display text that is to print in boldface type or underlined on output in reverse video (Figure 5–7a). Systems with high-resolution monitors allow text to appear in boldface and underlined right on the display screen (Figure 5–7b).

FIGURE 5–7 Word Processing: Displaying Boldface and Underlined Text
(a) Boldface and underline are displayed in reverse video on some monitors. (b) High-resolution monitors can display boldface and underlined text.

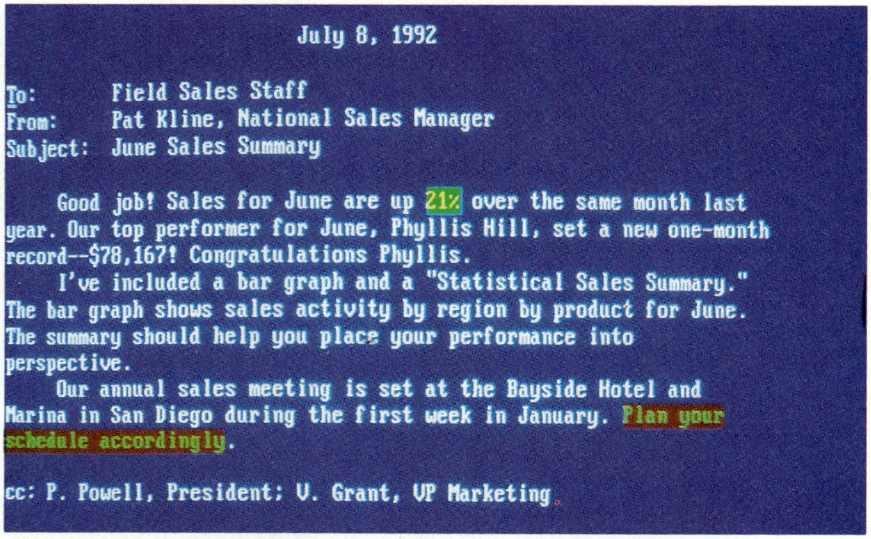

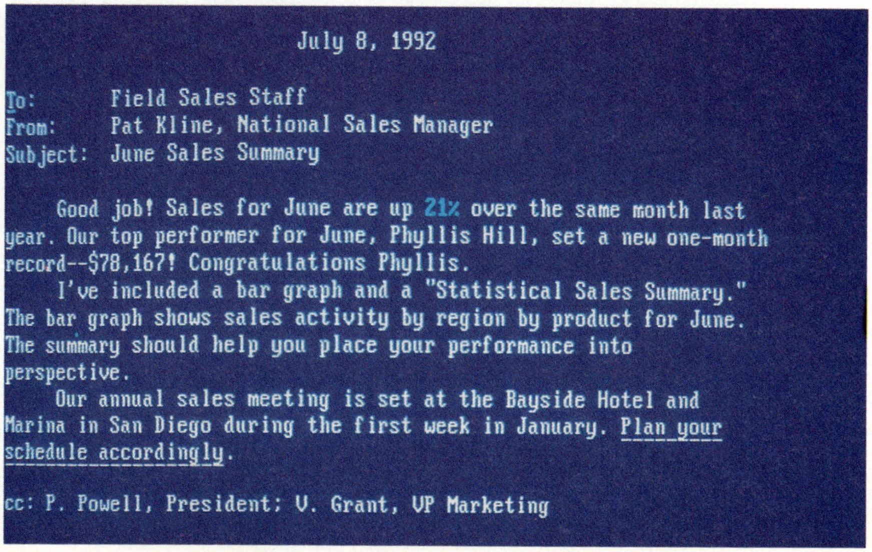

To enhance the appearance of a document, some people like to *justify* (align) text on the left or the right margin, or on both margins, like the print in newspapers and in this book. Word processing software is able to produce "clean" margins on both sides by adding small spaces between characters and words in a line as it is output. The right and left margins of the memo in Figure 5-6b are justified. However, Pat prefers the more traditional *ragged right* margin on personal letters. The first paragraph in Figure 5-8 is printed as ragged right.

FIGURE 5-8 Word Processing: Features Overview
Many of the more common capabilities of word processing software are illustrated in this printout.

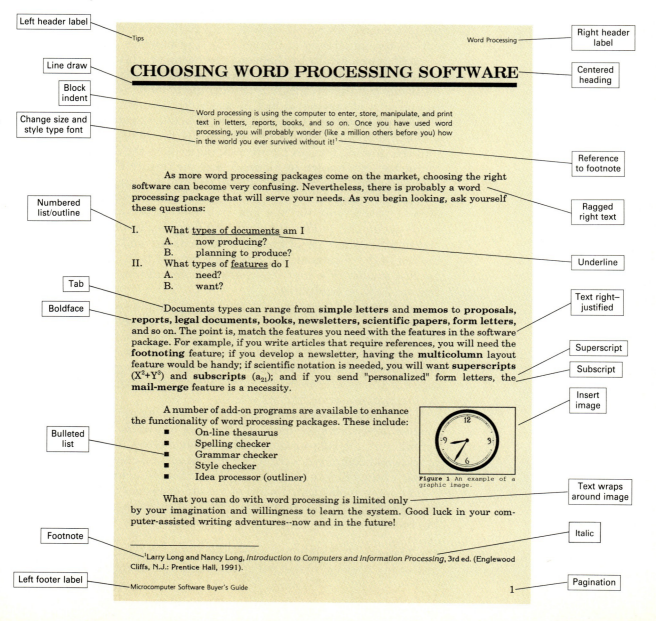

In creating the memo of Figure 5–6, Pat used many but not all the word processing features available to enhance its appearance and readability. Other such features are illustrated in Figure 5–8. Users can *indent* a block of text, cause *header* and *footer labels* to be printed on each page, and request that pages be numbered (*pagination* feature). On long reports, Pat usually repeats the report title at the top of each page (header label) and numbers each page at the bottom (pagination).

The example in Figure 5–8 also illustrates hyphenation, footnotes, numbered list/outline, bulleted list, line draw, superscripts and subscripts, and the insertion of an image into the running text. The *hyphenation* feature automatically breaks and hyphenates words to create a smoother appearing right margin. One of the most tedious typing chores, *footnoting*, is done automatically. Footnote spacing is resolved electronically before anything is printed. The *numbered list* and *outline* features enable descriptive items to be presented in a numbered list or in outline format (shown in Figure 5–8). The numbers and/or letters are inserted automatically by the word processing program. The *bulleted list* is created in a similar manner. Users can create special effects with the *line-draw* feature. This feature permits the drawing of vertical and horizontal lines of varying widths. *Superscripts* and *subscripts* are common in technical writing. One of the most popular features of the more sophisticated word processing programs is the ability to *insert images* into the running text. In Figure 5–8, notice how the text wraps around the image. Not shown in Figure 5–8 is the feature that permits *multicolumn output*, one or more columns of text on a single page.

Depending on the type of software and printer you have, you may even be able to mix the size and style of typefaces, called **fonts**, in a single document. In Figure 5–8, the heading, headers, footer, quotation, and figure caption are printed in a different size and style of type than the rest of the document. The heading is a larger type font and the others are in a smaller type font. Fonts are discussed in more detail in the section on desktop publishing.

Some word processing software contains sophisticated features for writers and people who are charged with the preparation of long, involved documents (strategic plans, annual reports, procedures manuals, and so on). A simple command creates a *table of contents* with page references for chapters and up to five levels of headings. An alphabetical *index of key words* can be compiled that lists the page numbers for each occurrence of user-designated words.

Some word processing packages have a *table* feature that expedites the tabular presentation of data. All the user has to do to set up a table format with the appropriate number of lined boxes is enter the number of rows and columns desired. Once data have been entered into the table, simple arithmetic can be performed (for example, column totals).

The more sophisticated word processing packages provide users with the capability of doing rudimentary *desktop publishing*. Desktop publishing is discussed in detail later in this chapter.

File Features. Certainly one of the most important features of a word processing package is the ability to store a document on disk for later recall. The stored version of a document is referred to as a *document file*. The *file* feature permits you to save, retrieve, and delete a text file. At a minimum, most word processing systems provide users with the save-, retrieve-, and delete-file options. No matter which option you choose, you are asked by the system to identify the file (document). You then enter an arbitrary name that in some way identifies the document (for example, MEMO). To retrieve or delete an existing file, you enter its file name.

Pat Kline "saved" the memo in Figure 5–6 (stored it on disk) under the file name MEMO. Because the memo is stored in electronic format on disk, Pat can retrieve and edit it to report the sales results for another month.

Printing a Document. To print a document, all you have to do is ready the printer and select the print option on the main menu. Some word processing systems present you with other options. For example, you can choose to print the document single- or double-spaced; you also could be given the option of printing specific pages or the whole document.

Most word processing packages are considered **WYSIWYG** (pronounced *WIZ e wig*), short for "What you see is what you get." What you see on the screen is essentially what the document will look like when it is printed. WYSIWYG is slightly misleading in that what you see while editing a document is *not exactly* what you get. For example, the text you see on the screen may not be right-justified. However, most of the new word processing packages have a *preview* feature that permits you to see what the document will look like when it is printed—almost. The display screen fonts may be slightly different than the printer fonts. These differences have prompted the occasional use of a more accurate term **WYSIWYG—MOL**, short for "What you see is what you get—more or less."

Add-on Capabilities. A number of programs are designed to enhance the functionality of word processing programs. These add-on capabilities are usually separate programs that can interface with a word processing package. They can be purchased separately or as part of the word processing package.

On-line thesaurus. Have you ever been in the middle of writing a letter or memo and been unable to put your finger on the right word? Some word processing packages have an **on-line thesaurus!** Suppose you have just written: *The Grand Canyon certainly is beautiful.* But *beautiful* is not quite the right word. Your electronic thesaurus is always ready with suggestions: *pretty, gorgeous, exquisite, angelic, pulchritudinous, ravishing,* and so on.

Spelling checker. If spelling is a problem, then word processing is the answer. Once you have entered the text and formatted the document the way you want it, you can call on the **spelling checker** capability. The spelling checker checks every word in the text against an **electronic dictionary** (usually from 75,000 to 150,000 words) and alerts you if a word is not in the dictionary. Upon finding an unidentified word, the spell function normally will give you several options:

1. You can correct the spelling.
2. You can ignore the word and continue scanning the text. Normally you do this when a word is spelled correctly but is not in the dictionary (for example, a company name such as Zimco).
3. You can ask for possible spellings. The spell function then gives you a list of words of similar spelling from which to choose. For example, assume that Pat left out the *o* in *month*. Upon finding the nonword *mnth*, the spelling checker might suggest the following alternatives: *math*, *month*, *moth*, *myth*, and *nth*.
4. You can add the word to the dictionary and continue scanning.

Grammar and style checkers. Grammar and style checkers are the electronic version of a copy editor. A **grammar checker** highlights grammatical concerns and deviations from conventions. For example, it highlights split infinitives, phrases with redundant words (*very highest*), misuse of capital letters (*JOhn* or *MarY*), subject and verb mismatches (*they was*), double words (*and and*), and punctuation errors. When applied to the memo in Figure 5-6, the grammar checker noted the incomplete sentence at the end of the first paragraph ("Congratulations Phyllis"). A **style checker** alerts users to such writing concerns as sexist words or phrases (*chairman*), long or complex sentence structures, clichés (*the bottom line*), and sentences written in the passive rather than the active voice.

Idea processor. Like word processing software, an **idea processor** permits the manipulation of text, but with a different twist. It deals with brief explanations of items—for example: ideas, points, notes, and so on.

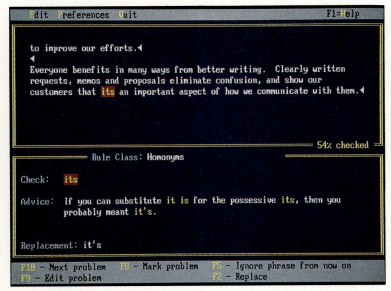

This screen illustrates how Grammatik IV handles a problem encountered while scanning a word processing document for grammar, style, usage, punctuation, and spelling errors. In the example, the program advises the user to replace its *with the homonym* it's. *The user has the option of taking no action and going on to the next problem; editing the problem; marking it for later examination; ignoring similar problems for the rest of the scan; or replacing* its *with* it's.

Idea processors, which are also called **outliners**, can be used to organize these brief items into an outline format. Some people have referred to the idea processor as an electronic version of the yellow notepad. When you use it, you can focus your attention on the thought process by letting the computer help document your ideas.

Document-conversion programs. Although a handful of word processing packages dominate the marketplace, about 30 are commonly used. It is not unusual for people within a company to use half a dozen incompatible word processing packages and, of course, these people frequently need to share text in their word processing documents. There are two ways to do this.

1. *Create an ASCII file.* When you save a word processing document, you save all the text in the file *plus* the hidden control characters that end paragraphs, start and end boldface, cause page breaks, and so on. These control characters are unique to each word processing package; therefore, one package cannot read a file produced by another. However, all word processing packages can read **ASCII files.** An ASCII file is a generic text file that is stripped of program-specific control characters. One way to pass text from one word processing package to another is to create a generic ASCII file with one and read it with another. Of course, when you do this, you lose everything (tabs, underlines, and so on) except the text in the transfer.
2. *Use a document-conversion program.* **Document-conversion programs** help solve the dilemma created when several word processing packages are used within a given company. This add-on converts documents generated on one word processing package into a format that is consistent with another. For example, document-conversion programs enable a Microsoft Word user to convert his or her files to WordPerfect files—control characters and all.

> **MEMORY BITS**
>
> *Word Processing*
> Entering text
> • Typeover mode
> • Insert mode
> Block operations on marked text
> • Move
> • Copy
> • Delete
> Search or find
> • Search only
> • Selective search and replace
> • Global search and replace
> Add-ons
> • On-line thesaurus
> • Spelling checker
> • Grammar and style checker
> • Idea processor
> • Document-conversion program

Use

Mail Merge. You can create just about any kind of text-based document with word processing: letters, reports, books, articles, forms, memos, tables, and so on. The features of some word processing packages go beyond the generation of text documents, however. For example, some word processing systems provide the capability of merging parts of a data base with the text of a document. An example of this **mail-merge** application is illustrated in Figure 5–9. In the example, Zimco Enterprises announced the enhanced version of its Qwert, one of its hottest selling items. Each regional sales manager sent a "personal" letter to every one of the thousands of Zimco customers in his or her region. Using word processing, a secretary enters the letter once, stores it on the disk, then simply merges the customer name-and-address file (also stored on the disk) with the letter. The letters then can be printed with the proper addresses and salutations. Figure 5–9 illustrates how the Qwert announcement letter could be merged with the customer name-and-address file to produce a "personalized" letter.

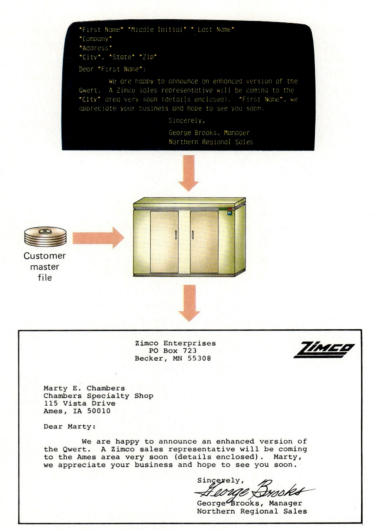

FIGURE 5–9 Merging Data with Word Processing
The names and addresses from a customer master file are retrieved from secondary storage and are merged with the text of a letter. In the actual letter, the appropriate data items are inserted for *First Name*, *Company*, *Address*, *City*, and so on. In this way, a "personalized" letter can be sent to each customer.

Boilerplate. The mail-merge example is a good illustration of the use of **boilerplate**. Boilerplate is existing text that can in some way be customized to be used in a variety of word processing applications. One of the beauties of word processing is that you can accumulate text on disk storage that eventually will help you meet other word processing needs. You can even *buy* boilerplate.

The legal profession offers some of the best examples of the use of boilerplate. Simple wills, uncontested divorces, individual bankruptcies, real estate transfers, and other straightforward legal documents may be as much as 95% boilerplate. Even more complex legal documents may be as much as 80% boilerplate. Once the appropriate boilerplate has been merged into a document, the lawyer edits the document to add transition sentences and the variables, such as the names of the litigants. Besides the obvious improvement in productivity, lawyers can be relatively confident that their documents are accurate and complete. Lawyers, of course, do not have a monopoly on boilerplate. Its use is common in all areas of business, education, government, and personal endeavor.

Integration of Text and Graphics. Most state-of-the-art word processing packages permit the integration of text and graphic images. For example, the text in Figure 5-10 refers to a "bar graph" and a "Statistical Sales Summary." Figure 5-10 shows how the memo, the bar graph (pro-

FIGURE 5-10 Integrating Text with Graphics
The bar graph and the "Statistical Sales Summary" referred to in the memo of Figure 5-6 are combined in the same word processing document and printed on a desktop page printer. The bar graph and summary were produced using electronic spreadsheet software.

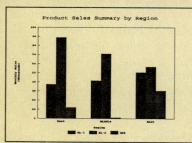

Many workers have become so accustomed to writing memos, preparing meeting agendas, and documenting ideas with word processing software that they take a portable computer along with them.

duced with electronic spreadsheet software), and the sales summary (from an electronic spreadsheet file) can be integrated into a single word processing document.

Summary. Word processing is the perfect example of how automation can be used to increase productivity and foster creativity. It minimizes the effort you must devote to the routine aspects of writing so you can focus your attention on its creative aspects. Most word processing users will agree that their writing styles have improved measurably. The finished product is less verbose, better organized, devoid of spelling errors, and, of course, more visually appealing.

5-2 DESKTOP PUBLISHING

Function

The ultimate extension of word processing is *desktop publishing*, sometimes abbreviated as **DTP**. Desktop publishing refers to the capability of producing *near-typeset-quality copy* from the confines of a desktop. The concept of desktop publishing is changing the way companies, government agencies, and individuals approach printing newsletters, brochures, user manuals, pamphlets, restaurant menus, periodicals, greeting cards, and thousands of other items.

Concepts

Traditionally, drafts of documents to be printed are delivered to commercial typographers to be typeset. The typeset text is physically pasted together with photos, artwork, ruled lines, and so on to achieve the final layout. Desktop publishing has made it possible to eliminate this typesetting and pasteup process for those documents that require only near-typeset quality (for example, those documents produced by desktop page printers with 300 to 1000 dots per inch). In practice, near-typeset-quality copy is acceptable for most printed documents. Relatively few need to be prepared using the expensive commercial phototypesetting process (which uses 1200 dpi or greater). The output of the desktop publishing process is called *camera-ready copy*. The camera-ready copy is reproduced by a variety of means, from duplicating machines to commercial offset printing.

The Components of Desktop Publishing. The components required for desktop publishing include:

- Document-composition software
- Microcomputer
- Desktop page printer
- Image scanner
- Typefaces and fonts
- Clip art

CHAPTER 5 Text and Image Processing: Word Processing, Desktop Publishing, and Graphics   143

Document-composition software. The document-composition software enables users to design and make up the page or pages of a document. When people talk of desktop publishing software, they are actually talking about document-composition software. Two of the most popular document-composition packages are Xerox's *Ventura Publisher* and Aldus Corporation's *PageMaker*.

Microcomputer. Of all of the microcomputer productivity tools, DTP is the most technologically demanding. A high-end microcomputer is a prerequisite for effective desktop publishing. The typical micro used for DTP will be fast (20 MHz or faster) and will be configured with a high-resolution *VGA monitor*, a *mouse*, at least 4 MB of RAM, and a *hard disk* with a capacity of at least 100 MB.

Desktop page printer. The overwhelming majority of desktop page printers configured with DTP systems are laser printers that print at 300 dpi. However, affordable desktop page printers with 1000 dpi resolution are available.

Image scanner. Image scanners (see Chapter 4, "Micro Peripheral Devices: I/O and Data Storage"), found on high-end DTP systems, are used to digitize images, such as photographs. Image scanners re-create an electronic version of text or an image (photograph or line drawing) that can be manipulated and reproduced under computer control.

Desktop publishing software certainly has captured the attention of the business community. Not only can users bypass the expense of professional typesetting and page layout, they also can drastically reduce the time needed to prepare a camera-ready document. Here a designer is creating an ad piece for an amateur photographers' convention. She used the image scanner (foreground) to scan an image into memory. Then she modified the image with a keyboard and mouse to fit the layout.

Typefaces and fonts. Most DTP-produced documents use a variety of **typefaces**. A typeface refers to a set of characters that are of the same type style (Helvetica, Courier, Swiss Light, Park Avenue, Dutch Roman, and so on). A *font* is described by its typeface, its height in points (8, 10, 14, 24, and so on; 72 points to the inch), and its presentation attribute (light, roman [or normal], medium, bold, italic, bold italic, extra bold, and so on). Most typefaces fall in one of two categories—*serif* and *sans serif*. Serif typefaces have short horizontal lines (serifs) appended at the ends of vertical elements of the characters. Sans-serif typefaces do not have serifs. A variety of typefaces and point sizes are illustrated in Figure 5–11.

Each font (such as 24-point Helvetica Bold) is stored on disk or in ROM (read-only memory). When needed to print a document, the **soft font** for a particular font is retrieved from disk storage and downloaded to the page printer's memory. A **resident font** is accessed directly from the printer's built-in ROM. Some printers have removable ROM cartridges, each of which contains a variety of fonts. The cartridges must be inserted manually in the printer when the fonts are needed for a print job. People engaged in DTP typically will have a minimum of a dozen soft or resident fonts available for use. The more sophisticated user will have access to at least a hundred fonts.

The latest round of high-speed micros have made it possible to generate fonts as they are needed. To do this, they use **scalable typefaces** that are stored in outline format. The outline is essentially a template, described in mathematical terms, from which fonts of any point size can be created. Scalable typefaces provide the user with tremendous flexibility in font selection. For example, you might elect to print your first-level headings in 20-point Old Goudy (bold) and your second-level headings in 16-point Old Goudy (bold). These two fonts are generated by the processor from the Old Goudy (bold) scalable typeface, then downloaded to the printer.

Scalable typefaces offer flexibility and save disk storage space; however, on some systems they must be generated internally and downloaded to the printer when they are needed for print jobs. Depending on the size of the font and the speed of the processor, the time it takes to generate a single font may be a minute or 15 minutes. The more sophisticated printer-typeface combinations are able to generate typefaces of any size *on the fly*—in seconds.

Clip art. No DTP environment would be complete without a healthy supply of **clip art**. Clip art refers to prepackaged electronic images that are stored on disk to be used as needed. The clock in Figure 5–8 is clip art. Clip art items could be a computer, a rose, two people talking, a hamburger, or just about anything you can imagine.

Desktop Publishing Files. Typically, a DTP-produced document such as a newsletter consists of several files. A long report or a book may be made up of hundreds of files. During the document-composition process, each file is assigned to a rectangular **frame**. A frame holds the text or an image of a particular file. Each page is a frame. There also can be frames within a frame (for example, figures and photos on a page).

▶ **MEMORY BITS**

Desktop Publishing Components
- Document-composition software
- Microcomputer
- Desktop page printer
- Image scanner
- Typefaces and fonts
- Clip art

Typefaces fall into three categories:

> Serif: those that have short crosslines projecting from the ends of the strokes.
> Sans Serif: those without serifs.
> *Decorative:* *those used for headlines and special effects.*

The lowercase *x* sits on the baseline and defines the x-height. That portion of a character that is below the baseline is the descender (as in *g, p* and *y*) and that which is above the x-height is the ascender (as in *d, f,* and *H*).

A typeface's style is defined in terms of

> Weight: light, **medium**, **heavy** or **bold** (with *extra* and *ultra* prefixes).
> Slant: *italic (for serif typefaces);* *oblique (for sans serif typefaces).*
> Proportion: condensed, **regular**, or extended.

Typeface families (those typefaces with similar shapes) are usually named for their designers (Frederick Goudy, Oswald **Cooper**) or their function (**Bookman**). Examples of the Claude Garamond family are illustrated below.

Garamond Book	***Garamond Bold Italic***
Garamond Book Italic	Garamond Book Condensed
Garamond Bold	*Garamond Book Condensed* Italic

A font refers to a particular typeface size and style. All previous fonts in this illustration are 12 point (72 points to an inch). Other fonts follow.

Brody: (4 point) and 8 point.

Chaucer (Old English): 24 point and 36 point.

Old Towne: 72 point.

Bitmapped fonts, which are made up of pixels, require a separate character set file for each point size. Outline fonts of any size (and orientation) for a particular typeface are generated from a single typeface file.

FIGURE 5–11 Typeface Tutorial

One of the most important components of a desktop publishing system is a desktop page printer. The printer enables the printing of near-typeset-quality camera-ready copy for a myriad of publications, such as a company newsletter.

A DTP document will involve one or more text files, perhaps one or more picture files, a style-sheet file, and a print file.

- *Text files.* The *text files* are created by a word processing program, such as WordPerfect. Although DTP software provides the facility to create and edit text, it is much easier to do these tasks with a word processing program.
- *Picture files. Picture files* are made up of clip art, line art, scanned-in graphics and photos, and renderings of screen displays (for example, the summary at the bottom of Figure 5–10).
- *Style-sheet file.* In the traditional approach to publishing, the designer of a print job (a book or a restaurant menu) creates a style sheet that provides the information needed by the typesetter (for example, typeface size and attributes for first-level headings). In DTP, the user creates a *style-sheet file* that tells the document-composition software what do with the text. To create the style-sheet file, the user must go into the document and *tag* each paragraph with the appropriate typographical attributes (such as typeface and size).
- *Print file.* The *print file* contains all the information needed to combine the text and picture files with the style sheet and print the document.

The Document-Composition Process. The document-composition process involves integrating graphics, photos, text, and other elements into a visually appealing *document layout*. With DTP, you can produce finished, professional-looking documents in four steps (see Figure 5–12).

1. *Prepare text and graphics.* Use your word processing software to create and edit the text of your document. For illustrations you can use clip art, computer-created graphics (such as a pie graph), or scanned images (photos).
2. *Create the style sheet.* Define the document format (for example, margins and number of columns) and text attributes. Once a style-sheet file for a particular job is created, it can be applied to similar text files (for example, monthly newsletters).
3. *Combine text and picture files.* Create and position needed frames, then insert text and picture files to fit your needs. The DTP display is WYSIWYG—that is, "What you see is what you get" when the document is printed. If what you see is not what you want, then you can use the mouse to reposition frames containing text and graphics to the desired locations.
4. *Print the document.* Once the WYSIWYG display shows what you want, use a desktop page printer to produce the finished camera-ready copy.

Desktop Publishing and Word Processing. Traditionally, users have combined the text manipulation capabilities of word processing software with the document-composition capabilities of DTP software to produce camera copy for reproduction. Word-processing produced text provides

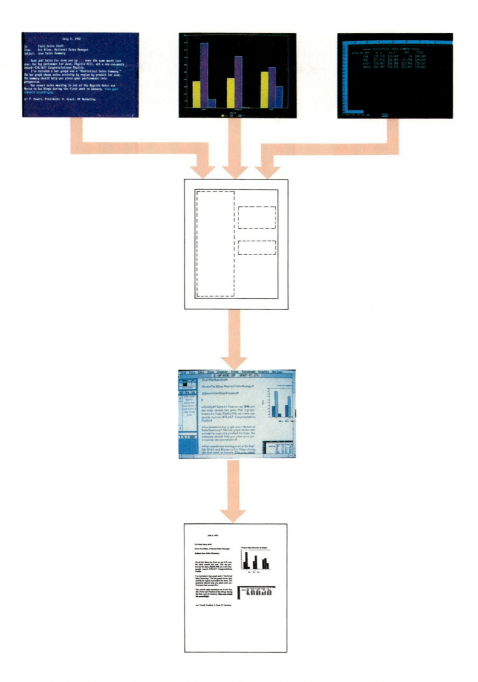

FIGURE 5–12 Preparing a Document with Desktop Publishing Software
Desktop publishing software combines text prepared using word processing software with images from a variety of sources and loads each into prepositioned frames. The graph and spreadsheet frames appear within the larger frame of the word processing text. The style sheet combines the elements, and the document is printed.

input to the document-composition process. This distinction may begin to blur in the near future. Already state-of-the-art word processing programs, such as Microsoft Word and WordPerfect, provide users with sophisticated DTP capabilities. Word processing users routinely produce camera-ready copy for everything from business cards to books—all without the aid of DTP software.

By now you are probably thinking, "If word processing software does it all, why do we need DTP software?" At this time, word processing software doesn't do it all. DTP software offers a full range of sophisticated capabilities that are not available with word processing software. For example, suppose the last sentence of a paragraph were, "The binary digits are 0 and 1." and "1." ended up alone on the last line. With DTP software, you can force the "1." onto the previous line. You can't with word processing software. In general, DTP software provides users with tremendous flexibility in formatting documents. The document-composition capabilities of word processing software are typically more cumbersome and time-consuming than similar DTP capabilities.

It is inevitable that future generations of high-end word processing software will incorporate more and more document-composition capabilities. In time, word processing software will be all that is needed for most jobs that require camera-ready copy. On the other hand, vendors of desktop publishing software are planning to incorporate advanced text manipulation capabilities; thereby eliminating the need for word processing–generated text. Look for the differences between the two to diminish over the next few years.

Use

Desktop publishing software is being used to produce the camera-ready copy for every conceivable type of printed matter, from graduation certificates to full-length books. One problem with desktop publishing is that the capability of producing camera-ready documents is now available to a large number of people, many of whom do not have the artistic skills needed to produce aesthetically pleasing and functionally readable copy. Recognizing this, many companies are adopting standards and policies that apply to all copy printed with the company logo that is released to the public.

5–3 GRAPHICS

A dollar may not buy what it used to, but a picture is still worth a thousand words. This time-honored maxim may be one of the many reasons for the explosion of **graphics software** as a productivity tool. Graphics software facilitates the creation and management of computer-based images. You can use graphics software to create pie graphs, line drawings, company logos, maps, clip art, blueprints, and just about anything else that can be drawn in the traditional manner.

The five dominant categories of graphics software are:

- Paint
- Draw
- Presentation graphics
- Computer-aided design
- Screen capture and graphics conversion

The function, concepts, and use of each is described in this section. However, before you can fully understand the capabilities of the various categories of graphics software, you need to know the fundamentals of how images are displayed.

Displaying and Printing Graphic Images

In Chapter 4, "Micro Peripheral Devices: I/O and Data Storage," we talked about how the PC displays are either in *text mode* or *graphics mode*. Depending on the software and hardware you are using, graphic images are maintained as **raster graphics** or **vector graphics**. In raster graphics, the image is composed of patterns of dots (pixels). (The enlarged view shown in Figure 5–15 in the Paint Software illustrates the pixel makeup of the original image.) In vector graphics, the image is composed of patterns of lines, points, and other geometric shapes (vectors). The naked eye cannot distinguish one method of graphics display from another; however, the differences are quite apparent when you try to manipulate them.

Raster Graphics. Raster graphics, which are displayed as dot patterns, are created by digital cameras, scanners, graphics paint software, presentation graphics software, and screen capture software. Dots on the screen are arranged in rows and columns. The ubiquitous VGA monitor, with 480 rows and 640 columns, has over 300,000 pixels. Very high-resolution monitors will have thousands of rows and columns and millions of pixels. Each dot or pixel on a VGA monitor is assigned a number that denotes its position on the screen grid (120th row and 323rd column) and its color. On a monochrome monitor, the pixel denotes the position and a shade of gray.

As with all internal numbers in a computer system, the numbers that describe the pixel attributes (position and color) are binary bits (1s and 0s). The number of bits needed to describe a pixel increases with the monitor's resolution and the number of colors that can be presented. Because the image is projected, or "mapped," onto the screen based on binary bits, the image is said to be **bit-mapped**. In conversation, the term *bit-mapped* may be used more frequently than the term *raster graphics*. A bit-mapped image and the display of a word processing document share many similarities. For example, compare a bit-mapped screen to a display of a word processing document filled with words such as *blue*, *green*, and *red* instead of dots. You could perform a global search-and-replace to change all *red*s to *orange*. Or you could mark a "paragraph" (a user-defined area of any shape in the graphics display) and change all *red*s to *orange* in that "paragraph" (or user-defined area). Carrying the

A computer artist used a computer and graphics software to create this remarkable image. Computer art emerged from the decade of the 1980s as a new art form.

analogy one step further, you also can do block operations—move, copy, and delete on a user-defined area in a graphics display.

Like television, a bit-mapped image is continuously projected onto the screen, one line of dots at a time. Any changes in the display are reflected immediately. **Animation**, or movement, is accomplished by rapid repositioning (moving) of an area of the screen. For example, animation techniques give life to video-game characters.

Vector Graphics. Vectors, which are lines, points, and other geometric shapes, are configured to create the vector graphics image. The vector graphics display, in contrast to the raster graphics display, permits the user to work with objects, such as a drawing of a computer. Draw software and computer-aided design software employ vector graphics to meet the need to manipulate individual objects on the screen.

Vector graphics images take up less storage than bit-mapped images. Each pixel in the bit-mapped image must be fully described, even the background colors. Vector graphics are defined in geometric shapes, each of which can define the attributes of many pixels.

Printing/Plotting Graphics Images. In general, printers and plotters provide higher resolution output than screen displays. The resolution of a 300-dpi page printer is four times that of a VGA monitor, and lines that may appear uneven on a monitor will be more uniform when printed.

Paint Software

Paint software provides the user with a sophisticated electronic canvas. Although you can perform amazing feats with paint software, one important similarity remains between it and the traditional canvas. Whatever you draw on either one becomes part of the whole drawing. You must erase or draw over any part of it you are dissatisfied with. This is because the canvas is a bit map and what you draw becomes part of the bit-mapped image. For example, suppose you draw a green circle. You would not be able simply to replace the circle with a blue square. The paint software does not remember the circle or any other representation of an object on the screen. To replace the circle with the square, you would have to draw over (or erase) the pixels that make up the green circle, then draw in the blue square.

The user interfaces of paint programs are similar. Once you are familiar with the six items in the user interface on a typical paint screen, you are ready to use the program. Paintbrush is a paint program distributed with Microsoft's Windows (discussed in Appendix B, "Windows Overview). The Paintbrush user interface is illustrated in Figure 5–13 and discussed here.

- *Drawing area*. The image is created in this area.
- *Graphics cursor*. Typically, the mouse is used to move the graphics cursor to draw images and to select options. However, other devices such as the joystick, track ball, digitizer tablet and pen, and light pen can be used to move the graphics cursor. When positioned in the

▶ **MEMORY BITS**

Graphic Images
- Raster graphics
    Image as pixels
    Bit-mapped image
- Vector graphics
    Image as line patterns and geometric shapes
    Permits manipulation of objects within image

CHAPTER 5 Text and Image Processing: Word Processing, Desktop Publishing, and Graphics

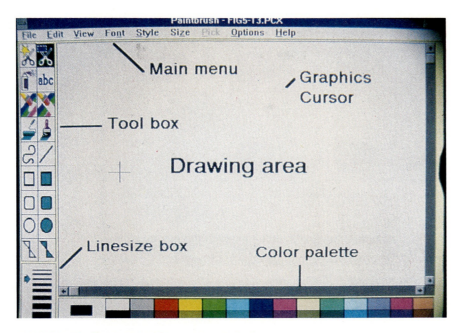

FIGURE 5–13 The Paint-Software User Interface
The user interface for Paintbrush, which is distributed with Windows, is representative of paint programs.

drawing area, the graphics cursor takes on a variety of shapes, depending on the tool selected. Outside the drawing area, it is an arrow.
- *Main menu.* Pull-down menus appear when any of the items in the main bar menu (top of screen) is selected. Go to the main menu to load and save drawings, zoom in on a particular area for detailed editing, change the attributes of the screen fonts, copy parts of the screen, and so on.
- *Tool box.* One of the tools in the tool box is active at any given time. Use the tools to draw; to move, copy, or delete parts of the screen; to create geometric shapes; to fill defined areas with colors; to add text; and to erase.
- *Linesize box.* This box contains the width options for the drawing line.
- *Color palette.* This box contains colors and patterns that are used with the drawing tools.

The examples in Figures 5–14, 5–15, and 5–16 illustrate some of the features of paint software. The screen in Figure 5–14 illustrates the steps in creating a PC image. Each step is described here.

Step A. The *box* and *rounded box tools* (see tool box in Figure 5–13) are used to create the outlines for the monitor and the processor unit. Notice that *text tool* was used to cross-reference the steps with letters.

Step B. The area containing the image created in Step A was *copied* to a position B, then the *paint roller tool* was used to fill in *background*

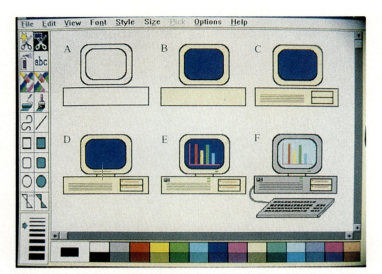

FIGURE 5–14 Creating an Image with Paint Software
This screen shows the various stages in the development of a PC image.

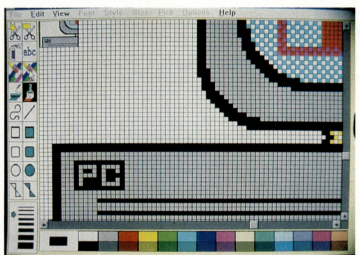

FIGURE 5–15 The Zoom Feature
In the illustration, the paint-software user has zoomed in on the upper left corner of the processor box and on the lower right corner of the screen in the completed PC image in Figure 5–14 (Step F). Each square is a pixel. Any changes that are made in the enlarged version of the image are reflected in the window in the upper left corner of the work area, which is the actual size, and in the actual image.

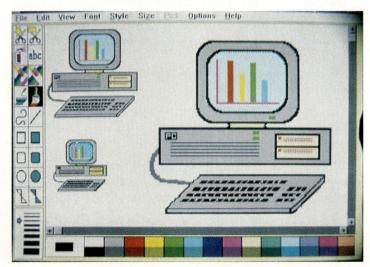

FIGURE 5–16 The Shrink-Grow Feature
The completed PC image in Figure 5–14 (Step F) is reduced and enlarged with the shrink-grow feature of paint software.

CHAPTER 5 Text and Image Processing: Word Processing, Desktop Publishing, and Graphics

colors. The image in each of the following steps was created from a copy of the image of the preceding step.

Step C. The *line tool* is used to draw the vents on the front of the processor unit. Drag the graphics cursor from one point to another and release the mouse button to draw the line. The two box areas for the microdisks were created with the box and line tools.

Step D. When the *brush tool* is active, the *foreground color* is drawn at the graphics cursor position. Use the brush tool for freehand drawing, such as the addition of the pedestal for the monitor. The microdisk slots and the disk-active lights are drawn with the line tool. Notice that the line width and the foreground color were changed to draw the slots and the lights.

Step E. A logo (upper left corner of processor box) and a bar graph are added. The *PC* in the black logo box was drawn one pixel at a time. The *zoom-in* feature explodes a small segment of the draw area to enable the user to draw one pixel at a time (see Figure 5–15). The bar graph is drawn with the line tool. Notice that each line is drawn with a different color from the color palette.

Step F. In this final step, the beige color was *erased* to gray. Paint software permits the user to selectively switch one color for another within a user-defined area or in the entire drawing area. The keyboard was drawn with the box, line, and erase tools, then *tilted* to give it a three-dimensional look.

Several other important paint software features are illustrated in Figure 5–16. The medium-sized micro in the upper left corner of Figure 5–16 is an exact duplicate of the Step F bit-mapped image from Figure 5–14. The original image was selected with the *cutout tool*, then saved to disk. The stored image was then loaded from disk and displayed in a clear drawing area. The paint software *shrink-grow* feature was employed to shrink and enlarge the image. Notice that parts of the image may be distorted when the image is shrunk (for example, the microdisk slots) and that image resolution suffers when the image is enlarged.

Once stored as a paint graphics file, images can be manipulated in many ways. For example, scanned images can be modified or colored. Even a frame from a video recording can be integrated into a paint drawing.

Draw Software

Both paint and **draw software** enable users to create imaginative images. Perhaps the best way to explain draw software is to address the differences between it and paint software. Consider the same example that was used in the paint software discussion—a drawing of a green circle, the latter to be replaced with a blue square. Draw software permits you to isolate and manipulate representations of individual objects, so you would simply delete the entire green circle and copy a blue square to that position. This is not possible with paint software.

This image was created by a computer artist. Just as a writer can edit a manuscript by using word processing software, an artist can easily make changes in computer art. For example, the artist could change the color of the awning from shades of blue to shades of green. Whether the artist uses a palette and easel or a computer, it still takes a creative mind and a keen eye to produce good art.

Draw software relies on vector graphics, so a specific object can be dealt with independently. An object can be moved, copied, deleted, rotated, tilted, flipped horizontally or vertically, stretched, and squeezed. A screen image produced by draw software is actually a collage of one or more objects.

Presentation Graphics

Using Technology to Make the Point. Computer-generated business graphics is one of the more recent applications of computers. With few exceptions, most computer-generated graphic outputs of a decade ago were for engineers and researchers. Managers of business units who wanted a pie graph or a bar graph had it produced manually by the drafting department. This could take anywhere from a few days to weeks. Most managers were not willing to wait, so they continued preparing reports and presentations in the traditional tabular manner— rows and columns of data.

Today managers of business units have powerful microcomputers and user-friendly **presentation graphics software** that allow them to create in seconds a wide variety of visually appealing and informative presentation graphics. To capture and reproduce these graphic images, they use printers and desktop plotters (for paper and transparency acetates), desktop film recorders (for 35-mm slides), and screen-image projectors (to project an image onto a large screen).

During the past decade, the use of presentation graphics has become a business imperative. A progressive sales manager would never consider reporting a sales increase in tabular format. A successful year that otherwise would be obscured in rows and columns of sales figures will be vividly apparent in a colorful bar graph. Those in other areas of business also want to "put their best foot forward." To do so, they use computer-generated presentation graphics.

A number of studies confirm the power of presentation graphics. These studies uniformly support the following conclusions:

- People who use presentation graphics to get their message across are perceived as being better prepared and more professional than those who do not.
- Presentation graphics can help persuade attendees or readers to adopt a particular point of view.
- Judicious use of presentation graphics tends to make meetings shorter. (Perhaps it's true that a picture is worth a thousand words!)

Whether you're preparing a report, a presentation, a newsletter, or any other form of business communication, it pays—immediately and over the long term—to take advantage of the capabilities of presentation graphics.

Output Options. With presentation graphics software, you can create a variety of graphics from data in a spreadsheet or a data base, or you can enter the data within the presentation graphics program. Among the most popular presentation graphics are **pie graphs** and **bar graphs** (as seen in Figures 5–17 and 5–18, respectively). It is also possible to produce other types of graphs, range bar charts, and scatter diagrams. Each can be annotated with *titles*, *labels*, and *legends*.

Most spreadsheet and database packages come with presentation graphics software. The functionality of graphs prepared by these integrated spreadsheet and database packages is no different from those prepared by presentation graphics packages, but the wider range of features available in dedicated presentation graphics packages can be used to prepare more dynamic and visually appealing graphics (such as three-dimensional pie and bar graphs). Dedicated presentation graphics packages provide users with the tools they need to customize their graphs. For example, a transportation company can add another dimension to a sales-summary bar graph by topping the bars with clip art that represents the sales area (a ship, an airplane, a truck).

In addition to traditional business graphs, presentation graphics software provides the ability to prepare *text charts* (such as lists of key points, see Figure 5–19), *organization charts* (such as block charts showing the hierarchical structure of an organization, see Figure 5–20), and *maps*.

FIGURE 5–17 Pie Graph

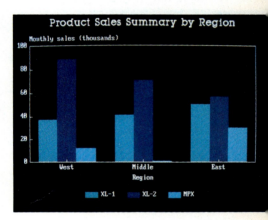

FIGURE 5–18 Bar Graph

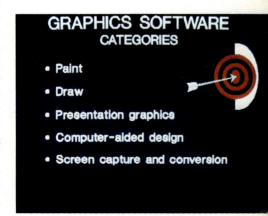

FIGURE 5–19 Text Chart

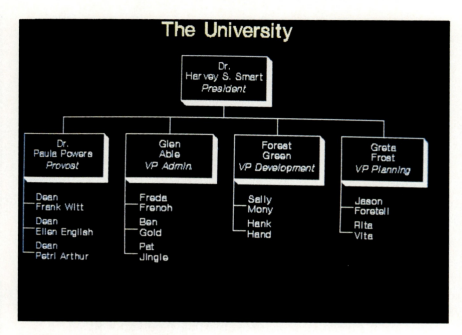

FIGURE 5-20 Organization Chart

Besides offering the ability to prepare graphs and charts from user-supplied data, some presentation graphics packages let you create and store original drawings. This capability is functionally similar to that of paint and draw packages, but without their sophisticated features. Companies frequently use this capability to draw and store the image of their company logo so it can be inserted on memos, reports, and graphs.

Another recently introduced feature of presentation graphics software is the *dynamic show* capability. The dynamic show capability enables you to assemble presentation graphics in a synchronized demonstration. The show is usually presented to a small group on a single PC, or it is projected onto a large screen with a screen-image projector. The dynamic show capability, which is also marketed as a stand-alone package, provides a visually interesting transition between the various graphics. For example, the current graph or image can be made to *fade out* (dissolve to a blank screen) while the next is fading in. Or the current image can be *wiped* away with the next.

The dynamic show can be further enhanced with rudimentary *animation*. Animating presentation graphics involves the rapid movement of an object, perhaps the image of an automobile, from one part of the screen to another. The animation is accomplished by moving the object in small increments of about ¼-inch in rapid succession, giving the illusion of movement. The judicious use of this capability can enliven any presentation.

Preparing a Business Graph. Usually the data needed to produce a graph already exist in a spreadsheet or data base. The graphics software leads you through a series of prompts, the first of which asks you what type of graph is to be produced—a bar graph, pie graph, line graph, and so on. You then select the data to be plotted. You can also enter names for the labels. Once you have identified the source of the data (perhaps a spreadsheet or a data base), have entered the labels, and perhaps have added a title, you can plot, display, and print the graph. The preparation of bar, pie, and line graphs from spreadsheet data is illustrated in Chapter 6, "Data Management: Spreadsheet and Database."

Presenting a Graph. The actual physical presentation of a graph depends on the available hardware (dot-matrix printer, color page printer, plotter, and so on). Computer-generated graphic images can be re-created on paper, transparency acetates, 35-mm slides, or they can be displayed on a monitor or projected onto a large screen. The use of sophisticated and colorful graphics adds an aura of professionalism to any report or presentation. Some of the more common approaches to presenting a graph are discussed below.

- Dot-matrix and ink-jet printers, both black on white and color, can be used to reproduce the graphic image on either paper or transparency acetates.
- Multi-pen plotters can be used to produce professional-quality presentation graphics (in color) on either paper or transparency acetates.
- Page printers, both black on white and color, enable very high-resolution (near-typeset-quality) hard copy.
- Desktop film recorders reproduce a high-resolution graphic image on 35-mm film in either black and white or color. Some models provide the facility for users to process and mount their own slides. Others require outside processing.

Micro users use graphics software to prepare professional-looking visuals. These graphs are frequently generated on color page printers. The images can be printed on paper or on acetates for use with overhead projectors.

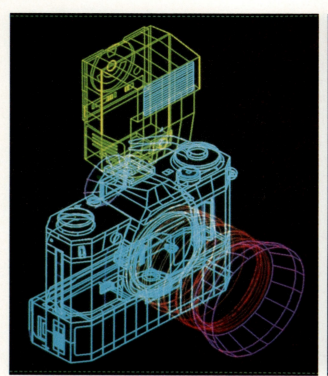 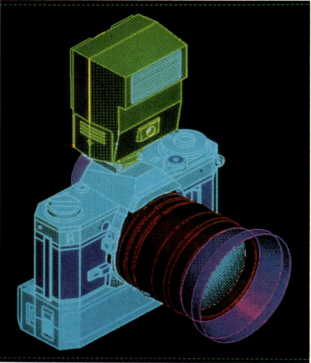

Computer-aided design (CAD) systems are used to design consumer goods, such as this 35-mm camera. In the design process, engineers create a framework (left), then the CAD software fills in between the lines to create the three-dimensional solid model (right).

- A less expensive alternative to a desktop film recorder is the hood, lens, and mounting brackets that enable the users to photograph the graphic image with an ordinary 35-mm camera. The quality of the resulting 35-mm slide depends, of course, on the resolution of the monitor.
- Screen-image projectors project the graphic image onto a large screen in much the same way that television programs are projected onto a large TV screen. Another device transfers the graphic image displayed on the monitor to a large screen using an ordinary overhead projector.

Computer-Aided Design

Until recently, sophisticated **computer-aided design (CAD)** was not possible in the PC environment. Now high-performance micros can be configured with very high-resolution large-screen monitors, a variety of pointing and drawing devices, plotters (of any size), and whatever else is needed to produce computer-aided graphics design. Traditionally, CAD applications have been associated with engineers and scientists; however, today PC-based CAD has opened the door to all who do design work.

Perhaps the best way to describe computer-aided design is visually, through its applications. Look at the adjacent photos to see how engineers design parts and assemblies, how artists design logos for television programs, how architects design buildings, and how others use CAD. Although generic CAD packages can accommodate almost any design application, in some application areas they can be cumbersome. In those areas where CAD has become a business imperative, specialized packages have emerged. For example, specialized CAD packages are available to help industrial engineers in plant layout, to help programmers and systems analysts with the design of an information system, to help architects with the design of buildings, and to help electrical engineers with the design of integrated circuits.

Screen Capture and Graphics Conversion

Screen-capture programs are memory-resident TSRs (terminate-and-stay-resident programs) that enable users to transfer all or part of the current screen image to a disk file. For example, you can capture the summary portion of a Lotus 1-2-3 display and integrate it into a report (a word processing document). A screen is captured as a bit-mapped image (pixel format). Once on disk, it can be recalled and manipulated with a paint program.

Unfortunately, there are no standards for the way graphic images are stored. Therefore, **graphics-conversion** programs are needed so that graphics files can be passed between programs. Most of the popular programs that create graphic images (paint, draw, presentation graphics, spreadsheet graphics) do so in their own unique formats. Graphics-conversion programs provide dozens of options. For example, you can convert an image created with a popular CAD program, AutoCAD (a vector graphics image), into Microsoft Windows Paintbrush (a bit-mapped image) for pixel-level editing. You also can convert a bit-mapped Harvard Graphics (presentation graphics program) file into a format that is compatible with a fax modem (an add-on board that can send and receive facsimile documents). If you do much work with graphics files, a good graphics-conversion program is invaluable.

SUMMARY OUTLINE AND IMPORTANT TERMS

5–1 **WORD PROCESSING.** Word processing is using the computer to enter, store, manipulate, and print text in letters, reports, books, and so on.

When you format a document, you are describing the size of the page to be printed and how you want the document to look when it is printed. To enter and edit text, you *toggle* between **typeover mode** and **insert mode. Word wrap** occurs when text that extends past the defined margins automatically wraps around to the next line. Word processing permits **full-screen editing.**

The block-move, the block-copy, and the block-delete commands are known collectively as *block operations*, the electronic equivalent of "cut and paste." The *search,* or *find,* feature permits the user to search the entire word processing document and identify all occurrences of a particular search string.

Word processing has several features that enable users to enhance the appearance and readability of their documents. These include left and/or right justification, automatic centering, boldface, underlining, indentation, header and footer labels, pagination, hyphenation, footnotes, numbered-list/outline format, bulleted-list format, line draw, superscripts and subscripts, the insertion of an image into the running text, a variety of **fonts**, and multicolumn text.

Some word processing packages enable the automatic generation of a table of contents and an alphabetical index of key words; have a table feature that expedites the presentation of tabular data; and enable rudimentary desktop publishing.

All word processing packages allow users to save, retrieve, and delete files that contain word processing documents. The print function transforms your electronic document into a hard-copy document.

Most word processing packages are considered **WYSIWYG**, short for "What you see is what you get." Some are **WYSIWYG—MOL**.

Several add-on programs are designed to enhance the functionality of word processing programs. An **on-line thesaurus** is always ready with synonyms for any word in a document. The **spelling checker** program checks every word in the text against an **electronic dictionary** and alerts the user when a word is not in the dictionary. A **grammar checker** highlights grammatical concerns and deviations from conventions. A **style checker** alerts users to such writing concerns as sexist words and hackneyed clichés. **Idea processors**, or **outliners**, can be used to organize single-line items into an outline format.

There are two ways to pass documents between different types of word processing programs—via **ASCII files** and the use of **document-conversion programs**.

Any kind of text-based document can be created with word processing software. **Boilerplate** is existing text that can in some way be customized so it can be used in a variety of word processing applications (for example, **mail merge**). Most state-of-the-art word processing packages enable the integration of text and graphic images.

5-2 DESKTOP PUBLISHING. Desktop publishing (**DTP**) refers to the capability of producing near-typeset-quality copy from the confines of a desktop. The components required for desktop publishing include: document-composition software, a high-end microcomputer, a desktop page printer, an image scanner, **typefaces** and fonts, and **clip art**.

Most DTP-produced documents use a variety of typefaces, all of which fall in one of two categories—*serif* and *sans serif*. **Soft fonts** are retrieved from disk storage and downloaded to the printer's memory as needed. A **resident font** is accessed directly from the printer's built-in ROM. **Scalable typefaces** give users the flexibility to scale them to any point size.

Typically, a DTP-produced document consists of several (often many) files. During the document-composition process, each file is assigned to a rectangular **frame**. A frame holds the text or an image of a particular file.

A DTP document will involve one or more text files, perhaps one or more picture files, a style-sheet file, and a print file. Text files are created by a word processing program. Picture files are made up of **clip art** and other images. The style-sheet file tells the document-composition software what to do with the text. The print file contains all the information needed to combine the text and picture files with the style sheet and print the document.

The document-composition process involves integrating graphics, photos, text, and other elements into a visually appealing layout. The steps are: (1) prepare text and graphics; (2) create the style sheet; (3) combine text and picture files; and (4) print the document.

5–3 GRAPHICS. **Graphics software** facilitates the creation and management of computer-based images. The five dominant categories of graphics software are: paint, draw, presentation graphics, computer-aided design, and screen capture and graphics conversion.

Graphic images are presented as **raster graphics** or **vector graphics**. In raster, or **bit-mapped**, graphics, the image is composed of patterns of dots (pixels). In vector graphics, the image is composed of patterns of lines, points, and other geometric shapes (vectors). **Animation**, or movement, is accomplished by rapidly repositioning an area of the screen.

Paint software provides the user with a sophisticated electronic canvas. Whatever you draw on either the traditional or the electronic canvas becomes part of the whole drawing. The six items in a paint program's user interface are the drawing area, graphics cursor, main menu, tool box, linesize box, and color palette.

Draw software permits you to create a screen image, then isolate and manipulate representations of individual objects within the overall image. Draw software relies on vector graphics, so a specific object can be dealt with independently.

User-friendly **presentation graphics software** enables users to create a wide variety of visually appealing and informative presentation graphics. Among the most popular are **bar graphs** and **pie graphs**. Presentation graphics software also permits the preparation of *text charts, organization charts, maps,* and original drawings. These graphic images are captured and reproduced on printers, desktop plotters, desktop film recorders, and screen-image projectors. Some sophisticated packages allow you to present *dynamic shows.*

High-performance microcomputers that support **computer-aided design (CAD)** are configured with very high-resolution large-screen monitors, a variety of pointing and drawing devices, plotters, and sometimes other design-oriented devices. CAD applications include everything from television graphics to engineering design.

Screen-capture programs are TSRs that enable users to transfer all or part of the current screen image to a disk file. **Graphics-conversion** programs help users pass graphics files between programs.

REVIEW EXERCISES

1. What is the function of word processing software?
2. What must be specified when formatting a document?
3. What is meant when a document is formatted to be justified on the right and on the left?
4. Text is entered in either of what two modes? What mode would you select to change *the table* to *the long table*? What mode would you select to change *pick the choose* to *pick and choose*?
5. What causes text to wrap around?
6. Give an example of when you might issue a global search-and-replace command.
7. When running the spelling checker, what options does the system present when it encounters an unidentified word?
8. What productivity software package has the capability of producing near-typeset-quality copy for printing jobs?
9. Name two software components and two hardware components of a desktop publishing system.
10. What is the shape of a desktop publishing frame?
11. What term is used to refer to prepackaged electronic images?
12. Which DTP file tells the document-composition software what do with the text?
13. What term is frequently used in place of *raster graphics*?
14. Which type of graphics software package provides a computer-based version of the painter's canvas?
15. What type of graphics software package enables the generation of a wide variety of presentation graphics?
16. What presentation graphics software capability enables users to assemble presentation graphics in a synchronized show?
17. What type of TSR program enables users to transfer all or part of the current screen image to a disk file?

SELF-TEST (by section)

5-1 a. Preset format specifications are referred to as _____.
   b. To add a word in the middle of an existing sentence in a word processing document, you would use the insert mode. (T/F)
   c. Which word processing feature enables the automatic numbering of pages of a document: (a) pagination, (b) page breaking, or (c) footers?
   d. The word processing feature that automatically breaks long words that fall at the end of a line is called _____.
   e. An on-line thesaurus can be used to suggest synonyms for a word in a word processing document. (T/F)

5-2 a. The type of printer normally associated with desktop publishing is the daisy-wheel printer. (T/F)
   b. The output of the desktop publishing process is _____ copy.

c. What device re-creates a black-and-white version of an image in an electronic format: (a) image scanner, (b) image-reduction aid, or (c) vision-entry device?
d. The height of a 36-point typeface is: (a) ¼ inch, (b) ½ inch, or (c) 1 inch?
e. Fontware is that component of the document-composition software that enables WYSIWYG display of DTP documents. (T/F)

5–3 a. Presentation graphics software allows users to create charts and line drawings. (T/F)
b. In raster graphics, the image is composed of patterns of: (a) vectors, (b) pictures, or (c) dots?
c. Which of the following would be an unlikely entry in a paint program's tool box: (a) create rectangle, (b) select color palette, or (c) erase?
d. _____ charts show the hierarchical structure of an organization.
e. Bit-mapped files cannot be converted to a format that is compatible with fax modems. (T/F)

Self-test answers. 5–1 (**a**) default settings; (**b**) T; (**c**) a; (**d**) hyphenation; (**e**) T. 5–2 (**a**) F; (**b**) camera-ready; (**c**) a; (**d**) b; (**e**) F. 5–3 (**a**) T; (**b**) c; (**c**) b; (**d**) Organization; (**e**) F.

CHAPTER 6

DATA MANAGEMENT: SPREADSHEET AND DATABASE

STUDENT LEARNING OBJECTIVES

- ▶ To describe the function, purpose, and applications of spreadsheet software.
- ▶ To discuss common spreadsheet concepts.
- ▶ To describe how presentation graphics can be created from spreadsheet data.
- ▶ To describe the function, purpose, and applications of database software.
- ▶ To discuss common database software concepts.

6–1 SPREADSHEET: THE MAGIC MATRIX

Function

The name *spreadsheet* describes this software's fundamental application. The spreadsheet has been a common business tool for centuries. Before computers, the ledger (a book of spreadsheets) was the accountant's primary tool for keeping a record of financial transactions. A professor's grade book is also set up in spreadsheet format.

Spreadsheets are simply an electronic alternative to thousands of traditionally manual tasks. No longer are we confined to using pencils, erasers, and hand calculators to deal with rows and columns of data. Think of anything that has rows and columns of data and you have identified an application for spreadsheet software: income (profit-and-loss) statements, personnel profiles, demographic data, and budget summaries, just to mention a few. Because spreadsheets parallel so many of our manual tasks, they are enjoying widespread acceptance.

All commercially available spreadsheet packages enable you to manipulate rows and columns of data. However, the *user interface*, or the manner in which you enter data and commands, differs from one package to the next. The conceptual coverage that follows is generic: It applies to all spreadsheets.

Concepts

Pat Kline, the national sales manager for a manufacturer of high-tech products, uses spreadsheet software to compile a monthly sales summary. We will use Pat's June sales summary, shown in Figure 6–1, to demonstrate spreadsheet concepts. Pat uses a monthly sales **template** each month. The template, simply a spreadsheet model, contains the lay-

FIGURE 6–1 Spreadsheet: A Monthly Sales Summary Template
This spreadsheet template is the basis for the explanation and demonstration of spreadsheet concepts.

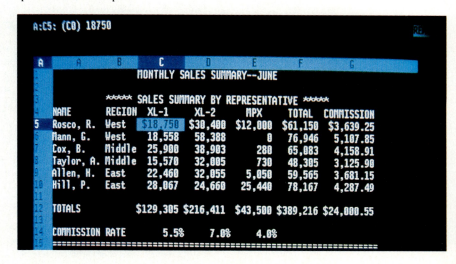

CHAPTER 6 Data Management: Spreadsheet and Database

out and formulas needed to produce the summary in Figure 6–1. Pat entered only the data for the current month (June in the example) and the spreadsheet template did all the needed calculations.

Viewing Data in a Spreadsheet. Scrolling through a spreadsheet is much like looking through a magnifying glass as you move it around a newspaper page. You scroll left and right (horizontal scrolling) and/or up and down (vertical scrolling) to see different portions of a large spreadsheet. In Figure 6–1, the entire sales summary can be displayed on a single screen. However, if five more products or 20 more salespeople were added, Pat would have to scroll horizontally and vertically to view the entire spreadsheet. Scrolling is discussed and illustrated in Chapter 2, "Interacting with Micros."

Organization. Spreadsheets are organized in a *tabular structure* with **rows** and **columns**. The intersection of a particular row and column designates a **cell**. As you can see in Figure 6–1, the rows are *numbered* and the columns are *lettered*. Single letters identify the first 26 columns; double letters are used thereafter (A, B, . . . Z; AA, AB, . . . AZ; BA, BB, . . . BZ). The number of rows or columns available to you depends on the size of your micro's RAM (random-access memory). Most spreadsheets permit hundreds of columns and thousands of rows.

Data are entered and stored in a cell at the intersection of a column and a row. During operations, data are referred to by their **cell address**. A cell address identifies the location of a cell in the spreadsheet by its column and row, with the column designator first. For example, in the monthly sales summary of Figure 6–1, C4 is the address of the column heading for product XL1, and D5 is the address of the total amount of XL2 sales for R. Rosco ($30,400).

Sometimes an electronic spreadsheet output is too wide for the printer. When this happens, it can be printed sideways. Shown is a 30-year financial projection.

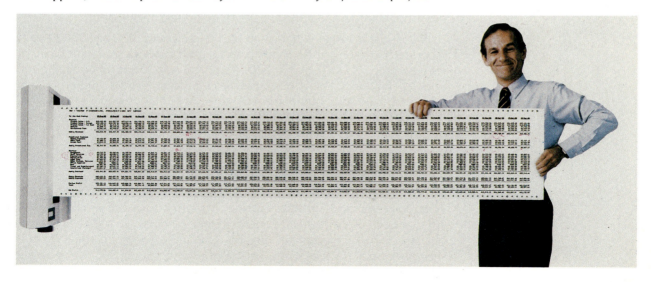

In the spreadsheet work area (the rows and columns), a movable highlighted area "points" to the *current cell*. This highlighted area, called the **pointer**, can be moved around the spreadsheet with the cursor-control keys to any cell address. To add or edit an entry at a particular cell, the pointer must be moved to that cell. The address and content of the current cell (the location of the pointer) are displayed in the user-interface portion of the spreadsheet, the area above and/or below the spreadsheet work area (above in Figure 6-1). Specifically, the information for a particular cell (Cell C5 in Figure 6-1) is displayed in a *cell status line*. The content, or resulting value (for example, from a formula), of each cell is shown in the spreadsheet work area. The current cell is displayed in reverse video (black on white or, for color monitors, black on a color). Also notice in Figure 6-1 that when the pointer is positioned at C5, the actual numeric value (18750) is displayed as the cell contents in the user interface, and an optional *edited* version ($18,750) is displayed in C5.

Cell Entries. To make an entry in the spreadsheet, simply move the pointer with the cursor-control keys to the appropriate cell, and key in the data. To *edit* or replace an existing entry, you also move the pointer to the appropriate cell. Key in the new or revised entry in the user-interface panel beside the cell address (see Figure 6-1). Once you have completed work on a particular entry, press the ENTER key or a cursor-control key to insert the entry in the actual spreadsheet.

Spreadsheet packages allow the user to vary the column width to improve readability. The width for Column A in Figure 6-1 is set at 11 positions; the width for Column B is set at 6 positions.

Ranges. Many spreadsheet operations ask you to designate a **range** of cells. The four types of ranges are highlighted in Figure 6-2:

a. A single cell (Example range is G12.)
b. All or part of a column of adjacent cells (Example range is A5..A10.)
c. All or part of a row of adjacent cells (Example range is C14..E14.)
d. A rectangular block of cells (Example range is C5..E10.)

A particular range is indicated by the addresses of the endpoint cells separated by two periods. (Some packages use only one period or a colon, for example: C5.E10 or C5:E10.) Any cell can comprise a single-cell range. The range for the commission percentages in Figure 6-2 is C14..E14, and the range for the row labels (salespeople's names) is A5..A10. The range of sales amounts for the three products is indicated by any two opposite-corner cell addresses (for example, C5..E10 or E5..C10).

When you want to copy, move, or erase a portion of the spreadsheet, you must first define the range you wish to copy, move, or erase.

Text, Numeric, and Formula Entries. An entry to a cell is classified as either a *text* (also called *label*) entry, a *numeric* entry, or a *formula* entry. (Strictly *numeric* entries fall into the formula category in some spreadsheet programs.) A text entry, or a label, is a word, phrase, or any string of alphanumeric text (spaces included) that occupies a particular cell. In

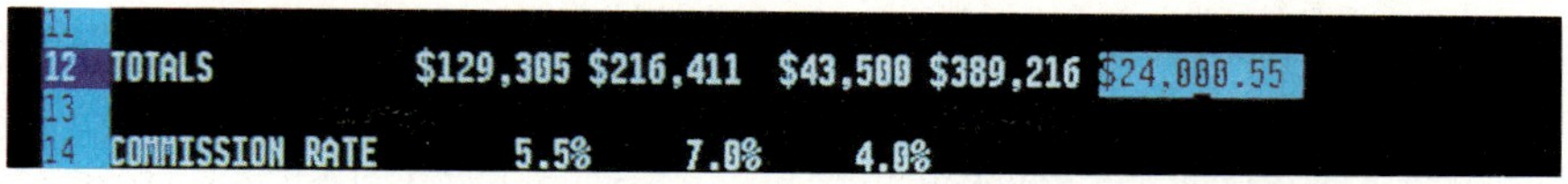

FIGURE 6-2 Spreadsheet: Ranges
The highlighted cells in these spreadsheet displays illustrate the four types of ranges: (a) cell (G12), (b) column (A5..A10), (c) row (C14..E14), and (d) block (C5..E10).

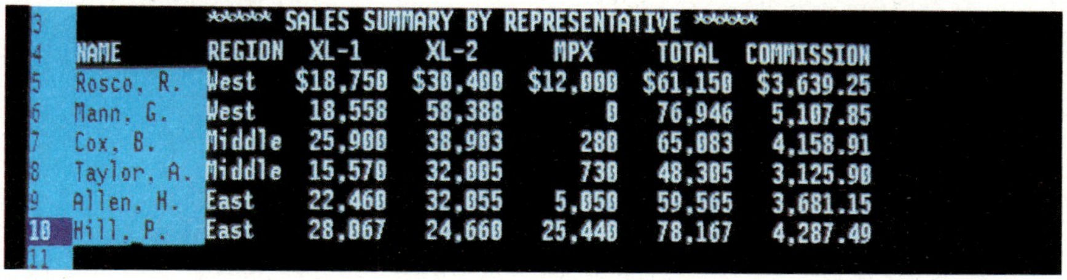

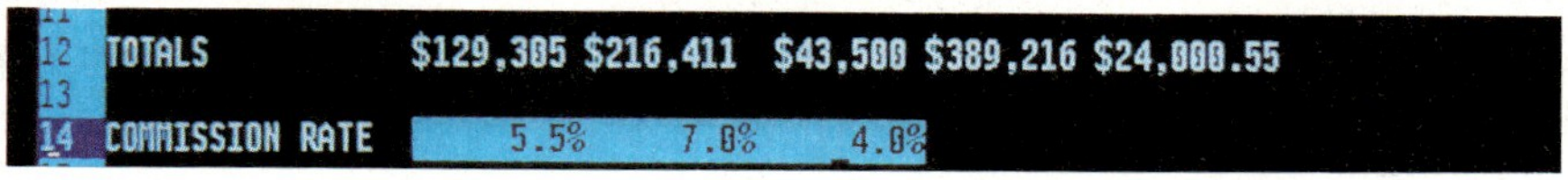

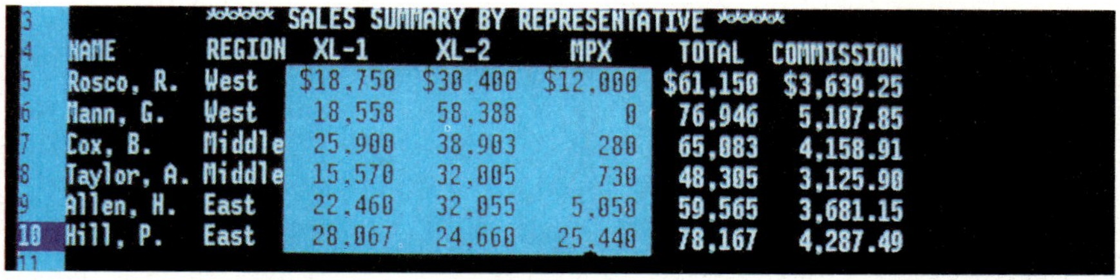

Figure 6-1, "NAME" in Cell A4 is a text entry, as is "COMMISSION" in G4 and "MONTHLY SALES SUMMARY—JUNE" in C1. Notice that the label in C1 extends across Columns C, D, and E. This is possible when the adjacent cells (D1 and E1) are blank. If an entry were made in D1, only the first nine positions (the width of Column C) of the entry in Cell C1 would be visible on the spreadsheet (that is, "MONTHLY S"). Unless otherwise specified, text entries are left-justified and numeric entries are right-justified (lined up on the right edge of the column). However, you can specify that any entry be left- or right-justified or centered in the column. In Figure 6-1 all column headings except "NAME" are centered.

In Figure 6-1, the dollar sales values in the range C5..E10 are numeric. The dollar sales values in the ranges F5..G10 and C12..G12 are results of formulas. Cell F5 contains a formula, but it is the numeric result (for example, $61,150 in Figure 6-3) that is displayed in the spreadsheet work area. With the pointer positioned at F5, the formula appears in the cell contents line in the user-interface panel, and the

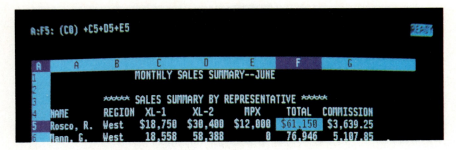

FIGURE 6–3 Spreadsheet: Formulas
The actual content of F5 is the formula in the user-interface panel in the upper left-hand part of the screen. The result of the formula appears in the spreadsheet at F5.

actual numeric value appears in the spreadsheet work area (see Figure 6–3). The formula value in F5 computes the total sales made by the salesperson in Row 5 for all three products (that is, total sales is +C5+D5+E5).

Spreadsheet formulas use standard notation for **arithmetic operators:** + (add), − (subtract), * (multiply), / (divide), ^ (raise to a power, or exponentiation). The formula in F5 (top of Figure 6–3) computes the total sales for R. Rosco. The range F6 .. F10 contains similar formulas that apply to their respective rows (+C6+D6+E6, +C7+D7+E7, and so on). For example, the formula in F6 computes the total sales for G. Mann.

Relative and absolute cell addressing. The formulas in the range G5..G10 (see Figure 6–4) compute the commission for the salespeople based on the commission rates listed in Row 14. The commission rates

FIGURE 6–4 Spreadsheet: Formulas with Relative and Absolute Cell Addresses
Each of the commission computation formulas in the range G5..G10 has the same multipliers—the commission rates in the range C14..E14. Because the relative positions between the commission formulas in G5..G10 and the commission rates in C14..E14 vary from row to row, the commission rates are entered as absolute cell addresses.

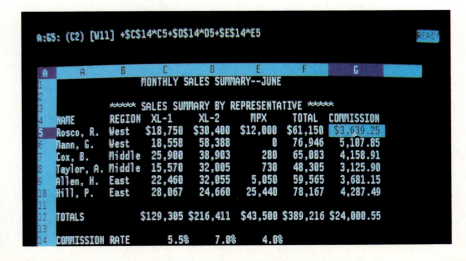

vary from month to month. The percentages in Row 14 reflect the rates for June. The commission for R. Rosco is computed by the following formula.

G5: +$C$14*C5+$D$14*D5+$E$14*E5

The distinction between the way the sales amounts and the commission-rate variables are represented in the formula highlights a very important concept in spreadsheets, that of **relative cell addressing** and **absolute cell addressing**. The dollar signs ($), which preface both the column and row in an absolute cell address ($C$14), distinguish it from a relative cell address (C5). *The relative cell address is based on its position relative to the cell containing the formula.* If the contents of a cell containing a formula are copied to another cell, the relative cell addresses in the copied formula are revised to reflect its new position, but the absolute cell addresses are unchanged.

The two types of cell addressing are illustrated in the spreadsheet in Figure 6-5. Suppose the formula B3*$E$1 is in Cell A1. B3 is a relative cell address that is one column to the right of and two rows down from A1. If this formula is copied to C2, the formula in C2 is D4*$E$1. Notice that D4 has the same relative position to the formula in Cell C2 as B3 has to the formula in Cell A1: one column to the right and two rows down. The absolute cell address ($E$1) remains the same in both formulas.

Copying formulas. In creating the spreadsheet template for the monthly sales summary, Pat Kline entered only one formula to compute salesperson commission—in G5 (see Figure 6-4). Then spreadsheet commands were selected that *copied*, or *replicated*, the formula into each cell in the range G6..G10. Notice in the following copied formulas for G. Mann and B. Cox how the absolute addresses ($C$14, $D$14, and $E$14) remained the same in each formula and the relative addresses were revised to reflect the applicable row.

G6: +$C$14*C6+$D$14*D6+$E$14*E6
G7: +$C$14*C7+$D$14*D7+$E$14*E7

The formula in G6 (above) applies to the sales data in the cells adjacent to G. Mann, not R. Rosco (as in the formula in G5). The same is true of other formulas in the range G5..G10.

FIGURE 6-5 Spreadsheet: Relative and Absolute Cell Addressing
*When the formula in A1 is copied to C2, the formula in C2 becomes D4*$E$1.*

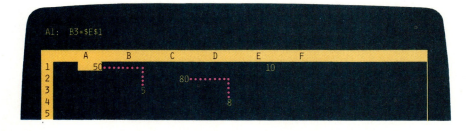

> **MEMORY BITS**

Spreadsheet Organization
- Tabular structure
  Numbered rows
  Lettered columns
- Row/column intersect at cell
- Cell address locates cell
- Pointer highlights current cell
- Cell entry types
  Text (label)
  Formula
  Numeric
- Cell addressing
  Relative
  Absolute

Creating Spreadsheet Formulas. This section expands on the use and application of formulas—the essence of spreadsheet operations. A formula enables the spreadsheet software to perform numeric and/or string calculations and/or logic operations that result in a numeric value (for example, 18750) or an alphanumeric character string (for example, *ABOVE QUOTA* or *BELOW QUOTA*). A formula may include one or all of the following: *arithmetic operations*, *functions*, *string operations*, and *logic operations*. The first two are discussed here in more detail. String operations (for example, joining, or *concatenating*, character strings) and logic operations (formulas that involve relational operators, such as < and >, and logic operators, such as *AND* and *OR*) are beyond the scope of this presentation.

When you design the spreadsheet, keep in mind where you want to place the formulas and what you want them to accomplish. Because formulas are based on relative position, you will need a knowledge of the layout and organization of the data in the spreadsheet. When you define a formula, you must first determine what you wish to achieve (for example, to calculate total sales for the first salesperson). Then select a cell location for the formula (for example, F5), and create the formula by connecting relative cell addresses, absolute cell addresses, and/or numbers with operators, as appropriate. In many instances, you will copy the formula to other locations (for example, in Figure 6–4, F5 was copied to each cell in F6..F10).

Spreadsheet applications begin with a blank screen and an idea. The spreadsheet you create is a product of skill and imagination. What you get from a spreadsheet depends on how effectively you use formulas.

Arithmetic operations. Formulas containing arithmetic operators are resolved according to a hierarchy of operations. That is, when more than one operator is included in a single formula, the spreadsheet software uses a set of rules to determine which operation to do first, second, and so on. In the hierarchy of operations illustrated in Figure 6–6, exponentiation has the highest priority, followed by multiplication-division and addition-subtraction. In the case of a tie (for example, * and /, or + and −), the formula is evaluated *from left to right*. *Parentheses*, however, override the priority rules. Expressions placed in parentheses have priority and are evaluated innermost first and left to right.

The formula that results in the value in G5 (3639.25) of Figure 6–4 is shown below:

G5: +$C$14*C5+$D$14*D5+$E$14*E5

FIGURE 6–6 Hierarchy of Operations

The Hierarchy of Operations	
OPERATION	OPERATOR
Exponentiation	^
Multiplication-Division	* /
Addition-Subtraction	+ −

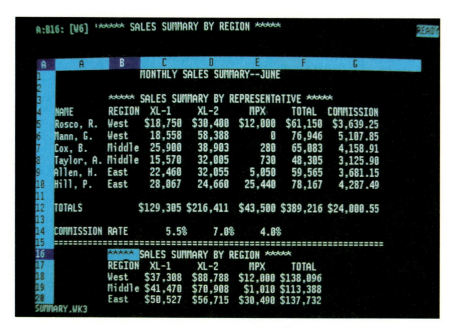

FIGURE 6-7 Spreadsheet: Adding a Regional Sales Summary
The "Sales Summary by Region" portion of the template is extrapolated from the data in the "Sales Summary by Representative" portion.

Following the hierarchy of operations, the three multiplications are performed first. The products are then added to arrive at the result in G5.

Pat Kline's monthly sales summary template also includes a "Sales Summary by Region" in Rows 16 through 20 (see Figure 6-7). All the formulas in the spreadsheet of Figure 6-7 are listed in Figure 6-8.

FIGURE 6-8 Spreadsheet: Actual Content of Formula Cells
This figure illustrates the actual content of the cells in Figure 6-7 that contain formulas. In an actual spreadsheet display, the formulas would be resolved when displayed (F5 would appear as $61,150).

	A	B	C	D	E	F	G	H	I
1			MONTHLY SALES SUMMARY--JUNE						
2									
3			***** SALES SUMMARY BY REPRESENTATIVE *****						
4	NAME	REGION	XL-1	XL-2	MPX	TOTAL		COMMISSION	
5	Rosco, R.	West	$18,750	$30,400	$12,000	+C5+D5+E5	+$C$14*C5+$D$14*D5+$E$14*E5		
6	Mann, G.	West	18,558	58,388	0	+C6+D6+E6	+$C$14*C6+$D$14*D6+$E$14*E6		
7	Cox, B.	Middle	25,900	38,903	280	+C7+D7+E7	+$C$14*C7+$D$14*D7+$E$14*E7		
8	Taylor, A.	Middle	15,570	32,005	730	+C8+D8+E8	+$C$14*C8+$D$14*D8+$E$14*E8		
9	Allen, H.	East	22,460	32,055	5,050	+C9+D9+E9	+$C$14*C9+$D$14*D9+$E$14*E9		
10	Hill, P.	East	28,067	24,660	25,440	+C10+D10+E10	+$C$14*C10+$D$14*D10+$E$14*E10		
11									
12	TOTALS		@SUM(C5..C10)	@SUM(D5..D10)	@SUM(E5..E10)	@SUM(F5..F10)	@SUM(G5..G10)		
13									
14	COMMISSION RATE		5.5%	7.0%	4.0%				
15	==								
16			***** SALES SUMMARY BY REGION *****						
17		REGION	XL-1	XL-2	MPX	TOTAL			
18		West	+C5+C6	+D5+D6	+E5+E6	+C18+D18+E18			
19		Middle	+C7+C8	+D7+D8	+E7+E8	+C19+D19+E19			
20		East	+C9+C10	+D9+D10	+E9+E10	+C20+D20+E20			

Functions. Spreadsheets offer users a wide variety of predefined operations called **functions**. These functions can be used to create formulas that perform mathematical, logical, statistical, financial, and character-string operations on spreadsheet data. To use a function, simply enter the desired function name (for example, SUM for "Compute the sum") and enter the **argument**. Some spreadsheet programs require the user to prefix the function with a symbol such as @. (The symbol may vary from one software package to the next). The argument, which is placed in parentheses, identifies the data to be operated on. The argument can be one or several numbers, character strings, or ranges that represent data.

In the spreadsheet in Figure 6–7, the "TOTALS" for each column (C12..G12) are determined by adding the amounts in the respective columns. For example, the total sales for the XL-1 is determined with the following formula.

C12: +C5+C6+C7+C8+C9+C10

Or the total sales for the XL-1 can be computed with a function and its argument:

C10: @SUM(C5..C10)

The use of predefined functions can save a lot of time. What if the range to be added was C5..C100? Other spreadsheet functions include trigonometric functions, square roots, comparisons of values, manipulations of strings of data, computation of net present value and internal rate of return, and a variety of techniques for statistical analysis.

Pat Kline has included a "Statistical Sales Summary" on the second screen of the spreadsheet template in Rows 21 through 27 (see Figure 6–9). The summary uses three common statistical functions: low or min-

FIGURE 6–9 Spreadsheet: Functions
The "Statistical Sales Summary" portion of the template is extrapolated from the data in the "Sales Summary by Representative" portion (see Figure 6–7). The statistical summary employs the minimum (@MIN), average (@AVG), and maximum (@MAX) functions (see Figure 6–10).

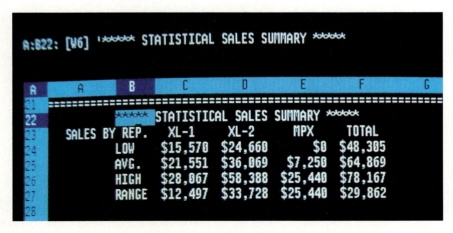

CHAPTER 6 Data Management: Spreadsheet and Database 175

```
     A        B          C            D            E            F
21  ===================================================================
22              ***** STATISTICAL SALES SUMMARY *****
23  SALES BY REP.   XL-1         XL-2         MPX         TOTAL
24           LOW   @MIN(C5..C10) @MIN(D5..D10) @MIN(E5..E10) @MIN(F5..F10)
25           AVG.  @AVG(C5..C10) @AVG(D5..D10) @AVG(E5..E10) @AVG(F5..F10)
26           HIGH  @MAX(C5..C10) @MAX(D5..D10) @MAX(E5..E10) @MAX(F5..F10)
27           RANGE +C26-C24      +D26-D24      +E26-E24      +F26-F24
```

FIGURE 6–10 Spreadsheet: Actual Content of Formula Cells
This figure illustrates the actual content of the cells in Figure 6–9 that contain formulas.

imum (@MIN), average (@AVG), and high or maximum (@MAX). For example, @MIN(C5..C10), the statistical function in C24 of Figure 6–9, determines the minimum sales amount for the XL-1. The actual formulas in Rows 21 through 27 are shown in Figure 6–10. Vendors of spreadsheet software create slightly different names for their functions.

Formatting Data for Readability. The appearance of data in the spreadsheet of Figures 6–7 and 6–9 has been modified to enhance readability. For example, the value .055 was entered as the rate of commission for the XL-1 in C14 (Figure 6–7), but it appears in the spreadsheet display as a percent (5.5%). This is because the range C14..E14 was *formatted* so the values are automatically displayed as percentages with one decimal place rather than as decimals.

All currency amounts entered in the spreadsheet template of Figure 6–7 were entered without commas or dollar signs. The currency amounts are formatted so that commas and a dollar sign (first row and totals) are inserted. For example, in Figure 6–7 the value for R. Rosco's XL-1 sales was entered as 18750 in C4, which is formatted for currency. Notice that it is displayed as $18,750.

The monthly sales summary example in the text is presented on a two-dimensional worksheet in rows and columns. Some electronic spreadsheet packages permit three-dimensional spreadsheets. A 3-D spreadsheet has multiple worksheets. This example contains a monthly sales summary for the current month (June) and the previous two months (May and April). The cell references in 3-D spreadsheets are prefaced with the letter of the worksheet. In the photo, the pointer is on Cell C:C1, the title of the report. The titles of the other two reports are in Cells A:C1 and B:C1. A quarterly sales summary can be compiled in a fourth worksheet (D) by adding like cells in Worksheets A, B, and C. For example, the XL-1 sales by R. Rosco for the quarter would be computed in Cell D:C5 by the formula A:C5+B:C5+C:C5.

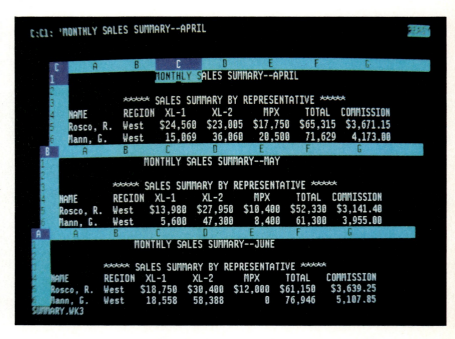

Numeric data can be defined so they are displayed with a fixed number of places to the right of the decimal point. In Figure 6–7, the format of the sales data in the range C5..F10 is currency with the number of decimal places fixed at zero. Numbers with more decimal digits than specified in the format are rounded when displayed. The amounts in the "COMMISSION" column of the spreadsheet of Figure 6–7 are formatted to be displayed as currency with two decimal places.

Use

The possibilities of what Pat Kline, you, and others can do with spreadsheet software and micros are endless. Find any set of numbers and you have identified a potential application for spreadsheet software.

Spreadsheet Templates. The spreadsheet in Figures 6–7 and 6–9 is a *template*, or a model, for Pat Kline's monthly sales summary. All Pat has to do is enter the sales data for the current month in the range C5..E10. All other data are calculated with formulas.

Most spreadsheet applications eventually take the form of a spreadsheet template. Once created, the template becomes the basis for handling a certain type of data (for example, monthly sales data).

Spreadsheet templates are modified easily. For example, any of these modifications of Figures 6–7 and 6–9 would require only a few minutes: Add another column to accommodate a new product; delete a row to accommodate one less salesperson; compute the standard deviation for XL-1 sales data; and change the rate of commission for the XL-1 to 6.0%.

"What If" Analysis. The real beauty of a spreadsheet is that if you change the value of a cell, all other affected cells are revised accordingly.

FIGURE 6–11 Spreadsheet: "What If" Analysis
"What if" each of the commission rates were increased by 0.5%? This spreadsheet reflects the commissions that would have been earned had the increase been in effect.

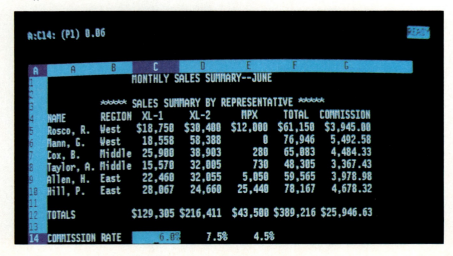

This capability makes spreadsheet software the perfect tool for "what if" analysis. For example, Pat Kline used the current data to assess how commissions might be affected if each of the rates of commission were increased by 0.5% (for example, from 5.5% to 6.0% for the XL-1). The resulting spreadsheet in Figure 6–11 indicates that the salesperson earning the highest commission (G. Mann) would have earned almost $400 more under the proposed commission rates.

Spreadsheet Graphics. Most commercial spreadsheet packages are *integrated packages*, combining spreadsheet, presentation graphics, and database capabilities. The graphics component enables users to present spreadsheet data as business graphs (see Chapter 5, "Text and Image Processing: Word Processing, Desktop Publishing, and Graphics"), the most popular of which are the *bar*, *pie*, and *line graphs* (as seen in Figures 6–13, 6–15, and 6–16, respectively). The user responds to a series of prompts to generate a graph. The first prompt asks the user to select the type of graph to be generated. The user then identifies the source of the data, enters labels and titles, and so on.

Pat Kline, the national sales manager who produced the monthly sales summary spreadsheet in the last section, is an avid user of spreadsheet and presentation graphics software. The spreadsheet segment in Figure 6–12 consists of Rows 15 through 20 of the monthly sales summary spreadsheet in Figure 6–7. The spreadsheet in Figure 6–12 is the basis for the preparation of bar, pie, and line graphs in the following sections.

The information contained in a page full of numbers is seldom obvious and, consequently, may not be apparent to the reader. However, trends, extraordinary efforts, and problem areas become easy to perceive when the same data are summarized in graph form.

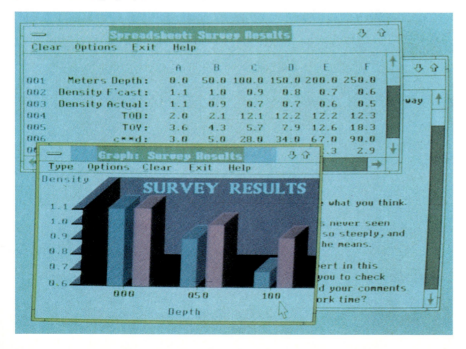

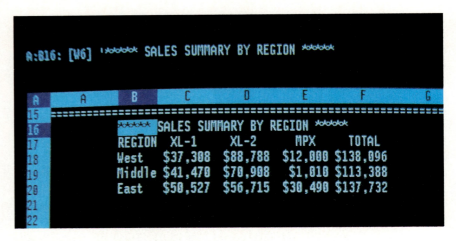

FIGURE 6–12 Spreadsheet: Sales Data for Graphs
The bar, pie, and line graphs of Figures 6–13 through 6–16 are derived from these sales figures.

Bar graphs. To prepare the bar graph in Figure 6–13, Pat had to specify appropriate ranges; that is, the values in the "TOTAL" column (Range F18..B20 of Figure 6–12) are to be plotted, and the region names (Range B18..B20 in Figure 6–12) are to be inserted as labels along the horizontal, or *x*, axis. Pat also added a title for the graph ("Monthly Sales Summary by Region"), and titles for the *x* axis ("Region"), and the vertical, or *y*, axis ("Monthly Sales").

The sales figures for each region in Figure 6–12 (Range C18..E20) can be plotted in a *stacked-bar graph*. The resulting graph, shown in Figure

FIGURE 6–13 Presentation Graphics: Bar Graph
The total sales for each region in Figure 6–12 are represented in this bar graph.

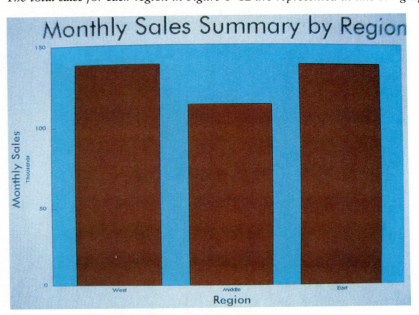

6–14, permits Pat Kline to better understand the regional distribution of sales. The *clustered-bar graph*, which includes a vertical bar for each product within each region, is an alternative to the stacked-bar graph in Figure 6–14. These bar graphs visually highlight the relative contribution each product has made to the total sales for each region.

Pie graphs. Pie graphs are the most basic of presentation graphics. A pie graph illustrates each "piece" of data in its proper relationship to the whole "pie." To illustrate how a pie graph is constructed and used, refer again to the monthly sales spreadsheet in Figure 6–12. Pat Kline produced the sales-by-region pie graph in Figure 6–15 by specifying that the values in the "TOTAL" column become the "pieces" of the pie. To emphasize the region with the greatest contribution to total sales, Pat decided to *explode* (or separate) the western region's piece of the pie.

Line graphs. A line graph connects similar points on a graph with one or several lines. Pat Kline used the same data in the spreadsheet of Figure 6–12 to generate the line graph in Figure 6–16. The line graph makes it easy to compare sales between regions for a particular product.

Spreadsheet Database Capabilities. The database component of an integrated spreadsheet package provides the user with many of the features of a dedicated database package—all within the context of the rows and columns of a spreadsheet. When used as a database tool, spreadsheet software organizes fields, records, and files into columns, rows, and tables,

FIGURE 6–14 Presentation Graphics: Stacked-Bar Graph
Regional sales for each of the three products in Figure 6–12 are represented in this stacked-bar graph.

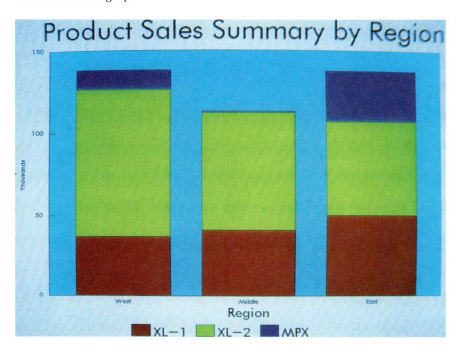

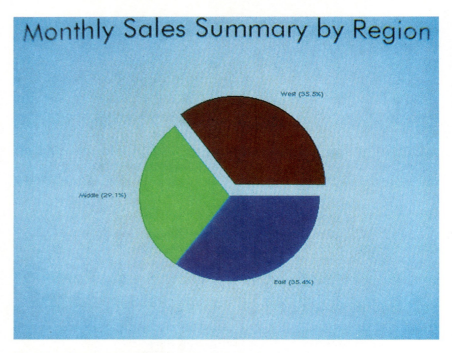

FIGURE 6–15 Presentation Graphics: Pie Graph
The total sales for each region in Figure 6–12 are represented in this pie graph. The western region's piece of the pie is exploded for emphasis.

FIGURE 6–16 Presentation Graphics: Line Graph
This line graph shows a plot of the data in Figure 6–12. A line connects the sales for each product by region.

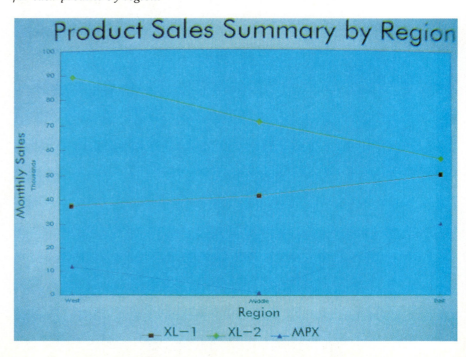

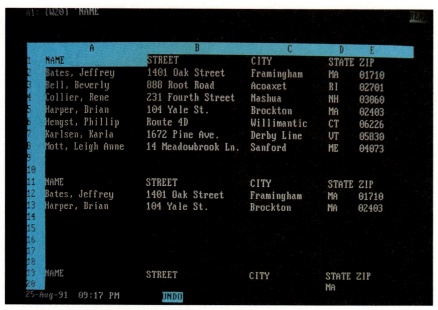

FIGURE 6–17 Spreadsheet: Database Format
This spreadsheet is organized as a data base (A1..E8). The name and permanent address data base contains a record for each student in a college dormitory. The labels for the fields in the record are listed in the first row (A1..E1). Each subsequent row contains one student record. This screen shows the results of an inquiry to the data base: List those students who live in Massachusetts (MA). *The criteria range (STATE="MA") is shown in A19..E20. The results of the inquiry are shown in the output range (A11..E13).*

respectively. For example, in the name-and-address file illustrated in Figure 6–17, each row in the spreadsheet after the first row contains the data items for each individual record (for example, Jeffrey Bates, 1401 Oak St., Framingham, MA 01710). The first row contains column headings that identify the fields in a record (name, address, city, state, zip). All the records are combined in a table of rows (records) and columns (fields) to make a file. Spreadsheet rows, or records, can be sorted or extracted based on preset conditions (for example, STATE="MA") to generate a variety of reports.

6–2 DATABASE: DYNAMIC DATA TOOL

Function

With database software you can create and maintain a data base and extract information from it. To use database software, you first identify the format of the data, then design a display format that permits interactive entry and revision of the data base. Once the data base is created, its data can be deleted or revised and other data can be added. Notice that *database* is one word when it refers to the software that manages

In the construction business, the accuracy of cost estimates may mean the difference between making or losing money. The historical and current cost data in a data base make it possible for this engineer to produce reliable estimates of project costs.

the data base. *Data base* is two words when the term refers to the highest level of the hierarchy of data organization (bit, character, field, record, file, and data base). The data hierarchy is discussed later.

All database software packages have these fundamental capabilities:

1. To create and maintain (add, delete, and revise records) a data base
2. To extract and list all records or only those records that meet certain conditions
3. To make an inquiry (for example, "What is the total amount owed by all customers?")
4. To sort records in ascending or descending sequence by primary, secondary, and tertiary fields
5. To generate formatted reports with subtotals and totals

The more sophisticated packages include a variety of other features, such as spreadsheet-type computations, presentation graphics, and programming.

Concepts

The Hierarchy of Data Organization: Bits to Data Bases. The six levels of the *hierarchy of data organization* are illustrated in Figure 6–18. They are *bit*, *character*, *field*, *record*, *file*, and *data base*. You are already familiar with several levels of the hierarchy. Bits and characters are discussed in some detail in Chapter 3, "Processors and Platforms."

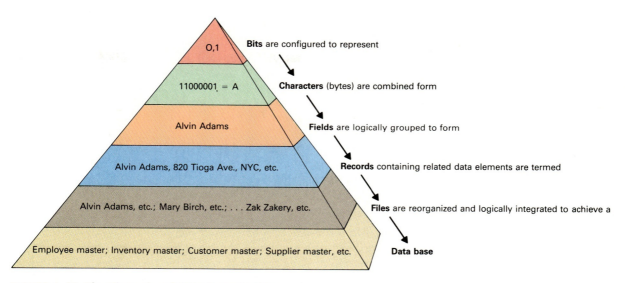

FIGURE 6–18 The Hierarchy of Data Organization

Each succeeding level in the hierarchy is the result of combining the elements of the preceding level (see Figure 6–18). Data are logically combined in this fashion until a data base is achieved. Bits—the first level—are handled automatically by the system. The other five levels are important design considerations for any information-processing activity. The following paragraphs explain each level of the hierarchy and how it relates to the succeeding level.

Bits and characters. A **character** is represented by a group of *bits* that are configured according to an encoding system, such as ASCII. Whereas the bit is the basic unit of primary and secondary storage, the character is the basic unit perceived by humans. When we enter a command, each character is automatically encoded into a bit configuration. The bit configurations are decoded on output so we can read and understand the output. In terms of data storage, a character is usually the same as a *byte*. (See Chapter 3 for more on bits, bytes, and encoding systems.)

Fields. The **field** is the lowest level *logical* unit in the data hierarchy. For example, a single character (such as *A*) has little meaning out of context. But when characters are combined to form a name (for example, *Alicia* or *Alvin*), they form a logical unit. A field is best described by example: social security number, first name, street address, marital status. These are all fields.

When it is stored in secondary storage, a field is allocated a certain number of character positions. The number of these positions is called the *field length*. The field length of a telephone area code is 3. The field length of a telephone number is 7.

Whereas the field is the general (or generic) reference, the specific content of a field is called the **data item**. For example, a social security number is a field, but *445487279* and *440214158* are data items. A street address is a field, but *1701 El Camino* and *134 East Himes Street* are data items.

Fields	Data Items
Employee/social security number	445447279
Last name	SMITH
First name	ALVIN
Middle initial	E
Department (coded)	ACT
Sex (coded)	M
Marital status (coded)	S
Salary (per week)	800.00

FIGURE 6–19 A Portion of an Employee Record
The fields listed are commonly found in employee records. Data items appear next to each field.

Records. A *record* is a description of an event (a sale, a hotel reservation) or an item (for example, a customer, a part). Related fields describing an event or item are logically grouped to form a record. For example, Figure 6–19 contains a partial list of fields for a typical employee record. It also shows the data items for an *occurrence* of a particular employee record (Alvin E. Smith): "Department," "Sex," and "Marital status" are *coded* for ease of data entry and to save storage space.

In general, the record is the lowest level logical unit that can be accessed from a file. For instance, if the personnel manager needs to know only the marital status of Alvin E. Smith, he will have to retrieve Smith's entire record from secondary storage and transmit it to primary storage for processing.

Files. A **file** is a collection of related records. The employee file contains a record for each employee. An inventory file contains a record for each inventory item. The accounts receivable file contains a record for each customer. The term *file* is also used to refer to a named area on a disk that contains a *program*, *textual material* (such as a letter), or even an *image*.

Data bases. The **data base** is the data resource for every computer-based information system. In essence, a data base is a collection of files that are in some way logically related to one another. In a data base, the data are integrated and related so that data redundancy is minimized. During the first three decades of computer-based automation, companies

These customer service representatives help customers when they have questions about a particular product. The first thing they do upon receiving a call from a customer is to retrieve the customer's record from the data base. The record can be retrieved and displayed by entering either of the two key fields—customer name or customer account number.

maintained **flat files**, or files with no formal association with one another. In the flat-file environment, the duplication of fields was commonplace. For example, if an employee moved, his or her address would have to be changed in all files that maintained address data, frequently 10 or more files. In a data base, employee-address data are stored only once. Therefore, only one update is needed when an employee changes his or her address.

The Relational Data Base. In contrast to the traditional flat-file approaches to data management, today's microcomputer database software packages access data by *content* rather than by *address*. That is, the database approach uses the computer to search the data base for the desired data rather than accessing data through a series of indices and physical disk addresses. In the data base example that follows, the data structures, or relationships between data, are defined in *logical* rather than *physical* terms. That is, the data base has no predetermined relationship between the data, such as records in the traditional file environment (see Figure 6–20). In this way, data can be accessed at the *data element* level. In traditional flat-file processing, the entire record must be retrieved to examine a single data element.

The following data base example should help you better understand the principles and advantages of database software. The example focuses on the book circulation activity in a library. The objective of a circulation system is to keep track of who borrows which books, then monitor their timely return. In the traditional flat-file environment, the record layout might be as shown in Figure 6–20. In this record, a library patron can borrow from one to four books. Precious storage space is wasted for patrons who borrow infrequently, and the four-book limit may force prolific readers to make more frequent trips to the library.

The **relational data base** has emerged as the most popular type of data base organization. The relational data base in Figure 6–21 contains two *tables*, each containing rows and columns of data. A row is roughly equivalent to a record in a traditional flat-file environment. The column headings, called *attributes*, are analogous to fields.

The first table contains patron data and the second table contains data relating to books out on loan. Each new patron is issued a library card with a number that can be read with an optical wand scanner. The patron's card number, name, and address are added to the data base. When the patron borrows a book, the librarian at the circulation desk uses a wand scanner to enter the card number and the book's ISBN (International Standard Book Number). These data and the due date, which are entered on a keyboard, become a row in the Books on Loan

FIGURE 6–20 Record Layout
This record layout is for a traditional book circulation file in a library.

Card No.	First Name	Last Name	Address				Book #1 (ISBN)	Due Date	Book #2 (ISBN)	Due Date	Book #3 (ISBN)	Due Date	Book #4 (ISBN)	Due Date
			Street	City	ST	ZIP								

Patron Data

Card No.	First Name	Last Name	Address			
			Street	City	ST	ZIP
1243	Jason	Jones	18 W. Oak	Ponca City	OK	74601
1618	Kay	Smith	108 10th St.	Newkirk	OK	74647
2380	Heather	Hall	2215 Pine Dr.	Ponca City	OK	74604
2644	Brett	Brown	1700 Sunset	Ponca City	OK	74604
3012	Melody	Beck	145 N. Brook	Ark. City	KS	67005
3376	Butch	Danner	RD#7	Tonkawa	OK	74653
3859	Abe	Michaels	333 Paul Ave.	Kaw City	OK	74641

Books-on-Loan Data

Card No.	Book No. (ISBN)	Due Date
1618	89303-530	4/7
1243	12-201702	4/20
3859	13-48049	4/9
2644	18-23614	4/14
2644	71606-214	4/14
2644	22-68111	4/3
1618	27-21675	4/12

FIGURE 6–21 A Relational Data Base Organization
The record layout of the traditional book circulation file of Figure 6–20 is reorganized and integrated into a relational data base with a Patron Data table and a Books-on-Loan Data table.

Data table. Notice that by using a relational data base there is no limit to the number of borrowed books the system can handle for a particular patron.

Suppose the circulation librarian wanted a report of overdue books as of April 8 (4/8). The query would be: "List all books overdue." (Query date is 4/8.) The search criterion of "due date < (before) 4/8" is applied to the Due Date column in the Books on Loan Data table (see Figure 6–22). The search reveals two overdue books; then the system uses the card numbers to cross-reference delinquent patrons in the Patron Data table to obtain their names and addresses. The report at the bottom of Figure 6–22 is produced in response to the librarian's query. Data on each book, including publisher, author, and ISBN, might be maintained in another table in the relational data base.

FIGURE 6–22 Queries to a Relational Data Base
The figure illustrates the resolution and output of an April 8 query to the data base: "List all books overdue." The card numbers in the "yes" response rows are cross-referenced to the Patron Data table in Figure 6–21 to produce the report.

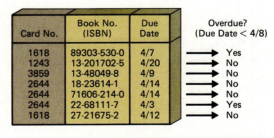

Creating a Data Base with Database Software. Many similarities exist between commercially available word processing packages and commercially available spreadsheet packages. With word processing, you see and manipulate lines of text. With spreadsheets, you see and manipulate data in numbered rows and lettered columns. This is not the case with database packages. All commercial software packages permit the creation and manipulation of data bases, but what you see on the screen may be vastly different from one package to the next. However, the concepts behind these database packages are very similar. The data base example that follows is generic and can be applied to all database packages. The displays in the accompanying figures are taken from Paradox (a product of Borland International).

The best way to illustrate and demonstrate the concepts of database software is by example. Pat Kline, the national sales manager from previous examples in this chapter and Chapter 5, uses a micro-based database software package to track product sales of important accounts. To do this, Pat created a KEY_ACCT data base (see Figure 6–23) that contains a record for each of the company's nine key accounts. Almost 30% of the company's worldwide sales comes from these key accounts. Each record in the KEY_ACCT data base contains the following fields:

- COMPANY (the name of a key account company)
- REGION (sales region: west, middle, or east)
- REP_NAME (name of field representative who services account)
- XL1_NO (the number of XL1s installed at the account)
- XL2_NO (the number of XL2s installed at the account)
- MPX_NO (the number of MPXs installed at the account)
- LAST_ORDER (the date of the last order for one or more XL1s, XL2s, or MPXs)

To create a data base, the first thing you do is to set up a *screen format* that enables you to enter the data for a record. The data-entry screen format is analogous to a hard-copy form that contains labels and blank

FIGURE 6–23 Database: The KEY_ ACCT Data Base
The KEY_ ACCT data base contains a record for each of a company's nine key accounts. The fields for each account (customer company) are described in the text.

COMPANY	REGION	REP. NAME	PRODUCTS			LAST ORDER
			XL1 NO.	XL2 NO.	MPX NO.	
Hi-Tech	West	Rosco	22	35	5	01/11/91
Electronic	East	Allen	48	21	15	02/06/91
Compufast	Middle	Taylor	103	67	42	02/07/92
Zapp. Inc.	West	Rosco	71	85	40	01/16/92
Whizzard	East	Hill	35	45	20	10/12/91
SuperGood	Middle	Cox	24	55	4	12/24/91
Bigco	East	Hill	38	50	21	09/09/91
Actionpak	Middle	Cox	24	37	14	11/01/91
Zimco	West	Mann	77	113	40	01/13/91

lines (for example, a medical questionnaire or an employment application). Data are entered and edited (deleted or revised) one record at a time with database software as they are on hard-copy forms.

The structure of the data base. To set up a data-entry screen format, you must first specify the *structure* of the data base by identifying the characteristics of each field in it. This is done interactively, with the system prompting you to enter the field name, field type, and so on (see Figure 6–24). The *field name* is "COMPANY," the *field length* is 10 positions, and the *field type* is alphanumeric, or character. An alphanumeric field type can be a single word or any alphanumeric (numbers, letters, and special characters) phrase up to several hundred positions in length. For numeric field types, you must specify the maximum number of digits (field length) and the number of decimal positions you wish to have displayed. Because the product sales are all defined in whole hours, the number of decimal positions for the XL1_NO, XL2_NO, and MPX_NO fields is set at zero.

Entering and editing a data base. The screen format for entering, editing, and adding records to the KEY_ACCT data base is shown in Figure 6–25. To create the KEY_ACCT data base, the sales manager issued a command that called up the data entry screen in Figure 6–25, entered the data for first record, then entered the second record, and so on. On most database systems, the records are automatically assigned a number as they are entered. Records can, of course, be added to the data base and edited (deleted or revised).

Query by Example. Database software also permits you to retrieve, view, and print records based on **query by example**. In query by example, you set conditions for the selection of records by composing one or more

FIGURE 6–24 Database: Structure of the KEY_ ACCT Data Base
This display shows the structure of the KEY_ ACCT data base for Paradox, a popular database software package. The KEY_ ACCT record has three alphanumeric (A) fields, three numeric (N) fields, and a data (D) field.

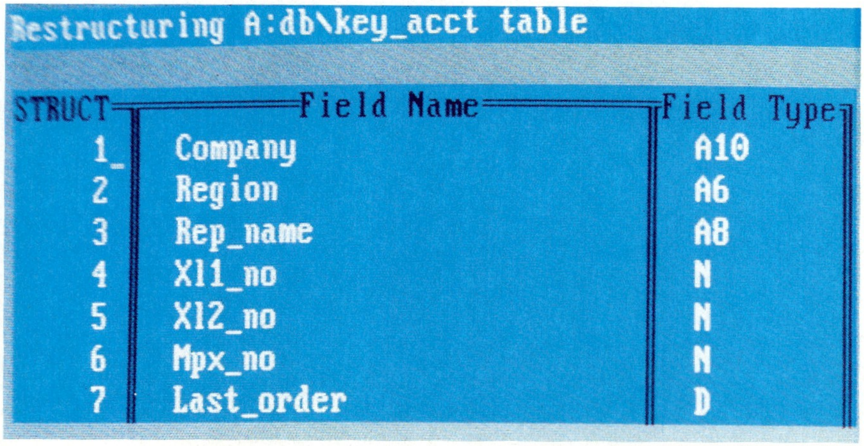

STRUCT	Field Name	Field Type
1	Company	A10
2	Region	A6
3	Rep_name	A8
4	Xl1_no	N
5	Xl2_no	N
6	Mpx_no	N
7	Last_order	D

Restructuring A:\db\key_acct table

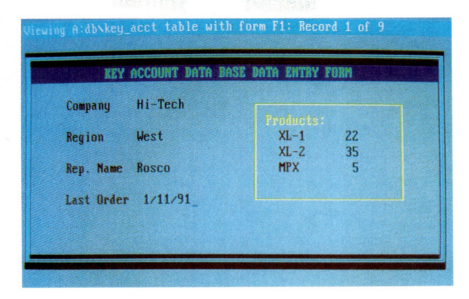

FIGURE 6–25 Database: Data Entry Screen Format
The screen format for entering, editing, and adding records to the KEY_ ACCT data base is illustrated.

example *relational expressions.* A relational expression normally compares one or more field names to numbers or character strings using the **relational operators** (= [equal to], > [greater than], < [less than], and combinations of these operators). Several conditions can be combined with **logical operators** (*AND, OR,* and *NOT*). Commonly used relational and logical operators are summarized in Figure 6–26.

Pat Kline wanted a listing of all key accounts in the eastern region, so the sales manager requested a list of all key accounts that meet the condition Region = East in the KEY_ACCT data base (see Figure 6–23). The result is shown in Figure 6–27. To produce the output in Figure 6–28, Pat Kline asks for the names of accounts in the Eastern region that

FIGURE 6–26 Relational and Logical Operators

Relational Operators	
COMPARISON	OPERATOR
Equal to	=
Less than	<
Greater than	>
Less than or equal to	<=
Greater than or equal to	>=
Not equal to	<>

Logical Operators AND and OR	
OPERATION	OPERATOR
For the condition to be true:	
Both subconditions must be true	AND
At least one subcondition must be true	OR

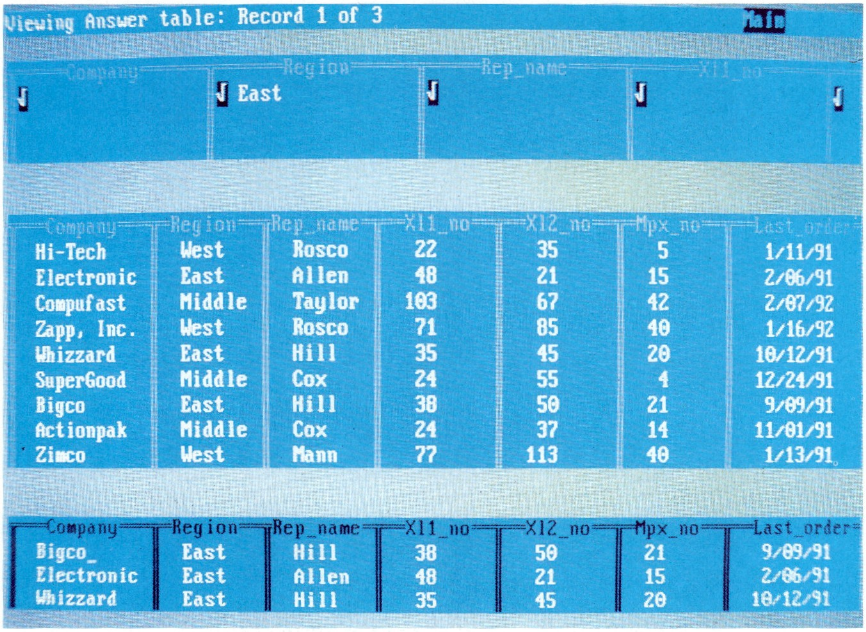

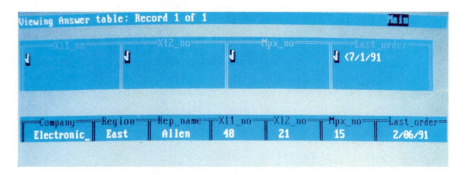

FIGURE 6-27 Database: Query by Example, One Condition
All records in the KEY_ ACCT data base (center of screen) that meet the condition REGION = East (top of screen) are displayed at the bottom of the screen.

FIGURE 6-28 Database: Query by Example, Two Conditions
All records in the KEY_ ACCT data base (see Figure 6-27) that meet the condition REGION = East and LAST_ ORDER < (is prior to) 7/1/91 are displayed. The LAST_ ORDER condition is added to the REGION=East condition noted in Figure 6-27.

have not posted an order since July 1, 1991 (REGION = East AND LAST_ORDER < 7/1/91). Of course, the output can be routed to a display screen or to a printer. In addition, the sales manager can select which fields are to be displayed as a result of a query. For example, in Figure 6-28, Pat may have wanted to display only the COMPANY and LAST_ ORDER fields.

The following relational expressions establish conditions that will select or extract records (noted to the right of the expression) from the KEY_ACCT data base in Figure 6–23.

COMPANY = Hi-Tech	(Hi-Tech)
XL1_NO > 40 AND XL2_NO > 30	(Compufast, Zapp, Zimco)
LAST_ORDER > 10/1/91 AND LAST_ORDER < 1/1/92	(Actionpak, SuperGood, Whizzard)
REGION = West OR Middle; MPX_NO = <5	(Hi-Tech, SuperGood)
REP_NAME NOT Rosco	(All but Hi-Tech and Compufast)

The process of selecting records by setting conditions is sometimes called *filtering*; those records or fields that you don't want are "filtered" out of the display.

Sorting Records. Data also can be sorted for display in a variety of formats. For example, the records in Figure 6–23 can be sorted by company, representative's name, or date of last order. Figure 6–29 illustrates how the KEY_ACCT data base in Figure 6–23 has been sorted by REP_NAME within REGION. This involves the selection of a *primary* and a *secondary key field*. The sales manager selected REGION as the primary key field but wanted the account records to be listed in ascending order by REP_NAME within REGION. To achieve this record sequence, Pat selected REP_NAME as the secondary key field. In most database packages, issuing a sort command results in the creation of a temporary data base. After the sort operation, the temporary data base contains the records in the order described in the sort command.

FIGURE 6–29 Database: KEY_ACCT Data Base Sorted by REP_NAME within REGION
This display is the result of a sort operation on the KEY_ACCT data base (Figure 6–23) with the REGION field as the primary key field and the REP_NAME field as the secondary key field.

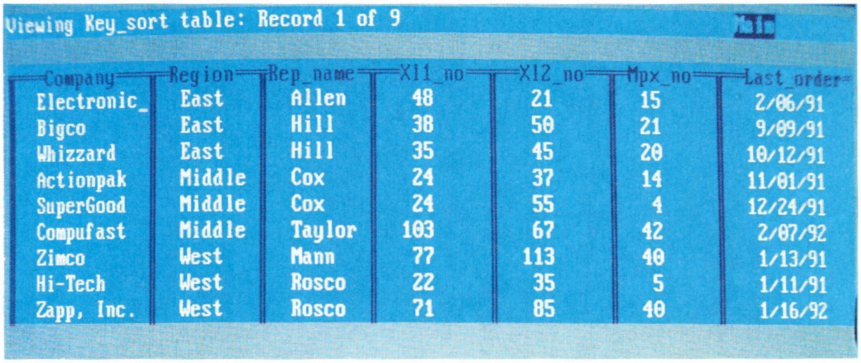

Company	Region	Rep_name	X11_no	X12_no	Mpx_no	Last_order
Electronic_	East	Allen	48	21	15	2/06/91
Bigco	East	Hill	38	50	21	9/09/91
Whizzard	East	Hill	35	45	20	10/12/91
Actionpak	Middle	Cox	24	37	14	11/01/91
SuperGood	Middle	Cox	24	55	4	12/24/91
Compufast	Middle	Taylor	103	67	42	2/07/92
Zimco	West	Mann	77	113	40	1/13/91
Hi-Tech	West	Rosco	22	35	5	1/11/91
Zapp, Inc.	West	Rosco	71	85	40	1/16/92

> **MEMORY BITS**
>
> *Database Inquiries*
> - Query by example (create relational expressions with)
>   Relational operators (=, >, <)
>   Logical operators (AND, OR, NOT)
> - Sorts (identify)
>   Primary sort field
>   Secondary sort field (if needed)

Customized Reports. Database software can create customized, or formatted, reports. This capability allows you to design the *layout* of the report. This means that you have some flexibility in spacing and can include titles, subtitles, column headings, separation lines, and other elements that make a report more readable. You describe the layout of the *customized* report interactively, then store it for later recall. The result of the description, called a *report form*, is recalled from disk storage and merged with a data base to create the customized report. Managers often use this capability to generate periodic reports (for example, monthly sales summary reports).

Once a month, Pat Kline generates several summary reports, one of which groups the key accounts by region and provides product subtotals and an overall total for each product (see Figure 6–30). This customized

FIGURE 6–30 Database: Formatted Report
This formatted report was compiled by merging a predefined report format with the KEY_ ACCT data base (Figure 6–23). The records are printed in alphabetical order by COMPANY within REGION.

```
                    KEY ACCOUNT SALES SUMMARY


     Company      Rep Name    XL-1    XL-2     MPX   Last Order
     =========================================================
         *** Key Acounts for Region:  East
     Bigco        Hill          38      50      21   9/09/91
     Electronic   Allen         48      21      15   2/06/91
     Whizzard     Hill          35      45      20   10/12/91
                                ------  ------  ------
           Region Totals       121     116      56

         *** Key Acounts for Region:  Middle
     Actionpak    Cox           24      37      14   11/01/91
     Compufast    Taylor       103      67      42   2/07/92
     SuperGood    Cox           24      55       4   12/24/91
                                ------  ------  ------
           Region Totals       151     159      60

         *** Key Acounts for Region:  West
     Hi-Tech      Rosco         22      35       5   1/11/91
     Zapp, Inc.   Rosco         71      85      40   1/16/92
     Zimco        Mann          77     113      40   1/13/91
                                ------  ------  ------
           Region Totals       170     233      85
                                ======  ======  ======
           Overall Totals      442     508     201
```

report was compiled by merging a predefined report format with the KEY_ACCT data base.

Use

Database Applications and Capabilities. Database software earns the "productivity tool" label by providing users with the capability of organizing data into an electronic data base that can be maintained and queried (can permit user inquiries) easily. The examples illustrated and discussed in the "Concepts" section merely "scratch the surface" of the potential of database software. With relative ease, you can generate some rather sophisticated reports that involve subtotals, calculations, and programming. In addition, data can be presented in the form of a graph (see Figure 6–31). You can even change the structure of a data base (for example, you can add another field). The programming capability of database software enables users to create their own microcomputer-based information systems.

Hypertext. The database software discussed in this chapter manipulates data within the context of a carefully structured data base. This type of structure can be used in thousands of applications in every industry type. Another type of data management software, called **hypertext**, addresses

FIGURE 6–31 Database: Presentation Graphics
Like spreadsheet packages, most database packages have the capability of preparing presentation graphics. The stacked-bar graph shown below, which is derived from the data in Figure 6–23, shows the contribution of each product to regional sales.

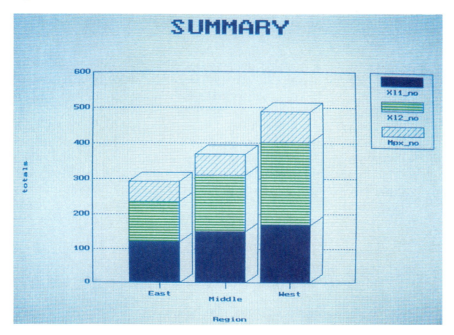

unstructured information. Hypertext software, which is still in the infant stages of use and development, provides links between *key words* in the kinds of unstructured text-based documents that we work with every day (letters, notes, boilerplate, and so on).

The theory behind hypertext is that it lets you work the way you think. For example, suppose you are a lawyer and one of your clients asked you to update his will. The information you need is computer-based, but in no particular format or file. Using the client's name as a key word, you might use hypertext links to assemble needed documents: client's address from client name and address file; random notes you took at the last meeting with your client; the most recent letters you wrote to or on behalf of your client; and the client's existing will. You might use other key word links to retrieve boilerplate text that can be used as the basis for the updated will and to access your appointment calendar to schedule a meeting with your clients. In effect, the computer responds to your requests in much the same way a legal assistant would.

SUMMARY OUTLINE AND IMPORTANT TERMS

6-1 THE SPREADSHEET: THE MAGIC MATRIX. Spreadsheets are simply an alternative to thousands of manual tasks that involve rows and columns of data. The primary example used in this chapter illustrates spreadsheet concepts in a spreadsheet **template** of a monthly sales summary.

Spreadsheets are organized in a tabular structure of **rows** and **columns**. The intersection of a particular row and column designates a **cell**. During operations, data are referred to by their **cell addresses**. The **pointer** can be moved around the spreadsheet to any cell with the cursor-control keys.

To make an entry, edit, or replace an entry in a spreadsheet, move the pointer to the appropriate cell. When in edit mode, revise the entry in much the same way you would revise the text in a word processing document.

The four types of **ranges** are a single cell, all or part of a column of adjacent cells, all or part of a row of adjacent cells, and a rectangular block of cells. A particular range is depicted by the addresses of the endpoint cells (for example, C5..E10).

An entry to a cell is classified as *text* (or *label*), *numeric,* or *formula*. A text entry is any string of alphanumeric text (spaces included) that occupies a particular cell. A numeric entry is any number. A cell may contain a formula, but it is the numeric results that are displayed in the spreadsheet. Spreadsheet formulas use standard programming notation for **arithmetic operators**.

The **relative cell address** is based on its position in relation to the cell containing the formula. When you copy, or replicate, a formula to another cell, the relative cell addresses in the formula are revised so they retain the same position in relation to the new location of the formula. When a formula is copied, the **absolute cell addresses** in the formula remain unchanged.

Predefined **functions** can be used to create formulas that perform mathematical, logical, statistical, financial, and character-string operations on spreadsheet data.

The appearance of data in a spreadsheet can be modified to enhance readability by adjusting the column width and formatting the individual numeric entries.

A spreadsheet template can be used over and over for different purposes by different people. If you change the value of a cell in a spreadsheet, all other affected cells are revised accordingly. This capability makes spreadsheet software the perfect tool for "what if" analysis.

Integrated spreadsheet packages include a presentation graphics software module. This capability enables users to create a variety of presentation graphics from data in a spreadsheet. Among the most popular presentation graphics are bar graphs (including the stacked-bar and clustered-bar graphs), pie graphs, and line graphs. Each of these graphs can be annotated with titles, labels, and legends.

6-2 DATABASE: DYNAMIC DATA TOOL. Database software permits users to create and maintain a data base and extract information from it. Once the data base is created, its data can be deleted or revised, and other data can be added to it.

The six levels of the hierarchy of data organization are bit, **character** (or byte), **field**, record, **file**, and **data base**. The last five levels are integral to the design of any information-processing activity. A string of bits is combined to form a character. Characters are combined to represent the content of fields—**data items**. Related fields are combined to form records. Records with the same data elements combine to form a file. The data base is the company's data resource for all information systems. Traditional **flat files** have no formal association with one another.

The **relational data base** is made up of *tables*, each containing rows and columns of data. The column headings are called *attributes*.

In database software, the user-defined structure of a data base identifies the characteristics of each field in it. The screen format for entering, editing, and adding records to a data base is generated automatically from the specifications outlined in the structure of the data base.

Database software also permits you to retrieve, view, and print records based on **query by example**. To do this, users set conditions for the selection of records by composing a *relational expression* containing **relational operators** that reflects the desired conditions. Several expressions can be combined into a single condition with **logical operators**.

Records in a data base can be sorted for display in a variety of formats. To sort the records in a data base, select a *primary key field* and, if needed, *secondary* and *tertiary key fields*. In most database packages, issuing a sort command results in the compilation of another data base.

Database software can create customized, or formatted, reports. The user describes the layout of the customized report interactively, then stores it for later recall.

Hypertext software provides links between *key words* in the kinds of unstructured text-based documents that we work with every day. People use hypertext to assemble information from letters, notes, boilerplate, and other computer-based documents.

REVIEW EXERCISES

1. Describe the layout of a spreadsheet.
2. Give an example of a cell address. Which portion of the address indicates the row and which portion, the column?
3. Give an example of each of the four types of ranges.
4. Give examples of the three types of entries that can be made in a spreadsheet.
5. Write the equivalent formula for AVG(A1..D1) without the use of functions.
6. If the formula B2*$B$1 is copied from C1 to E3, what is the formula in E3? If the formula in E3 is copied to D45, what is the formula in D45?
7. List three different descriptors for the range A4..P12.
8. What formula would be entered in A5 to add all numbers in the range A1..A4?
9. Name three types of graphs commonly used for presentation graphics.
10. Name two sources of data for generating pie graphs and bar graphs.
11. Name and draw two variations of the bar graph.
12. What is shown when a portion of a pie chart is "exploded"?
13. What characteristics describe a field in a data base record?
14. What is the lowest level logical unit in the hierarchy of data organization?
15. The attribute of a relational data base is analogous to which level of the hierarchy of data organization?
16. What is the purpose of setting conditions for a data base?
17. What is the relationship between a field, a record, and the structure of a data base?
18. Give examples and descriptions of at least two other fields that might be added to the record for the KEY_ACCT data base.
19. If the KEY_ACCT data base (Figure 6–23) were sorted so that the primary and secondary key fields were REGION and LAST_ORDER, respectively, what is the company name for the third record?
20. What records would be displayed if the selection condition for the KEY_ACCT data base (Figure 6–23) were XL1_NO > 20 AND MPX_NO <= 5?

SELF-TEST (by section)

6–1 a. The term *spreadsheet* was coined at the beginning of the personal computer boom. (T/F)
    b. Data in a spreadsheet are referred to by their cell _____.
    c. The spreadsheet pointer highlights the: (a) relative cell, (b) status cell, or (c) current cell?
    d. D20..Z40 and Z20..D40 define the same spreadsheet range. (T/F)
    e. When the spreadsheet formula +H4*$Z$18 is copied from A1 to A3, the formula in A3 is _____.

    f. The spreadsheet formula SUM(A1..A20) results in the computation of the sum of the values in the range A20..A1. (T/F)
    g. A model of a spreadsheet designed for a particular application is sometimes called a _____.
    h. Among the most popular presentation graphics are bar graphs, pie graphs, and _____ graphs.
    i. An alternative to the clustered-bar graph is the _____ graph.

6-2 a. If the KEY_ACCT data base in Figure 6–23 is sorted in descending order by XL1_NO, the third record would be Zapp, Inc. (T/F)
    b. The specific content of a field is called the _____.
    c. The definition of the structure of a data base would not include which of the following: (a) field names, (b) selection conditions for fields, (c) field lengths?
    d. The relational operator for greater than or equal to is _____.
    e. What record(s) would be selected from the KEY_ACCT data base in Figure 6–23 for the condition REGION = West and MPX_NO>15: (a) Zapp, Inc., Zimco; (b) Compufast; or (c) no records are selected?
    f. _____ enables users to assemble information from unstructured computer-based documents.

Self-test answers.   6–1 **(a)** F; **(b)** addresses; **(c)** c; **(d)** T; **(e)** +H6*$Z$18; **(f)** T; **(g)** template; **(h)** line; **(i)** stacked-bar.   6–2 **(a)** F; **(b)** data item; **(c)** b; **(d)** >=; **(e)** a; **(f)** Hypertext.

CHAPTER 7
DATA COMMUNICATIONS AND NETWORKS

STUDENT LEARNING OBJECTIVES

- ▶ To describe the concept of connectivity.
- ▶ To demonstrate an understanding of data communications terminology and applications.
- ▶ To detail the function and operation of data communications hardware.
- ▶ To describe the types of data transmission services.
- ▶ To illustrate the various kinds of computer networks.
- ▶ To describe the purpose, use, and applications of communications software.

7–1 DATA COMMUNICATIONS

From One Room to the World

In the 1960s computers numbered in the tens of thousands. Today, with the explosion of microcomputers, they number in the tens of millions. Information is everywhere. The challenge of the next decade is to make this information more accessible to a greater number of people. To do this, the business and computer communities are seeking ways to interface, or connect, a diverse set of hardware, software, and data bases.

This is the nerve center of EDSNET, Electronic Data Systems Corporation's global communications system. EDSNET facilitates data, voice, and video communication between computers, many of which are PCs, at a quarter of a million sites on five continents. Here in Plano, Texas, (near Dallas) more than 100 operators manage the system. Operators view 12-by-16-foot screens to keep abreast of system activity. Fourteen smaller screens provide detailed information for troubleshooting situations, and 13 clocks display times from around the world.

Connectivity, as it is called, is necessary to facilitate the electronic communication between companies, end user computing, and the free flow of information within an enterprise. This chapter focuses on connectivity concepts and the base technologies of connectivity—data communications and networks.

Data communications is, very simply, the collection and distribution of the electronic representation of information from and to remote facilities. The information can appear in a variety of formats: data, text, voice, still pictures, graphics, and video. Prior to transmission, the raw information must be digitized. (For example, data and text might be translated into their corresponding ASCII codes.) Ultimately all forms of information are sent over the transmission media as a series of binary bits (1s and 0s). Information is transmitted from computers to terminals and other computers over land via optical fiber, through the air by microwave signal, and under the sea through coaxial cable. The technical aspects of data communications are discussed later in this chapter.

Several other terms describe the general area of data communications. **Telecommunications** encompasses not only data communications but any type of remote communication, such as transmitting a television signal. **Teleprocessing**, or **TP**, is the combination of *tele*communications and data *processing*; it often is used interchangeably with the term *data communications*. The integration of computer systems, terminals, and communication links is referred to as a **computer network**.

Through the mid-1960s, a company's computing hardware was located in a single room called the *machine room*. The only people who had direct access to the computer were those who worked in the machine room. Since that time, microcomputers, terminals, data communications, and computer networks have made it possible to move hardware and information systems "closer to the source"—to the people who use them. Before long, terminals and micros, which can serve as terminals, will be as much a part of our work environment as desks and telephones are now.

Communications Software versus Other Micro Software

People with little or no computer experience can readily identify with memos, sales reports, bar graphs, and name-and-address files—applications for word processing, spreadsheet, graphics, and database software. These applications are part of our everyday business and domestic experiences. Because of this familiarity, we are able to jump right in and begin the conceptual discussions of the various software packages. However, the application for communications software is data communications, a technical area that is a mystery to most micro users. This jump-right-in approach is inappropriate for the subject of data communications software.

To effectively use the capabilities of communications software, it is important that you be familiar with the fundamental concepts associated with data communications. Therefore, much of this chapter is devoted to familiarizing you with the concepts and trends associated with data communications.

7-2 THE BEGINNING OF AN ERA: COOPERATIVE COMPUTING

Intracompany Networking

This is the era of **cooperative computing**. Information is the password to success in today's business environment. To get meaningful, accurate, and timely information, businesses have decided they must cooperate internally and externally to take full advantage of what is available. To promote internal cooperation, they are moving in the direction of *intracompany networking* (see Figure 7-1). For example, information maintained in the personnel department is readily accessible to people throughout the company on a *need-to-know* basis. The same is true of information maintained by purchasing, engineering, or any other department. At the individual level, managers or knowledge workers create microcomputer-based systems and data bases to help them do their jobs. When these personalized systems and data bases have the potential of benefiting other people in the company, they can be made a part of the company's computer network to permit the sharing of these information resources.

Intercompany Networking

Companies have recognized that they must cooperate with one another to compete effectively in a world market. They are doing this via *intercompany networking* (Figure 7-1) or, more specifically, **electronic data interchange (EDI)**. EDI uses computers and data communications to transmit data electronically between companies. Invoices, orders, and many other intercompany transactions, including the exchange of information, can be transmitted from the computer of one company to the

FIGURE 7-1 Intracompany and Intercompany Networking

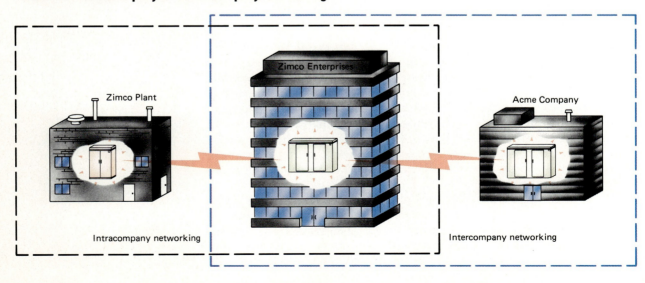

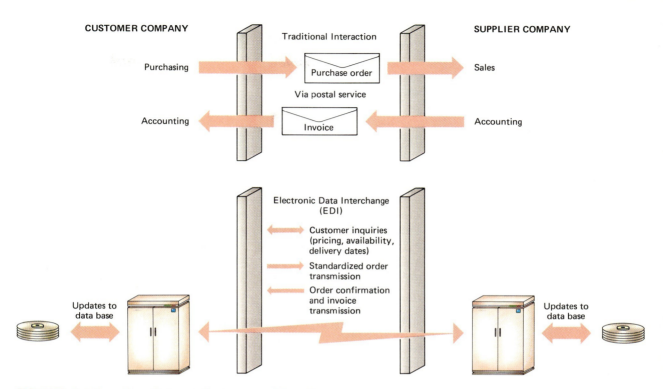

FIGURE 7-2 Interactions Between Customer and Supplier
In the figure, the traditional interaction between a customer company and a supplier company is contrasted with similar interactions via electronic data interchange (EDI).

computer of another. For example, at General Foods, over 50% of all shipments result from computer-to-computer order processing—customers submitting their orders to General Foods via EDI. Figure 7-2 contrasts the traditional interaction between a customer and supplier company with interactions via EDI. EDI is a strategic advantage that some companies have over their competitors.

- It reduces paper-processing costs and delays.
- It reduces errors and correction costs.
- It minimizes receivables and inventory disputes.
- It improves relations between trading partners.

Executives are no longer debating whether or not to implement EDI; they are more concerned about the speed at which it can be put to work in their companies.

External Computing Support: Service via Computer

The phenomenal growth of the use of micros in the home is causing companies to expand their information system capabilities to permit linkages with home and portable PCs. This form of cooperative computing increases system efficiency while lowering costs. For example, in

This office is located at one of 12 regional warehouses. Over 80% of the company's orders are sent to vendors via EDI (electronic data interchange).

over 100 banks, services have been extended to home micro owners in the form of home banking systems. Subscribers to a home banking service use their personal computers as terminals linked to the bank's mainframe computer system to pay bills, transfer funds, and inquire about account status.

The Internal Revenue Service (IRS) now permits tax returns to be filed by professional preparers from their PCs. This service saves both the taxpayer and the IRS time and money. For the taxpayer and the preparer, the on-line system performs all the necessary table searches and computations, and it even cross-checks the accuracy and consistency of the input data. For the IRS, no further data entry or personal assistance is required. Brokerage firms now permit customers to access up-to-the-minute stock market quotations and to issue buy/sell orders directly through their personal computers. Several supermarkets are experimenting with electronic shopping. In the 1990s virtually every type of industry will provide the facility for external links to their mainframe computer systems.

Connectivity: Linking Hardware, Software, and Data Bases

Connectivity refers to the degree to which hardware devices can be linked functionally to one another. Some people expand the scope of connectivity to include software and data bases. It has become such an important consideration that virtually all future decisions involving hardware, software, and data base management must be evaluated with respect to connectivity.

Connectivity is implemented in degrees. To achieve almost any level, technical specialists must juggle **communication protocols** (rules for transmitting and receiving data), official and de facto standards, different approaches to data base design, different computer system architectures, and user information requirements. Each of these considerations poses formidable technological hurdles.

The ideal implementation of intracompany connectivity would be to make all corporate computer and information resources accessible from each worker's terminal. This ideal is referred to as **total connectivity**. Realistically, industry analysts are predicting that total connectivity is still a decade or more away. Nevertheless, almost every company has made a commitment to strive for a higher level of connectivity.

7-3 DATA COMMUNICATIONS HARDWARE

Data communications hardware is used to transmit data between terminals and computers and from one computer to another in a computer network. This hardware includes modems, down-line processors, and front-end processors. The integration of these devices with terminals and computer systems is illustrated in Figure 7–3 and discussed in the paragraphs that follow.

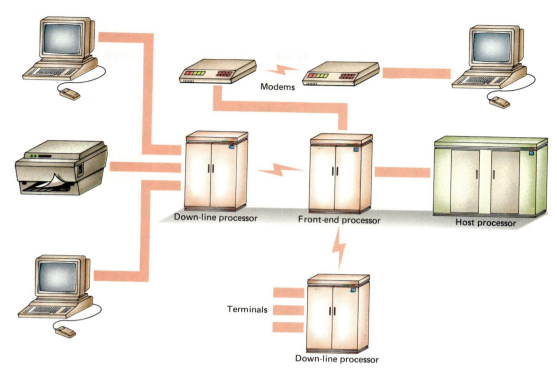

FIGURE 7–3 Hardware Components in Data Communications
Devices that handle the movement of data in a computer network are the modem, down-line processor, front-end processor, and host processor.

The Modem

If you have a micro, you have the capability of establishing a communications link between your microcomputer and any remote computer system in the world. However, to do this you must have ready access to a telephone line and your micro must be equipped with a *modem*. Currently, a little over 50% of all PCs are equipped with modems.

Telephone lines were designed for voice communication, not data communication. The **modem** (*m*odulator-*dem*odulator) converts micro-to-computer and terminal-to-computer electrical *digital* signals into *analog* signals so that the data can be transmitted over telephone lines (see Figure 7–4). The digital electrical signals are modulated to make sounds similar to those you hear on a touch-tone telephone. Upon reaching their destination, these analog signals are demodulated by another modem into computer-compatible electrical signals for processing. The procedure is reversed for computer-to-terminal or computer-to-micro communication. A modem is always required when you dial up the computer on a telephone line. The modulation-demodulation process is not needed when a micro or terminal is linked directly to a network.

Internal and External Modems. There are two types of modems for micros and terminals: *internal* and *external*. Most micros and terminals

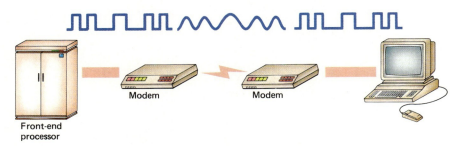

FIGURE 7–4 The Modulation/Demodulation Process
Electrical digital signals are modulated into analog signals for transmission over telephone lines and then demodulated for processing at the destination.

have internal modems; that is, the modem is on an optional add-on circuit board that is simply plugged into an empty expansion slot in the micro's processor unit or the terminal's housing. The external modem is a separate component, as illustrated in Figure 7–4, and is connected via a serial interface port (see Chapter 2, "Interacting with Micros"). To make the connection with a telephone line and either type of modem, you simply plug the telephone line into the modem just as you would when connecting the line to a telephone.

At the end of each month, this plant manager uses an external modem (under the telephone) to download cost data from the company's mainframe computer to the plant's minicomputer. He then compares the expenditures of the Boston plant with those of the Phoenix and Indianapolis plants.

Smart Modems. Modems have varying degrees of "intelligence" produced by embedded microprocessors. For instance, some modems can automatically dial up the computer (*auto-dial*), establish a link (*log on*), and even answer incoming calls from other computers (*auto-answer*). **Smart modems** also have made it possible to increase the rate at which data can be transmitted and received.

Acoustical Couplers. If you need a telephone hookup for voice conversations on the same telephone line used for data communication and do not want to disconnect the phone each time, you can purchase a modem with an **acoustical coupler**. To make the connection, you mount the telephone handset directly on the acoustical coupler. Acoustical couplers are essential items for travelers who routinely make micro-mainframe connections from public telephones.

The Down-Line Processor

The **down-line processor**, also called a **cluster controller**, is remote from the **host processor**. The host processor, which normally would be a minicomputer, a mainframe, or a supercomputer, is responsible for the overall control of a computer system. The down-line processor collects data from a number of low-speed devices, such as terminals and serial printers. It then "concentrates" the data—sending the data over a single communications channel (see Figure 7–5).

FIGURE 7–5 "Concentrating" Data for Remote Transmission
The down-line processor "concentrates" the data from several low-speed devices for transmission over a single high-speed line. At the host site, the front-end processor separates the data for processing. Data received from a front-end processor are interpreted by the down-line processor and routed to the appropriate device.

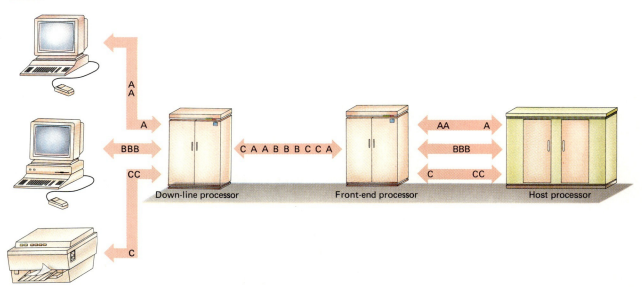

The down-line processor is an economic necessity when several low-speed terminals are located at one remote site. One high-speed line connecting the down-line processor to the host is considerably less expensive than several low-speed lines connecting each terminal to the host. An airline reservations counter might have 10 terminals. Each terminal is connected to a common down-line processor, which in turn is connected to a central **host computer**. The host computer has direct control over the terminals, processors, and peripheral devices that are linked to them. An airline might have one or several down-line processors at a given airport, depending on the volume of passenger traffic.

A microcomputer can be made to emulate the function of a down-line processor. This often occurs when a network of micros is linked to a mainframe computer.

The Front-End Processor

The terminal or computer sending a **message** is the *source*. The terminal or computer receiving the message is the *destination*. The **front-end processor** establishes the link between the source and destination in a process called **handshaking**.

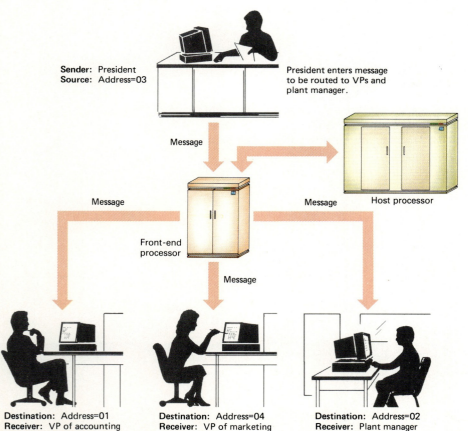

FIGURE 7–6 Message Routing
In the illustration, the president sends a message to two vice presidents and the plant manager. The front-end processor accepts the president's message for processing and routes it to the appropriate addresses.

If you think of messages as mail to be delivered to various points in a computer network, the front-end processor is the post office. Each computer system and terminal is assigned an **address**. The front-end processor uses these addresses to route messages to their destinations. The content of a message could be a prompt to the user, a user inquiry, a program instruction, an "electronic memo," or any type of information that can be transmitted electronically—even the image of a handwritten report. Figure 7–6 illustrates how a memo would be sent from the president of a company to two vice presidents and the plant manager. It is not uncommon for a front-end processor to control communications between a dozen down-line processors and 100 or more micros or terminals.

The front-end processor relieves the host processor of communications-related tasks, such as message routing, parity checking, code translation, editing, and cryptography (the encryption/decryption of data). This processor specialization permits the host to operate more efficiently and to devote more of its resources to processing applications programs.

> **MEMORY BITS**
>
> *Hardware for Data Communications*
> - Modem
> - Down-line processor
> - Front-end processor

7–4 THE DATA COMMUNICATIONS CHANNEL: DATA HIGHWAYS

Transmission Media

A **communications channel** is the facility through which electronic signals are transmitted between locations in a computer network. Data, text, and digitized images are transmitted as combinations of bits (0s and 1s). A *channel's capacity* is rated by the number of bits it can transmit per second. A regular telephone line can transmit up to 9600 **bits per second** (**bps**), or 9.6-K bps (thousands of bits per second). Under normal circumstances, a 9.6-K bps line would fill the screen of a typical video monitor with text in one or two seconds.

In practice, the word **baud** is often used interchangeably with bits per second (bps). But in reality they are quite different. Baud is a measure of the maximum number of electronic signals that can be transmitted via a communications channel. It is true that a 300-bps modem operates at 300 baud, but both 1200-bps and 2400-bps modems operate at 600 baud. A technical differentiation between baud and bits per second is beyond the scope of this book. Suffice it to say that when someone says *baud* and he or she is talking about computer-based communications, that person probably means bits per second. The erroneous use of *baud* is so common that some software packages that facilitate data communication ask you to specify baud when they actually want bits per second.

Data rates of 1500-K bps are available through common carriers such as American Telephone & Telegraph (AT&T). The channel, also called a **line** or a **data link**, may comprise one or a combination of the transmission media discussed next.

Telephone Lines. The same transmission facilities we use for voice communication via telephones can also be used to transmit data. This capa-

Copper wire in the telephone network eventually will replace the more versatile optical fiber. Laser-generated light pulses are transmitted through thin glass fibers. A pair of optical fibers can carry 1344 voice conversations and interactive data communications sessions simultaneously.

bility is provided by communications companies throughout the country and the world.

Optical Fiber. Very thin transparent fibers have been developed that eventually will replace the copper wire traditionally used in the telephone system. These hairlike **optical fibers** carry data faster and are lighter and less expensive than their copper-wire counterparts.

The differences between the data transmission rates of copper wire and optical fiber are tremendous. In the time it takes to transmit a single page of *Webster's Unabridged Dictionary* over copper wire (about 6 seconds), the entire dictionary could be transmitted over a single optical fiber.

Another of the many advantages of optical fiber is its contribution to data security. It is much more difficult for a computer criminal to intercept a signal sent over optical fiber (via a beam of light) than it is over copper wire (an electrical signal).

Coaxial Cable. **Coaxial cable** contains electrical wire and is constructed to permit high-speed data transmission with a minimum of signal distortion. Coaxial cable is laid along the ocean floor for intercontinental voice and data transmission. It is also used to connect terminals and computers in a "local" area (from a few feet to a few miles).

Microwave repeater stations, such as these atop the Haleakala Crater in Maui, Hawaii, relay voice, data, and television signals to transceivers or other repeater stations.

Microwave. Communications channels do not have to be wires or fibers. Data also can be transmitted via **microwave radio signals**. Transmission of these signals is *line-of-sight*; that is, the radio signal travels in a direct line from one repeater station to the next until it reaches its destination. Because of the curvature of the earth, microwave repeater stations are placed on the tops of mountains and towers, usually about 30 miles apart.

Satellites have made it possible to minimize the line-of-sight limitation. Satellites routinely are launched into orbit for the sole purpose of relaying data communications signals to and from earth stations. A satellite, which is essentially a repeater station, is launched and set in a **geosynchronous orbit** 22,300 miles above the earth. A geosynchronous orbit permits the communications satellite to maintain a fixed position relative to the surface of the earth. Each satellite can receive and retransmit signals to slightly less than half of the earth's surface; therefore, three satellites are required to cover the earth effectively (see Figure 7–7). The big advantage of satellites is that data can be transmitted from one location to any number of other locations anywhere on (or near) our planet.

FIGURE 7–7 Satellite Data Transmission
Three satellites in geosynchronous orbit provide worldwide data transmission service.

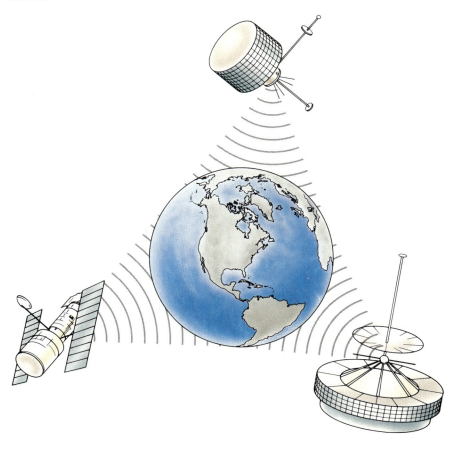

CHAPTER 7 Data Communications and Networks

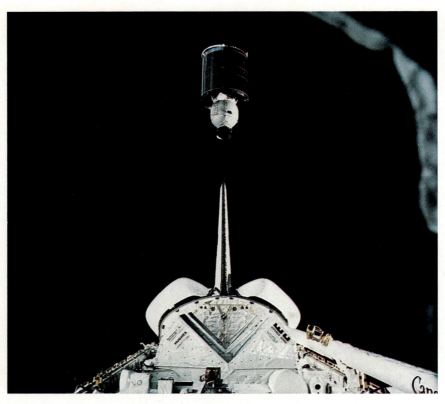

This communications satellite is being released from the space shuttle en route to a geosynchronous orbit 22,300 miles above the earth.

In satellite communications, data are transmitted first to an earth station where giant antennae route the signals to another earth station via a communications satellite. The signals are then transmitted to their destination over a different type of communications channel.

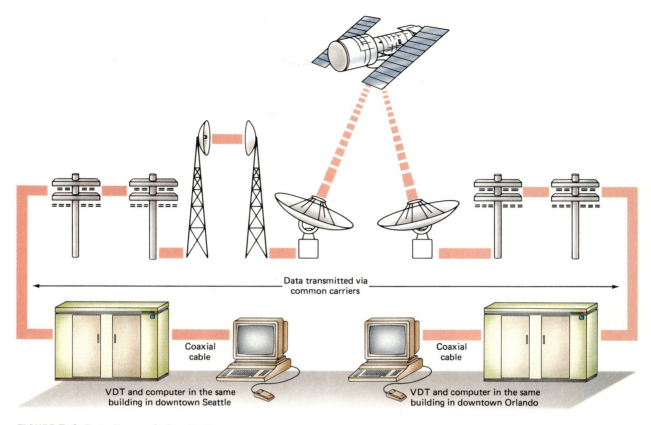

FIGURE 7-8 Data Transmission Path
It's more the rule than the exception that data are carried over several transmission media between source and destination.

Data Transmission in Practice

A communications channel from Computer A in Seattle, Washington, to Computer B in Orlando, Florida (see Figure 7-8), usually would consist of several different transmission media. The connection between Computer A and a terminal in the same building is probably coaxial cable. The Seattle company might use a communications company such as AT&T to transmit the data. AT&T then would send the data through a combination of transmission facilities that might include copper wire, optical fiber, and microwave radio signals.

7-5 DATA TRANSMISSION SERVICES

Common Carriers

It is impractical, not to mention illegal, for companies to string their own coaxial cables between two locations, such as Philadelphia and New York City. It is also impractical for them to set their own satellites in orbit. Therefore, companies turn to **common carriers** such as AT&T

and Western Union to provide communications channels. Communications common carriers, which are regulated by the Federal Communications Commission (FCC), offer two basic types of service: private lines and switched lines.

A **private line** (or **leased line**) provides a dedicated data communications channel between any two points in a computer network. The charge for a private line is based on channel capacity (bps) and distance (air miles).

A **switched line** (or **dial-up line**) is available strictly on a time-and-distance charge, similar to a long-distance telephone call. You make a connection by "dialing up" the computer, then a modem sends and receives data.

As a rule of thumb, a private line is the least expensive alternative if you expect to use the channel more than three hours a day and you do not need the flexibility to connect with several different computers.

Specialized Common Carriers

A **specialized common carrier**, such as a **value-added network** (**VAN**), may or may not use the transmission facilities of a common carrier, but in each case it "adds value" to the transmission service. The value added over and above the standard services of the common carriers may include electronic mail, data encryption/decryption, access to commercial data bases, and code conversion for communication between incompatible computers. Not only do VANs such as Tymshares's Tymnet and GTE's Telenet offer expanded services but the basic communications service provided by the VAN also may be less expensive than the same service from a common carrier.

7–6 NETWORKS: LINKING COMPUTERS AND PEOPLE

Network Topologies

Each time you use the telephone, you use the world's largest computer network—the telephone system. A telephone is an endpoint, or a **node**, connected to a network of computers that route your voice signals to any one of the 500 million telephones (other nodes) in the world. In a computer network the node can be a terminal or another computer. Computer networks are configured to meet the specific requirements of an organization. The basic computer **network topologies**—star, ring, and bus—are illustrated in Figure 7–9. A network topology is a description of the possible physical connections within a network. The topology is the configuration of the hardware and indicates which pairs of nodes are able to communicate.

The **star topology** involves a centralized host computer connected to a number of smaller computer systems. The smaller computer systems communicate with one another through the host and usually share the host computer's data base. Both the central computer and the distributed computer systems (usually microcomputers or minicomputers) are connected to terminals (micros or video display terminals). Any terminal can

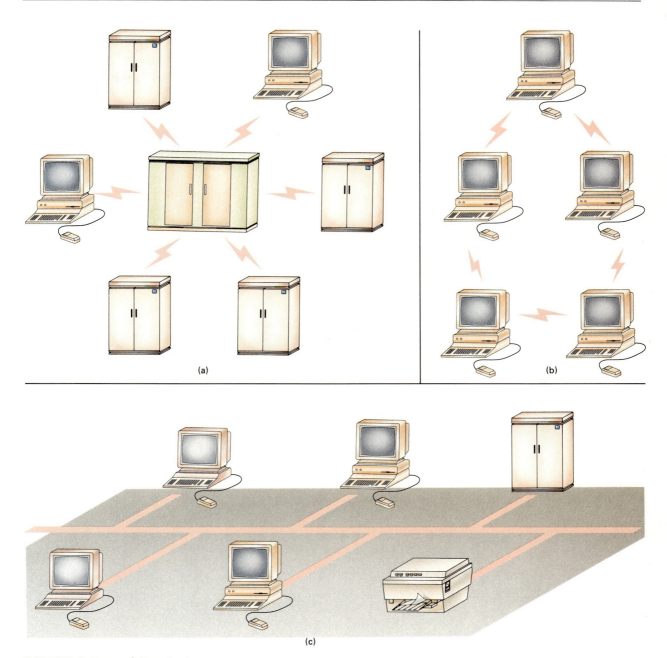

FIGURE 7-9 Network Topologies
(a) star; (b) ring; (c) bus.

communicate with any other terminal in the network. Banks usually have a large home-office computer system with a star network of minicomputer or microcomputer systems in the branch banks.

The **ring topology** involves computer systems that are approximately the same size, with no one computer system as the focal point of the network. When one system routes a message to another system, it is passed around the ring until it reaches its destination.

The **bus topology** permits the connection of terminals, peripheral devices, and microcomputers along a central cable called a **transmission medium**. It is easy to add devices or delete them from the network. Bus topologies are most appropriate when the linked devices are physically close to one another. (See the discussion of local area networks that follows.)

A pure form of any of these three topologies is seldom found in practice. Most computer networks are *hybrids*—combinations of topologies.

The Micro-Mainframe Link

Micros, initially designed for use by a single individual, have even greater potential when they can be linked with mainframe computers. To give micros this dual-function capability, vendors have developed the necessary hardware and software to enable some **micro-mainframe links**. There are three types of micro-mainframe links:

1. The microcomputer serves as a "dumb" terminal (that is, I/O only with no processing) linked to the mainframe. Micros can be set up via software to emulate (act like) any popular terminal. When acting like a terminal, the micro is said to be in **terminal emulation mode**.
2. Microcomputer users request that data and/or programs be *downloaded* (mainframe-to-micro transmission of data) from the mainframe to their micros for processing. Upon completion of processing, user data may be *uploaded* from their microcomputers to the mainframe.
3. Both microcomputer and mainframe work together to process data and produce information.

Micro-mainframe links of the first two types are well within the state of the art, but achieving the third is more involved. The tremendous differences in the way computers and software are designed make complete integration of micro-mainframe activities difficult and, for some combinations of micros and mainframes, impossible.

7-7 LOCAL AREA NETWORKS

LAN Defined

A **local area network** (**LAN**), or **local net**, is a system of hardware, software, and communications channels that connects devices in close proximity, such as in a suite of offices. A local net permits the movement of data (including text, voice, and graphic images) between mainframe computers, personal computers, terminals, and I/O devices. For example, your micro can be connected to another micro, to mainframes, and to shared resources such as printers and disk storage. The distance separating devices in the local net may vary from a few feet to a few miles. As few as two and as many as several hundred micros can be linked on a single local area network.

The unique feature of a local net is that a common carrier is not necessary for transmitting data between computers, terminals, and shared resources. Because of the proximity of devices in local nets, a company can install its own communications channels (such as coaxial cable or optical fiber).

The ability to share valuable resources is the fundamental reason that the trend is to incorporate more and more PCs into local area networks. Currently about 20% of all PCs are part of a LAN. Industry forecasters are predicting that the percentage will grow rapidly during the decade of the 1990s, perhaps to 70% or 80%. In a LAN, data, applications software, links to mainframes, communications capabilities (for example, modems), CD-ROM data bases (for example, an on-line national telephone directory), add-on boards (for example, fax boards), and other resources can be shared among users of the system. LANs make good business sense because available resources can be shared. For example, the cost of a LAN-based spreadsheet is far less than the cost of a spreadsheet for each PC in the LAN. Also, in a normal office setting, a single page printer can service the printing needs of up to 10 micro users.

LANs have opened the door to applications impossible in the one-person, one-computer environment. For example, users on the network can send electronic mail to one another. When everyone's calendar is on-line, scheduling meetings is a snap.

A local area network links microcomputers at this company so that managers and administrative staff can share hardware, software, and data base resources.

Like computers, automobiles, and just about everything else, local nets can be built at various levels of sophistication. At the most basic level, they permit the interconnection of PCs in a department so that users can send messages to one another and share files and printers. The more sophisticated local nets permit the interconnection of mainframes, micros, and the gamut of peripheral devices throughout a large but geographically constrained area, such as a cluster of buildings.

In the near future you will be able to plug a terminal into a communications channel just as you would plug a telephone line into a telephone jack. This type of data communications capability is being installed in the new "smart" office buildings and even in some hotel rooms.

Local nets are often integrated into "long-haul" networks. For example, a bank will link home-office teller terminals to the central computer via a local net. But for long-haul data communication, the bank's branch offices must rely on common carriers.

LAN Hardware and Software

The three basic hardware components in a PC-based LAN are the network interface cards, or NICs; the cables that connect the nodes in the network; and the servers.

- *Network interface cards.* The NIC, which was described briefly in Chapter 3, "Processors and Platforms," is an add-on card that facilitates and controls the exchange of data between the micros in a LAN. Each PC in a LAN must be equipped with an NIC. As an add-on card, the NIC is connected directly to the PC's bus. The cables that link the PCs are physically connected to the NICs.

    The physical transfer of data and programs between nodes is controlled by the access method embedded in the network interface card's ROM. The two most popular access methods are *token-ring* and *Ethernet.*

    In a token-ring network, an electronic *token* travels around a ring of nodes in the form of a *header* (see Figure 7–10). The header contains control signals, including one specifying whether the token is "free" or carrying a message. A sender node captures a free token as it travels from node to node, changes it to "busy," and adds the message. The resulting *message frame* travels around the ring to the addressee's NIC, which copies the message and returns the message frame to the sender. The sender's NIC removes the message frame from the ring and circulates a new free token.

    Ethernet, which employs the *CSMA/CD* (Carrier Sense Multiple Access/Collision Detection) access method, is based on the bus network topology. To gain access to the network, a node with a message to be sent automatically requests network service from the network software. The request might result in a "line busy" signal, in which case the node waits a fraction of a second and tries again, and again, until the line is free. Upon assuming control of the line, the node sends the message and then relinquishes control of the line to another node.

CHAPTER 7 Data Communications and Networks

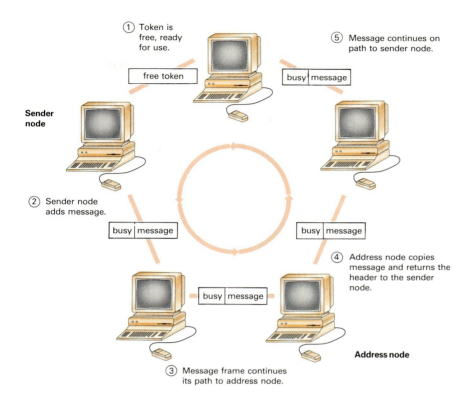

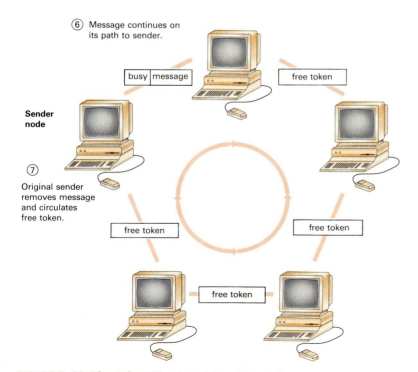

FIGURE 7–10 The Token-Ring Local Area Network

- *Cables.* Three kinds of cables are connected to the network interface cards: twisted-pair cable (the same four-wire cables used to connect telephones in a home), coaxial cable, and optical fiber.
- *Servers.* A **server** is a LAN component that can be shared by users on the LAN. The three most popular servers are the **file server**, **print server**, and **communications server**. These server functions may reside in a single micro or they can be distributed among the micros that make up the LAN. When the server functions are consolidated, the server micro usually is *dedicated* to servicing the LAN and, therefore, is not used for applications. Until recently, you would purchase a traditional single-user micro and make it a dedicated server. This continues to be a viable option with small to medium-sized LANs, but not in large LANs with 100 or more users. Recently micro vendors began manufacturing powerful micros designed specifically as network servers. These micros can comfortably handle hundreds of micros on a single LAN.

The file server normally is a dedicated micro with a high-capacity disk for storing the data and programs shared by the network users. For example, the master client file, word processing software, spreadsheet software, and so on would be stored on the server disk. When a user wants to begin a spreadsheet session, the spreadsheet software is downloaded from the file server to the user's RAM.

The print server typically is housed in the same dedicated micro as the file server. The print server handles user print jobs and controls at least one printer. If needed, the server *spools* print jobs to disk until the requested printer is available.

The micros at this engineering firm are on a LAN. The tower micro on the floor doubles as a file server for the entire network. All applications software is downloaded from the file server.

The communications server provides communications links external to the LAN—that is, micro-mainframe links and links to other networks. To accomplish this service, the communications server controls one or more modems.

The **LAN operating system**, which is the nucleus of a local area network, is actually several pieces of software. Each processing component in the LAN has a piece of the LAN operating system resident in its RAM. The controlling software resides in the file server's RAM. The pieces interact with one another to enable the nodes to share resources and communication. Two of the most popular LAN operating systems are Novell's *NetWare* and Microsoft's *LAN Manager*.

The individual user in a LAN might appear to be interacting with an operating system, such as MS-DOS or OS/2. However, the resident LAN software *redirects* certain requests to the appropriate LAN component. For example, a print request would be redirected to the print server.

> **MEMORY BITS**
>
> *Networking*
> - Network topologies
>   Star
>   Ring
>   Bus
> - Micro-mainframe link
> - Local area network
>   Also called LAN or local net
>   Components: NICs, cables, and servers

Bridges and Gateways

Companies with established networks use gateway and bridge technologies to achieve connectivity in the various networks. **Gateways** help alleviate the problems of linking incompatible micros, minis, and mainframes. A gateway is a combination of hardware and software that permits networks using different communications protocols (sets of rules by which data are transmitted) to "talk" to one another. The use of a gateway normally implies a requirement for a protocol conversion. Most commercially available gateways connect microcomputer-based local area networks to mainframes.

Some companies have many small and medium-sized departmental local area networks, all of the same type. Instead of integrating these microcomputer-based LANs into a large one, they use **bridges** to enable these LANs to continue operation in their present format with the added advantage of being able to "talk" to each other. Bridges are hardware devices that permit communication between devices in local area networks of the same type. Because all connected LANs use the same communication protocol, bridges are said to be protocol-independent. Bridges provide a relatively straightforward solution to enable LANs of the same type to communicate with one another.

For the foreseeable future, many connectivity questions can be answered with planning, restrictive policies, gateways, and bridges. However, with total connectivity the goal of most progressive companies, the computer community will continue to focus its sights on overcoming the barriers to it.

7–8 LINE CONTROL: COMMUNICATIONS PROTOCOLS

Communications protocols are rules established to govern the way data are transmitted in a computer network. A number of different protocols are in common use. For example, X.12 is the standard for electronic data interchange (EDI); X.25 is used for packet switching; X.75 is used for

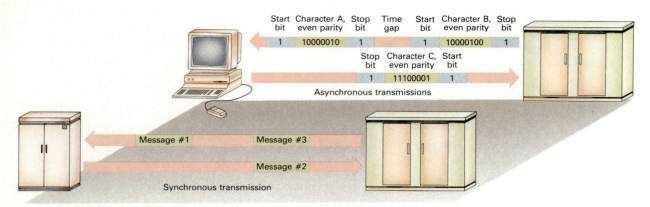

FIGURE 7–11 Asynchronous and Synchronous Transmission of Data
Asynchronous data transmission takes place at irregular intervals. In asynchronous transmission, the message is typically a single character. Synchronous data transmission requires timed synchronization between sending and receiving devices. The message is typically a block of characters.

interconnections between networks of different countries; XON/XOFF is the de facto standard for microcomputer data communications; and XMODEM is the defacto standard for uploading files from and downloading files to microcomputers. Protocols fall into two general classifications, **asynchronous** and **synchronous** (see Figure 7–11).

Asynchronous Transmission

In asynchronous transmission, data are transmitted at irregular intervals on an as-needed basis. A modem is usually involved in asynchronous transmission. *Start/stop bits* are appended to the beginning and end of each message. The start/stop bits signal the receiving terminal/computer at the beginning and end of the message. In microcomputer data communications, the message is a single byte or character. Asynchronous transmission, sometimes called *start/stop transmission*, is best suited for data communication involving low-speed I/O devices, such as serial printers and micros functioning as remote terminals.

Both sending and receiving devices maintain and coordinate data communications through *handshaking*. They do this by sending and receiving data in accordance with the rules set forth in a data communications protocol. In the microcomputer environment, the **XON/XOFF** (pronounced *ex ON ex OFF*) data communications protocol is the de facto standard. There are other protocols for data communications, but the most important thing to remember is that both the sending and receiving devices must adhere to the same data communications protocol.

The protocol used to upload and download files may be different from the data communications protocol. The **XMODEM** protocol is the de facto standard for file transfer activities to and from micros. Again, the sending and receiving devices must follow the same file transfer protocol.

Synchronous Transmission

In synchronous transmission, the source and destination operate in timed synchronization to enable high-speed data transfer. Start/stop bits are not required in synchronous transmission. Data transmission between computers, including those in a LAN, and between down-line processors and front-end processors is normally synchronous.

7-9 USING MICRO-BASED COMMUNICATIONS SOFTWARE

The Function of Communications Software

Communications software expands the capability of a microcomputer. With communications software, a micro becomes more than a small stand-alone computer: It becomes capable of interacting with a remote computer, in the next room or in Japan.

In a nutshell, communications software performs two basic functions.

1. *Terminal emulation.* Communications software transforms a micro into a video display terminal (VDT) that can be linked to another computer.
2. *File transfer.* Communications software enables the transfer of files between a micro and another computer.

Before accomplishing either of these functions, an electronic link must be established between the micro and the other computer. To establish this link the micro user initiates the **log-on procedure**. Typically, the log-on procedure involves the following.

1. A remote computer (another micro or a mainframe) is dialed up via the telephone system. The remote computer answers with a high-pitched tone.
2. A preassigned **password** and **personal identification number**, or **PIN**, is entered. The use of passwords and PINs helps protect a computer system against unauthorized access and use.

Once the remote computer validates the password, PIN, or both, the link is established. At this time, the remote computer normally will prompt the end user to enter a command or it will present the user with a menu of options.

Terminal Emulation. Supercomputers, mainframes, minis, and multiuser micros are host processors that can provide service to remote terminals. Supercomputers and mainframes can serve thousands of end users at remote terminals. Multiuser micros can serve about a dozen end users. When an end user at a terminal logs onto (establishes a link) a host computer, the host immediately responds by asking the end user to enter the type of terminal he or she is using. Of course, a micro is not a terminal, but with the aid of communications software, a micro can emulate, or act like, one of the terminals that can be interfaced with the host. Com-

This executive is using communications software to enable his PC to emulate a VT-100 terminal. By doing this he can establish an on-line link to his company's mainframe computer.

munications software can transform a micro into any of a variety of popular terminals.

The two most distinguishing characteristics of terminals are the keyboard layout and the manner in which they send and receive data. When a micro is in **terminal emulation mode**, the keyboard, monitor, and data interface function like that of the terminal being emulated. From the host computer's perspective, the workstation being serviced is a terminal (for example, the DEC VT-100 terminal), not a micro.

Most terminals are *dumb terminals*; that is, they do not have stand-alone processing or storage capabilities. Communications software transforms a micro into an *intelligent terminal* that can provide capabilities above and beyond that of the terminal being emulated: For example, it can store an interactive session on a disk file.

File Transfers. Once the link between the micro and host has been established, data, program, or text files can be downloaded from disk storage on the host computer to disk storage on the micro. Files also can be uploaded. The file transfer capability afforded by communications software can be invaluable when you need to transfer files between computers.

Preparing for an Interactive Session with a Remote Computer

When you use a PC, a modem, and data communications software to establish a link with another computer, the communications software will prompt you to specify the *telephone number* to be called and certain data communications **parameters**. A parameter is a descriptor that can take on different values. These parameters may include:

- *Terminal emulation.* Specify the type of terminal to be emulated. The options might include the generic TTY, the DEC VT-100, DEC VT-52, IBM 3101, and others.
- *Communications protocol.* Select protocol (for example, XON/XOFF, XMODEM).
- *Data flow.* Select half or full duplex. Communication channels that transmit data in both directions, but not at the same time, are called **half-duplex**. A channel that transmits data in both directions at the same time is called **full-duplex**. A full-duplex line is simply two half-duplex lines dedicated to the same link. Half-duplex channels do not permit the echoing of user keystrokes on the display screen.
- *Data bits.* Specify the number of bits in the message (the bits within the start/stop bits). Typically, the character is transmitted with *seven* or *eight bits*.
- *Parity checking.* In data communications, data in the form of coded characters are continuously transferred at high rates of speed between the micro and the remote computer. Each device uses a built-in checking procedure to help ensure that the transmission is complete and accurate. This procedure is called **parity checking**.

Logically, an ASCII character may be represented using *seven bits*, but physically there are actually *eight bits* transmitted between computers. Confused? Don't be. The extra **parity bit**, which is not part of the character code, is used in the parity-checking procedure to detect whether a bit has been accidentally changed, or "dropped," during transmission. A dropped bit results in a **parity error**.

To maintain **odd parity** (see Figure 7–12), the extra parity bit is turned *on* when the seven-bit ASCII byte has an *even* number of on-bits. When the ASCII byte has an *odd* number of on-bits, the parity bit is turned *off*. The receiving device checks for this condition. A

FIGURE 7–12 Parity Checking
The letter B is entered and transmitted to a remote computer for processing. Because the ASCII B has an even number of bits, an on-bit must be added to maintain odd parity. The remote computer checks the parity before accepting the transmission for processing.

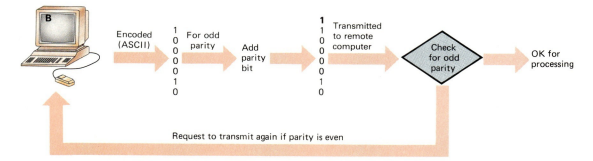

parity error occurs when an even number of on-bits is encountered. When the receiving device detects a parity error, it sends a message to the sending device requesting that the message be transmitted again. Some computer systems are designed to maintain **even parity**, but odd and even parity work in a similar manner.

Parity checking is optional when using communications software. As a rule, if the message length (number of **data bits**) is specified as seven bits, parity checking is activated, but if it is specified as eight, parity checking is not activated. If activated, the parity-checking procedure must be the same (even or odd) for both the sending and receiving devices.

In response to the parity checking parameter, select *odd*, *even*, or *none*, as appropriate.

- *Bits per second* (sometimes labeled as *baud*). Select the appropriate transmission rate: 300, 1200, 2400, 4800, or 9600 bps.
- *Stop bits*. Stop is actually a misnomer in that it is actually a timing unit. Usually you would select *1* for micro-based data communications. Other options might be *1.5* or *2*.
- *Echo*. Typically, the host computer will **echo,** or return, the characters that are received from a micro; that is, the characters entered at the micro appear on the micro's monitor in the context of those originated by the host computer. In effect, the entire interactive session is displayed when the echo is on. When the host does not echo characters, the user will have to specify *local echo* to display characters entered via the keyboard.

Depending on the protocol and communications package, you may need to specify other parameters as well.

Communications software offers a variety of handy, time-saving features. For example, you can store the settings (parameters) for a particular bulletin board, information service, or mainframe computer in a *communications profile*. To establish a link with another computer, simply recall and activate the appropriate communications profile. From there, the communications software takes over and automatically dials and logs onto the remote computer. It will even redial if it gets a busy signal. A micro with a modem and communications software can be on the receiving end as well: It can automatically answer "calls" from other computers.

Most communications software packages provide the feature that enables the micro to *capture* all input/output during an interactive session in an ASCII file on disk. At a later time the user can recall the session from disk storage with word processing software and browse through it at a more leisurely pace. Of course, all or part of the information gathered during an interactive session can be integrated into word processing documents, such as memos, letters, and reports.

Communications Software in Practice

Information Services, Bulletin Boards, and E-mail. A variety of *information services* are available to microcomputer owners with communications capabilities. A few of these services include up-to-date real estate information, interactive health information, and movie reviews, to mention a few. You can even shop at home in the comfort of your own living room for just about anything from microcomputers to automobiles. These and other services are discussed in Chapter 1, "Micros and Personal Computing."

Most cities with a population of 25,000 or more have at least one electronic *bulletin-board system*, often sponsored by a local computer club. Members "post" messages, announcements, for-sale notices, and so on, "on" the computer bulletin board by transmitting them to a central computer—usually another micro. To scan the bulletin board, members again use communications software to link to the central computer. There are hundreds of regional and national special-interest bulletin boards that focus on anything from matchmaking to UFOs.

Communications software also enables you to send and receive *electronic mail*, or *E-mail*, either through a local bulletin board, a public electronic mail service, or an information service.

Information services, bulletin boards, and E-mail are the tip of the applications iceberg. Communications software lets you **fax** text and images (send an electronic version) directly from an electronic file to a remote **facsimile** machine or another micro. Facsimile equipment transfers images of hard-copy documents via telephone lines to a remote location. Communications software also enables managers to tap into their company's mainframe-based information resources.

Telecommuting and the Cottage Industry. In the coming years, we will probably see a shift to smaller briefcases. Why? With communications software and an ever-growing number of home computers, people won't need to lug their paperwork between home and office every day. A great many white-collar workers at all levels do much of their work on computers. Working at home is simply a matter of establishing a link between their home and office computers. This is sometimes referred to as **telecommuting**. In the years to come, many white-collar workers will elect to telecommute at least one day a week.

The combination of microcomputers and communications software has fueled the growth of *cottage industries*. The world has been made a little more compact with the computer revolution. Stockbrokers, financial planners, writers, programmers, and people from a wide variety of professions may not need to "go to the office," so they can live wherever they choose. Micros make it possible for these people to access needed information, communicate with their clients, and even deliver their work (programs, stories, reports, or recommendations).

Summary. Microcomputers have placed the power of computers at our fingertips. Communications software expands that capability by enabling micro users to become a part of any number of computer networks. Once part of the network, a user can take advantage of the awesome power of mainframe computers, the information in their data bases, and the opportunity to communicate electronically with others on the network.

This stockbroker uses his micro and communications software to telecommute at least one day a week; that is, he commutes to work via data communications. Once on-line, he can keep in touch with office activities and retrieve critical information.

SUMMARY OUTLINE AND IMPORTANT TERMS

7-1 DATA COMMUNICATIONS: FROM ONE ROOM TO THE WORLD. **Connectivity** facilitates the electronic communication between companies, end user computing, and the free flow of information within an enterprise. Modern businesses use **data communications** to transmit data and information at high speeds from one location to the next. Data communications, **teleprocessing (TP)**, and **telecommunications** make an information system more accessible to the people who use it. The integration of computer systems via data communications is referred to as a **computer network**.

7-2 THE BEGINNING OF AN ERA: COOPERATIVE COMPUTING. This is the era of **cooperative computing**. To obtain meaningful, accurate, and timely information, businesses have decided they must cooperate internally and externally to take full advantage of available information. To encourage internal cooperation, they are promoting intracompany networking. To compete in a world market, they are encouraging intercompany networking, or **electronic data interchange (EDI)**.

Connectivity refers to the degree to which hardware sevices can be functionally linked to one another. Some people expand the scope of connectivity to include other aspects of information systems, such as software and data bases. Technical specialists must juggle **communication protocols** to achieve varying degrees of connectivity. The ideal implementation of connectivity is referred to as **total connectivity**.

7-3 DATA COMMUNICATIONS HARDWARE. The data communications hardware used to facilitate the transmission of data from one remote location to another includes **modems, down-line processors** (also called **cluster controllers**), and **front-end processors**. Modems modulate and demodulate signals so that data can be transmitted over telephone lines. Down-line processors and front-end processors are special-function processors; they not only convert the signal to a format compatible with the transmission facility but also relieve the **host processor** of a number of processing tasks associated with data communications. One of the duties of the front-end processor is to establish the link between source and destination for sending and receiving messages in a process called **handshaking**.

7-4 THE DATA COMMUNICATIONS CHANNEL: DATA HIGHWAYS. A **communications channel** (**line**, or **data link**) is the facility through which data are transmitted between locations in a computer network. A channel's capacity is rated by the number of bits it can transmit per second (**bits per second**, or **bps**). In practice, the word **baud** is often used interchangeably with bits per second; in reality, they are quite different.

A channel may consist of one or more of the following transmission media: telephone lines, **optical fiber**, **coaxial cable**, and **microwave radio signals**. Satellites are essentially microwave repeater stations that maintain a **geosynchronous orbit** around the earth.

7-5 DATA TRANSMISSION SERVICES. **Common carriers** provide communications channels to the public, and lines can be arranged to suit a particular application. A **private**, or **leased**, **line** provides a dedicated communications channel. A **switched**, or **dial-up**, **line** is available on a time-and-dis-

CHAPTER 7 Data Communications and Networks   **229**

tance-charge basis. **Specialized common carriers**, such as **value-added networks (VANs)**, offer expanded transmission services.

7–6 **NETWORKS: LINKING COMPUTERS AND PEOPLE.** Computer systems, or **nodes**, are linked together to form a computer network. The basic patterns for configuring computer systems within a computer network are **star topology**, **ring topology**, and **bus topology**. In practice, most networks are actually *hybrids* of these **network topologies**.

The connection of microcomputers to a mainframe computer is called a **micro-mainframe link**. When acting like a terminal, the micro is said to be in **terminal emulation mode**. With this link, microcomputer users download/upload data from/to the mainframe as needed.

7–7 **LOCAL AREA NETWORKS.** A **local area network (LAN)**, or **local net**, is a system of hardware, software, and communications channels that connects devices in close proximity and does not involve a common carrier. A local net permits the movement of data between mainframe computers, personal computers, terminals, and I/O devices. The ability to share valuable resources is the fundamental reason that the trend is to incorporate more and more PCs into local area networks.

The three basic hardware components in a PC-based LAN are the network interface cards, or NICs; the cables that connect the nodes in the network; and the servers. The physical transfer of data and programs between LAN nodes is controlled by the access method embedded in the network interface card's ROM, usually the *token-ring* or *Ethernet* access method.

A **server** is a LAN component that can be shared by users on the LAN. The three most popular servers are the **file server**, **print server**, and **communications server**.

The **LAN operating system** is actually several pieces of software, a part of which resides in each LAN component's RAM.

Companies with established networks use **gateway** and **bridge** technologies to achieve connectivity within the various networks.

7–8 **LINE CONTROL: COMMUNICATIONS PROTOCOLS.** Communications protocols are rules for transmitting data. The **asynchronous** protocol begins and ends each message with start/stop bits and is used primarily for low-speed data transmission. The de facto standard protocols for microcomputer data communications are **XON/XOFF** and **XMODEM**. The **synchronous** protocol permits the source and destination to communicate in timed synchronization for high-speed data transmission.

7–9 **USING MICRO-BASED COMMUNICATIONS SOFTWARE.** Communications software performs two basic functions: *terminal emulation* and *file transfer*. Typically, the **log-on procedure** involves dialing the remote computer and entering a **password** and **personal identification number**, or **PIN**.

When a micro is in **terminal emulation mode**, the keyboard, monitor, and data interface are like that of the terminal that is being emulated. Communications software transforms a micro into an *intelligent terminal* that can provide capabilities above and beyond that of the terminal being emulated.

When using communications software, specify the following **parameters**: type of terminal to be emulated, communications protocol, data flow (**half-duplex** or **full-duplex**), data bits, **parity checking** activated (typically activated when the message length, or number of **data bits**, is specified to be 7 bits), type of **parity checking** (**odd parity**, **even parity**, or none), bits per second (sometimes labeled as *baud*), stop bits, and **echo**. Communications software allows you to store the settings for a particular remote computer in a communications profile.

A variety of information services are available to microcomputer owners with communications capabilities. *Bulletin-board systems* are popular throughout the country. Communications software also opens the door to sending and receiving electronic mail.

In the years to come, many white-collar workers will elect to **telecommute** at least one day a week. The combination of microcomputers and communications software has fueled the growth of cottage industries.

REVIEW EXERCISES

1. Would EDI be more closely associated with intercompany networking or intracompany networking?
2. What is meant by *geosynchronous orbit*, and how does it relate to data transmission via satellite?
3. What is the unit of measure for the capacity of a data communications channel?
4. Expand the following acronyms: TP, bps, VAN, and LAN.
5. What is the purpose of a down-line processor?
6. What is the relationship between data communications and a computer network?
7. At what channel capacity is the bits per second equal to the baud?
8. What computerese term refers to the degree to which hardware devices can be functionally linked to one another?
9. What device converts digital signals into analog signals for transmission over telephone lines? Why is it necessary?
10. Why is it not advisable to increase the distance between microwave relay stations to 200 miles?
11. What is the ideal implementation of connectivity called?
12. What is the purpose of the X.12 communications protocol?
13. Describe circumstances in which a leased line would be preferable to a dial-up line.
14. Consider this situation: A remote line printer is capable of printing 800 lines per minute (70 characters per line average). Line capacity options are 2.4-K, 4.8-K, or 9.6-K bps. Data are transmitted according to the ASCII encoding system (seven bits per character). What capacity would you recommend for a communications channel to permit the printer to operate at capacity?
15. What are the two basic functions performed by communications software?
16. Describe what is involved in a typical log-on procedure.
17. What is the advantage of a communications profile?
18. Which LAN access method passes a token from node to node?

SELF-TEST (by section)

7-1 a. The general area of data communications encompasses telecommunications. (T/F)
  b. The integration of computer systems, terminals, and communication links is referred to as a _____.

7-2 a. Using computers and data communications to transmit data electronically between companies is called: (a) EDI, (b) DIE, or (c) DEI?
  b. A company either has total connectivity or it has no connectivity. (T/F)

7-3 a. The modem converts computer-to-terminal electrical _____ (digital *or* analog) signals into _____ (digital *or* analog) signals so that the data can be transmitted over telephone lines.
  b. The terminal sending a message is the source, and the computer receiving the message is the destination. (T/F)
  c. Another name for a front-end processor is cluster controller. (T/F)

7-4 a. It is more difficult for a computer criminal to tap into an optical fiber than a copper telephone line. (T/F)
  b. A 9600-bits-per-second channel is the same as a: (a) 9.6-kps line, (b) 9.6-K bps line, or (c) dual 4800X2-K bps line.

7-5 a. The two basic types of service offered by common carriers are a private line and a leased line. (T/F)
  b. A value-added network will always use the transmission facilities of a common carrier. (T/F)

7-6 a. An endpoint in a network of computers is called a _____.
  b. When acting like a terminal, the micro is said to be in _____ mode.
  c. The central cable called a transmission medium is most closely associated with which network topology: (a) ring, (b) star, or (c) bus?

7-7 a. A LAN is designed for "long-haul" data communications. (T/F)
  b. Which of the following is not a popular LAN access method: (a) token-ring, (b) Ethernet, or (c) parity checking?
  c. The LAN operating system resides entirely in the server processor's RAM. (T/F)

7-8 a. In asynchronous data transmission, start/stop bits are appended to the beginning and end of each message. (T/F)
  b. The _____ communications protocol is the standard for electronic data interchange.

7-9 a. Parity checking is mandatory when downloading data but it is optional when uploading data. (T/F)
  b. A micro with a modem and communications software can make calls to other computers but it cannot receive calls. (T/F)
  c. A channel that transmits data in both directions at the same time is called _____.

Self-test answers. **7-1** (a) F; (b) computer network. **7-2** (a) a; (b) F. **7-3** (a) digital, analog; (b) T; (c) F. **7-4** (a) T; (b) b. **7-5** (a) F; (b) F. **7-6** (a) node; (b) terminal emulation; (c) c. **7-7** (a) F; (b) c; (c) F. **7-8** (a) T; (b) X.12. **7-9** (a) F; (b) F; (c) full-duplex.

CHAPTER 8
MICROCOMPUTER SYSTEMS

STUDENT LEARNING OBJECTIVES

- ▶ To discuss the principles and use of information systems, decision support systems, and expert systems.
- ▶ To describe and order the major activities that take place during each phase of system development.
- ▶ To demonstrate an understanding of the principles and use of system and program design techniques.
- ▶ To describe the steps to program development.
- ▶ To distinguish between the different approaches to system conversion.
- ▶ To explain the concept of prototyping.
- ▶ To identify points of security vulnerability for the computer and for information systems.

8-1 TYPES OF MICRO SYSTEMS

Information Systems

Timesaving microcomputer productivity tools, such as word processing and spreadsheet, represent only one facet of a micro's processing potential. Micros also collect and analyze experimental data; they help us learn; they monitor the environmental and security systems in our homes; and they support our personal, departmental, and corporate **information systems**. An information system is a computer-based system that provides *data processing capability* and *information for making decisions*.

We combine *hardware*, *software*, *people*, *procedures*, and *data* to create an *information system* (see Figure 8–1). A micro-based information system provides an individual, department, or small company with *data processing* capabilities and with *information* that people need to make better, more informed decisions. The data processing capability, or the handling and processing of data, is only one facet of an information system. A complete information system provides decision makers with on-demand reports and inquiry capabilities as well as routine periodic

FIGURE 8–1 Information System Ingredients and Capabilities

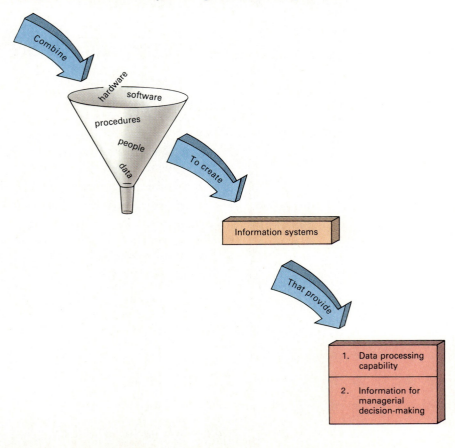

The need for information exists in all fields of endeavor, not just business. These astrophysicists rely on computer-generated information to help them in their study of the formation and growth of galaxies.

reports. Because an information system helps management make business decisions, it is sometimes called a **management information system** (**MIS**). In practice, the terms *information system*, *management information system*, and *MIS* are used interchangeably.

A little historical perspective may help you relate micros to business information systems. During the 1950s, first-generation computers handled the computing needs of large banks, automobile manufacturers, and major corporations in other industries. Early commercial computers were behemoths that occupied huge rooms and were leased from the computer manufacturer for as much as $30,000 a month (about $200,000 of today's dollars). These computers, however, did mostly *data processing*; that is, updating inventory, printing payroll checks, and so on. Computers of that era simply were not powerful enough to perform the processing needed to generate information for decision making purposes. Not until the third generation of computers (mid-1960s) were computers able to provide meaningful *management information*—thus began the era of information systems, systems that provided both data processing and information for decision making. Today's state-of-the-art micros have about the same processing capability as high-end third-generation mainframes that cost millions of dollars in the 1960s. This processing power gives them the ability to support a wide variety of information systems for individuals or entire corporations.

Most micro-based information systems are designed to run on only one microcomputer, just as most mainframe-based systems operate on only one mainframe computer.

- A planner at a land development company in Utah has his own personal micro-based information system. His company develops properties in resort locations. The planner's system, which addresses his unique processing and information needs, enables him to track and monitor the status of each parcel of land under development (for example, whether it has road access, water service, and so on.) The planner has only to press a few keys to determine the building status of a lot in a particular cul de sac in a particular development area.
- A 50-employee distributor of tin-plate steel products in Illinois has annual sales in excess of $20 million, and its accounting department does all accounting on a PC. The information system handles all accounting (general ledger, accounts payable, and accounts receivable), tax reporting, budgeting, and payroll. The system is designed to enable management to make "what if" inquiries to the system and to generate color graphics that highlight business trends.
- A beverage distributor in Oklahoma relies on a microcomputer-based system to handle the inventory and dollar accounting for 150 delivery routes. Drivers log the data related to each sale into a portable data entry unit. Upon returning to the warehouse, the data are dumped (transferred) to the micro and processed. These data provide the basis for inventory management, payroll, customer billing, and critical management information. Managers routinely make inquiries to the system to determine what brands are selling, who is buying them, how rising temperatures have an impact on sales, and much more.

In medium-sized and large companies, you often will find people or groups of people who perform essentially the same functions. For example, at the individual level, commercial loan officers in a bank perform similar functions. At the group level, the administration offices for distribution warehouses perform similar functions. Companies with opportunities such as these create **common systems** that can be installed and run on micros in several locations.

- Each of over 200 field sales representatives for a New Jersey–based publisher of college textbooks has a portable micro. The same micro-based information system is installed on all portable computers. The system helps representatives service their accounts by expediting the sampling of review copies and monitoring the textbook needs of hundreds of professors in a variety of disciplines. At the end of each business day, representatives upload transaction data (for example, books to be sampled) to the publisher's mainframe computer in New Jersey via data communications.
- Common micro-based information systems handle the day-to-day processing and information needs of a chain of sporting goods stores in California. The common system, which was developed by headquarters staff and installed in 25 stores, does sales reporting, inventory management, accounting, payroll, ordering, billing, and tax reporting. Management reports can be generated in all application areas. Appropriate data are uploaded to corporate headquarters each night.

Micro-based information systems are fundamental to the daily operation of tens of thousands of organizations, both small and large. For a few thousand dollars, medical clinics, auto salvage yards, and independent insurance agencies can have the same sophisticated information systems that only large corporations could afford in the 1960s and 1970s. Of course, large hospitals, automobile manufacturers, and insurance companies are developing a variety of micro-based information systems to complement their mainframe-based systems.

Decision Support Systems

The term **decision support system** (**DSS**) generally refers to user-friendly software that produces and presents information to help support management in the decision-making process. DSS software often involves the latest technological innovations (for example, color graphics and database management systems), planning and forecasting models, and user-oriented **fourth-generation languages**, sometimes called **4GLs**. Fourth-generation languages use high-level, English-like instruc-

Decision-support systems provide these product marketing managers with direct access to the information necessary to make critical decisions about the timing of promotional campaigns. A DSS can supply the information when they want it and in the form they want it.

tions to retrieve and format data for inquiries and reporting. With fourth-generation languages, the user tells the computer what to do, *not* how to do it. In contrast, a professional programmer might employ the COBOL programming language and write instructions for what to do *and* how to do it.

Decision support systems help remove the tedium of gathering, analyzing, and presenting data. No longer are managers strapped with such laborious tasks as manually entering and extending numbers (adding rows and columns of numbers) on spreadsheet paper. Graphics software enables managers to generate illustrative bar and pie graphs in minutes. And now, with the availability of a variety of DSSs, managers can get the information they need without having to depend on direct technical assistance from a computer professional.

Managers spend much of their day requesting and analyzing information before making a decision. Decision support systems help close the information gap so managers can improve the quality of their decisions.

Expert Systems

Perhaps the ultimate decision support system is the **expert system**. Expert systems provide "expert" advice and guidance on a wide range of activities, from locomotive maintenance to surgery. Until the mid-1980s expert systems were created and implemented in the mainframe environment. However, with recent advances in micros, more and more expert systems are being developed for micros. An expert system is an interactive system that responds to questions, asks for clarification, makes recommendations, and generally helps in the decision-making process. At the heart of an expert system is a **knowledge base**.

A knowledge base is *not* a data base. The key-account data base illustrated in Figure 6–18 in Chapter 6, "Data Management: Spreadsheet and Database," deals with data that have a *static* relationship between the elements. That is, the company name and region fields have a fixed relationship with the company record. A knowledge base is created by *knowledge engineers*, who translate the knowledge of human experts into rules and strategies. A knowledge base is *heuristic*—it provides the expert system with the capability of recommending directions for user inquiry. It also encourages further investigation into areas that may be important to a certain line of questioning but are not apparent to the user.

A knowledge base grows because it "learns" from user feedback. An expert system learns by "remembering": It stores past occurrences in its knowledge base. For example, a recommendation that sends a user on a "wild goose chase" is thereafter deleted as a workable strategy for similar future inquiries. Expert systems simulate the human thought process. To varying degrees they can reason, draw inferences, and make judgments.

Computer-based expert systems have fared well against expert human physicians in the accuracy of their diagnoses of illnesses. Other expert systems help crews repair telephone lines, financial analysts counsel their clients, computer vendors configure computer systems, and geologists explore for minerals.

> ▶ **MEMORY BITS**
>
> *Microcomputer Systems*
> - Information system
> - Decision support system
> - Expert system

CHAPTER 8 Microcomputer Systems 239

8-2 THE SYSTEMS DEVELOPMENT PROCESS

Traditionally, the systems development process has been a cooperative effort of users and computer professionals to create information systems that would run on minicomputers and mainframe computers. On one hand, computer professionals are familiar with the technology and how it can be applied to meet a business's information processing needs. On the other, users have in-depth familiarity with their respective functional areas and information processing needs. The skills and knowledge of these two groups complement each other and can be combined to create any type of information system during the systems development process. Now, with the current generation of micros and their user-friendly software, users can create their own information systems, often without the assistance of computer professionals.

If the scope of a proposed micro-based information system extends past an individual to a department or even the entire company, systems development typically becomes a team effort. When this happens, the best approach is to follow a standardized **systems development methodology**. The methodology, which is similar for mainframe and micro development projects, provides a framework for cooperation. This step-by-step approach to systems development is essentially the same, be it for an international mainframe-based airline reservation system or a micro-based, department-level, fixed-asset inventory system. As members of a **project team** progress through the procedures outlined in a systems development methodology, the results of one step provide the input for the next step and/or subsequent steps. The project team for a micro-based information-system development effort, which is the focus of this discussion, could be only users. However, depending on the complexity of the project, one or more computer professionals may be involved. Although a mainframe-based information system may have in excess of 25 people on the project team, the project team in the micro environment is usually one, two, or, at most, three people.

Two important advantages of following the methodological approach to systems development are:

- Managers can more easily coordinate the efforts of people engaged in a complex process.
- Project team members can feel secure that they will "leave no stone unturned."

The activities of the systems development process typically are grouped in phases, often labeled *systems analysis*, *systems design*, *programming*, *systems conversion*, and *implementation*. Each phase is examined in the following discussions.

Systems Analysis: Understanding the System

The systems analysis phase of the systems development process produces the following results:

At the start of a project, it is always a good idea for the project team leader to assemble the team, go over the system development methodology, and make sure responsibility areas are clearly understood.

- Existing system review
- System objectives
- Design constraints
- Requirements definition

Each of these results defines an activity that is to take place.

Existing System Review. Before designing a new or enhanced information system, the members of the project team must have a good grasp of the existing work and information flow, be it manual or computer-based. To do this, the team conducts interviews with others who might use the system and observes the present system in operation. Then the team documents the work and information flow of the system by reducing it to its basic components—*input*, *processing*, and *output*. A variety of design techniques can be used to graphically depict the logical relationships between these parts. Perhaps the most popular, although not necessarily the best for all situations, is **flowcharting**. Flowcharting and a more structured technique that produces **data flow diagrams** are introduced later in this chapter.

System Objectives. Once the existing system is documented, the project team can begin to identify the obvious and not-so-obvious problem areas, including procedural bottlenecks, inefficiencies in information flow and storage, duplication of effort, deficiencies in information dissemination, worker discontent, problems with customer interaction, inaccuracy of operational data, and so on. Once these are identified, project team members can concentrate their energies on identifying opportunities for the coordination of effort, the integration of systems, and the use of information. This knowledge is formalized as system objectives.

Design Constraints. The proposed system, sometimes referred to as the target system, will be developed subject to specific constraints. The purpose of this activity is to detail, at the onset of the systems development process, any cost, hardware, schedule, procedural, software, data base, and operating constraints that may limit the definition and design of the target system. For example, cost constraints include any limits on developmental, operational, or maintenance costs.

Requirements Definition. In this activity the project team completes a *needs analysis* that results in a definition of the data processing and information requirements for the target system. To accomplish this task, the project team begins by gathering information. User feedback from interviews is the basis for the project team's **functional specifications** for system input, processing, and output requirements (information needs). The functional specifications describe the logic of the system (input/output, work, and information flow) from the perspective of the user.

At this point the emphasis turns toward *output requirements.* In the systems development process, the project team begins with the desired output and works backward to determine input and processing requirements. Outputs are typically printed reports, terminal displays, or some kind of transaction (for example, purchase order, payroll check). At this time, outputs are described functionally. The actual **layout** (spacing on the screen or page) and detailed content of a display screen or report is specified during the system design phase.

Systems Design: A Science or an Art?

The systems design stage of the systems development process produces the following results:

- General system design
- Data base design
- Detailed system design

Each of these results defines an activity that is to take place.

General System Design

System design: The creative process. The design of an information system is more of a challenge to the human intellect than it is a procedural challenge. Just as an author begins with a blank page and an idea, the members of the project team begin with empty RAM (random-access memory) and the information requirements definitions. From here they must create what can sometimes be a complex information system. The number of ways in which a particular information system can be designed is limited only by the imagination of the project team members.

> **MEMORY BITS**
>
> *Results of Systems Analysis Phase*
> - Existing system review
> - System objectives
> - Design constraints
> - Requirements definition

Software packages are available that enable project team members to design systems interactively at their workstations. Automated design tools, such as Teamwork/SA from Cadre Technologies Inc., have helped programmers and systems analysts make significant strides in productivity improvement. With Teamwork/SA, systems analysts can show the work and information flow in a system that uses any of a variety of structured design techniques.

Completing the general system design. The project team analyzes the existing system, assesses information processing requirements, and then develops a **general system design** for the target system. The general system design, and later the detailed design, involve continuous communication between members of the project team and others who will use or be affected by the system. After evaluating several different approaches, the project team translates the system specifications into a general system design.

At a minimum, the documentation of the general design of the target system includes the following:

- A graphic illustration that depicts the fundamental operation of the target system (for example, data flow diagrams).
- A written explanation of the illustration.
- General descriptions of the outputs to be produced by the system, including display screens and hard-copy reports and documents. (The actual layout—for example, spacing on the page or screen—is not completed until the detailed system design.)

Data Base Design. The data base is the common denominator of any system. It contains the raw material (data) necessary to produce the output (information). In manufacturing, for example, you decide what you are going to make, then you order the raw material. In the process of developing an information system, you decide what your output requirements are, then you determine which data are needed to produce the output. In a sense, output requirements can be thought of as input to data base design. Data bases are discussed in Chapter 6, "Data Management: Spreadsheet and Database."

Detailed System Design. The **detailed system design**—the detailed input/output, processing, and control requirements—is the result of the analysis of user feedback on the general system design. The general system design depicts the relationship between major processing activities and is detailed enough for users to determine whether or not that is what they want. The detailed design includes *all* processing activities and the input/output associated with them.

The detailed design is the cornerstone of the systems development process. It is here that the relationships between the various components of the system are defined. The system specifications are transformed with the project team's imagination and skill into an information system. The detailed system design is the culmination of all previous work. Moreover, it is the *blueprint* for all project team activities that follow.

A number of techniques help project team members in the design process. Each of these techniques enables the system design to be illustrated graphically. One of these techniques, data flow diagrams, is briefly discussed here.

Structured system design. It is much easier to address a complex design problem in small, manageable modules than as one big task. This is done using the principles of **structured system design**. The structured approach to system design encourages the top-down design technique: That is, the project team divides the system into independent modules for ease of understanding and design. The **structure chart** in Figure 8–2 illustrates how a payroll system can be conceptualized as a hierarchy of modules. Eventually the logic for the modules is represented in detail in step-by-step diagrams that illustrate the interactions between input, processing, output, and storage activities for a particular module.

FIGURE 8–2 Structure Chart
This structure chart breaks a payroll system down into a hierarchy of modules.

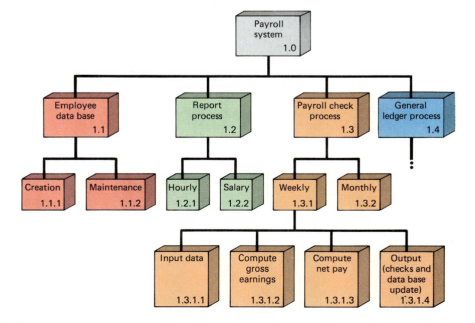

Data flow diagrams. **Data flow diagrams**, or **DFD**s, enable analysts to design and document systems using the structured approach to systems development. Only four symbols are needed for data flow diagrams: entity, process, flow line, and data storage. The symbols are summarized in Figure 8–3 and their use is illustrated in Figure 8–4.

- *Entity.* The entity symbol, a square with a darkened "shadow," is the source or destination of data or information flow. An entity can be a person, a group of people (for example, customers or employees), a department, or even a place (such as a warehouse).
- *Process.* Each process symbol, a rectangle with rounded corners, contains a description of a function to be performed. Process symbols also can be depicted as circles. Typical processes include *enter data, calculate, store, create, produce,* and *verify.* Process-symbol identification numbers are assigned in levels. (For example, Processes 1.1 and 1.2 are subordinate to Process 1.)
- *Flow line.* The flow lines indicate the flow and direction of data or information.
- *Data storage.* These open-ended rectangles identify storage locations for data, which could be a file drawer, a shelf, a data base on magnetic disk, and so on.

In Figure 8–4, a data flow diagram documents that portion of a personnel system that produces payroll checks. Processes 1 and 2 deal with the employee data base, but in Process 3 the actual payroll checks are produced. In the bottom portion of Figure 8–4, Process 3 is *exploded* to show greater detail. Notice that the second-level processes within the explosion of Process 3 are numbered 3.1, 3.2, 3.3, and 3.4. Process 3.1 could be exploded to a third level of processes to show even greater detail (for example, 3.1.1, 3.1.2, and so on).

There is no one best analytical or design technique. Design techniques are just tools. Your skill and imagination make an information system a reality.

The presentation of information. Information can be presented in many ways within the context of an information system. During the system design process, members of the project team work in close cooperation with those who will use the system to describe each output to be generated from the target system. An output could be a hard-copy report, a display of information, or a transaction document (an invoice). Transaction documents are typically periodic (monthly invoices). Gen-

FIGURE 8–3 Data Flow Diagram Symbols

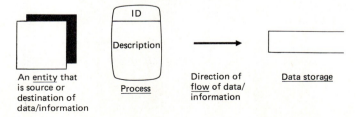

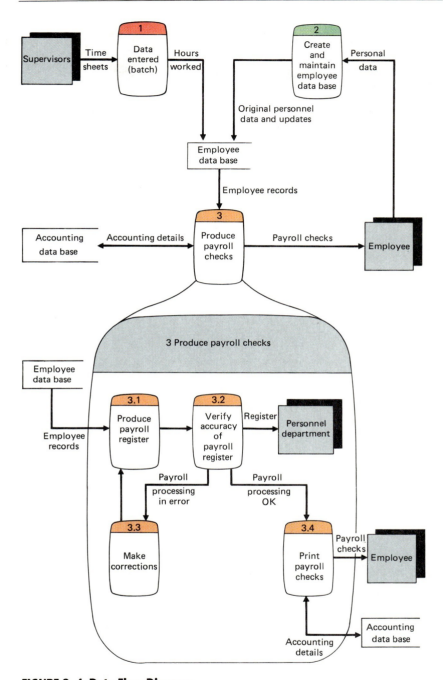

FIGURE 8–4 Data Flow Diagram
In this data flow diagram of a payroll system, Process 3 is exploded to show greater detail.

erally, reports are the presentation of information in either hard-copy or soft-copy format. They can be either *periodic* or *ad hoc* (to meet an immediate information need).

Of course, not all reports contain numbers and text. Some of the most effective ways of presenting information involve the use of graphics.

▶ **MEMORY BITS**

Results of Systems Design Phase
- General system design
- Data base design
- Detailed system design

Programming: Ideas Become Reality

The next challenge is to translate the system design and specifications into instructions that can be interpreted and executed by the computer. This, of course, is the programming phase of the systems development process.

In Chapter 2, "Interacting with Micros," three levels of command interaction are identified: *menu*, *macro*, and *programming*. An elementary information system can be created using only the macro capability of productivity software packages, such as spreadsheet and database. (See Chapter 2, "Interacting with Micros," for a discussion of macros and programming.) However, most micro-based information systems will involve programming, the highest level of command interaction. In the micro environment, programming tools fall into three categories.

1. *Programming languages associated with productivity software tools.* Many major software products, especially spreadsheet and database, come with their own programming languages. When you purchase a spreadsheet package (for example, Lotus 1-2-3 or Quatro) or a database package (such as Paradox or dBASE IV), you also receive the package's programming language.

KnowledgeWare, Inc., provides an integrated CASE (computer-aided software engineering) environment for the planning, analysis, design, and construction of information systems. The KnowledgeWare tools function both as an integrated set and independently as stand-alone products. The windows in the screen illustrate the capabilities of the Analysis Workstation, an integrated set of diagrammatic tools for requirements analysis. The techniques incorporated into the software include decomposition diagrams (top left), data flow diagrams (top right), entity relationship diagrams (middle), and action diagrams (bottom left).

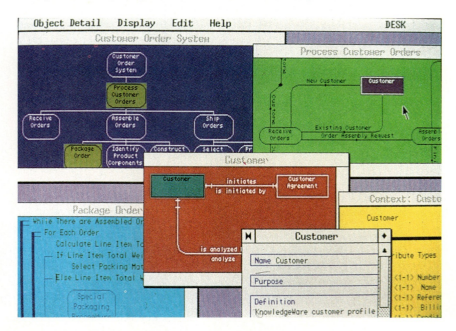

2. *Third-generation languages.* **Third-generation programming languages** were the dominant information system implementation tools during the 1960s, 1970s, and most of the 1980s. The flexibility of third-generation languages permits programmers to model almost any scientific or business procedure. Instructions are **coded**, or written, sequentially and processed according to program specifications. In the mainframe environment, the majority of the existing systems are implemented in **COBOL**. Micro-based information systems are often implemented in **BASIC**. COBOL, **C,** and **Pascal** are also popular with micro users.
3. *Fourth-generation languages.* The trend in systems development is toward using high-level, user-friendly, *fourth-generation languages* (4GLs). There are two types of fourth-generation languages.
   - *Production-oriented fourth-generation languages.* Production-oriented fourth-generation languages are designed primarily for computer professionals and are used for the most part in the mainframe environment.
   - *User-oriented fourth-generation languages.* This type of fourth-generation language is designed primarily for the end user in both the mainframe and micro environments. Users write fourth-generation language programs to query (extract information from) a data base and to create personal or departmental information systems.

   Fourth-generation languages use high-level, English-like instructions to retrieve and format data for inquiries and reporting. Most of the procedure portion of a fourth-generation language program is generated automatically by the computer and the language software. That is, for the most part, the user specifies what to do, *not* how to do it. In contrast, a COBOL or BASIC programmer writes instructions for what to do *and* how to do it.

The programming phase of the systems development process produces the following results:

- System specifications review
- Program identification and description
- Program coding, testing, and documentation

Each of these results defines an activity to be completed. With detailed specifications in hand, the project team members are now ready to write the programs needed to make the target system operational.

System Specifications Review. During the programming phase, programming becomes the dominant activity. The system specifications completed during the system analysis and design phases are all that is necessary for project team members to write, or *code,* the programs to implement the information system. But before getting started, team members should review the system specifications (layouts, design, and so on) created during system analysis and design.

Program Identification and Description. An information system needs an array of programs to create and update the data base, print reports, permit inquiry, and so on. Depending on the scope of the system, as few as three or four or as many as several hundred programs may need to be written before the system can be implemented. At this point, all programs necessary to make the system operational are identified and described. A typical program description would include:

- Type of programming language (dBASE IV, BASIC, and so on)
- A narrative of the program, describing the tasks to be performed
- Frequency of processing (for example, daily, weekly, on-line)
- Input to the program (data and their source)
- Output produced by the program
- Limitations and restrictions (for example, sequence of input data)
- Detailed specifications (for example, specific computations and logical manipulations, tables)

Program Coding, Testing, and Documentation. Armed with system specifications and program descriptions, team members can begin the actual coding of programs. The development of a program is really a project within a project. Just as there are certain steps the project team takes to develop an information system, there are steps that a programmer takes to write a program. These steps are described briefly in the following sections. In a micro environment, the programmer is often a user, not a professional programmer.

Step 1: Describe the problem. Identify exactly what needs to be done.

Step 2: Analyze the problem. In this step you break the programming problem into its basic components for analysis. Remember to "divide and conquer." Although different programs have different components, a good starting place for most is to analyze the *output*, *input*, *processing*, and *file-interaction* components.

FIGURE 8–5 Program Structure Chart
The logic of a payroll program to print weekly payroll checks can be broken down into modules for ease of understanding, coding, and maintenance.

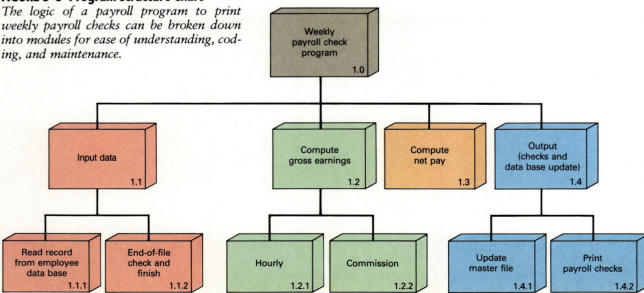

CHAPTER 8 Microcomputer Systems

Steps 3 and 4: Design the general and detailed logic of the program. Now you need to put the pieces together in the form of a logical program design. A program is designed in a hierarchical manner—that is, from general to the specific.

The *general* design (Step 3) of the program is oriented primarily to the major processing activities and the relationships between these activities. The **structure chart** of Figure 8–5 and the **flowchart** of Figure 8–6

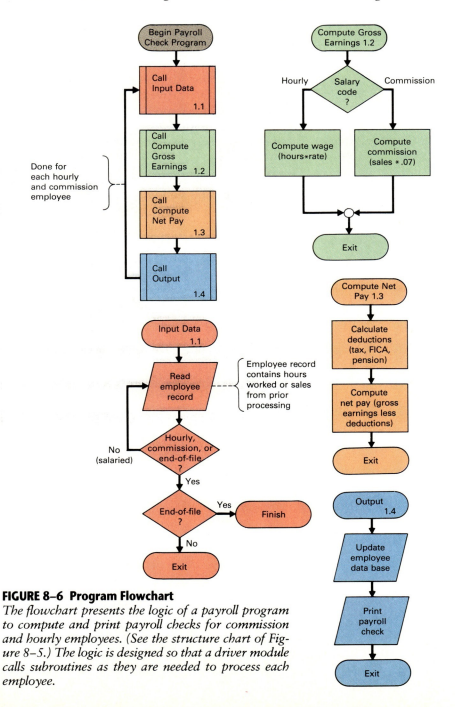

FIGURE 8–6 Program Flowchart
The flowchart presents the logic of a payroll program to compute and print payroll checks for commission and hourly employees. (See the structure chart of Figure 8–5.) The logic is designed so that a driver module calls subroutines as they are needed to process each employee.

illustrate the general design of a weekly payroll program to compute and print paychecks. Figure 8–7 summarizes the most frequently used program flowchart symbols. By first completing a general program design, you make it easier to investigate different design approaches. Once you are confident of which approach is best, you may complete a more detailed design.

The *detailed* design (Step 4) results in a graphic representation of the program logic that includes *all* processing activities and their relationships, calculations, data manipulations, logic operations, and all input/output.

Step 5: Code the program. Whether you "write" or "code" the program is a matter of personal preference. In this context, the terms are the same. In Step 5, the graphic and narrative design of program-development Steps 1 through 4 are translated into machine-readable instructions, or programs. If the logic is sound and the design documentation (flowcharts, structure charts, and so on) is thorough, the coding process is relatively straightforward.

Step 6: Test and debug the program. Once the program has been entered into the system, it is likely that you will encounter at least one of those cantankerous **bugs**. A bug is either a *syntax error* (violation of

FIGURE 8–7 Common Flowchart Symbols

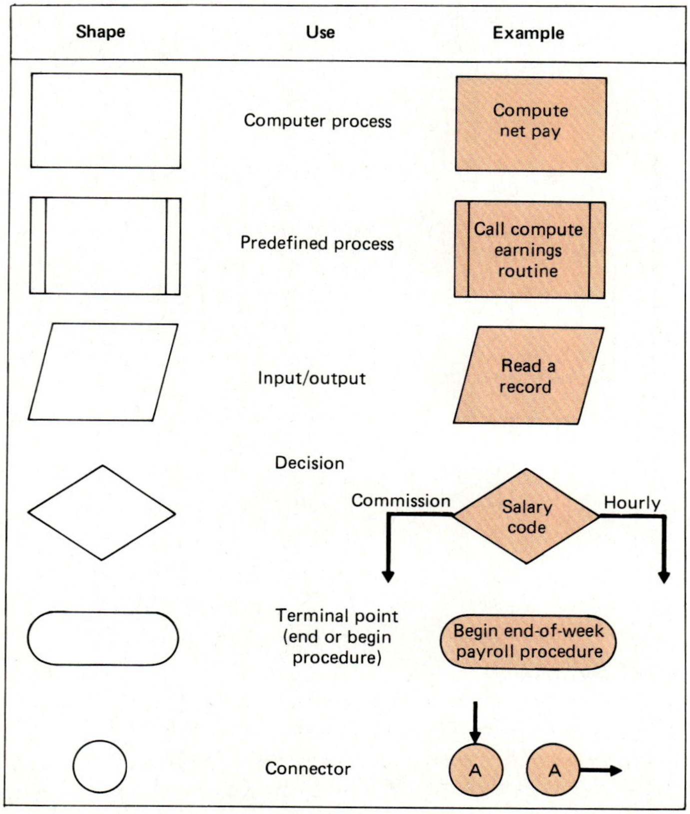

Shape	Use	Example
▭	Computer process	Compute net pay
▯	Predefined process	Call compute earnings routine
▱	Input/output	Read a record
◇	Decision	Salary code (Commission / Hourly)
⬭	Terminal point (end or begin procedure)	Begin end-of-week payroll procedure
○	Connector	A A

Computer "showrooms" have made it easier for retailers to buy fashions for the next season. Rather than thumb through thousands of garments, buyers enter their fashion needs (for example, type, style, cost, fabric, and so on) into the apparel selection system, and garments that meet their specifications, along with the location and seller for each garment, are displayed.

one of the rules for writing instructions) or a *logic error*. Ridding a program of bugs is the process of **debugging**.

Step 7: Document the program. Procedures and information requirements change over the life of a system. For example, because the social security tax rate is revised each year, certain payroll programs must be modified. To keep up with these changes, programs must be updated periodically, or *maintained*. Program maintenance can be difficult if the program documentation is not complete and up-to-date. *Documentation* is part of the *programming process*. It's not something you do after the program is written.

System Conversion and Implementation

System Testing. The first step of the system conversion and implementation phase of the system development process is system testing. System testing encompasses everything that makes up the information system—the hardware, the software, the end users, the procedures (for example, user manuals), and the data. If needed, the interfaces between the system and other systems are tested as well.

During the programming phase of systems development, programs are written according to system specifications and are individually tested. Although the programs that comprise the software for the system have undergone **unit testing** (individual testing) and have been debugged,

▶ **MEMORY BITS**

Results of Programmed Phase
- System specifications review
- Program identification and description
- Program coding, testing, and documentation

there is no guarantee that the programs will work as a system. To ensure that the software can be combined into an operational information system, the project team performs integrated **systems testing**.

To conduct the system test, the project team compiles and thoroughly tests the system with test data. In this first stage, tests are run for each subsystem (one of the functional aspects of the system) or cycle (weekly or monthly activities). The test data are judiciously compiled so all program and system options and all error and validation routines are tested. The tests are repeated and modifications are made until all subsystems or cycles function properly. At this point the entire system is tested as a unit. Testing and modifications continue until the components of the system work as they should and all input/output is validated.

The second stage of system testing is done with *live data* by several of the people who eventually will use the system. Live data have already been processed through the existing system. Testing with live data provides an extra level of assurance that the system will work properly when implemented.

Approaches to System Conversion. Once systems testing is complete, the project team can begin to integrate people, software, hardware, procedures, and data into an operational information system. This normally involves a conversion from the existing system to the new one. An organization's approach to system conversion depends on its *willingness to accept risk* and the *amount of time available* for the conversion. Four common approaches are parallel conversion, direct conversion, phased conversion, and pilot conversion. These approaches are illustrated in Figure 8–8 and discussed in the paragraphs that follow.

Parallel conversion. In **parallel conversion**, the existing system and the new system operate simultaneously, or in parallel, until the project team is confident that the new system is working properly. Parallel con-

FIGURE 8–8 Common Approaches to System Conversion

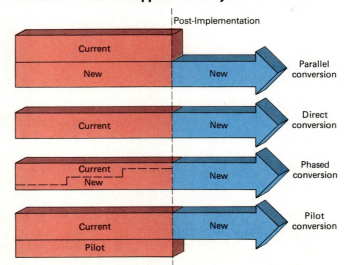

version has two important advantages. First, the existing system serves as a backup if the new system fails to operate as expected. Second, the results of the new system can be compared to the results of the existing system.

There is less risk with this strategy because the present system provides backup, but it doubles the workload of personnel and hardware resources during the conversion. Parallel conversion usually takes one month or a major system cycle. For a retail outlet, this might be one complete billing cycle, which is usually a month.

Direct conversion. Some companies forego parallel conversion in favor of a **direct conversion.** Direct conversion involves a greater risk because there is no backup in case the system fails. Companies select this "cold turkey" approach when there is no existing system or when the existing system is substantially different. Most micro systems are implemented "cold turkey" because they provide processing capability and information that never existed in the past.

Phased conversion. In **phased conversion**, an information system is implemented one module at a time by either parallel or direct conversion. For example, in a system for a retail outlet, the first phase might be to convert the sales-accounting module. The second phase could involve the inventory-management module. The third phase might be the credit-check module.

Phased conversion has the advantage of spreading the demand for resources to avoid an intense demand. The disadvantages are that the conversion takes longer and an interface must be developed between the existing system and the new one.

Pilot conversion. In **pilot conversion**, the new system is implemented by parallel, direct, or phased conversion as a pilot system in only one of the areas for which it is targeted. Suppose a beverage distributor wants to implement a route accounting system in each of its four distribution warehouses. One warehouse would be selected as a pilot, and the new information system would be implemented there first.

The advantage of pilot conversion is that the inevitable bugs in a system can be removed before the system is implemented at the other locations. The disadvantage is that the implementation time for the total system takes longer than if the entire system were implemented at one time.

The System Becomes Operational. Once the conversion has been completed, the micro-based information system becomes operational, serving the information needs of the individual, department, or company.

Post-Implementation Activities

Just as a new automobile will need some screws tightened after a few hundred miles, an information system will need some fine-tuning just after implementation. Thereafter and throughout the production stage of the system life cycle, the system will be modified many times to meet the changing needs of the individual, department, or company. The pro-

Three to six months after the hardware, software, people, procedures, and data have been integrated into an operational information system, key members of the project team are conducting a post-implementation evaluation to assess the overall effectiveness of a risk evaluation system for commercial loans.

cess of modifying an information system to meet changing needs is known as **system maintenance.**

An information system cannot live forever. The accumulation of modifications and enhancements eventually will make any information system cumbersome and inefficient. Depending on the number of minor modifications, known as **patches,** and enhancements, an information system will remain operational from four to seven years.

8–3 PROTOTYPING: CREATING A MODEL OF THE TARGET SYSTEM

Throughout the twentieth century manufacturers have built prototypes of everything from toasters to airplanes. Automobile manufacturers routinely build prototypes according to design specifications. Scaled-down clay models are made to evaluate aesthetics and aerodynamics. Ultimately, a full-size, fully functional prototype is created that enables the driver and passengers to test all aspects of the car's functionality. If engineers see possibilities for improvement, the prototypes are modified and retested until they meet or exceed all specifications. The prototype approach to development is now being embraced by the computer and information system communities. Prototyping is emerging as an enhancement of or an alternative to the phased approach to systems development discussed in the last section.

The Prototype System

The three objectives of **prototyping** are:

1. To analyze the current situation
2. To identify information needs
3. To develop a scaled-down model of the target system

The scaled-down model, called a **prototype system**, normally would handle the main transaction-oriented procedures, produce the critical reports, and permit rudimentary inquiries. The prototype system gives users an opportunity to actually work with the functional aspect of the target system before the system is implemented. Once users gain hands-on familiarity with the prototype system, they are in a position to be

For years automobile manufacturers have built prototype models that could be tested for aerodynamics, aesthetics, and functionality. Only recently has prototyping become popular with information systems development. Now over 70% of all new information systems emerge from a prototype system, and the percentage is increasing each year.

more precise when they relate their information processing needs to the project team.

A prototype system can be anything from a nonfunctional demonstration of the input/output of a target information system to a full-scale operational system. These models are tested and refined until the users are confident that what they see is what they want. In some cases, the software developed to create a prototype system is expanded to create a fully operational information system. However, in most cases, the prototype system provides an alternate vehicle for completing the functional specifications activity of a systems development methodology. Incomplete and/or inaccurate user specifications have been the curse of systems development methodologies. Many companies have exorcised this curse by integrating prototyping into their methodologies.

Creating the Prototype System

To create a prototype information system, project team members rough out the logic of the system and how the elements fit together with an *automated design tool*. The resulting logic usually is depicted in the form of data flow diagrams. Then the project team works with the end users to define the I/O interfaces (the system interaction with the user). During interactive sessions, project team members and users create whatever interactive display screens are required to meet the user's information processing needs. To do this, project team members use applications development tools such as fourth-generation languages to create the screen images (menus, reports, inquiries, and so on) and to generate much of the programming code.

Users actually can sit down at a terminal and evaluate portions of and eventually all of the prototype system. Invariably they have suggestions for improving the user interfaces and/or the format of the I/O. And without fail their examination reveals new needs for information.

The prototype system is the beginning. From there the system is expanded and refined to meet the users' total information needs. Prototyping software tools are limited in what they can do, so the typical system may require a considerable amount of custom coding, probably written in third- and fourth-generation languages.

8–4 COMPUTER AND SYSTEM SECURITY

One of the most important considerations in the development and ongoing operation of an information system is security. This is especially true with micro-based information systems because micros are often located in areas where access is not controlled. The individual, department, and company must be extremely careful not to compromise the integrity of the system. They must be equally careful with the "engine" for the information system—the microcomputer. A micro with all its software and data can be easily stolen when security is lax.

CHAPTER 8 Microcomputer Systems

An information system has many points of vulnerability, and too much is at stake to overlook threats to its security. These threats take many forms: white-collar crime, natural disasters (such as earthquakes and floods), vandalism, and carelessness. This section is devoted to discussing system security considerations.

Points of Vulnerability in the Micro Computing Environment

Points of vulnerability exist in five areas: *hardware*, *software*, *files/data bases*, *data communications*, and *personnel*. These are summarized in Figure 8-9 and briefly discussed here.

- *Hardware*. If the hardware fails, the information system fails. The threat of failure can be minimized by implementing security precautions that prevent access by unauthorized personnel and by taking steps to keep all hardware operational.
  Common approaches to securing the premises from unauthorized entry include closed-circuit TV monitors, alarm systems, and com-

FIGURE 8-9 Security Precautions
Some or all of the security precautions noted in the figure are in force in most computer centers. Each precaution helps minimize the risk of an information system's or a computer system's vulnerability to crime, disasters, and failure.

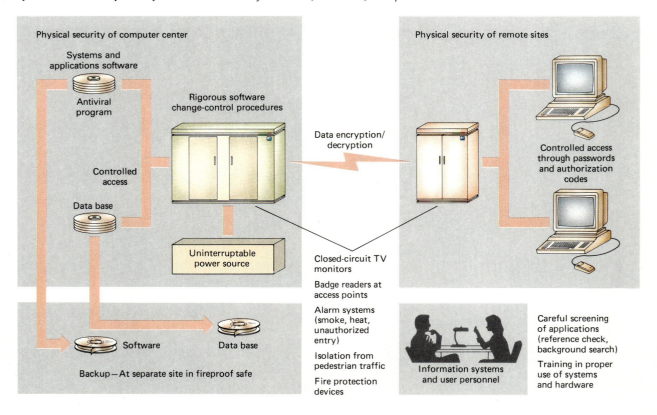

puter-controlled devices that check employee badges, fingerprints, or voice prints before unlocking doors at access points. Micros with critical systems and data also should be isolated from pedestrian traffic. Some micro systems that process sensitive information can be configured with a badge reader.

Micros must have a "clean," continuous source of power. To minimize the effects of "dirty" power or power outages, a micro can be equipped with an **uninterruptible power source** (**UPS**). A UPS system serves as a buffer between the external power source and the computer system. In a UPS system, the computer is powered by batteries that deliver clean power, which in turn are regenerated by an external power source. If the external power source fails, the UPS system enables operation to continue for a period of time after an outage.

- *Software*. Unless properly controlled, the software for an information system can be modified for personal gain. Thus, close control over software development and the documentation of an information system is needed to minimize the opportunity for computer crime. Operational control procedures that are built into the design of an information system will constantly monitor processing accuracy.

With microcomputers proliferating throughout most companies, computer crime has become a major concern. Prospective employees who are expected to work with sensitive data must undergo intensive screening before being offered a job.

- *Files/data bases.* The data base contains the raw material for information. In some cases, the files/data bases are the lifeblood of a company and must be protected. Having several *generations of backups* (backups to backups) to all files is not sufficient insurance against loss of files/data bases. The backup files should be stored in fireproof safes in separate rooms, preferably in separate buildings.
- *Data communications.* The mere existence of data communications capabilities, where data are transmitted via communications links from one computer to another, poses a threat to security. Some companies use *cryptography—encryption/decryption* hardware that scrambles messages and unscrambles messages.
- *Personnel.* Managers are paying close attention to who gets hired for positions with access to computer-based information systems and sensitive data.

Information Systems Security

Information systems security is classified as physical or logical. *Physical security* refers to hardware, facilities, magnetic disks, and other things that could be illegally accessed, stolen, or destroyed.

Logical security is built into the software by permitting only authorized persons to access and use the system. Logical security for information systems is achieved primarily by **passwords** and **authorization codes**. Only those with a "need to know" are told the password and given authorization codes.

Level of Risk

No amount of security measures will completely remove the vulnerability of a microcomputer or an information system. Each individual and company must determine an acceptable level of risk.

SUMMARY OUTLINE AND IMPORTANT TERMS

8-1 **TYPES OF MICRO SYSTEMS.** An **information system** is a computer-based system that provides *data processing capability* and *information for making decisions*. We combine *hardware, software, people, procedures,* and *data* to create an information system, sometimes called an **management information system (MIS)**.

Most micro-based information systems are designed to run on only one microcomputer. Some companies create **common systems** that can be installed and run on more than one micro.

The term **decision support system (DSS)** generally refers to user-friendly software that produces and presents information to help support management in the decision-making process. **Fourth-generation languages (4GLs)** use high-level, English-like instructions to retrieve and format data for inquiries and reporting.

Expert systems are interactive systems that respond to questions, ask for clarification, make recommendations, and generally help in the decision-making process. At the heart of an expert system is a heuristic **knowledge base**.

8–2 **THE SYSTEMS DEVELOPMENT PROCESS.** The systems development process is a cooperative undertaking by users who know the functional areas and computer professionals who know the technology. The step-by-step **systems development methodology** provides the framework for system development.

During the systems analysis phase of the systems development process, the following activities take place.

- *Existing system review.* The work and information flow of the present system is documented by reducing the system to its basic components—input, processing, and output. System design techniques include **flowcharting** and other more structured techniques such as **data flow diagrams**.
- *System objectives.* The project team arrives at general system objectives by engaging in discussions with all end user managers ultimately affected by the target system.
- *Design constraints.* The target information system must be developed within the boundaries of any applicable hardware, cost, schedule, procedural, software, data base, and operating constraints.
- *Requirements definition.* User feedback provides the basis for the **functional specifications** for system input, processing, and output requirements. These specifications describe the logic of the system from the perspective of the user.

During the systems design phase of the systems development process, the following activities are completed.

- *General system design.* At a minimum, the documentation of the **general system design** includes a graphic illustration and explanation of the fundamental operation of the target system and general descriptions of the outputs to be produced by the system.
- *Data base design.* During systems development, designers describe the output requirements and determine which data are needed to produce the output.
- *Detailed system design.* The **detailed system design** includes all processing activities and the input/output associated with them. When adhering to **structured system design**, designers divide the system into independent modules for ease of understanding and design. **Data flow diagrams** enable analysts to design and document systems using the structured approach to systems development. The four symbols used in **DFDs** are entity, process, flow line, and data store. Reports, or the general presentation of information, can be either *periodic* or *ad hoc*.

During the programming phase of the systems development process, programs are written to create the software necessary to make the information system operational. In the micro environment, the tools of programming fall into three categories: programming languages associated with productivity software tools; **third-generation programming languages** (**BASIC**, **COBOL**, **C**, and **Pascal**); and fourth-generation lan-

guages (4GLs). During the programming phase, the following activities take place.
- *System specifications review.* Programmers review the system specifications created during system analysis and design.
- *Program identification and description.* A typical program description would include the type of programming language, a narrative description, frequency of processing, input/output, limitations and restrictions, and detailed specifications.
- *Program coding, testing, and documentation.* For each program, the programmer describes the problem; analyzes the problem; designs the general, then the detailed logic (often via **structure charts** and **flowcharts**); and codes, tests, and documents the program.

Although the programs that make up an information system have been **debugged** on an individual basis (**unit testing**), they must be combined and subjected to integrated **systems testing** prior to implementation.

The four common approaches to system conversion are **parallel conversion**, **direct conversion**, **phased conversion**, and **pilot conversion**. The approach that an organization selects depends on its willingness to accept risk and the amount of time available for the conversion.

The post-implementation review, which is a critical examination of the system after it has been put into production, is conducted three to six months after implementation.

An information system is dynamic and must be responsive to the changing needs of the company and those who use it. The process of modifying, or **patching**, an information system to meet changing needs is known as **system maintenance**.

8-3 PROTOTYPING: CREATING A MODEL OF THE TARGET SYSTEM. The three objectives of **prototyping** are to analyze the current situation, to identify information needs, and to develop a scaled-down model of the target system. A **prototype system** normally would handle the main transaction-oriented procedures, produce the critical reports, and permit rudimentary inquiries.

Ideally, users should experiment and familiarize themselves with the operation of a target system as early in the development process as possible. The prototyping process enables users to relate accurate information processing needs to the project team from the early phases of the project.

8-4 COMPUTER AND SYSTEM SECURITY. The threats to the security of computer centers and information systems call for precautionary measures. A computer center can be vulnerable in its hardware, software, files/data bases, data communications, and personnel. A variety of tools and procedures are used to minimize the threat to computer and system security. Information systems security is classified as physical security or logical security (achieved primarily by **passwords** and **authorization codes**).

REVIEW EXERCISES

1. Name the four symbols used in data flow diagrams.
2. The functional specifications describe the logic of a proposed system from whose perspective?

3. What is the design philosophy called that enables complex design problems to be addressed in small, manageable modules?
4. Name two system design techniques.
5. What are the objectives of prototyping?
6. Which comes first during system testing, testing with live data or testing with test data?
7. List three areas addressed during a post-implementation review.
8. The mere fact that a system uses data communications poses a threat to security. Why?
9. What advantage does direct conversion have over parallel conversion? Parallel over direct?
10. Draw the flowcharting symbols for predefined process, terminal point, and decision.
11. Name two types of program errors.
12. What differentiates a decision support system from an information system?
13. Who translates the knowledge of human experts into rules and strategies for an expert system's knowledge base?
14. Name three of the five phases of the systems development process.
15. Name three third-generation programming languages.

SELF-TEST (by section)

8-1 a. We combine hardware, software, people, procedures, and data to create an _____.
   b. A system designed to run on more than one micro is called: (a) a conventional system, (b) a common system, or (c) a standard system?

8-2 a. A standardized _____ provides the framework for cooperation during the systems development process.
   b. Which of the following is not a design technique: (a) flowcharting, (b) data flow diagrams, or (c) phased conversion?
   c. Functional specifications include system input, _____, and processing requirements.
   d. The _____ (general/detailed) system design includes all processing activities and the input/output associated with them.
   e. A typical program description would *not* include which of the following: (a) the type of programming language, (b) the output produced by the program, or (c) the data base design?
   f. Once all the syntax errors have been removed from a program, no further testing is required. (T/F)
   g. When programming in COBOL, you tell the computer what to do and how to do it. (T/F)
   h. Individual program testing is known as: (a) unit testing, (b) module testing, or (c) hierarchical testing?
   i. In the _____ approach to system conversion, the existing system and the new system operate simultaneously until the project team is confident the new system is working properly.

j. The post-implementation evaluation normally is conducted one year after system implementation. (T/F)

8-3 a. A prototype system is essentially a complete information system without the data base. (T/F)

b. A prototype system normally would permit rudimentary inquiries. (T/F)

8-4 Logical security for microcomputer systems is achieved primarily by _____ and authorization codes.

Self-test answers. **8-1 (a)** information system; **(b)** b. **8-2 (a)** systems development methodology; **(b)** c; **(c)** output; **(d)** detailed; **(e)** c; **(f)** F; **(g)** T; **(h)** a; **(i)** parallel; **(j)** F. **8-3 (a)** F; **(b)** T. **8-4** passwords.

CHAPTER

9

MICROCOMPUTERS AND SOCIETY

STUDENT LEARNING OBJECTIVES

- ▶ To put society's dependence on computers in perspective.
- ▶ To understand and appreciate emerging PC-related trends.
- ▶ To identify and discuss controversial PC-related issues.

9–1 COMPUTERS: CAN WE LIVE WITHOUT THEM?

Computers in general and microcomputers in particular have enhanced our lifestyles to the point that most of us take them for granted. There is nothing wrong with this attitude, but we must recognize that society has made a very real commitment to computers. Whether it is good or bad, society has reached the point of no return in its dependence on computers. And stiff business competition means their use will continue to grow. On a more personal level, we are reluctant to forfeit the everyday conveniences made possible by computers. More and more of us find that our personal computers are an integral part of our daily activities, whether at work or at home.

At this television station, a newsroom automation system controls programming flow, monitors the electronic teleprompter display, and operates studio camera movement through robotics. This and other television stations are very dependent on computers.

Turn off the computer system for a day in almost any company and observe the consequences. Most companies would cease to function. Turn off the computer system for several days, and many companies would cease to exist. Recognizing their dependence on computers, most firms have made contingency plans that provide for backup computers in case of disaster. We as individuals are experiencing this same dependence. For example, a sales manager would never consider making an important presentation without the help of presentation graphics software. Customers are conditioned to accept nothing less than a certain level of professionalism and sophistication.

Ask a secretary to trade a word processing system for a typewriter. Ask an attorney to give up her on-line case research capability. Ask a certified public accountant if there is a realistic manual alternative to tax accounting. Ask a marketing manager if his company can remain competitive without the benefit of timely computer-generated information. Ask yourself if you would give up the convenience and effectiveness of your PC.

Our dependence on food has evolved into the joy of eating gourmet food—and so it is or can be with computers. Dependence is not necessarily bad as long as we keep it in perspective. We can't passively assume that computers will continue to enhance the quality of our lives. It is our obligation to learn to understand them so we can better direct their application for society's benefit.

With the prospect of increased productivity, manufacturing companies have been rushing to install more and more applications that involve industrial robots. The processors in many industrial robots are similar to the processors in PCs. In the photo, an industrial robot positions materials for assembly in a pick-and-place application.

9–2 MICROCOMPUTER TRENDS AND ISSUES

PC Trends

Several trends are sure to have an impact you and others who are just joining the microcomputer revolution. Four significant trends are discussed in the following sections.

Telecommuting and the Electronic Cottage. Traditionally, people get up in the morning, get dressed, and fight rush-hour traffic to get to the office because that is where the work is. However, for many *knowledge workers*, work is really at a micro or terminal, whether it is at the office or at home. Knowledge workers are people who work with information. More and more knowledge workers (and employers) are beginning to question the wisdom of going to the office in the traditional sense. Many would prefer to telecommute and work in the more comfortable surroundings of home. **Telecommuting** is "commuting" to work via a data communications link between home and office.

In theory, millions of people could telecommute to work at least a few days a week. People whose jobs involve considerable interaction with a computer system are perfect candidates (such as those who process insurance claims and programmers). Managers who need a few hours or perhaps a few days of uninterrupted time to accomplish tasks that do not require direct personal interaction are beginning to consider the merits of telecommuting.

At present, telecommuting is seldom an employee option. Most companies that permit telecommuting are restricting it to management and computer professionals. However, it is only a matter of time before self-motivated individuals at all levels and in a variety of disciplines are given the option of telecommuting at least part of the time. Most workers would view telecommuting and the accompanying flexible work hours as "perks" of employment. The company that does not offer them may be at a disadvantage in recruiting quality workers.

There is definitely a trend toward an increased level of telecommuting, especially with the proliferation of micros, facsimile (fax) machines, and sophisticated telephone systems that include voice mail and call forwarding. In effect, a knowledge worker's home office could function much like his or her "at work" office. In many situations, the "at work" office could be eliminated.

Everyone has a different reason for wanting to telecommute. A programmer with two school-age children says, "I want to say good-bye when the kids leave for school and greet them when they return." A writer goes into the office once a week, the day before the magazine goes to press. He says, "I write all my stories from the comfort of my home. For me, an office that puts out a weekly magazine is not conducive to creative thinking." A financial analyst telecommutes to prepare quarterly financial statements. He says, "All the information I need is at my fingertips, and I finish in one day at home what used to take me a week at the office." The president of the same company stated emphatically, "I got sick and tired of spending nights up in my office. By telecom-

Many insurance companies say they are quick to process claims, but some are more effective than others. This insurance claims adjuster does not have to go to the office to fill out claims forms. He brings a cellular laptop, which is capable of transmitting voice, data, and images, plus a video camera to the site of an accident or a natural disaster. While writing up the claim, he transmits videos, frame by frame, to the company's home office. Normally, electronic approval for issuing a check is sent to him via his laptop. He then issues a check on the spot to the policyholder.

muting, I'm at least within earshot of my wife and kids. Also, I like to get into more comfortable clothes." The director of an MIS department describes one of many telecommuting applications: "Every Monday evening I write out the agenda for my Tuesday morning staff meeting. I then send a summary of the agenda via electronic mail to my managers so they will see it first thing Tuesday morning when they log on." Of course, there are differing opinions. One sales manager says, "I'm more productive working at the office, where household and family distractions fade into the distance."

Telecommuting may never catch on as a general alternative to working in the office, but for some applications it has proved to be a boon to productivity. As a personnel director observed: "With the elimination of travel time, coffee breaks, idle conversations, and numerous office distractions, we have found that conscientious, self-motivated employees can be more productive at home when working on certain projects." However, management at this company encourages workers to select their telecommuting activities carefully. Telecommuting is fine for interaction with the computer and the data base, but for interaction with other people, it has its limitations. Telecommuting does not permit "pressing of the flesh" and the transmittal of the nonverbal cues that are so essential to personal interaction.

Electronic Mail. Every third micro is linked to a computer network, mostly local area networks, and most of the remaining micros have the capability of establishing a communications link with a network. The number of networked micros is growing daily. One of the many advantages of computer networks is that they enable us to route messages to each other. A message can be a note, letter, report, chart, or even the

When the potential for forest fires is high, this forest ranger alerts appropriate people via electronic mail.

manuscript of a book. Each person in a company can be assigned an "electronic mailbox" in which messages are received and stored on secondary storage, such as magnetic disk. To "open" and "read" electronic mail, or E-mail, the user simply goes to his or her micro or terminal and recalls the message from storage.

The trend toward greater use of E-mail is accelerating as its benefits become apparent.

- *E-mail is quick*. E-mail travels at electronic speeds via data communications.
- *E-mail is flexible*. The sender can route a message to one person or to many people.
- *E-mail is direct*. The message is placed in the addressee's electronic mailbox and the addressee is alerted to the fact that mail needs to be opened (recalled from storage and displayed).

These benefits are illustrated in the following example. Within minutes, a national sales manager can inform eight regional sales managers of a price reduction via electronic mail. Moreover, the manager can avoid the time-consuming ritual of "telephone tag." The message is entered by the sales manager at the national headquarters and routed to the electronic mailboxes of the regional managers. Each manager "opens the mail" by displaying the message on his or her workstation.

Information Services. As the percentage of homes with micros increases, so does the use of commercial information services. Information services, a number of which exist today, make a variety of services available to micro users. The micro user has only to establish a communications link to an information service's mainframe computer. Several currently available functions offered by information services are described in Chapter 7, "Data Communications and Networks." The two-way system provides the micro user with information (for example, airline flight schedules) and permits the user to enter data (such as a flight number to make a reservation).

The four components of an information service are the *central computer* (usually a mainframe), the *network* (the communications links), the *data base*, and the *microcomputers*. The central computer system is accessed by micro users who desire a particular service. The data base contains data and screens of information that are presented to users. For example, a buying-service display might combine the graphic rendering of a refrigerator with price and delivery information.

As microcomputers proliferate, a greater variety of information services will be available to more and more people. Even now some hotel rooms are equipped with microcomputers that can access these services. Hotel guests can communicate with their homes, companies, clients, or virtually anyone else. They can obtain theater or airline tickets, shop or order gifts, scan restaurant menus, and even play video games. In a few years all major hotels will provide their guests with access to microcomputers and information services.

Commercially available information services have an endless number of applications. Let's take real estate as an example. Suppose you live in

Tucson, Arizona, and have been transferred to Salt Lake City, Utah. It is only a matter of time before you will be able to gain access to a nationwide information service that maintains an up-to-date listing of every home in the country that is for sale. Here is how it will work. You will enter your purchase criteria: Salt Lake City, Utah; $130,000 to $190,000; no more than one mile from an elementary school; double garage; four bedrooms; and so on. The system then presents pictures and specifications of those homes that meet your criteria.

Computer Competency as a Requirement for Employment. Computer competency, which is described in Chapter 1, "Micros and Personal Computing," is rapidly becoming a prerequisite skill for most management and professional positions, most administrative and clerical positions, and now many blue-collar jobs. Job descriptions at all levels and in most disciplines are being revised to include computer competency as a skill requirement. Within a few years a micro will be within arm's reach of every employee. In an accounting firm, a knowledge of spreadsheets and tax-preparation software is as important as a knowledge of the principles of accounting. The previous generation of civil engineers spent months analyzing the stress points in bridges; today's civil engineers use the computer to expedite this laborious process. The portable PC is the constant companion of journalists. Today's automated factories demand that shop-floor supervisors understand the computer systems that control the flow of materials.

Computer competency has emerged as a prerequisite for employment in many fields. Much of the work done at this land development company revolves around microcomputers; therefore, all employees must be computer competent.

Today's competitive international market demands that companies make the most effective use of available technology. To do so, they must have people who understand and can use the technology. In a high-tech society a person's education is incomplete until computer competency is achieved.

PC Issues

Intense controversy is a by-product of the computer and microcomputer revolution. The emotions of both the general public and the computer community run high on computer-related issues. Some of the more heated issues are discussed here.

The Misuse of Personal Information. The issue of greatest concern to the general public is the privacy of personal information. Some people fear that computer-based record-keeping offers too great an opportunity for the invasion of an individual's privacy. There is indeed reason for concern.

Sources of personal data. Enormous amounts of personal data are maintained on you by the IRS, your college, your employer, your creditors, your hospital, your insurance company, your broker, and on and on. Each day your name and personal information is passed from computer to computer. Depending on your level of activity, this could happen 20 or more times a day. Thousands of public- and private-sector organizations maintain data on individuals. The data collection begins before you are born and does not end until all your affairs are settled and those maintaining records on you are informed of your parting.

It is hoped that information about us is up-to-date and accurate. Unfortunately, much of it is not. Laws permit us to examine our records, but first we must find them. You cannot just write to the federal government and request to see your files. To be completely sure that you examine all your federal records for completeness and accuracy, you would have to write and probably visit each of the approximately 5800 agencies that maintain computer-based files on individuals. The same is true of computer-based personal data maintained in the private sector. With the explosion of PCs in recent years, the number of computers maintaining personal information has soared into the millions!

Violating the privacy of personal information. Most people will agree that the potential exists for abuse, but are these data actually being misused? Some say yes. Personal information has become the product of a growing industry. Companies have been formed that do nothing but sell information about people. Not only are the people involved not asked for permission to use their data, they are seldom even told that their personal information is being sold! A great deal of this personal data can be extracted from public records. For example, one company sends employees to county courthouses all over the United States to gather publicly accessible data about people who have recently filed papers to purchase a home. Mailing lists are then generated from microcomputer-based data bases and sold to local insurance companies, landscape com-

Personal information is a by-product of credit-card businesses. These companies have an obligation to deal with this information in a responsible manner.

panies, public officials seeking new voters, lawyers seeking new clients, and so on. Those placed on the mailing list eventually become targets of commercial and special-interest groups. You be the judge. Is the sale of such a list an abuse of personal information?

The use of personal information for profit and other purposes is growing at such a rapid rate that for all practical purposes the abuse of this information has slipped out from under the legislative umbrella. Antiquated laws, combined with judicial unfamiliarity with computers, make policing and prosecuting abuses of the privacy of personal information difficult and, in many cases, impossible.

Securing the integrity of personal information. Computer experts feel that the integrity of personal data can be more secure in computer data bases than in file cabinets. They contend that we can continue to be masters and not victims if we implement proper safeguards for the maintenance and release of this information and enact effective legislation to cope with the abuse of it.

Computer Crime. Computer crime is on the rise. There are many types of computer crimes, ranging from the use of an unauthorized password by a student to a billion-dollar insurance fraud. It is estimated that each year the total money lost from computer crime is greater than the sum total of that taken in all robberies. In fact, no one really knows the extent of computer crime because much of it is either undetected or unreported (most often the latter). In those cases involving banks, officers may elect to write off the loss rather than announce the crime and risk losing the goodwill of their customers.

The microcomputer is one of the primary tools of the computer criminal. Because it can simulate almost any type of terminal, the PC has been used to gain illegal access to a variety of computer networks, including top-secret military networks. The PC's processing power enables computer criminals to decipher security codes and to change records and extract valuable information for personal gain.

Computer crime requires the cooperation of an experienced computer specialist. A common street thug does not have the knowledge or the opportunity to be successful at computer crime. The sophistication of the crime, however, makes it no less criminal.

Computer crime is a relatively recent phenomenon. Legislation, the criminal justice system, and industry are not yet adequately prepared to cope with it. Only a few police and FBI agents in the entire country have been trained to handle cases involving computer crime. And when a case comes to court, few judges or juries have the background necessary to understand the testimony.

Recognizing the potential impact of computer crime, the legal system and industry are trying to speed up precautionary measures. Some say we are still moving too slowly and that it will take a major catastrophe to force government and business to take computer crime seriously.

The academic environment is conducive to the origination and propagation of viruses. One virus wreaked havoc at several universities. It infected the operating systems of IBM-compatible microcomputers, specifically the DOS COMMAND.COM file. When booted, the infected disk would replicate itself to an uninfected COMMAND.COM file. After repeating the replication four times, the original software virus would destroy itself—and all the files on its diskette. The other infected disks would continue to reproduce.

COMPUTER CRIMES: CATEGORIES AND TECHNIQUES

Computer crimes can be grouped into seven categories.

- *Crimes that create havoc inside a computer.* Trojan horses, computer viruses, and logic bombs fall into this category. A *Trojan horse* is a set of unauthorized instructions hidden in a legitimate program, such as an operating system. The intent of Trojan horse programmers is, by definition, malicious or criminal. The Trojan horse is a carrier of computer viruses and logic bombs. A *virus* is a Trojan horse that propagates versions of itself into other computer systems. A virus can result in the display of a harmless political message or in the devastating loss of all programs and data. A *logic bomb* is a Trojan horse that is executed when a certain set of conditions are met. For example, a disgruntled employee might plant a logic bomb to be "exploded" on the first Friday the thirteenth after his or her record is deleted from the personnel data base.

- *Crimes that involve the manipulation of computer systems and their data.* Embezzlement and fraud fall into this category. Embezzlement concerns the misappropriation of funds, and fraud involves obtaining illegal access to a computer system for the purpose of personal gain.

    The *salami technique* for embezzlement requires that a Trojan horse (unauthorized code in a legitimate program) be planted in the program code of a financial system that processes a large number of accounts. These covert instructions cause a small amount of money, usually less than a penny, to be debited periodically from each account and credited to one or more dummy accounts. A number of less sophisticated computer-manipulation crimes are the result of *data diddling*. Data diddling is changing the data, perhaps the "ship to" address, on manually prepared source documents or during entry to the system.

- *Crimes that involve telecommunications.* Illegal bulletin boards (for example, one that distributes confidential access codes and passwords), misuse of the telephone system, and any unauthorized access to a computer system, including eavesdropping (tapping into communications channels), fall into this category.

    Unauthorized entry to a computer system is achieved in a variety of ways. The most common approach is *masquerading*. People acquire authorization codes and personal information that will enable them to masquerade as an authorized user. The *tailgating* technique is used by vendors and company outsiders to gain access to sensitive information. The perpetrator simply begins using the terminal or microcomputer of an authorized user who has left the room without terminating his or her session.

    The more sophisticated user might prefer building a trap door, scanning, or superzapping. A *trap door* is a Trojan horse that permits unauthorized and undetected access to a computer system. *Scanning* involves the use of a computer to test different combinations of access information until access is permitted (for example, stepping through a four-digit access code from 0000 to 9999). *Superzapping* involves using a program that enables someone to bypass the security controls.

- *Crimes that involve the abuse of personal information.* The willful release or distribution of personal information that is inaccurate would fall into this category.

- *Crimes that involve negligence.* Companies that employ computers to process data must do so in a responsible manner. Irresponsible actions that result in the deletion of a bank account or the premature discontinuation of electrical service would fall into this category. Lax controls and the availability of sensitive information invites scavenging. *Scavenging* is searching for discarded information that may be of some value on the black market, such as a printout containing credit-card numbers.

- *Crimes that support criminal enterprises.* Money laundering and data bases that support drug distribution would fall into this category.

- *Crimes that involve the theft of hardware or software.* Software piracy, theft of computers or computer components, and the theft of trade secrets belong in this category.

A few hackers and computer professionals have chosen computer crime as a profession. But the threat from managers and consultants may be even greater because they are in the best position to commit computer crime successfully. They know how the systems operate, and they know the passwords needed to gain access to the systems.

There is a growing concern that the media is glorifying the illegal entry and use of computer systems by overzealous hackers, most of which use microcomputers. These "electronic vandals" have tapped into everything from local credit agencies to international banking systems. The evidence of unlawful entry, perhaps a revised record or access during nonoperating hours, is called a **footprint**.

Computer Viruses. Some malicious hackers leave much more than a footprint—they infect the computer system with a virus. A **computer virus** is a program that literally "infects" other programs and data bases. Viral programs are written with malicious intent and are loaded to the computer system of an unsuspecting victim. Viruses have been found at all levels of computing, from PCs to large mainframe computers. The micro computing environment is particularly susceptible to virus infiltration because of its lack of system controls.

The virus is so named because it can spread from one system to another like a biological virus. There are many types. Some act quickly by erasing user programs and data bases. Others grow like a cancer, destroying small parts of a data base each day. Some viruses act like a time bomb: They lay dormant for days or months but eventually are activated and wreak havoc on any software in the system. Some viruses attack hardware and have been known to throw the mechanical components of a computer system, such as disk access arms, into costly spasms.

In the microcomputer environment, there are three primary sources of computer viruses (see Figure 9–1).

- *Electronic bulletin-board systems.* The most common source of viral infection is the public electronic bulletin board through which users exchange software. Typically, a user logs onto the bulletin board and downloads what he or she thinks is a game, a utility program, or some other enticing piece of freeware, but gets a virus instead. One virus frequently distributed via electronic bulletin boards displays "Gotcha" on the user's monitor, then erases all programs and data from accessible disk storage.
- *Diskettes.* Viruses are also spread from one system to another via common diskettes. For example, a student with an infected applications disk might infect the fixed disks of one or more laboratory PCs. These PCs then infect the applications software of other students.
- *Computer networks.* In a computer network, viruses usually are planted in legitimate code, often the communications software. The virus is then transmitted via communications channels to other computers in the network, many of which are microcomputers.

Since first appearing in the mid-1980s, viruses have erased bank records, damaged hospital records, destroyed the programs in thousands of

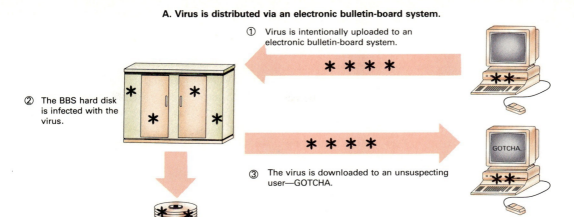
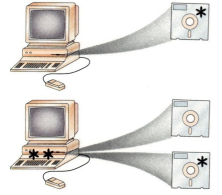
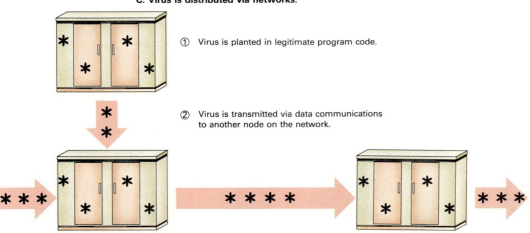

FIGURE 9-1 The Ways in Which Viruses Are Spread

microcomputers, and even infected part of the systems at NORAD (strategic defense) and NASA. Disgruntled employees have inserted viruses in disks that were distributed to customers. The motives of those who would infect a system with a virus run from electronic vandalism to revenge to terrorism. There is no monetary reward, only the "satisfaction" of knowing that their efforts have been very costly to individuals, companies, and governments.

Viruses are a serious problem. They have the potential of affecting an individual's career and even destroying companies. Antiviral programs, called **vaccines**, exist, but they can be circumvented by a persistent (and malicious) programmer. The best way to cope with viruses is to recognize that they exist and to take precautionary measures. For example, one company requires micro users to turn off their micros and reload their personal copies of the operating system before each use.

The Effects of Automation on Jobs. Concern about the effects of automation began 200 years ago with the Industrial Revolution, and the public is still apprehensive. To many people, computers mean automation, and automation means loss of jobs. Just as the Industrial Revolution created hundreds of new job opportunities, so will the "Information Revolution."

There is no doubt that the emergence of computer technology has resulted in the elimination of jobs involving routine, monotonous, and sometimes hazardous tasks. However, the loss of these jobs has been off-

The nature of the work and the availability of specially designed microcomputers have made computer careers particularly inviting to the physically disabled. These managers monitor construction projects to keep them on schedule and within budget.

set by the creation of more challenging ones. Many people whose jobs have been eliminated have been displaced to jobs carrying greater responsibilities and offering more opportunities. It is common for bookkeepers to become systems analysts, for drafters to advance to computer-aided design, and for secretaries to become specialists in a myriad of computer applications from word processing to data management. This pattern is repeated thousands of times each month.

Automation will continue to eliminate and create jobs. Historically, any advancement in technology has increased overall productivity in certain areas, thereby cutting the number of workers needed. But this also produces a wave of new jobs in the wake of cutbacks in traditional areas. With the cost of labor increasing and the cost of computers decreasing, the trend toward the automation of routine activities probably will continue. However, to realize a smooth transition to an automated environment, industry and government must recognize that they have a social responsibility to retrain those who will be displaced by the loss of their jobs.

9–3 YOUR CHALLENGE

Having mastered the contents of this book and this course, you are now in a position to exploit the benefits of microcomputers in your personal and professional life. This course, however, is only the beginning. The

Microcomputers and productivity software have become fixtures in every business, educational, and government environment. On board the space shuttle Columbia, astronaut Bonnie Dunbar relies on her laptop computer to help her analyze and document the results of a fluids experiment.

computer learning process is ongoing. The dynamics of a rapidly advancing computer technology demands a constant updating of skills and expertise. Perhaps the excitement of technological innovation and the ever-changing opportunities for application is part of the lure of computers.

By their very nature, computers bring about change. However, you and others who use them are the agents of this change. Society is counting on you to use your imagination and your newly acquired microcomputer skills to bring about positive change, both at home and at work. This is your challenge.

SUMMARY OUTLINE AND IMPORTANT TERMS

9-1 COMPUTERS: CAN WE LIVE WITHOUT THEM? Society has reached a point of no return in its dependence on computers. Business competition demands their use. Individuals are also reluctant to give up those personal conveniences made possible by the computer. Only through understanding can we control the misuse or abuse of computer technology.

9-2 MICROCOMPUTER TRENDS AND ISSUES. Several trends are sure to have an impact on you and others who are just joining the microcomputer revolution. More and more people are electing to **telecommute** to work via a data communications link between home and office. The trend toward greater use of E-mail is accelerating as its benefits become apparent—it's quick, flexible, and direct. The number of people using information services increases as the percentage of homes with micros increases. The four components of an information service are the *central computer*, the *network*, the *data base*, and the *microcomputers*. As microcomputers proliferate, a greater variety of information services will be made available to more and more people. Also, there is a trend toward making computer competency a prerequisite skill for many jobs.

The emotions of both the general public and the computer community run high on computer-related issues. The abuse of personal information is perhaps the issue of greatest concern. Enormous amounts of personal data are maintained by the IRS, colleges, employers, creditors, hospitals, insurance companies, brokers, and others, some of which may be inaccurate. The use of personal information for profit and other purposes is growing at such a rapid rate that for all practical purposes the abuse of this information has slipped out from under the legislative umbrella.

Computer crime is on the rise. In fact, no one really knows the extent of computer crime because much of it is either undetected or unreported. The evidence of unlawful entry to a computer system is called a **footprint**.

A **computer virus** is a program that "infects" other programs and data bases. The virus is so named because it can spread from one system to another like a biological virus. In the microcomputer environment, there are three primary sources of computer viruses: electronic bulletin-board systems, common diskettes, and computer networks. Antiviral programs, called **vaccines**, help minimize the damage done by computer viruses.

The emergence of computer technology has resulted in the elimination of jobs involving routine, monotonous, and sometimes hazardous tasks;

however, the loss of these jobs has been offset by the creation of more challenging ones.

9-3 YOUR CHALLENGE. The dynamics of a rapidly advancing computer technology demands a constant updating of skills and expertise.

REVIEW EXERCISES

1. Has society reached the point of no return in its dependence on computers?
2. Why are managers and consultants in a good position to commit computer crimes?
3. Name three PC trends.
4. What name is given to those people who work with information?
5. What is telecommuting?
6. Approximately what percentage of micros is linked to a computer network?
7. What are the four components of a commercial information service?
8. Describe one way in which the microcomputer can benefit the computer criminal.
9. What are the three primary sources of computer viruses?
10. Name five organizations that maintain personal data on you.

SELF-TEST (by section)

9-1 a. It would take at least a month to retool a typical automobile assembly line so it could function without computers. (T/F)
  b. If the number of computer applications continues to grow at the present rate, our computer-independent society will be dependent on computers by the year 2000. (T/F)
9-2 a. It is estimated that each year the total monetary loss from computer crime is greater than the sum total of all robberies. (T/F)
  b. The trend to telecommuting is being dampened by the proliferation of fax machines. (T/F)
  c. To open E-mail, the user recalls the message from storage and displays it. (T/F)
  d. Computer competency will never become a requirement for employment in the field of accounting. (T/F)
  e. Which of the following is not a PC issue: (a) computer crime, (b) computer viruses, or (c) computer cottages?
  f. Antiviral programs are called _____.
  g. The number of federal agencies that maintain computer-based files on individuals is between: (a) 50 and 100, (b) 500 and 1000, or (c) more than 5000?
  h. The evidence of unlawful entry to a computer system is called a _____.

9-3 The computer learning process is ongoing. (T/F)

Self-test answers.   9-1 **(a)** F; **(b)** F.   9-2 **(a)** T; **(b)** F; **(c)** T; **(d)** F; **(e)** c; **(f)** vaccines; **(g)** c; **(h)** footprint.   9-3 T.

APPENDIX A

MS-DOS TUTORIAL AND EXERCISES

- ▶ A–1 Introduction
- ▶ A–2 Files, Directories, and Paths
- ▶ A–3 Booting the System
- ▶ A–4 DOS Commands
- ▶ A–5 DOS Keyboard Functions
- ▶ A–6 Backup
- ▶ A–7 Batch Files

APPENDIX A MS-DOS Tutorial and Exercises

A-1 INTRODUCTION

This tutorial focuses on features of the MS-DOS operating system that are fundamental to the use and application of microcomputer productivity software. MS-DOS, often referred to as "DOS" (rhymes with *boss*), is the primary operating system for IBM-compatible PCs. General operating system concepts are discussed in Chapter 2, "Interacting with Micros." If you have not already done so, you should read and familiarize yourself with the material in Chapter 2.

Interspersed throughout the discussion of MS-DOS are *step-by-step* tutorial boxes that lead you, *keystroke-by-keystroke*, through the execution of the most commonly used DOS commands. These tutorial boxes enable you to interact with the computer and actually do what is being discussed.

Microcomputers can be configured with or without a hard disk. (Virtually all micros will have at least one diskette or microdisk drive; some have one of each.) However, because almost all micros manufactured in recent years are configured with a permanently installed hard disk, *this tutorial and the productivity software tutorials that accompany this book assume that you are using a hard-disk-based PC*. When you are interacting with the hard disk during a DOS session, the DOS prompt for you to enter a command is either C> or C:\>.

MS-DOS and the productivity software (for example, WordPerfect) normally are stored on the hard disk. In learning situations, students usually keep their personal data files on interchangeable diskettes. If the PC you plan to use does not have a hard disk, read the material in the adjacent box entitled "Performing Tutorials on Diskette-Based PCs."

▶ PERFORMING THE MS-DOS TUTORIAL ON DISKETTE-BASED PERSONAL COMPUTERS

Disregard this box item if the PC on which you intend to do the MS-DOS tutorial has a permanently installed hard disk. The tutorial is designed for this environment and needs no modification.

- *If you are using a diskette-based PC with only one diskette*, MS-DOS, the application software, and your data diskette must share Disk Drive A. Therefore, the initial DOS prompt will be A> or A:\>. To use the tutorial in this book, simply read the C:\> prompt in the tutorial as an A> prompt and insert the appropriate diskette (MS-DOS, productivity software, or data), as needed.

  Some DOS commands, called *external commands*, must be loaded to RAM from disk on each use. Prior to issuing an external DOS command, you will need to insert the diskette containing DOS into Disk Drive A. Once the command has been loaded to RAM you probably will need to exchange the DOS diskette in Disk Drive A with your application or data diskette.

- *If you are using a diskette-based PC with two diskettes*, let MS-DOS and your applications software share Disk Drive A. Use Disk Drive B for your data disk. To use the tutorial in this book, simply read the C:\> and the A:\> prompts in the tutorial as A> and B>, respectively. Insert the appropriate diskette (MS-DOS, productivity software, or data) in the appropriate disk drive (A or B), as needed.

  Some DOS commands, called *external commands*, must be loaded to RAM from disk on each use. Prior to issuing an external DOS command, you will need to insert the diskette containing DOS into Disk Drive A. Once the command has been loaded to RAM you probably will need to exchange the DOS diskette in Disk Drive A with your application or data diskette.

A–2 FILES, DIRECTORIES, AND PATHS

One of the prerequisites to understanding DOS commands is an understanding of how DOS deals with files.

Naming Files

On a microcomputer, a **file** is related information that is stored on disk as a unit. A file can be a program, data for an electronic spreadsheet, a database of names and addresses, the text of a report, or even a game. Each file is given a name, either by a user or someone else (for example, a software vendor). The name of a file includes:

- A *filename* of up to eight characters.
- An optional *extension* of up to three characters.

The filename and extension are separated by a period (.). The extension identifies files with a certain application. For example, word processing packages often append the extension DOC (for document) to a user-supplied filename (such as LETTER.DOC). The extension appended to BASIC program filenames is BAS (PAYROLL.BAS). The following are "legal" filenames:

NAMEADDR.DB   SALES.WK1   A

These are not legal (DOS will not accept them):

N+A.DB	*(The symbols + . = ∧ [ ] : | < > = ; , are not allowed.)*
FIRSTQUARTERSALES	*(There are more than eight characters.)*
.out	*(There is no filename.)*

Referencing Files

The *file specification* includes the disk drive, the filename, and the extension. A file (such as SALES.WK1) is stored on a user-designated disk drive. The diskette drives are labeled A and B. The hard-disk drive is labeled C.

One of the disk drives is designated as the *active drive* (or default drive); that is, the DOS commands you issue apply to the active drive unless you state otherwise in the command. The DOS prompt indicates which drive is the active drive. (For example, a DOS prompt of A:\> tells you that the active drive is A.) If the desired file (SALES.WK1) is on Drive A and the active drive is A, the *drive specifier* can be omitted. If the active drive is C (the DOS prompt is C:\>), and the desired file (SALES.WK1) is on Drive A, the entire file specification, including the drive specifier, is necessary in order to reference the file: A:SALES.WK1.

Active Drive	File Reference
A:\>	SALES.WK1
C:\>	A:SALES.WK1

Directories and Subdirectories

A **directory** is simply a list of the names of the files stored in a named area on a hard disk or diskette. A disk can have any number of directories and subdi-

---

▶ **MEMORY BITS**

File Specification (filename.ext)
- Filename
  Up to eight valid characters
  Valid characters:
  A–Z 0–9 ~!#$%&()-'{}
- Extension
  Optional
  Separated from filename by a period
  Up to three valid characters

rectories. The directory feature of DOS enables us to group related files in a directory. For example, we can create a directory into which we would store only word processing document files and another directory into which we would store only spreadsheet files.

It is not uncommon for a hard disk to contain hundreds of files in 20 or more directories. To make file management and inquiries easier, users organize their files into a hierarchy, or *tree*, of directories and **subdirectories**. At the highest level of the "upside-down tree" is the **root directory** (typically C:\ for a hard-disk drive and A:\ or B:\ for a diskette drive). All other directories are subordinate to the root directory. When you load DOS to RAM, the root directory is the *active directory*.

Consider the directory tree illustrated in Figure A–1. Two marketing managers, Ted and Amy, and their assistant, Dennis, share the same personal computer. To keep their programs and files separate, they established directories as shown in Figure A–1. They created the subdirectories \LOTUS and \WP to which they could assign subordinate subdirectories for their personal files. The subdirectory \LOTUS contains the software for LOTUS 1-2-3 and two subordinate directories for Ted's (\LOTUS\TED) and Amy's (\LOTUS\AMY) Lotus 1-2-3 data files (such as SALES.WK1, BOOKFILE.WK1, and so on). The subdirectory \WP contains the software for WordPerfect and three subordinate directories for Ted's (\WP\TED), Amy's (\WP\AMY), and Dennis's (\WP\DENNIS) WordPerfect documents and graphics (such as MEMO.DOC, REPORT.TXT, FIGURE1.WPG, and so on).

The relationship between a directory at a higher level to one at a lower level is that of a *parent* to *child* or *children*. In Figure A–1, the root (C:\) is the parent of the \LOTUS and \WP. The subdirectory \LOTUS is the parent of both \LOTUS\TED and \LOTUS\AMY. In the hierarchy, no directory has more than one parent. The root does not have a parent.

Files of any kind can be stored in the root directory or in any subdirectory. When working with files stored on a disk with a hierarchy of directories, you need to specify the **path**. The path is the logical route that DOS must follow in order to locate the specified file on a disk. In the example in Figure A–1, the path to one of Ted's Lotus 1-2-3 files, SALES.WK1, would be *from* the root directory (C:\) *to*:

FIGURE A–1 Example Directory Tree
The first-level subdirectories \LOTUS and \WP have two and three second-level subdirectories, respectively.

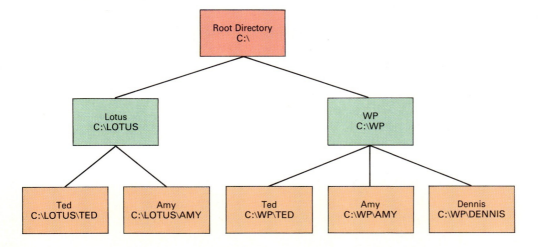

- the Lotus 1-2-3 subdirectory (C:\LOTUS) *to*
- Ted's subdirectory (C:\LOTUS\TED) *to*
- the specific file (C:\LOTUS\TED\SALES.WK1).

The filename is always the last entry in the path.

DOS, Directories, and Local Area Networks

Today 20% of all PCs are part of a local area network (LAN), and this percentage is growing rapidly. A LAN, or local net, is a system of hardware, software, and communications channels that connects devices in close proximity, such as in a suite of offices. LANs are discussed in detail in Chapter 7, "Data Communications and Networks." If you plan to use a PC that is part of a LAN for the keystroke tutorials, you may wish to read Section 7–7 of Chapter 7.

LANs offer two fundamental advantages over the single-user environment. First, resources such as printers, data, and applications software can be shared among the nodes on the network. Second, LANs enable the use of **groupware**—software whose application is designed to benefit a group of people. Electronic mail, electronic bulletin-board, on-line appointment calendar, and project/resource scheduling software are examples of groupware.

PCs on most LANs are equipped with a network interface card (see Chapter 3, "Processors and Platforms") and interact with a central file server to use groupware or load applications programs such as WordPerfect or Lotus 1-2-3. When a LAN-based PC is booted, memory-resident software that enables the use of the network interface card, communication with the file server, and interaction with DOS is loaded to RAM. Depending on how the LAN system administrator configured the LAN, you may need to enter an ID (usually your name) and a password. Again, depending on how the LAN is set up, you may see a menu of available groupware and applications software on the file server, or you may see a DOS prompt. Frequently, the file server is given the disk-drive specifier *F*. When DOS prompt is F:\> or F:*directory*>, the active directory is on the file-server disk. When the DOS prompt is A:\>, B:\>, or C:\>, the active directory is on one of the disks on your PC.

In addition to the DOS commands presented in this appendix, LAN-based PCs can execute network commands. Network commands are often similar to DOS commands. For example, NDIR may be the network version of the DOS DIR (list directory) command.

Wildcards

There are many times you might wish to issue a DOS command that applies to a group of related files. For such operations we use DOS **wildcard** characters, the asterisk (*) or the question mark (?).

* When used in a filename.extension combination, the * is a generic reference to any combination of legal characters.
? When used in a filename.extension combination, the ? is a substitute for any single character.

A wildcard reference applies only to those files in the current or named directory. For example, suppose the following files are on the root directory (A:\>) on the diskette in the active drive (A).

SALES1Q.WK1	LETTER.WP	SALES3Q.WK1	MEMO2.WP
IDEA.OUT	SALES2Q.WK1	SALES4Q.WK1	THOUGHTS.OUT
NET.WK1	REPORT.WP	MEMO14.WP	NAMES.DB

▶ KEYSTROKE CONVENTIONS USED IN THE STEP-BY-STEP TUTORIAL

Boxed keystroke tutorial are interspersed throughout this MS-DOS appendix and all skill modules that accompany this text (WordPerfect, Lotus 1-2-3, dBASE III PLUS, and so on). These keystroke tutorial are designed to give you hands-on experience with DOS and a variety of application software packages. The keystroke conventions are similar to what you might find in the vendor-supplied documentation for a particular software package.

Standard Type, Boldface, Outlined Keys, and Italic

Portions of the keystroke tutorial displayed by the program are shown in standard type. User-entered data and text commands are shown in **boldface** type.

Enter new date (mm-dd-yy): **12-14-93** ⏎

For the foregoing, you would enter "12-14-93" in response to the prompt and tap the ⏎, or ENTER key.

Keystroke or keystroke combination commands are boxed. Inline instructions or clarifications that are not displayed on the screen in response to an input are shown in italics (such as **Y**es). Italicized instructions or clarifications that are not extensions of commands are in italics and enclosed in parentheses, for example (*15 times*).

|HOME| **/W**orksheet **C**olumn **S**et-Width
Enter column width (1..240): → (*15 times*) ⏎

For the above, you would tap the HOME key, "/", "W", "C", "S", the right cursor-control key 15 times, and ⏎.

Summary of Keystroke Conventions

Keystroke(s)	Action
⏎	Tap ENTER, RETURN, CR (carriage return).
← → ↑ ↓	Tap the left, right, up, or down cursor-control (arrow) key indicated.
|F1|	Tap Function Key 1 (or the number indicated). Boxed keys refer to specific keys (F5, HOME, ESC).
/File **S**ave	Tap "/", then "F", then "S". Clarifications and instructions displayed by the program are in standard print.
|ESC| **E**nd **Q**uit	Tap escape (ESC), then "E", then "Q". Clarifications and instructions not displayed by the program are in italics.
|CTRL| + |PRTSC|	Press keys linked with a plus (+) symbol simultaneously (press and hold CTRL, then tap PRTSC). (*Note: Until recently, key combinations were hyphenated; however, the emerging convention is to link them with the plus, or add, symbol.*)

Simply stated, you tap only those characters that are in boldface type, the cursor-control keys, the ENTER key, and the boxed keys. All other characters are provided for clarification or explanation.

The following demonstrates three common uses of the * and ? wildcard characters.

Wildcard File Reference	Files Referenced			
*.WP	LETTER.WP	REPORT.WP	MEMO2.WP	MEMO14.WP
SALES?Q.WK1	SALES1Q.WK1	SALES2Q.WK1	SALES3Q.WK1	SALES4Q.WK1
MEMO*.*	MEMO2.WP	MEMO14.WP		
MEMO?.*	MEMO2.WP			
.	all files in directory			

The two wildcard references to the MEMO files (MEMO *.* and MEMO?.*) illustrate the difference between the * and the ?. Because MEMO14.WP has two characters between "MEMO" and the dot (.), it is not included for the MEMO?.* reference.

A-3 BOOTING THE SYSTEM

Before you can use a microcomputer, you must load DOS, or "boot the system." When you boot the system, the computer "pulls itself up by its own bootstraps." The procedure for booting the system on most micros is simply to load the operating system from disk storage into main memory.

- Turn on the monitor and the printer (if needed).
- Turn on the computer. (On a diskette-based system, insert the DOS disk in Disk Drive A [top or left drive], close the door, and turn on the computer.)
- After a short period, a beep signals the end of the system check, and DOS is loaded from disk to RAM.
- At the date prompt, enter the date in the month (mm), day (dd), year (yy) format. At the time prompt, enter the time in the HOURS:MINUTES format.

Note: Use the backspace key, as needed, to make corrections while entering data or commands.

STEP 1 DATE and TIME

Boot the system and, if needed, enter today's date and time.

    Enter new date (mm-dd-yy): **12-14-93** ↵
    Enter new time: **13:35** ↵
    C:\>

Figure A-2 shows the display of the DOS sequence in Step 1. The entries are for December 14, 1993, and 1:35 P.M. To omit these entries tap (ENTER) after the prompts. Change or request the date and time at any time during a session by issuing the DATE and TIME commands (for example, C:\>DATE).

Note: If your system is configured with a battery-powered clock, the date and time prompts may not appear after booting the system.

The C:\> prompt on the monitor's display indicates that the system is ready to receive user commands.

Note: These tutorials assume that your micro is configured to display the DOS prompt with a colon and a backslash (C:\>). If your prompt is C>, you

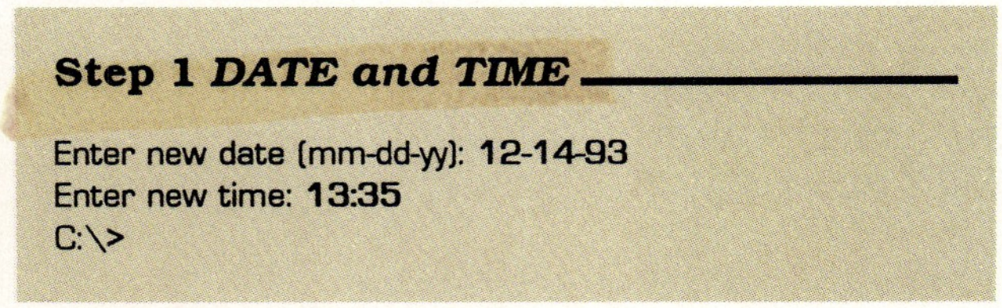

Step 1 DATE and TIME

Enter new date (mm-dd-yy): **12-14-93**
Enter new time: **13:35**
C:\>

FIGURE A-2 DOS Sequence in Step 1: Booting the System
Systems that are not configured with battery-powered clocks will request that date and time be entered at the conclusion of the booting procedure.

APPENDIX A MS-DOS Tutorial and Exercises

*may find it helpful to enter **prompt pg** at the DOS prompt (that is, C>
prompt pg). The DOS PROMPT command enables the user to change the
DOS prompt to better meet processing needs. The $p option causes the active
directory to be displayed with the root directory (C:\WP) and the $g option
adds the > to prompt (C:\WP>). Plan on entering **prompt pg** any time
that your work calls for manipulating files in several directories.*

A-4 DOS COMMANDS

We use *DOS commands* to run our application programs, make systems inquiries, and manage files. DOS provides us with about 60 commands; however, the typical user will use no more than 25% of them. These frequently used commands are the focus of this DOS appendix.

Internal and External Commands

DOS commands are of two types, *internal* and *external*. Internal commands are memory-resident; that is, they are stored in memory when you load DOS. Internal commands are available to the user at any time. In contrast, external commands must be loaded to memory from the directory containing the DOS files. If you are working on a PC with a hard disk, the internal/external distinction is less apparent because all DOS commands are readily accessible. However, if DOS is loaded from an interchangeable diskette, you must make sure that the diskette containing DOS is inserted in the active disk drive (Disk Drive A or B) before issuing an external DOS command. The DOS Command Summary box indicates which commands are internal and which are external.

Changing the Active Disk Drive

If you wish to change the active, or logged, drive, simply type the desired drive letter followed by a colon (:) at the DOS prompt. For example, if C is the active drive, and you wish to make A the active drive, make sure you have a diskette in Drive A.

> **STEP 2** *Change the Active Drive*
>
> Change the active drive from C to A.
>
>   C:\> **a:**↵
>   A:\>
>
> Now make Drive C the active drive again.
>
>   A:\> **c:**↵
>   C:\>

Figure A-3 shows an example display of the DOS sequence in Steps 2 through 12. Periodically check your interactive session against the general flow in this example. Your display will differ slightly from the example because of differences in hardware configuration, level of DOS used, and the mix of programs and files.

Step 2 *Change the Active Drive*

C:\>a:
A:\>c:
C:\>

Step 3 *FORMAT a Disk*

C:\>format
Insert new diskette for drive A:
and press ENTER when ready...

Format complete

Volume label (11 characters, ENTER for none)?

   362496 bytes total disk space
   362496 bytes available on disk

    1024 bytes in each allocation unit
     354 allocation units available on disk

Volume Serial Number is 0C78-10F2

Format another (Y/N) ?**y**

Insert new diskette for drive A:
and press ENTER when ready...

Format complete

Volume label (11 characters, ENTER for none)?

   362496 bytes total disk space
   362496 bytes available on disk

    1024 bytes in each allocation unit
     354 allocation units available on disk

Volume Serial Number is 4527-0DE2

Format another (Y/N) ?**n**

Step 4 *DIRectory List*

C:\>dir

  Volume in drive C is DOS400
  Volume Serial Number is 160F-17F9
  Directory of C:\

COMMAND COM   37557   05-12-89   12:00a
WINDOWS   <DIR>   08-21-90   11:41p
123   <DIR>   02-12-90   10:26p
      .
      .

AUTOEXEC BAT   343   03-28-91   12:01a
    93 File(s) 9238528 bytes free

C:\>**dir/p**

  Volume in drive C is DOS400
  Volume Serial Number is 160F-17F9
  Directory of C:\

COMMAND COM   37557   05-12-89   12:00a
WINDOWS   <DIR>   08-21-90   11:41p
123   <DIR>   02-12-90   10:26p
      .
SUPER   <DIR>   04-18-90   12:43a
Press any key to continue...
      .

Press any key to continue...
      .

AUTOEXEC BAT   343   03-28-91   12:01a
    93 File(s) 9238528 bytes free

C:\>**dir/w**

  Volume in drive C is DOS400
  Volume Serial Number is 160F-17F9
  Directory of C:\

COMMAND COM   WINDOWS   123
      .
TALKS   COLLEGE   AUTOEXEC BAT
    93 File (s) 9238528 bytes free

Step 5 *MD (Make Directory)*

C:\>a:
A:\>**md wp**
A:\>**md ss**
A:\>**md db**
A:\>**md extra**
A:\>dir

  Volume in drive A has no label
  Volume Serial Number is 0C78-10F2
  Directory of A:\

WP   <DIR>   05-29-91   10:11a
SS   <DIR>   05-29-91   10:11a
DB   <DIR>   05-29-91   10:11a
EXTRA   <DIR>   05-29-91   10:12a
    4 File(s) 358400 bytes free

FIGURE A–3 DOS Sequence in Steps 2 through 12: DOS Commands

APPENDIX A MS-DOS Tutorial and Exercises

Step 6 CD (Change Directory)

A:\>cd extra

Step 7 RD (Remove Directory)

A:\EXTRA>cd\
A:\>rd extra
A:\>dir

Volume in drive A has no label
Volume Serial Number is 0C78-10F2
Directory of A:\

```
WP           <DIR>        05-29-91   10:11a
SS           <DIR>        05-29-91   10:11a
DB           <DIR>        05-29-91   10:11a
       3 File(s)    359424 bytes free
```

Step 8 CLS (Clear Screen); COPY CON

A:\>cls
A:\>cd wp
A:\WP>copy con file1.txt
This one-sentence text file is created
and manipulated in this DOS tutorial.
(F6 for end-of-file marker.)^Z
        1 File(s) copied

A:\WP>dir

Volume in drive A has no label
Volume Serial Number is 0C78-10F2
Directory of A:\WP

```
.            <DIR>        05-29-91   10:11a
..           <DIR>        05-29-91   10:11a
FILE1        TXT      79  05-29-91   10:17a
       3 File(s)    358400 bytes free
```

Step 9 TYPE

A:\WP>type file1.txt
This one-sentence text file is created
and manipulated in this DOS tutorial.

Step 10 COPY and Wildcard Characters

A:\WP>copy file1.txt file2.txt
        1 File(s) copied

A:\WP>dir/w

Volume in drive A has no label
Volume Serial Number is 0C78-10F2
Directory of A:\WP

```
.                ..               FILE1    TXT     FILE2    TXT
       4 File(s)    357376 bytes free
```

A:\WP>copy *.* \ss
FILE1.TXT
FILE2.TXT
        2 File(s) copied

A:\WP>dir \ss

Volume in drive A has no label
Volume Serial Number is 0C78-10F2
Directory of A:\SS

```
.            <DIR>        05-29-91   10:11a
..           <DIR>        05-29-91   10:11a
FILE1        TXT      79  05-29-91   10:17a
FILE2        TXT      79  05-29-91   10:17a
       4 File(s)    355328 bytes free
```

A:\WP>cd\ss

A:\SS>dir file*.*

Volume in drive A has no label
Volume Serial Number is 0C78-10F2
Directory of A:\SS

```
FILE1        TXT      79  05-29-91   10:17a
FILE2        TXT      79  05-29-91   10:17a
       2 File(s)    355328 bytes free
```

Step 11 DELete

A:\SS>del file1.txt
A:\SS>dir

Volume in drive A has no label
Volume Serial Number is 0C78-10F2
Directory of A:\SS

```
.            <DIR>        05-29-91   10:11a
..           <DIR>        05-29-91   10:11a
FILE2        TXT      79  05-29-91   10:17a
       3 File(s)    356352 bytes free
```

FIGURE A-3 (cont'd)

Step 12 *REName*

```
A:\SS>ren file2.txt file3.txt
A:\SS>cls
A:\SS>dir

 Volume in drive A has no label
 Volume Serial Number is 0C78-10F2
 Directory of A:\SS

.            <DIR>         05-29-91   10:11a
..           <DIR>         05-29-91   10:11a
FILE3        TXT       79  05-29-91   10:17a
         3 File(s)    356352 bytes free

A:\SS>dir \wp

 Volume in drive A has no label
 Volume Serial Number is 0C78-10F2
 Directory of A:\WP

.            <DIR>         05-29-91   10:11a
..           <DIR>         05-29-91   10:11a
FILE1        TXT       79  05-29-91   10:17a
FILE2        TXT       79  05-29-91   10:17a
         4 File(s)    356352 bytes free
```

FIGURE A–3 *(cont'd)*

FORMAT: Preparing a Disk for Use

The *external* FORMAT command prepares a new disk for use. A new disk is coated with a surface that can be magnetized easily to represent data; however, before the disk can be used, it must be formatted. The FORMAT command causes the disk to be initialized with the DOS recording format. Specifically, it:

- Creates sectors and tracks (see Chapter 4, "Micro Peripheral Devices: I/O and Data Storage").
- Sets up an area for the file and directory allocation tables. (The tables tell the system where to find the directories and files that you will eventually store on the disk.)

If the computer you are using has a hard disk, it probably has been configured to accept external DOS commands from any directory, including the root directory (C:\). If this is not the case, your instructor will provide you with specific instructions.

You will need two interchangeable disks for the Step 3 tutorial. The disks can be new or used. A new disk is blank; however, a used disk may contain files. *Formatting an already used disk erases everything that was previously stored on it*, so make sure that the files on a used disk are of no value to you.

STEP 3 *Format a Disk*

Insert and FORMAT one of the disks in Drive A.

    C:\> **format a:** ↵
Insert new diskette for drive A:

    and press ENTER when ready... ↵

DOS should reply with a message that the disk is being formatted. If your version of DOS prompts you for a *volume label*, tap ↵ ENTER to indicate "none" or no volume label for this disk. As you begin using applications software, you might opt to enter internal volume (disk) labels on your newly formatted disks.

    Format complete
    Volume label (11 characters, Enter for none)? ↵

APPENDIX A MS-DOS Tutorial and Exercises

The system responds with a disk-space summary and a "Format another?" prompt (see Figure A–3). The disk-space summary varies depending on the type of disk formatted. Answer *y*, or yes, to the "Format another?" prompt when it appears. Remove the first disk from Drive A and insert the second. After the second disk has been successfully formatted, answer *n*, or no, to the "Format another?" prompt.

> Format another (Y/N)?**y** ↵
> *(Replace the newly formatted disk with another disk.)*
> Insert new diskette for drive A:
> and press ENTER when ready... ↵
> Format complete
> Volume label (11 characters, Enter for none)? ↵
> Format another (Y/N)?**n** ↵
> C:\>

In practice, the way you use FORMAT depends on the version of DOS you have, the disk to be formatted, and the disk drive. To accommodate these varying circumstances, the FORMAT command permits the user to enter descriptive *parameters* (options). For example, you might enter **format a:/4** to format a DS/DD 5¼-inch 360-KB diskette in a DS/HD (1.2-MB) disk drive or enter **format a:/t:80/n:9** to format a DS/DD 3½-inch 720-KB diskette in a DS/HD (1.44-MB) disk drive. Your instructor will tell you if the FORMAT sequence is other than that depicted in the keystroke tutorial.

From now on, we'll refer to the disks you have just formatted as the *data disk* and the *backup disk*. Use the data disk for all keystroke tutorials in this appendix and in applications tutorials that accompany this book. Use a soft felt-tipped pen to write "Data Disk" and "Backup Disk" on the two disk labels. Include other information as appropriate (name, phone number, course number, and so on). Use the backup disk in Step 16 and to make periodic backups of your data disk.

Creating, Changing, and Removing a Directory

Figure A–4 is provided to help you keep abreast of the status of your data disk as you progress through the DOS tutorials. The status of the data disk is shown following those steps that result in file and/or directory changes.

DIR: Directory Command. The *internal* DIR, or directory command, causes a list of all entries on the current directory to be displayed on the monitor, including the names of all files and subdirectories (indicated by a <DIR>). The listing also includes such useful information as the size of each file (in bytes) and the number of bytes on the disk that are still available to the user.

Several DOS commands have switches. A **switch** is a parameter that modifies the basic command. A DOS switch is prefaced by a forward slash (/). Two frequently used switches for the DIR command are the /w, or *wide*, option (C:\> **dir/w**) and the /p, or *pause*, option (C:\> **dir/p**). Use the /w switch if you want a list that includes only the names of the files and subdirectories on the current directory. The wide option (/w) results in a multicolumn list that runs across the screen. Use the /p switch if you wish to scroll through a long

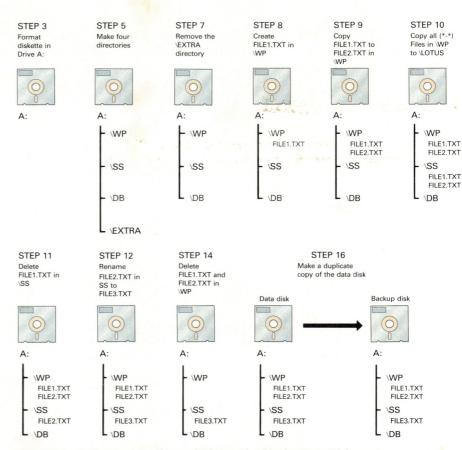

FIGURE A–4 Changes to Files and Directories on the Data Disk
The content of the data disk is altered in Steps 3, 5, 7, 8, 9, 10, 11, 12, 14, and 16. The directory tree below a diskette portrays the content of the data disk at the conclusion of the step noted above the diskette. In addition, the tree reflects the status of the disk at the beginning of the next sequential step and the next step in the figure.

directory one screen at a time. Both of these switches and others, if needed, can be appended to a DIR command (C:\> **dir/w/p**).

Note: Two types of slashes are used. One is a backslash (\) and the other, a forward slash (/).

STEP 4 *DIRectory List*

View the C:\ directory using the DIR command and the /p and /w switches.

    C:\> **dir** ↵
    C:\> **dir/p** ↵ *(Tap any key to advance to the next screen.)*
    C:\> **dir/w** ↵

The actual list of files and subdirectories will vary markedly from computer to computer.

APPENDIX A MS-DOS Tutorial and Exercises

MD: Make Directory Command. The *internal* MD, or make directory command, is used to create a new directory.

> **STEP 5** MD (Make Directory)
>
> Create four directories on your newly formatted data disk. Name these directories WP (for word processing files), SS (for spreadsheet files), DB (for database files), and EXTRA. Use the DIR command to confirm that these subdirectories to the root directory A:\ have been created.
>
>   C:\> **a:** ↵
>   A:\> **md wp** ↵
>   A:\> **md ss** ↵
>   A:\> **md db** ↵
>   A:\> **md extra** ↵
>   A:\> **dir** ↵
>
> *Note: Should you wish to create subdirectories to any of these directories, simply make the parent directory the active directory (see Step 6) and issue the make directory (MD) command. For example, to create a PERSONAL subdirectory to the \WP directory, enter* **md personal** *after the A:\WP> prompt. The path to this directory would be A:\WP\PERSONAL.*

[handwritten margin notes: MAKE DIRECTORY ↓ A: MD WP ↵ ; sub-directory A:\WP\Personal]

CD: Change Directory Command. The *internal* CD, or change directory command, is used to change the active directory.

> **STEP 6** CD (Change Directory)
>
> Make EXTRA the current directory.
>
>   A:\> **cd extra** ↵
>   A:\EXTRA> ↵ *(Tapping ENTER simply repeats the prompt.)*

[handwritten margin note: Change Dir ↓ A: CD EXTRA]

Notice that the new prompt shows the entire path: root directory (A:\) and subdirectory (EXTRA).

Note: If your DOS prompt does not reflect the active directory (A:\EXTRA), enter **prompt pg** *at the A:\> prompt.*

RD: Remove Directory Command. The *internal* RD, or remove directory command, is used to remove a directory. To remove a directory, it must be empty (that is, contain no files or subdirectories). Also, the directory to be removed cannot be the current directory.

> **STEP 7** *RD (Remove Directory)*
>
> Use *cd* to change to the root directory, then remove the directory named EXTRA. The backslash (\) is the symbol for the root directory.
>
>   A:\EXTRA> **cd** ↵
>   A:\> **rd extra** ↵
>   A:\> **dir** ↵

[Margin note: REMOVE DIR]

Only three directories (\WP, \SS, and \DB) are listed for the root directory (A:) by the DIR command. Keep and use this data disk in the remaining DOS keystroke tutorials.

Working with DOS Files and Directories

COPY CON: Copy Input from Keyboard to Disk. To complete the DOS tutorial, we'll need a file to manipulate. A "quick-and-dirty" way to create a file on disk is to use the COPY command to "copy" whatever you enter via the keyboard to a disk file. Use COPY to create a file called FILE1.TXT in the \WP directory. The system-defined name for the keyboard (the source of the file) is CON: (for *con*sole keyboard). We'll use this form of the COPY command just to create this file. We'll look at more conventional uses of COPY later in the DOS tutorial.

Note: In lieu of creating FILE1.TXT with COPY CON, your instructor may ask you to copy an existing file from the hard disk to the A:\WP directory. If so, perform the first two commands in Step 8 then, at the A:\WP> prompt, enter **copy c:\file1.txt**. *This command copies an existing file from C: to A:\WP. Skip the remainder of Step 8.*

> **STEP 8** *CLS (Clear Screen); COPY CON*
>
> Clear the screen, make \WP the active directory, and create a text file named FILE1.TXT.
>
>   A:\> **cls** *(Clear the screen.)* ↵
>   A:\> **cd wp** ↵
>   A:\WP> **copy con file1.txt** ↵
>
> Key in the following sentence. Tap ↵ after "created", the period, and the ^Z.
>
>   **This one-sentence text file is created** ↵
>   **and manipulated in this DOS tutorial.** ↵
>   [F6] *(F6 inserts an end-of-file marker)* ^Z ↵
>   A:\WP> **dir**

[Margin notes: Clear → A:\> cls; Change Dir. → A:\> cd wp]

Whenever you create, copy, or delete files, confirm that you did what you wanted to do by issuing the DIR command. FILE1.TXT should be the only named file on the newly formatted disk. Figure A-3 shows the display of the

APPENDIX A MS-DOS Tutorial and Exercises

DOS sequence in Step 8. The dot (. <DIR>) and the double dot (.. <DIR>) entries at the beginning of the DIR listing are references to the root directory and the parent directory for A:\WP.

The TYPE command is handy when you want a quick preview of the contents of a particular text file.

STEP 9 *TYPE*

View the contents of FILE1.TXT.

A:\WP> **type file1.txt** ↵
This one-sentence text file is created
and manipulated in this DOS tutorial.

← CTRL + S TO PAUSE

PRINTING

Note: The DOS PRINT command works in much the same way as the TYPE command except that the output is printed rather than displayed on the monitor. To PRINT FILE1.TXT, enter **print file1.txt** *at the A:\> prompt.*

COPY: Copying Files. The *internal* COPY files command copies one or more files to the directory specified in the command. Remember these three points about the COPY command.

- The *source* file(s) specification is listed first and the *target* file(s) specification is listed second.
- If not stated in the file specification, the current directory is assumed.
- If you omit the filename(s) in the target specification, the duplicate file(s) is given the same name as the source file(s).

STEP 10 *COPY and Wildcard Characters*

Use COPY to create a duplicate copy of FILE1.TXT, called FILE2.TXT, on the same \WP subdirectory. Invoke the "wide" option on the directory command.

A:\WP> **copy file1.txt file2.txt** ↵
A:\WP> **dir/w** ↵

Now use the * (asterisk) wildcard character to copy all files on the directory \WP to the directory \SS and give these files the same name.

A:\WP> **copy *.* \ss** ↵

Now request a DIR listing for A:\SS. Because you are logged into A:\WP, you must qualify your DIR request by specifying \SS. Also, use the asterisk (*) wildcard character to request a listing of only those files in \SS that begin with *file*.

A:\WP> **dir \ss** ↵
A:\WP> **cd\ss** ↵
A:\SS> **dir file*.*** ↵

> **MEMORY BITS**
>
> *Frequently Used DOS Commands*
> - Disk
>   FORMAT (E)
>   CHKDSK (E)
>   DISKCOPY (E)
> - Directory
>   DIR (I)
>   MD (I)
>   CD (I)
>   RD (I)
> - File
>   COPY (I)
>   ERASE, DEL (I)
>   REN (I) — Rename
> - Output
>   TYPE (I)
>   CLS (I)
>
> I = internal command   E = external command

Note: When you wish to change to a subdirectory (CD command) of the active directory (or the root directory), the destination directory need not be prefaced by a backslash (\) such as illustrated in Steps 6 and 8. However, in the Step 10 example, you are asked to change the active directory from A:\WP to A:\SS, both of which are subdirectories of the root directory (A:). When this occurs, preface the destination directory with a backslash (\).

DEL or ERASE: Deleting Files. The *internal* DEL or ERASE command deletes the specified file(s) from disk storage. You now have two directories with exactly the same content—two files named FILE1.TXT and FILE2.TXT.

STEP 11 DELete

Use DEL or ERASE, which are identical commands, to delete FILE1.TXT from directory A:\SS.

   A:\SS> **del file1.txt** ↵
   A:\SS> **dir** ↵

REN: Rename a File. The *internal* REN command renames an existing file.

STEP 12 REName

Use REN to change the name of the remaining file on \SS from FILE2.TXT to FILE3.TXT.

   A:\SS> **ren file2.txt file3.txt** ↵
   A:\SS> **cls** (Clear the screen.) ↵
   A:\SS> **dir** ↵
   A:\SS> **dir\wp** ↵

Figure A–3 shows the display of the DOS sequence in Step 12.

A-5 DOS KEYBOARD FUNCTIONS

DOS provides you with internal functions that can be invoked with a single keystroke or a keystroke combination.

Output Control Keys

SHIFT+PRTSC: Print Screen. Press SHIFT+PRTSC (press and hold the SHIFT key, then tap PRTSC) to print what is currently being displayed on the screen.

CTRL+PRTSC: Printer Echo. Press CTRL+PRTSC (press and hold the CTRL key, then tap PRTSC) to begin echoing, or repeating, on the printer what is

APPENDIX A MS-DOS Tutorial and Exercises

displayed on the screen. Press CTRL+PRTSC to discontinue printer-echo mode. Use this function to get a line-by-line hard copy of your interaction with the computer.

CTRL+S: Pause Screen. Press CTRL+S (press and hold the CTRL key, then tap S) to stop the scrolling of the text, and tap any key to continue. This pause-screen function is often used with the TYPE and DIR commands that result in multiple-screen listings.

STEP 13 SHIFT+PRTSC, CTRL+PRTSC, and CTRL+S

Use output key combinations to print the current screen, to begin and end printer-echo mode, and to stop/continue scrolling.

A:\SS>**cd** ↵

A:\>**c:** *(Change the root directory from A: to C:.)* ↵

(Check that printer is turned on.)

C:\> **dir *.bat** *(List BAT files only.)* ↵

[SHIFT]+[PRTSC] *(Print the current display.)*

[CTRL]+[PRTSC] *(Begin printer echo.)*

C:\> **type a:\ss\file3.txt** ↵

[CTRL]+[PRTSC] *(End printer echo.)*

C:\> **dir** ↵

[CTRL]+[S] *(Stop scrolling of C: directory.)*

Any key *(Continue scrolling.)*

Note: When the PRTSC key is used in conjunction with a page printer, the page is not printed until it is filled. If you wish to print a page prior to its being filled, you may need to press the form-feed button on the printer.

Note: A directory with at least 30 entries (files and/or directories) is needed to demonstrate scrolling control. If C:\> does not have enough entries, ask your instructor to identify one that does.

Figure A-5 shows the display of the DOS sequence in Steps 13 through 15.

DOS Function Keys

The most commonly used DOS function keys are F1, F3, and F6.

F1 and F3: Repeat DOS Command. Tap the F3 function key to invoke a command that causes the most recently entered DOS command to be repeated after the DOS prompt. Tap F1 to repeat the most recently entered DOS command one character at a time.

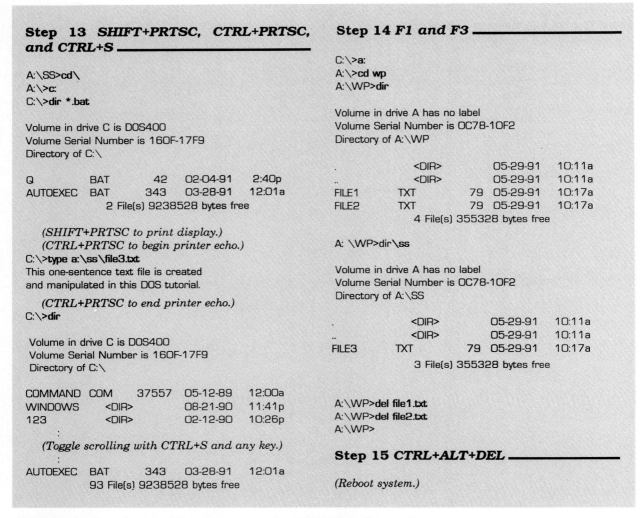

FIGURE A-5 DOS Sequence in Steps 13 through 15: DOS Keyboard Functions

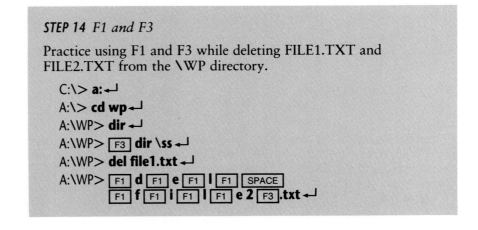

APPENDIX A MS-DOS Tutorial and Exercises   301

F6: Insert End-of-File Marker. Tap the F6 function key to insert an end-of-file marker (^Z) at the end of a DOS-generated text file. The use of F6 was demonstrated earlier in Step 8 with the use of COPY CON to create a text file.

System Control Keys

CTRL+BREAK: Break. Always terminate an application program in accordance with its normal exit procedure. However, if the program fails and you get *locked up* (the program no longer accepts your commands), the CTRL+BREAK provides a way to return to DOS without having to reboot the system. When you get locked up, enter CTRL+BREAK to terminate the program and return to the DOS prompt.

CTRL+BREAK performs a similar function during DOS sessions. Enter CTRL+BREAK to abort the current DOS command and return you to the DOS prompt. For example, if you enter CTRL+BREAK during a directory listing, the DIR command is terminated and you are returned to the DOS prompt.

CTRL+ALT+DEL: Restart DOS. Press and hold down CTRL+ALT, then tap DEL to reload DOS to memory. Use this keystroke combination when the computer is already on or when you are running an applications program that has no orderly *exit* (leaving the program) to DOS. The CTRL+ALT+DEL procedure is sometimes referred to as a *warm boot*. The *cold boot* procedure involves turning on the computer with the DOS diskette in place.

STEP 15 CTRL+ALT+DEL

Perform a warm boot. If you are using a diskette-based system, make sure that the DOS disk is in Drive A.

(*Remove your data disk from Drive A.*)
A:\WP> [CTRL]+[ALT]+[DEL]
(*The warm boot clears RAM and reloads DOS.*)
C:\>

Note: The startup program in read-only memory (ROM) begins its search for DOS programs with the disk in Drive A. It then searches the disk in Drive B and finally the hard drive (C:). If your data disk is left in Drive A or B, the boot procedure is halted and a system message informs you that a nonsystems disk was encountered.

A–6 BACKUP

DISKCOPY: Copy a Diskette

The *external* DISKCOPY command makes a duplicate copy of a diskette. In the DISKCOPY command the source diskette is listed first and the target diskette is second. If the target diskette is a new disk, it is automatically formatted prior to the copy operation.

STEP 16 DISKCOPY

Use DISKCOPY to make a backup copy of your data disk. Issue the DISKCOPY command to copy the data disk (source diskette) in Drive A to a backup disk (target diskette), which will share Drive A with the source diskette.

Note: If your PC is configured with two diskette drives of the same type (both 5¼-inch or both 3½-inch), enter **diskcopy a: b:** *and place the source diskette in Drive A and the target diskette in Drive B.*

    C:\> **diskcopy a: a:** ↵
    (Insert data disk.)
    Insert SOURCE diskette in drive A:
    Press any key to continue . . . ↵
    (Insert backup disk.)
    Insert TARGET diskette in drive A:
    Press any key to continue . . . ↵
    Copy another diskette (Y/N)?**n**
    C:\>

Figure A–6 shows the display of the DOS sequence in Steps 16 and 17.

FIGURE A–6 DOS Sequence in Steps 16 and 17: DISKCOPY and CHKDSK

Step 16 *DISKCOPY*	Step 17 *CHKDSK (Check Disk)*
C:\>diskcopy a: a:	C:\>chkdsk a:
Insert SOURCE diskette in drive A:	Volume Serial Number is 4527-0DE2
Press any key to continue...	362496 bytes total disk space
	3072 bytes in 3 directories
Copying 40 tracks	3072 bytes in 3 user files
9 Sectors/Track, 2 Side(s)	356352 bytes available on disk
Insert TARGET diskette in drive A:	1024 bytes in each allocation unit
	354 total allocation units on disk
Press any key to continue...	348 available allocation units on disk
Volume Serial Number is 4527-0DE2	655360 total bytes memory 525568 bytes free
Copy another diskette (Y/N)? n	C:\>

APPENDIX A MS-DOS Tutorial and Exercises

CHKDSK: Check the Disk

The *external* CHKDSK command displays a status report of disk contents and storage space and of memory.

> **STEP 17** CHKDSK (Check Disk)
>
> Check the disk in Drive A.
>
> C:\> **chkdsk a:** ↵
> C:\>

A-7 BATCH FILES

Batch files permit users to customize their system to best meet their processing needs. A batch file is a user-created disk file that can contain any one or all of the following: DOS commands, filenames for executable programs, and batch file commands. All batch filenames must have the extension BAT (for example, BATCHFIL.BAT). If you want to execute the commands and/or programs in BATCHFIL.BAT, a batch file on Disk Drive A, you simply enter **batchfil** at the A:\> prompt (the .BAT extension is optional on input). BATCHFIL.BAT is loaded to RAM and the commands and/or programs listed in the batch file are executed in the order in which they appear, unless otherwise specified by a batch file command.

The AUTOEXEC.BAT File

All batch files are named by the user except one—the **AUTOEXEC.BAT** file. As soon as DOS is loaded to RAM, DOS searches for this special batch file on the startup disk (usually C:). If such a file exists, the commands and/or programs listed in AUTOEXEC.BAT are *AUTO*matically *EXEC*uted in *BAT*ch mode (in sequence, starting with the first command or program). A user who primarily does word processing might create the following AUTOEXEC.BAT file.

```
ECHO OFF
REM This is an AUTOEXEC.BAT file.
REM Search for executable commands in these directories
PATH C:\MOUSE;C:\BATCH;C:\CALENDAR;C:\WORDPROC
REM Change the system prompt from C> to C:\ACTIVE>
PROMPT $P$G
REM Redirect printer output from parallel to serial port
MODE COM1:96,N,8,1,P
MODE LPT1:=COM1:
REM Load the memory-resident mouse software
MOUSE
REM Load terminate-and-stay-resident (TSR) calendar
CAL
REM Load word processing program
WP
```

The above batch file contains batch file commands (ECHO, REM), DOS commands (PATH, PROMPT, and MODE), and three executable program files (MOUSE.COM, CAL.EXE, and WP.EXE).

- *ECHO OFF* is a batch file command that suppresses the display (or echo) of batch commands/programs. *ECHO ON* starts the echo feature. When ECHO is OFF the text following the ECHO command is displayed when the batch file is executed (see Step 18).
- *REM*, another batch file command, gives users the capability of inserting comments in the batch file. REM lines do not affect the batch file.
- *PATH*, a DOS command, informs DOS which directories to search for executable program files (those with extensions COM, EXE, and BAT). Unless directed to do otherwise, DOS searches only the active directory.
- *PROMPT*, a DOS command, changes the default DOS prompt (C>) to display the active directory followed by a > (for example C:\WP>).
- *MODE*, a DOS command, defines serial port protocols (first MODE) and causes printer output to be redirected from the system default parallel port (LPT1) to the first serial or communications port (COM1).
- *MOUSE*, *CAL*, and *WP* are executable program files (MOUSE.COM, CAL.EXE, and WP.EXE). The system begins its search for MOUSE in the startup directory (usually C:), then expands it search to those directories listed in the PATH command. Upon finding MOUSE, it is loaded to RAM. CAL is loaded to RAM in a similar manner. The mouse software remains active and the TSR calendar program can be recalled at any time with a hot key (a unique key combination). Finally, WP is found and executed, leaving the user in the word processing program.

The AUTOEXEC.BAT is executed each time the system is booted (cold or warm boot).

Other Batch Files

Batch files save you time. They enable you to execute a frequently used sequence of DOS commands and programs by simply entering the name of the batch file at the DOS prompt. For example, you might wish to create a batch file, called SSBACKUP.BAT, that copies all spreadsheet files from the A:\SS to a backup disk. Or, you might create two batch files, called CONFIG1.BAT and CONFIG2.BAT, that enable you to switch easily between two system configurations. The variety of batch files is limited only by processing needs and your imagination.

Creating and Executing Batch Files

At this point in your PC learning experience, perhaps the best way to create a batch file is to use the COPY command to copy from CON (the keyboard console) to a disk file; that is, key in the commands and store these commands on a disk file. The COPY CON command is demonstrated in Step 8.

APPENDIX A MS-DOS Tutorial and Exercises

STEP 18 *Creating a Batch File*

Create a batch file to display the content of FILE3.TXT in the A:\SS directory on your data disk. Store the file on root directory A:.

    C:\> **copy con a:typefile.bat** ↵
    ECHO OFF ↵
    REM Display A:\SS\FILE3.TXT ↵
    CLS ↵
    REM Display message ↵
    ECHO Insert data disk in Drive A: ↵
    PAUSE ↵
    REM Change to A: from any root directory ↵
    CD ↵
    A: ↵
    CD SS ↵
    TYPE FILE3.TXT ↵
    [F6] *(F6 inserts an end-of-file marker)* ^Z ↵

    The *PAUSE* batch file command temporarily suspends execution of the batch file and displays "Strike any key when ready. . . ." Figure A–7 shows the display of the DOS sequence in Steps 18 and 19.

FIGURE A–7 DOS Sequence in Steps 18 and 19: Batch Files

Step 18 *Creating a Batch File* ───────

```
C:\>copy con a:typefile.bat
ECHO OFF
REM Display A:\SS\FILE3.TXT
CLS
REM Display message
ECHO Insert data disk in Drive A:
PAUSE
REM Change to A: from any root directory
CD\
A:
CD SS
TYPE FILE3.TXT
```

(F6 for end-of-file marker.)^Z
    1 File(s) copied

Step 19 *Executing a Batch File* ───────

```
C:\>a:
A:\>typefile
A:\>ECHO OFF
Insert data disk in Drive A:
Press any key to continue...

This one-sentence text file is created
and manipulated in this DOS tutorial.
A:\SS>
```

▶ DOS COMMAND/KEY SUMMARY

DOS Command	Description	Steps in Which Used
A:, B:, C:	Change the active drive.	2, 13, 14, 19
Batch file	Batch file commands.	18, 19
CD (I)†	Change current directory.	6, 7, 8, 10, 13, 14
CLS (I)	Clear the screen.	8, 12
CHKDSK (E)	Check disk.	17
COPY (I)	Copy file(s).	10
COPY CON (I)	Copy from keyboard to disk.	8, 18
DATE (I)	View or change date.	1
DEL (I)	Delete file(s) (also ERASE).	11, 14
DIR (I)	List contents of directory.	4, 5, 7, 8, 10, 11, 12, 13, 14
DIR/P (I)	Pause during directory listing.	4
DIR/W (I)	Abbreviated directory listing.	4, 10
DISKCOPY (E)	Copy disk.	16
ERASE (I)	Delete file(s) (also DEL).	11
FORMAT (E)	Format a disk.	3
MD (I)	Make a directory.	5
RD (I)	Remove a directory.	7
REN (I)	Rename file.	12
SHIFT+PRTSC	Print screen.	14
TIME (I)	View or change time.	1
TYPE (I)	Display file content.	9, 13
* and ?	Wildcard characters.	10, 13, 14

DOS Keyboard Functions	Description	Steps in Which Used
CTRL + ALT + DEL	Restart DOS (warm boot).	15
CTRL + BREAK	Terminate program prematurely.	
CTRL + PRTSC	Printer echo.	13
CTRL + S	Pause screen.	13
F1	Repeat previous DOS command, one character at a time.	14
F3	Repeat previous DOS command.	14
F6	Insert end-of-file marker.	8, 18
SHIFT + PRTSC	Print screen.	13

†Internal—I, External—E

APPENDIX A MS-DOS Tutorial and Exercises

> **STEP 19** *Executing a Batch File*
>
> Execute the TYPEFILE.BAT batch file.
>
> C:\ **a:** ↵
> A:\> **typefile** ↵
> A:\> ECHO OFF ↵
> Insert data disk in Drive A:
> Press any key to continue . . .
> This one-sentence text file is created
> and manipulated in this DOS tutorial.
> A:\SS>
>
> This is the last DOS tutorial. Remove all diskettes and turn off the monitor, the printer (if needed), then the computer. Store your data disk and its backup in a safe place. You will be using them again if you plan to do the word processing, spreadsheet, and database tutorials that accompany this book.

You would use this same approach to create a batch file that would display the AUTOEXEC.BAT file. As you gain familiarity with DOS, occasionally you will need to view your AUTOEXEC.BAT file.

Modifying Batch Files

The COPY CON command cannot be used to modify a batch file. The only way to change an existing batch file with COPY CON is to rekey the entire file. Fortunately, most batch files are short.

The best way to create and modify batch files is with word processing software. When you save a word processing document, you save the text that you have keyed in plus many hidden control characters, such as tabs and page breaks. Most word processing packages permit users to store and retrieve files in *ASCII*, or *DOS text*, format, the same format required of batch files. ASCII files, which contain only the user-entered text, are discussed in Chapter 5, "Text and Image Processing: Word Processing, Desktop Publishing, and Graphics."

REVIEW EXERCISES

1. What is meant by booting the system? *Load Oper. System to main memory*
2. Name two external and two internal DOS commands. *Inter: Available Any Time / External must be loaded.*
3. Explain why the following could not be valid DOS filenames.
   NAME.LAST   firstname   I/O   <filenm>.ext
4. What are the major functions of a microcomputer operating system?
5. List and describe one DOS command for each of these categories: disk, directory, file, and output.
6. What happens if you omit the filename in the target specification of a COPY file command?

7. The files on the disk in the active drive contain word processing (WP) and database (DB) files.

   LETTER1.WP   LETTER2.WP   INVENTORY.DB   DRAFT.WP
   NAMEADDR.DB   REPORT.WP   BIO.WP   LETTER3.WP

   What wildcard reference would refer to
   a. All files.
   b. Only word processing files.
   c. Only database files.
   d. Only LETTER word processing files.
8. Just after DOS is loaded to RAM in a hard-disk-based micro, which directory is the active directory? Which would be the active directory on a diskette-based micro?
9. Create three filenames that would be included within the wildcard reference EXAMPLE?.*.
10. Describe circumstances that might encourage you to use the DOS pause-screen (CTRL+S) function.
11. What makes batch files named AUTOEXEC.BAT unique?
12. What the logical route called that DOS would follow to locate a specified file?
13. What is the DOS command that clears the screen?

STEP-BY-STEP TUTORIAL EXERCISES

1. Complete Steps 1 through 7 of the keystroke tutorials in this appendix to boot the system, format a diskette, and create three subdirectories on the data disk.
2. Complete Steps 8 through 12 of the keystroke tutorials in this appendix to practice creating and manipulating files. Use the data disk from Exercise 1.
3. Complete Steps 13 through 15 of the keystroke tutorials in this appendix to practice using common DOS keyboard functions. Use the data disk from Exercise 2.
4. Complete Steps 16 and 17 of the keystroke tutorials in this appendix to make a backup disk of the data disk from Exercise 3.
5. Complete Steps 18 and 19 of the keystroke tutorials in this appendix to create a batch file on the root directory of the data disk from Exercise 4.

PRACTICE

1. a. Format a new or blank disk (*not* your data disk). After formatting is complete, examine the directory on your work disk to confirm that no files exist on the disk. Print the screen image.
   b. Clear the screen, then use the COPY CON command (Step 8) to create the following text file on your work disk.

   This is a "hands-on exercise" text file.

   Name the file THREE.TXT, and store it on your newly formatted work

APPENDIX A MS-DOS Tutorial and Exercises 309

disk. Confirm that THREE.TXT is stored on your disk by displaying the contents of the file. Print the screen image and clear the screen. Save this and all printer output as exercise documentation.

c. Create a duplicate copy of THREE.TXT and call it TWO.TXT. Confirm that the copy was successful by examining the directory of your work disk.

d. Rename THREE.TXT to be ONE.TXT. Confirm that only two files, ONE.TXT and TWO.TXT, are stored on the disk. Print the screen image.

2. a. On the work disk from Exercise 6, create two subdirectories. Name them \ALPHA and \BETA.

b. Use the asterisk (*) wildcard character to copy ONE.TXT and TWO.TXT to both of the newly created directories.
(Hint: Use the F1 key to facilitate the keying of the second COPY command.)

c. Rename the ONE.TXT and TWO.TXT on \ALPHA to be THREE.TXT and FOUR.TXT. Rename the ONE.TXT and TWO.TXT on \BETA to be FIVE.TXT and SIX.TXT. Clear the screen and confirm that the copy operations were successful by examining the appropriate directories. Print the screen image.

d. Consolidate all six TXT files on the root directory (A:\>). Use a wildcard file reference to copy the four TXT files on \ALPHA and \BETA to the root directory.

e. Delete the TXT files from the subdirectories \ALPHA and \BETA.

f. Remove the \BETA directory. Clear the screen and confirm that the root directory contains six TXT files and an empty \ALPHA directory. Print the screen image.

3. a. On the work disk from Exercise 7, create two subdirectories for \ALPHA. Name them \GAMMA and \DELTA.

b. With the printer on, activate the printer echo and display the directories for the root directory and \ALPHA. Deactivate the printer echo. On the printout, identify all parent/child relationships between the directories on the work disk by drawing a line between each parent/child relationship.

c. Copy ONE.TXT to \ALPHA\GAMMA as SEVEN.TXT, and copy TWO.TXT to \ALPHA\DELTA as EIGHT.TXT.

d. Clear the screen and confirm that \ALPHA and \GAMMA contain the TXT files. Print the screen image.

4. a. You will need a blank disk for this exercise. Use the DISKCOPY command to make a backup of the work disk from Exercise 8.

b. With the printer on, activate the printer echo and display the directory for the backup diskette. Deactivate the printer echo.

c. What is the total capacity (in bytes) of the diskette in Drive A? How many bytes of disk storage are taken up by the six user files? What is the total capacity (in bytes) of your microcomputer's memory (RAM)?

d. What is the total capacity (in bytes) of the hard disk?

5. a. Locate the directory on your PC that contains the AUTOEXEC.BAT file. *(Hint: For hard-disk-based systems, AUTOEXEC.BAT is normally on C:\. For diskette-based systems, it is on the root directory of the diskette containing DOS.)*

b. Create a batch file, called SHOWAUTO.BAT, that will display the AUTOEXEC.BAT file. Insert a sequence of commands that will enable the file to be executed from any directory.
(Hint: The batch file in Step 18 performs a similar function.)
c. Clear the screen and use the TYPE command to display SHOWAUTO.BAT. Print the screen image.
d. Activate the printer echo and execute SHOWAUTO.BAT. Deactivate the printer echo.

APPENDIX B

WINDOWS OVERVIEW

- ▶ B–1 About Windows
- ▶ B–2 Windows Concepts
- ▶ B–3 Windows Applications
- ▶ B–4 Windows Accessory Applications
- ▶ B–5 Using Windows

B–1 ABOUT WINDOWS

Windows is the dominant graphical user interface (GUI) for the MS-DOS environment. Although millions of copies of Microsoft's Windows have been sold, only now is it beginning to live up to its unprecedented prerelease promotion. As we settle into the 1990s, there are more high-performance micros in use that can take full advantage of the potential of Windows. Also, a healthy array of software applications for Windows is available to Windows users, with more being introduced each month.

The Windows discussion that follows assumes that the reader has been exposed to fundamental MS-DOS concepts (see Appendix A, "MS-DOS Tutorial and Exercises").

What Is Windows?

The name *Windows* describes basically how the software functions. It runs one or more applications in "windows"—rectangular areas displayed on the screen. Other Windows capabilities are described in this section.

The Windows Platform. Windows, itself a commercial software package, is more than just another application for micros. It also defines a new platform for which other application software packages are written. MS-DOS and OS/2, both operating systems, define platforms. The overwhelming majority of application software packages are written to run under MS-DOS, a single-user

Microsoft's Windows enables you to switch between several open applications, each of which is displayed in a window. The open applications in the screen are word processing, database, and the Windows Program Manager. The icons in the Program Manager window—the active window—represent applications (Paintbrush, Calendar, Clock, Calculator, and so on).

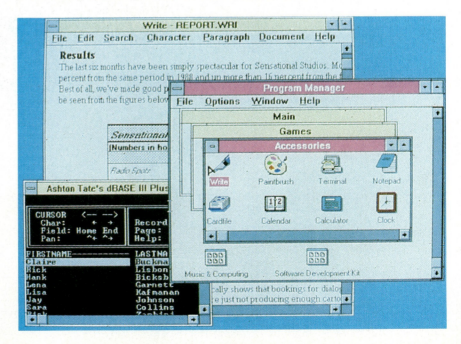

operating system. MS-DOS is still the dominant platform in use today, but it is over a decade old and it is not designed to take advantage of modern PC technology. Windows offers some very inviting solutions to the limitations of MS-DOS.

1. *Windows is user-friendly.* Windows employs a graphical user interface (GUI). With a GUI the user "points" to the desired option, file, program, and so on with a mouse or other pointing device. In contrast, MS-DOS users must enter what are often cryptic commands to the microcomputer system via the keyboard. (Microsoft refers to Windows as a "graphical environment.")
2. *Windows enables multiple programs to be run simultaneously.* This multitasking feature permits a user to print out a WordPerfect report while engaged in a Lotus 1-2-3 session. If the same user were running under the MS-DOS platform, she or he would need to exit Lotus 1-2-3 and load WordPerfect to print out the report. To return to a Lotus 1-2-3 session, the user would have to exit WordPerfect and reload Lotus 1-2-3 to RAM.
3. *Windows enables users to work with large files.* Data bases, spreadsheet files, and word processing documents can be as big as available memory will permit. Some micros have over 30 MB of random-access memory. With Windows, the text in this book (about 1 MB of memory) and many other books could be loaded to RAM—simultaneously! Without Windows, a file containing one or two chapters of this book might not fit into available RAM.
4. *Windows permits information to be passed between applications.* With Windows, text in a word processing document can be transferred in seconds to a data base record. A pie chart from a graphics program can be inserted into a word processing document just as easily. These types of information transfers, though not impossible, are cumbersome and time-consuming with MS-DOS.

Although Windows establishes a new platform, virtually all of the thousands of application software packages created for MS-DOS can run under Windows.

De Facto Standard. Windows is being so wholeheartedly embraced by the microcomputer community, including software vendors, that the GUI, the terms, and the concepts introduced by Windows are emerging as de facto standards in the industry. Of course, the Windows platform uses many traditional tools (for example, the mouse) and techniques (such as windows, bar menus, and default options). However, Windows has introduced a number of new terms and concepts, all of which apply to the hundreds of software packages that have been and are being developed to run under Windows. These are discussed in this appendix.

Non-Windows versus Windows Applications

Non-Windows Applications. Any software application that does not adhere to the Windows user-interface conventions is a **non-Windows application**. Many popular applications—such as WordPerfect 5.1; Lotus 1-2-3, version 2.2; and Paradox 3.5—are non-Windows applications. In fact, most available software falls into the non-Windows category. Non-Windows applications will run under Windows but these software packages cannot take advantage of many helpful Windows features. Windows has become such a powerful force in the PC software industry that those vendors who are without a Windows version of their MS-DOS products are working night and day to do so.

Windows Applications. Programs that adhere to Windows conventions are **Windows applications**. These conventions describe:

- *Type and style of window*. A window is a rectangular box superimposed over the screen image.
- *Arrangement and style of menus*.
- *Use of the keyboard and mouse*.
- *Format for screen-image display*. Windows is a graphics-based application (as opposed to text-based). In a graphics-based software package, the text and all images are made up of patterns of pixels. This permits tremendous flexibility in the integration and presentation of information.

In other words, all Windows applications have a common user interface. The GUI for Windows versions of Word, CorelDRAW, WordPerfect, Ventura Publisher, and all other Windows applications have the same look and feel. *When you learn the GUI for Windows, you also learn the GUI for hundreds of different software packages.*

The Windows graphical user interface employs both the mouse and the keyboard as input devices. Interaction with Windows or a Windows application is most efficient when options are chosen with a mouse and characters are entered via the keyboard. All Windows commands can be activated with the keyboard, but keyboard-only interaction can be slow and cumbersome for many operations.

When working with the mouse (see Chapter 2, "Interacting with Micros") in Windows:

- Point and *click* the left button to **select** an item (an applications program, a menu option, box, and so on). When you select an item, the item is in some way highlighted. *Generally, selection does not result in the initiation of a processing activity.*
- Point and *double-click* the left button to **choose** an item. *Choosing an item results in some kind of action.*
- Point and *drag* to move or resize a window on the display screen.

When working with the keyboard in Windows:

- Enter text as needed (for example, a path for a file: **c:\wp\wp.exe**).
- Activate the current menu bar with function keys.
- Enter the underlined letter of menu option in the active menu to choose that option.
- Use the cursor-control keys to highlight menu options in an active menu.
- Use "shortcut" key combinations (for example, ALT+F4) to highlight items and to navigate between applications.

B-2 WINDOWS CONCEPTS

The Desktop

The screen upon which icons, windows, and so on are displayed is known as the **desktop**. The Windows desktop may contain a *background*, *one active window*, *one or more inactive windows*, and *icons* (see Figure B-1). The background can be anything from a single-color screen to an elaborate artistic image, such as a 3-D chess board. The user can choose from a number of backgrounds. All windows and icons are superimposed over the background, be it plain or an artistic image.

APPENDIX B Windows Overview

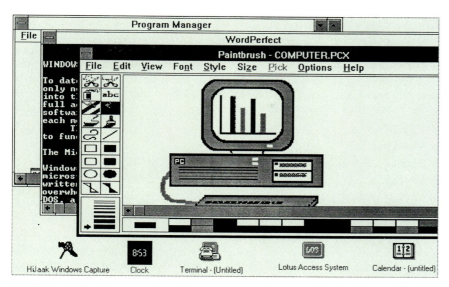

FIGURE B-1 The Windows Desktop
The appearance of the Windows desktop depends on the user's application mix and visual needs at a particular time. This user has three open application windows (Program Manager, WordPerfect, and Paintbrush, the active window) and five applications that have been shrunk to application icons (Hijaak Windows Capture, Clock, Terminal, Lotus Access System, and Calendar) at the bottom of the desktop.

Windows allows users to choose their own colors and wallpaper (the background color or pattern) for the Windows desktop. This wallpaper pattern is called Ribbons. You choose from a variety of wallpaper patterns, including Chess, Pyramids, Party, and others. Or you can create your own.

The Windows Window. A typical rectangular Windows **application window** is illustrated in Figure B-1. An application window contains a running application, such as Paintbrush or WordPerfect. Several applications can be running simultaneously, but there is only one **active window** at any given time. (Paintbrush is the active window in Figure B-1.) Commands issued via the keyboard or mouse apply to the active window, which is highlighted. The elements of the application window are:

- Title bar
- Menu bar
- Application workspace
- Scroll bars
- Corners and borders

Each is described in the following sections and illustrated in Figure B-2.

Title bar. The horizontal **title bar** at the top of each window runs the width of the window. From left to right (see Figure B-2), the elements of the title bar are the *control menu box, window title and active filename*, and *maximize/minimize buttons*. Point and click the mouse on these elements to change the presentation of the window.

- *Control menu box.* Point and click on the control menu box to display the pull-down control menu (see Figure B-3), which is also called the *system menu*. Most of the options on the control menu are available without having to display the menu. For example, one of the options is *Move*. To move a window, the user simply uses the mouse to point to the window title area then drags the window to the desired location. The keyboard user would need to choose the *Move* option and use the cursor-control keys to move the window. Control menu options vary, depending on the type of application being displayed in the window, but most will have some or all of the following options.

  Restore   When available, users can restore an enlarged window to its previous size (a window or an icon). The *Restore* option is **dimmed** and not available unless the window is enlarged. The term *dimmed* is used to describe an option that is visible but

FIGURE B-2 Elements of an Application Window

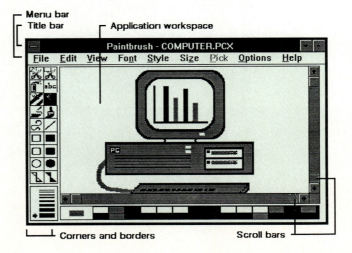

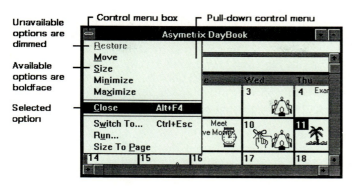

FIGURE B–3 The Control Menu

	not as dark as the available options (*Restore* is dimmed in Figure B–3).
Move	The *Move* option enables the user to use the cursor-control keys to reposition the active window on the desktop.
Size	The *Size* option enables the user to change the height or width of the active window with the cursor-control keys.
Minimize	The *Minimize* option **shrinks** the active window to an icon at the bottom of the desktop (see Figure B–1). That is, the application in the window is deactivated and the window disappears from the screen, but the application remains open in the form of an icon.
Maximize	The *Maximize* option enlarges the active window to fill the entire screen.
Close	Choosing *Close* deactivates and removes the active window from the desktop.
Switch to	Choosing the *Switch to* option results in the display of the Task List. The Task List lists open applications (see Figure B–4). Use the mouse to point, and double-click the application you want to make the active application.
Next	Choose *Next* to rotate among active **document windows** and document windows that have been shrunk to icons. Document windows, which are explained and illustrated in the "File Manager" portion of Section B–3, are windows within applications windows.
Edit	Choosing *Edit* results in a **cascading menu** that permits users to transfer information between windows. A cascading menu is a pop-up menu that is displayed when a command from the active menu is chosen. *Edit* operations are discussed in Section B–5.

- *Window title and active filename*. The title of the application is contained in the center portion of the title bar ("Paintbrush" in Figure B–2). To the right of the title is the name of the file displayed in the application workspace ("COMPUTER.PCX" in Figure B–2).
- *Maximize/minimize/restore buttons*. Mouse users can point and click on the maximize (▲) and minimize (▼) buttons (on the right end of the title bar in Figure B–2) to enlarge the window to fill the screen or shrink it to an icon. The restore button (↕), replaces the maximize button (▲) when the window is enlarged.

FIGURE B–4 Task List
The Task List provides a list of open applications.

Menu bar. The **menu bar** for an application window runs the width of the window just below the title bar (see Figure B–2). The menu bar lists the menus available for that application. Choosing an option from the menu bar results in a pull-down menu. The *File*, *Edit*, and *Help* menus are available for most applications. Other menu options depend on the application.

Certain conventions apply to user interactions with any Windows menu, whether a menu bar, pull-down menu, or cascading menu.

- *Only the boldface options can be chosen.* Dimmed options are not available for the current circumstances. For example, the *Copy* option would not be available in an Edit menu if nothing had been identified to be copied.
- *Choosing a menu option followed by an ellipsis (. . .) results in a dialog box.* The text in the pop-up **dialog box** asks the user to choose parameters or enter further information. Often the dialog box appears when the user must choose among more options before the chosen menu option can be executed. For example, choosing the *Paste From* menu option from Figure B–5 produces a dialog box. In the box, the user is asked to enter the file specification of the source file (the file to be copied into the workspace).

  The Task List in Figure B–4 provides another example of a dialog box. The Task List dialog box asks the user to choose which of the open applications is to be made the active application.
- *Corresponding shortcut keys are presented adjacent to many options in Windows menus.* The **shortcut key** is a key combination that can be executed without displaying a menu. For example, the Cut option on the Edit menu in Figure B–5 can be executed by the Shift+Del shortcut key combination, that is, tap Del while holding down Shift.
- *Choosing a menu option followed by an arrow (▶) results in a cascading menu.* For example, the Edit option on Control menus for non-Windows applications results in a cascading menu (Cut, Copy, Paste, and so on).
- *A user-recorded check mark (√) to the left of the menu option indicates that the option is active and applies to any related commands.* For example, in the Windows File Manager application, the View option lets the user check the options that apply when the files are listed (for example, alphabetical *By Name* or *By Type* of extension).
- *There are three ways to choose a menu option.*

FIGURE B–5 A Pull-Down *Edit* Menu
The Edit *menu is pulled down from the Paintbrush menu bar. Point and click the underlined letter with the mouse or key to choose an option. Options followed by an ellipsis (. . .) result in a pop-up dialog box. Shortcut key combinations for* Undo *(Alt+BackSpace),* Cut, *and* Copy *enable users to perform these activities from the keyboard without calling up the* Edit *menu.*

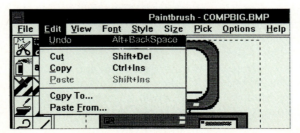

1. Point and click the mouse on the option.
2. Use the keyboard cursor-control keys to select (highlight) the option and tap the Enter key to choose it.
3. Use the keyboard to enter the underlined letter of the menu option. For example, in Figure B-5, enter U (Undo), T (Cut), and so on.

On most application windows, the last option on the menu bar is *Help*. Choose the on-line Help menu whenever you need context-sensitive information regarding basic Windows skills, key shortcuts, procedures, features, or commands.

Workspace. The **workspace** is the area in a window below the title bar or menu bar (see Figure B-2). Everything that relates to the application noted in the title bar is displayed in the workspace. For example, in Figure B-2, a microcomputer has been drawn in the workspace of the Paintbrush paint program. The workspace of a word processing program contains the word processing document.

Scroll bars. Depending on the size of a window, the entire application may not be visible. When this happens the window is outfitted with **vertical** and/or **horizontal scroll bars** (see Figure B-2). Each bar contains a **scroll box** and two **scroll arrows**. Use the mouse or keyboard to move a box up/down or left/right on a scroll bar to display other parts of the application. To move the scroll box with the mouse, simply drag it to another location on the scroll bar or click the scroll arrows.

Corners and borders. To resize a window, use the mouse and point to a window's border or corner. The graphics cursor changes to a double arrow when positioned over a border or corner. Drag the border or corner in the directions indicated by the double arrow to the desired shape. When dragging a corner, the two sides linked to the corner move. To resize with the keyboard, display the Control menu and choose Size.

Types of Windows. The three types of windows in the Windows graphical environment are the *application window*, the *document window*, and the *dialog box*, all of which have been introduced in earlier sections. The document window and the dialog box require further explanation.

Document windows, which are windows within an application window, are displayed in the parent application window's workspace. For example, the Windows File Manager application normally will have document windows into which the Directory Tree and various directories are displayed. In Figure B-6,

FIGURE B-6 Application and Document Windows
In this display, the Windows File Manager application has four open document windows: the Directory Tree (the active document window) and three directory windows.

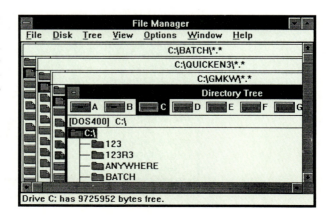

a portion of the directory tree for the root directory (C:) is displayed in the active document window along with the title bars of three open directory windows (C:\BATCH, C:\QUICKEN, and C:\GMKW). Being a subordinate window, the document window does not have a menu bar. However, the menu bar for the active application is applicable to the active document window. Note in Figure B–6 that the title bars of both the active application (File Manager) and the active document window (Directory Tree) are highlighted.

Typically, entries in the dialog box must be okayed or revised by the user before a command can be executed. The dialog may contain any of these seven elements (see Figures B–7 and B–8).

1. *Text box.* Enter text information in the text box or accept the default entry that is displayed. Often, the user is asked to enter a number (see Figure B–7) or the path for a file (C:\WP51\WP.EXE).
2. *Command buttons.* Point and click to the *OK* rectangular command button to carry out the command with the information provided in the dialog box. Choose *Cancel* to retain the original information (see Figure B–7).

FIGURE B–7 Elements of a Dialog Box
Five of the seven dialog box elements are shown in the Desktop dialog box (see also Figure B–8).

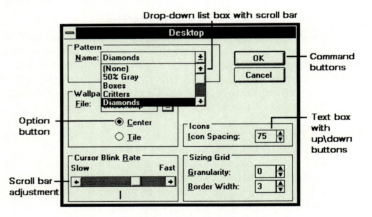

FIGURE B–8 Elements of a Dialog Box
The list box *and* check box *dialog box elements are shown in the Printers dialog box (see also Figure B–7).*

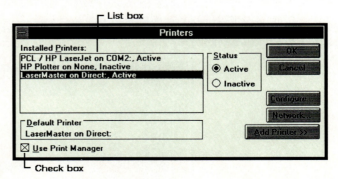

3. *Option buttons.* Circular option buttons preface each item in a list of mutually exclusive items (only one can be marked). Point and click a button to insert a black dot in the button and activate the option (see Figure B-7).
4. *Drop-down list boxes.* The drop-down list box is used as an alternative to the list box (see Figure B-8 and Item 6, following) when the dialog box is too small for a list box to be displayed. The existence of a drop-down list box is indicated by a button containing an underlined down arrow. The button is positioned to the right of the current choice in the dialog box. Point and click on the button to display a drop-down list box (see Figure B-7).
5. *Scroll bar adjustment.* The scroll bar adjustment enables users to change parameters with an infinite number of possible settings, such as the speed at which the cursor blinks (see Figure B-7).
6. *List boxes.* A list box displays a list of available choices for a particular option. For example, one list box lists the printers that are installed on the system (see Figure B-8). Long lists will have a vertical scroll bar. In contrast with the drop-down list box (see Figure B-6 and Item 4, above), the list box is part of the original dialog box display. The drop-down list box must be requested by the user.
7. *Check boxes.* Check boxes preface options that can be switched off or on as needed. Point and click on a box to insert an *X* and activate the option (see Figure B-8).

Icons. Icons, the graphical representation of a Windows element, play a major role in the Windows environment. The most commonly used icons are in the following four categories: *application- and program-item icons*, *document icons*, *disk-drive icons*, and *file icons*.

Application and program-item icons. An active application window can be minimized, or shrunk, to an **application icon**, thereby making it inactive. The application icon, usually a graphic rendering of the software package's logo, is positioned at the bottom of the desktop (see Figure B-1). Point and double-click on the icon to restore the window and the application to active status. Typically, you would minimize application windows that may not be needed for a while to make room on the desktop for other windows.

An application icon that has not been opened is called a **program-item icon**. An application icon and a program-item icon for a particular application, such as Venture Publisher, look exactly the same. Their location indicates whether the application is opened or closed. Program-item icons are discussed and illustrated in the Program Manager portion of Section B-3.

Document icons. The active document window, which is a window within an application window, can be minimized to a **document icon**. For example, in Figure B-9, three of the document windows in Figure B-6 are minimized to document icons in the File Manager application window. The graphic for the document-window icon usually provides some insight into the function of the document window. For example, in the File Manager application window of Figure B-9, the directory icons look like lists. Point and double-click on the document icon to restore the document window.

Disk-drive icons. The disk-drive icons graphically represent five disk-drive options: floppy, hard, network (hard), RAM, and CD-ROM. The floppy (A and B) and hard-disk (C through I) icons shown in Figure B-9 resemble the faceplates of the two most popular types of disk drives.

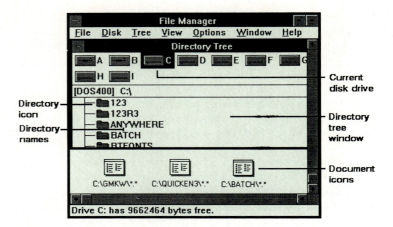

FIGURE B-9 Document Icons
Windows uses a variety of icons to represent everything from disk drives to applications. In this File Manager example, the three directory windows in Figure B-6 are minimized to document icons.

File icons. File icons are found in the document windows within the Windows File Manager application (see Figures B-6 and B-9). These windows typically list disk content. The four types of file icons are:

    Directory icon. The directory icon (shown in the Directory Tree document window in Figure B-9) denotes a directory.

    Program and file icon. The program and file icon denotes files that can start an application—that is, they have EXE, COM, PIF, and BAT extensions to their filenames.

    Document icon. The document icon indicates an association with a particular application program (for example, the WIN.INI file and other files with the INI extension are associated with Windows).

    Generic icon. All other files are denoted by the generic icon.

Viewing Windows. Windows is designed to enable you to view multiple applications in windows on the desktop display. An application window can be opened in several ways, usually by pointing and clicking on the application icon in the Program Manager window. Once open, a window can be resized, shrunk (and restored), maximized (and restored), and, finally, closed.

Essentially, any application software written to run under Windows can be:

- Viewed and run in a window, the shape and size of which is determined by the user.
- Run full-screen, that is, filling the entire screen, with no other application windows or icons showing.

Some non-Windows applications run only as full-screen applications and cannot be run in a window. When multiple applications are running, the user can use the Move and Resize capabilities to arrange and size the windows to meet viewing needs. Of course, open windows can be minimized to free viewing space on the desktop.

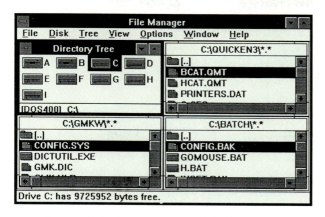

FIGURE B-10 Tile Arrangement of Windows
The File Manager document windows in Figure B-6 are shown in a tile arrangement. Contrast this arrangement with the cascade arrangement in Figure B-6.

Within a given application window, such as the Program Manager, multiple document windows can be sized, shrunk, and arranged by the user within the workspace. As an alternative, the user can request that the document windows be automatically presented as **cascading windows** (see Figure B-6) or **tiled windows** (see Figure B-10). Choose these options from the Windows menu in the menu bar. The Cascade option overlaps open document windows so that all title bars are visible. The Tile option fills the workspace in such a way that no document window overlaps another. Scroll bars are provided on those document windows for which the space is not adequate to display the windows content.

B-3 WINDOWS APPLICATIONS

The Microsoft Windows software package comes with a number of applications, two of which are integral to running the program: Program Manager and File Manager.

Program Manager

The Program Manager is the nucleus of the Windows operating environment. When you start Windows, the Program Manager is opened as the active window and remains open until you exit Windows. The Program Manager window contains document windows, each of which may be displayed or minimized to a document icon (see Figure B-11). Each document window contains icons for a group of related applications. For example, one document window might contain those icons for applications that are related to CorelDRAW, a popular graphics package (Figure B-11). These icons are called *program-item icons*. When opened, they become application windows, which can be minimized to *application icons*. Program-item icons represent dormant applications. The document windows within the Program Manager sometimes are called **group windows** because they contain groups of program-item icons.

> ▶ **MEMORY BITS**
>
> *Viewing Windows*
> - Display of windows
>   In windows
>   Shrunk to icons
> - Arrangement of windows
>   User-determined shape and position
>   Cascading windows
>   Tiled windows

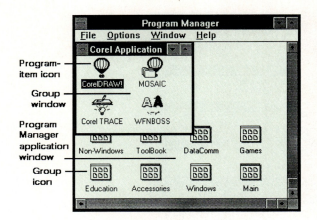

FIGURE B-11 Program Manager Window
In the example, the Corel Application group window is open within the Program Manager application. All other application groups are presented as group icons.

There are five predefined group windows in the Program Manager.

- *Main group.* The main group includes Windows system applications, such as the File Manager and DOS Prompt.
- *Accessories group.* This group contains several helpful applications that do not relate directly to the running of Windows applications, such as the clock, calendar, drawing, and so on.
- *Games group.* Microsoft includes a couple of fun and instructive games (Solitaire and Reversi).
- *Windows applications group.* This group is set aside for any Windows-based application.
- *Non-Windows applications group.* This group is set aside for any non-Windows application.

Windows permits program items to be added to, deleted from, or moved between group windows. In addition, users can define their own groups. For example, in Figure B-11, group windows are defined for "Education" and "DataComm" (data communications).

To run an application from the Program Manager, open the appropriate group window by pointing and double-clicking the icon. Then point and double-click the desired program-item icon. When you exit an application, such as CorelDRAW, its application window is removed from the desktop.

To exit Windows, close all open applications except the Program Manager (which cannot be closed), then point and double-click the menu control box on the Program Manager title bar. A *confirmation dialog box* asks you for confirmation in this and many other circumstances that may result in loss of data.

File Manager

The Windows File Manager application is a user-friendly file-management tool. Users who are familiar with the cryptic, command-driven MS-DOS approach to file management will appreciate the ease with which File Manager allows files to be moved, copied, deleted, and generally organized for more efficient retrieval. The File Manager application is opened from the Main Group window within the Program Manager application (see Figure B-11).

File Manager has two types of document windows.

- *Directory tree window.* This window graphically illustrates the organization of directories and subdirectories for any given disk drive (see Figure B–12).
- *Directory windows.* This window lists the contents of a user-selected directory or subdirectory (see Figure B–13).

FIGURE B–12 The Directory Tree
In the directory tree, directories with subordinate directories can be expanded (indicated with a "−") or collapsed (indicated with a "+") to meet the needs of the user.

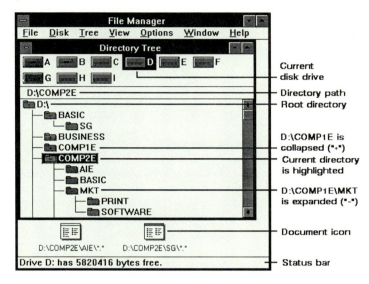

FIGURE B–13 File Manager Directory Window Showing File Details
The document icons in Figure B–12 are restored in this display. The active document window is shown with file details.

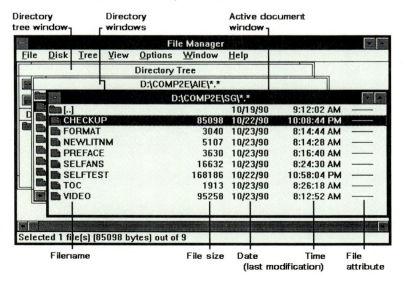

Files and directories are listed next to four types of icons: directory icon, program- and batch-file icon, document-file icon, and generic-file icon (see Figures B–10 and B–13).

The Directory Tree Window. In Figure B–12 the disk-drive icons under the title bar of the directory tree window show the available lettered root directories and the disk-drive type associated with each root directory. Point and click the desired disk-drive icon to display the corresponding directory tree document window. When displayed, the "tree" looks more like a list of directories. It becomes a tree when one or more directories with subdirectories are *expanded* to show the subdirectories (see Figure B–12). Directories with one or more subdirectories are marked with a "+" within the icon. Point and click the already selected directory icon to expand it. Or, select the Tree menu-bar option to expand or *collapse* the entire directory. Directory icons that have been expanded to show subdirectories are marked with a "−" (see Figure B–12).

The Directory Window. Point and double-click a directory icon in the directory tree window (see Figure B–12) to open that particular directory window (see Figure B–13). The directory window contains a list of all files and subdirectories in the selected directory. You can open as many directory windows as you want. Simply point and click the desired directory window or the directory tree window to make it the active document window.

The user has the option of displaying all files and subdirectories in the directory, or he or she can use check boxes to tell the system which types to display (directories, programs, documents, and/or others). The user also can request that file details be displayed (see Figure B–13) or only the filename (see Figure B–14). The file-details list can include any or all of the following along with the filename.

- Size of file (in bytes)
- Last modification date
- Last modification time
- File attributes (hidden or not available to the user; read-only, archive, or system files)

FIGURE B–14 File Manager Directory Window Showing Filename Only
The directory document windows for D:\COMP2E\SG and D:\COMP2E\AIE (both paths abbreviated in the figure) show only the filename.

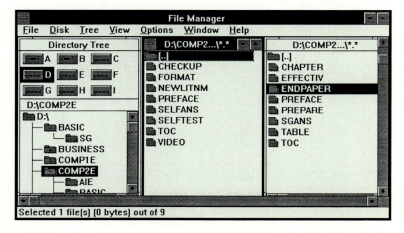

The File Manager permits the user to choose the order in which files are displayed in the directory window. The Sort By dialog box, which is displayed when you chose the Sort By option from the View menu bar item, has four mutually exclusive option buttons from which to choose (*Name*, *Type* of file, *Size*, and *Last Modification Date*). Figure B–13 illustrates a directory that contains all file details and is sorted by filename.

Working with Directory and Directory Tree Windows. The File Manager's menu bar is applicable to document windows, such as the directory and directory tree windows.

The file menu. Choosing the File Manager menu bar's File option presents the user with several important file management capabilities. Most options require that a file or files be selected before the command can be executed. Typically, choosing an option in the pull-down File menu results in a pop-up dialog box (see Figure B–15) in which the user is asked to enter information and/or is asked to confirm that the selected file is correct. The most frequently used File menu commands are the following.

- Run (execute a program)
- Print
- Search (for a user-specified file or files)
- Move (files or directories)
- Copy (files or directories)
- Delete (files or directories)
- Rename (files or directories)
- Create directory

A quick way to execute a program file is to open the directory window containing the file, then point and double-click the desired file.

Perhaps the most efficient way to move and copy files/directories is to open the desired directory windows, then choose the tile window arrangement so that the source and destination directory windows are visible. (In Figure B–14 the directory windows are visible, but titles are abbreviated: D:\COMP2E\SG is in the middle window and D:\COMP2E\AIE is in the right window.) For example, if you wanted to move ENDPAPER (the selected file in D:\COMP2E\SG, the source directory) to the directory D:\COMP2E\AIE (the destination

FIGURE B–15 Pop-up Dialog Box
Choosing Rename *in the* File *menu results in a pop-up dialog box.*

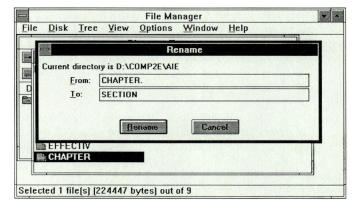

> **MEMORY BITS**
>
> *Windows and Icons*
> Types of windows
> - Application window
> - Document window
> - Dialog box
>
> Program Manager
> - Group window
>   Program-item icons
>   Applications in window
>   are closed
>   Can be shrunk to a group
>   icon
> - Open applications
>   Application windows
>   Foreground (contains
>   active window)
>   Background
>   Application icons
>
> File Manager
> - File icons
>   Directory icon
>   Program and file icon
>   Document icon
>   Generic icon
> - Disk-drive icons
> - Document windows
>   Directory tree window
>   Directory window

directory), point to the selected file icon and drag it with the mouse to the destination directory while holding down the ALT key. (In the Figure B–14, the directory names are abbreviated to fit within the tiled arrangement. The left directory window is Copy a file(s) in a similar manner, except that you drag the desired icon(s) between source and destination directories while holding down the CTRL key. In keeping with the user-friendly philosophy of Windows, a *confirmation message* asks users to confirm most file operations.

The disk menu. Choosing the menu bar's Disk option presents the user with commands that enable the maintenance of hard disks and diskettes. The most frequently used commands in the Disk menu are the *Format Diskette* and *Copy Diskette* commands. The format command prepares the diskette in the designated drive to store MS-DOS files. Copy Diskette performs the same function as the MS-DOS diskcopy command; that is, it permits the entire contents of a diskette to be copied to a like diskette (of the same size and density). These commands result in the destruction of all data on the formatted diskette and the destination diskette, so caution is recommended when using these commands.

B–4 WINDOWS ACCESSORY APPLICATIONS

Windows comes with a variety of helpful accessory applications and desktop software, all of which are run from the Accessories Group window in the Program Manager (see Figure B–11). The applications include Write (an executive word processing program), Paintbrush (a paint graphics program), and Terminal (a communications program). The handy desktop tools include a pop-up calculator, cardfile (an on-line "card file"), clock, notepad, and recorder (for creating Windows macros). Windows also is distributed with two interactive games, both of which are run from the Games Group window. These applications, desktop tools, and games are discussed in this section.

Write

Write is a full-function word processing package that provides users with the capability of creating most common documents such as letters, memos, and straightforward reports. Write is an easy-to-learn and easy-to-use package that provides most common word processing features (text entry and editing, text formatting, search and replace). It is not intended to offer the sophisticated capabilities of mainline packages such as Word and WordPerfect so, of course, the latter may require more time to learn and use. The function and use of word processing software is discussed and illustrated in detail in Chapter 5, "Text and Image Processing: Word Processing, Desktop Publishing, and Graphics."

Paintbrush

Paintbrush is a paint graphics package. It provides the user with an electronic canvas on which you can depict anything that can be drawn on a traditional canvas. Because Paintbrush is a paint graphics package, the end result of whatever you draw in the workspace becomes part of the whole drawing. If you wish to change a portion of the drawing, you can erase it or draw over it.

The Paintbrush user interface features six items (see Figure B–16).

APPENDIX B Windows Overview

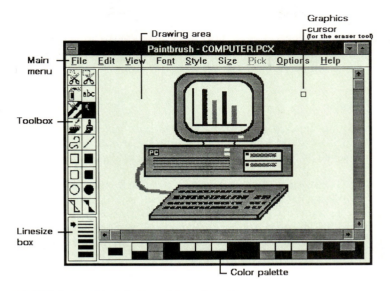

FIGURE B–16 The Paintbrush User Interface

- *Drawing area.*
- *Main menu.* A pull-down menu appears when any of the items in the Bar menu is selected.
- *Toolbox.* One of the tools in the toolbox (left of workspace) is active (the erasure tool in Figure B–16) at any give time. Use the tools to draw; to move, copy, or delete parts of the screen; to create geometric shapes; to fill defined areas with colors; to add text; and to erase.
- *Graphics cursor.* Use the mouse to use the graphics cursor to draw images and to select options. The graphics cursor takes on different shapes based on the tool selected.
- *Linesize box.* This box contains the width options for the drawing line.
- *Color palette.* This box contains colors and patterns that are used with the drawing tools.

The function and use of paint software is discussed and illustrated in detail in Chapter 5.

Terminal

Terminal is a communications software package that adds two basic functions to a microcomputer system.

- *Terminal emulation.* Communications software transforms a micro into a video display terminal (VDT) that can be linked to another computer.
- *File transfer.* Communications software enables the transfer of files between a micro and another computer.

Before either of these functions can be activated, an electronic link must be established between the micro and the other computer, and the micro must be equipped with a modem and have access to a telephone line. The function and use of communications software is discussed in detail in Chapter 7, "Data Communications and Networks."

Terminal opens the door to a wide variety of on-line information services (for example, movie reviews, home banking, and airline reservations), bulletin boards, and electronic mail. Many people use Terminal to telecommute to work or operate a cottage industry.

Desktop Software

The Accessory Group window in the Program Manager has six other handy desktop tools: Calculator, Clock, Calendar, Notepad, Cardfile, and Recorder. These tools are opened as windows or application icons in Figure B–17.

Calculator. The Calculator tool is presented in a window that when opened and, like other windows, can be shrunk to an icon and restored as needed. The user can opt for a standard calculator for simple arithmetic operations or a scientific calculator for scientific and statistical operations. Both work in much the same way as a hand-held calculator except that the user points and clicks the calculator's buttons rather than pressing them.

Clock. Many Windows users open the Clock and display it as an application icon. Unlike most icons, the Clock icon is active, showing the current time in analog or digital format within the icon (see Figure B–17).

Calendar. The Calendar tool provides users with an on-line calendar. A user can log hour-by-hour daily appointments as they become known. He or she can toggle between a day view and a month view. The day view shows user-entered appointments and notes and the month view shows the traditional monthly calendar.

Notepad. Notepad is a text editor that can be used to "jot down" ideas, activities, things-to-do, or anything else that you might write on a notepad. Notepad can even add the date and time to your note. The Notepad text file is an ASCII file so the filename, when saved, automatically is given a TXT extension. ASCII files are generic text files that are stripped of program-specific control characters. They are handy because they can be read by any word processing package, they can be used as MS-DOS batch files, and they can be interpreted by programming languages.

FIGURE B–17 Tools in the Accessory Group Window

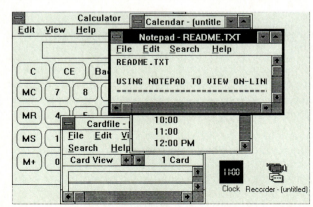

APPENDIX B Windows Overview

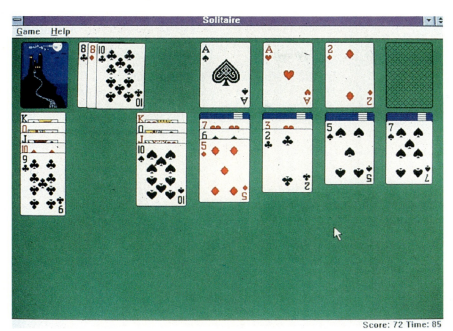

One of the games included with Windows is Solitaire. The electronic version of Solitaire has a number of advantages: You have 12 brightly colored decks from which to choose; the deck is shuffled automatically; you don't have to worry about cards sticking together; and players must adhere to all rules.

Cardfile. The Cardfile tool is an electronic alternative to a stack of 3-by-5-inch index cards. Each card has an index, or title, and space for anything from a recipe for cherry pie to notes for a speech. The cards are always sorted by index and can be accessed by searching the index or the information area for key words. Cardfile already has helped many people clean up their desk drawers.

Recorder. The Recorder enables users to record and play back any sequence of keystroke/mouse operations. In effect, the Recorder tool provides a vehicle for generating simple macros in the Windows environment. To record a sequence of operations, tell the Recorder to begin recording, perform the desired Windows operations using the keyboard and/or mouse, then tell the Recorder to stop recording. To repeat the sequence of operations, tap the assigned hot keys or choose from a list of available user-defined macros.

Games

Windows comes with two games, Solitaire and Reversi. Solitaire is played just like the traditional single-player card game, except the computer shuffles and deals the "cards," and you move the cards by dragging them with a mouse. Reversi pits you against the computer in a game of wits. Both games are excellent tools for practicing basic Windows skills.

B–5 USING WINDOWS

Windows is designed to be easy to learn and easy to use but, like any other skill, you need a solid understanding of its underlying principles and you need plenty of practice.

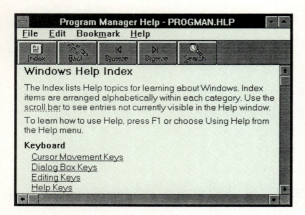

FIGURE B-18 The Windows Help Window
Help windows are context-sensitive—that is, they pertain to the active application. The Help window has five buttons to facilitate navigation within the Help feature: Index (for the application), Back (click to retrace path), Browse ◀◀ (click to view the previous topic in a series of related topics), Browse ▶▶ (click to view the next topic in a series of related topics), and Search (click on any item in an alphabetical listing of key words and phrases to view information on the topic).

The Help Feature

When using Windows, your best source of information about common operations is the Help command. The on-line Help feature is available whenever the Help command button is displayed or whenever the Help option is included in the menu bar. In any Help window display (see Figure B–18), point and click any green item (on color monitors) to get detailed information on that topic. Of course, Help information applies to the active application. Standard options found on the pull-down Help menu include the following.

- *Index*. A list of Help topics.
- *Keyboard*. Applicable key combinations.
- *Comnands*. Command explanations.
- *Procedures*. Step-by-step explanations of application procedures.
- *Using Help*. Information on how to use Help. (This option explains how to navigate within the Help window.)

Switching Between Windows

Windows allows users to open as many applications as available RAM will permit. It is not unusual for Windows users to have from two to 10 applications running at any given time. For example, a user might open these applications and keep them open during the working day: Program Manager, File Manager, WordPerfect, CorelDRAW, Calculator, Clock, and Calendar. When running multiple applications, the user can elect to display them as windows or application icons. In Figure B–19, several open applications are shrunk to application icons and restored to windows as needed.

The active window is always highlighted in the **foreground.** When in the foreground all parts of the window are visible. Other open windows are in the **background,** or behind the foreground. There are three ways to switch between open applications.

- Point and click anywhere on the desired inactive window or point and double-click the desired application icon.
- Tap ALT+ESC to toggle between open windows and application icons.
- Tap CTRL+ESC to display the Task List box (see Figure B–4), then point and click the name of the application you want to make the active window.

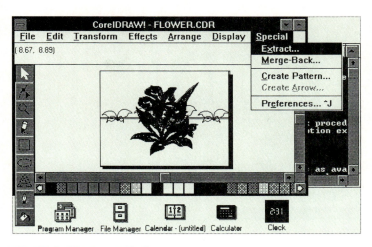

FIGURE B-19 Open Windows
In this display, CorelDRAW, the active window, is running in the foreground. Six other applications are running in the background, five of which are shrunk to application icons.

Transferring Information Between Applications

One of the most inviting aspects of the Windows environment is the ability to copy and move information (text, graphics, or a combination) from one application to another. This is done via the Windows Clipboard and the Edit option. Edit is an option in the menu bar of most Windows-based applications and an option in the Control menu of most non-Windows applications. Choosing Edit results in a pull-down menu from the Bar menu and a cascading menu from the Control menu. Options common to most Edit menus are Cut, Copy, Paste, and Delete. The source and destination windows can contain dissimilar applications. For example, text in a word processing document can be copied into a cell in a spreadsheet. As another example, a block of text from a WordPerfect document can be copied into a Paintbrush workspace.

The procedure for transferring information is as follows.

1. *Mark the information.* Point and hold the mouse button on one corner of the information to be cut or copied, then drag the graphics cursor to the opposite corner of the area and release the mouse button. The information to be transferred is highlighted.
2. *Cut or copy the marked information to the Clipboard.* Choose Edit in the source application's Bar menu or Control menu to display the options (usually Cut and/or Copy). Choosing the Cut option causes the specified information to be removed from the source application and placed on the Windows Clipboard. (Think of the Clipboard as an intermediate holding area for information en route to another application.) The Copy option causes the specified information in the source application to be placed on the Windows Clipboard, leaving the source application unchanged.
3. Switch to the destination application and place the graphics cursor at the desired insertion point.
4. *Paste the marked information.* Choose Edit in the destination application's Bar menu or Control menu to display the applicable options. Choosing the

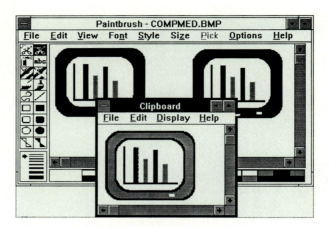

FIGURE B–20 The Windows Clipboard
In a cut or copy operation, information is transferred to the Windows clipboard. In the example, a Paintbrush image of a monitor is copied to the clipboard, then pasted from the clipboard to the original Paintbrush image to complete the copy operation.

Paste option causes the contents of the Clipboard to be copied to the cursor position in the destination application. The Clipboard contents remain unchanged and can be pasted as many times as needed.

The Clipboard also can be used to move or copy information within a single application (see Figure B–20). The Clipboard window does not have to be opened to perform information transfers.

Terminating an Application and a Windows Session

Perform three operations before ending a Windows session.

1. *Save your work.* Most applications offer two options on the File menu: *Save* and *Save as*. More often than not, users work with existing files. The Save option updates the existing file to reflect the changes made during the session. The Save as option allows users to save the current file under another filename. This feature is handy when you want to retain the working file in its original format (as it was at the beginning of the session).
2. *Close all open windows (except Program Manager).* After saving your work, exit each window by pointing and double-clicking the control menu box in the title bar.
3. *Exit the Program Manager application and Windows.* After all windows are closed, only the Program Manager remains. Close it and exit Windows.

Summary

This Windows overview is intended to introduce you to fundamental Windows concepts, terminology, and capabilities. Hundreds of software packages written specifically for the Windows environment have adopted the same concepts and terminology and are designed to take advantage of Windows capabilities. Once you understand the Windows environment, you will feel comfortable with the user interfaces of all software written for Microsoft Windows.

APPENDIX B Windows Overview

Use the Help feature and what you have learned in these pages to learn the use and operation of Windows, Windows applications, and Windows accessories. Once you gain familiarity with the environment, you may wish to customize Windows to meet your computing needs and maximize system throughput.

REVIEW EXERCISES

1. How is a Windows item, such as an applications program or a menu option, selected with a mouse? How is the item chosen?
2. In Windows, what is the screen area called upon which icons, windows, and so on are displayed?
3. List four elements of the Windows application window.
4. Briefly describe what happens when the Minimize option in the Windows control menu is chosen.
5. What area is just below the Windows title bar or menu bar?
6. What is displayed in a Windows Program Manager group window?
7. Name the three types of windows in the Windows graphical environment.
8. Name four categories of Windows icons.
9. What results when a Windows menu option, which is followed by an ellipsis (. . .), is chosen?
10. Which window arrangement in Windows enables the user to view at least a portion of the content of each window?
11. Briefly describe how a menu option is chosen from the keyboard.
12. What are the two types of document windows in the Windows File Manager?
13. When using a mouse to move a selected file from one Windows directory window to another, which key is held down during the drag operation?
14. The color palette and toolbox are found in which Windows accessory application?
15. Is the active Windows window highlighted in the foreground or the background?
16. Name three handy desktop tools found in the Windows Accessory Group window.
17. What is the intermediate holding area called through which information is transferred between Windows applications?

APPENDIX C

BUYING MICROCOMPUTERS AND THEIR PERIPHERAL DEVICES

- ▶ C-1 Where to Buy PCs
- ▶ C-2 Steps in Buying a Microcomputer
- ▶ C-3 Factors to Consider When Buying a Micro
- ▶ C-4 PC Buyer's Worksheet

APPENDIX C Buying Microcomputers and Their Peripheral Devices

C-1 WHERE TO BUY PCs

Each year millions of people go through the process of buying a microcomputer, micro peripheral devices, and various types of software. During the last few years the PC has emerged as the third most significant purchase—right behind homes and automobiles. The information presented here will help those planning to purchase a microcomputer to spend their money wisely.

PC Retailers

Ten years ago, micros were considered a highly technical specialty item and were sold almost exclusively through microcomputer retail outlets. Today micros have emerged as a popular consumer item. Microcomputers and associated hardware and software can be purchased at thousands of convenient locations.

- *Computer retailers.* About a dozen national retail chains, such as ComputerLand (over 500 locations), ENTRE (over 200 locations), and MicroAge (over 200 locations), and many regional retail chains specialize in the sale of microcomputer hardware and software. Most market and service a variety of small computer systems. Radio Shack stores carry and sell their own line of computers. This chain has over 400 computer specialty stores and over 10,000 electronics stores, all of which sell computers. There are also over a thousand computer stores that are not affiliated with a national or regional chain.

    Most computer specialty stores offer customers the option of leasing or buying. Depending on your willingness to accept the risk of obsolescence and your tax situation, leasing may be a viable alternative to purchasing.
- *Department stores.* Micros and micro software are sold in the computer departments of most department store chains, such as Sears and Walmart.
- *Discount stores.* Discount stores, such as SAM's and Service Merchandise, sell a wide range of micro hardware and software.
- *Other retail stores.* Many office supply stores, college bookstores, audio/video stores, and other specialty retailers sell computers and computer products, too.
- *Mail-order services.* The alternative to buying a computer and related products at a retail outlet is to purchase them from a mail-order service. If you know what you want, you can call any of several mail-order services, give your credit-card number, and your order will be delivered to your doorstep.
- *Direct marketers.* Some manufacturers of micro hardware and/or software are direct marketers; that is, they sell directly to the customer. For the most part, the direct marketer's "store window" is an advertisement in a PC trade magazine. The customer telephones, faxes, or mails the order and the direct marketer sends the requested product(s) by return mail. DELL Computer Corporation is a direct marketer.
- *Manufacturer.* Some manufacturers will sell directly to the customer via mail order, usually at list price. However, most will direct you to the nearest retail outlet that handles their product.
- *Used-computer retailers.* The demand for used computers has spawned a new industry during the past few years. The used-computer retailer was as inevitable as the used-car dealer. A computer that is no longer powerful enough for one user may have more than enough power for another. The used-computer dealer makes the mutually beneficial exchange possible.

Salespeople at computer retail stores are usually happy to give you an overview of the most popular micro productivity software packages. Available in most retail stores are "demo disks" that, when loaded to a PC, demonstrate the features of a software package.

- *Classified ads.* Frequently, people wishing to upgrade will opt to advertise their existing systems in the classified ad sections of their local newspapers.

The sale price of a microcomputer, a peripheral device, or a software package may vary substantially from one source to another. It pays to shop around. A word processing package may be offered at list price ($500) from the manufacturer, at $350 from one local computer retailer, at $325 from another, and at $265 from a mail-order service. Of course, the selling price does not tell the whole story. For example, the local retailers may promise to provide some technical support after the sale.

The "Perks" of Employment

You might be able to acquire a micro through your employer. Many companies offer their employees a "computer perk." In cooperation with vendors, companies make volume purchases of PCs and software at discount rates, then offer them to employees at substantial savings. Many colleges sponsor similar programs to benefit students and professors. The employee-purchase program is so popular in some organizations that they set up internal computer stores.

C–2 STEPS IN BUYING A MICROCOMPUTER

Buying a microcomputer can be a harrowing experience or it can be a thrilling and fulfilling one. If you approach the purchase of a micro haphazardly, expect the former. If you go about the acquisition methodically and with purpose,

APPENDIX C Buying Microcomputers and Their Peripheral Devices

expect the latter. This section contains a 10-step procedure to help you evaluate and select a microcomputer system.

Step 1: Achieve Computer Competency. You do not buy an automobile before you learn how to drive, and you should not buy a microcomputer without a good understanding of its capabilities and how you intend to use it. In effect, this book is a comprehensive buyer's guide: The informed buyer will know and understand its content. Every college and vocational college offers courses leading to computer competency. (*Computer competency* is defined in Chapter 1, "Micros and Personal Computing.") Generally speaking, the price you pay for hardware or software is for the product. Any advice or instruction is extra.

Step 2: Determine How Much You Are Willing to Spend. Microcomputer systems can be purchased for as little as a few hundred dollars or as much as $40,000. Assess your circumstances and decide how much you are willing to commit to the purchase of a microcomputer system.

Step 3: Determine Your Information and Computer-Usage Needs. There is an adage: "If you don't know where you are going, any road will get you there." The statement is certainly true of choosing a PC and its software. Knowing where you are going can be translated into: "How do you plan to use the PC?"

Determine which general application areas you wish to have supported on the proposed PC (spreadsheet, accounting, word processing, data communications, home banking, graphics, or others). Applications in personal computing are discussed in detail in Chapter 1, "Micros and Personal Computing."

If you want to write your own programs, you must select the programming language best suited to your skills and application needs. The most popular programming languages for micros are BASIC, C, COBOL, and Pascal.

Step 4: Assess the Availability of Software and Information Services. Determine what software and information services are available to meet your needs. Good sources of this type of information include general computer periodicals (*PC, Byte, Software, Computerworld,* and *Personal Computing,* to name a few), application- and product-specific periodicals (*Publish* and *WordPerfect: The Magazine*), salespeople at computer stores, your computer/software instructor, a local computer club, your colleagues at work, and acquaintances who have knowledge in the area.

Several hundred micro productivity software packages are available commercially, and they vary greatly in capabilities and price. Software with essentially the same capabilities may have price differences of several hundred dollars. Some graphics software creates displays of graphs in seconds, while others take minutes. Some software packages are easy to learn and are accompanied by good documentation, while others are not. Considering the amount of time you might spend using micro software, any extra time you devote to evaluating the software will be time well spent.

Step 5: Determine Which Platform to Follow. At this point in the PC decision process you will need to decide on a platform. Platforms are important because software is written to run under a particular platform. The various platforms are discussed in detail in Chapter 3, "Processors and Platforms." In the IBM-PC–compatible single-user environment, the dominant options are MS-DOS, MS-DOS/Windows, or OS/2. In the multiuser environment it is

The decision that confronts most people in the market for a microcomputer is whether to go with one of the IBM-compatible options or one of the Apple Macintosh options (several are shown here). A number of companies produce the former, but only Apple sells Macintoshes.

UNIX. High-end users will need to decide between MCA and EISA architectures. Appendix B, "Windows Overview," is devoted to the Windows platform. Of course, the Apple Macintosh platform is another option.

Step 6: Investigate Microcomputer System Options. If you select a specific proprietary software product (for example, desktop publishing or a general accounting system for a clinical laboratory), your selection may dictate the general microcomputer-system configuration requirements and, in some cases, a specific microcomputer system. However, if you are like most people and want to take advantage of the wide variety of microcomputer productivity software, you will have a dozen or more micro alternatives available to you. Become familiar with the features and options of at least three of these systems. For example, assess the availability of expansion slots, parallel ports, and serial ports.

Step 7: Determine the Processor Features You Want. You can go with a basic processor or, if your budget allows, you can select a more powerful processor and add a few "bells and whistles." Expect to pay for each increase in convenience, quality, and speed. For example, you may wish to enhance your processor's capability by increasing the size of the random-access memory (RAM), adding a coprocessor, and including some add-on capabilities (for example, a modem for data communications or a fax board). RAM, coprocessors, and add-on boards are discussed in Chapter 3, "Processors and Platforms."

Step 8: Determine the Peripheral Devices You Want. Generally speaking the only necessary peripheral devices are the disk drive, monitor, keyboard, mouse, and printer. However, these and other peripheral devices come in a wide variety of speeds, capacities, and qualities. The peripherals you select depend on your specific needs, volume of usage, and the amount of money you are willing to spend. Most people will pay a little extra for the added convenience of a two-disk system (usually a floppy and a hard disk), although one disk will suf-

APPENDIX C Buying Microcomputers and Their Peripheral Devices

The first disk (introduced in the late 1950s) would have to be cut down to fit in a micro. This 3½-inch disk platter, which is ready to be installed in a Winchester disk drive, has many times the capacity of the earlier disk. Fixed disks are manufactured in rooms 1000 times cleaner than operating rooms in hospitals. The various types of micro storage options are discussed in detail in Chapter 4, "Micro Peripheral Devices: I/O and Data Storage."

fice. On the other hand, a color monitor may be an unnecessary luxury for some applications. You can pay $150 for a printer or $10,000 for a desktop typesetter. This choice depends on the anticipated volume of hard-copy output; whether you need graphics output, letter-quality print, color output; and so on.

These standard peripheral devices and other devices, such as a joystick, optical scanner, speech-recognition device, vision-input system, plotter, desktop film recorder, screen-image projector, speech synthesizer, and tape drive, are discussed in detail in Chapter 4, "Micro Peripheral Devices: I/O and Data Storage."

Step 9: "Test-Drive" Several Alternatives. Once you have selected several software and hardware alternatives, spend enough time to gain some familiarity with them. Do you prefer one keyboard over another? Does a word processing system fully implement the hardware features? Is one system easier to understand than another?

Many software packages have demonstration and/or tutorial disks. When you load the demo or tutorial disk on the micro, an instructional program interactively "walks you through" a simulation (demonstration) of the features and use of the software. It is a good idea to work through the demo to get a feeling for the product's features and ease of use.

Salespeople at most retail stores are happy to give you a "test drive"—just ask. Use these sessions to answer any questions you might have about the hardware or software.

Step 10: Select and Buy. Apply your criteria, select, and then buy your hardware and software.

The type of printer you choose depends very much on its intended application. For example, you may need to print bar code labels on continuous-feed paper. This printer prints bar codes as well as traditional text output. Printers and other input/output devices are discussed in detail in Chapter 4.

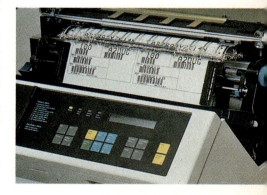

> **MEMORY BITS**
>
> *Steps in Buying a Microcomputer*
>   1. Achieve computer competency.
>   2. Determine how much you are willing to spend.
>   3. Determine your information and computer-usage needs.
>   4. Assess availability of software and information services.
>   5. Determine which platform to follow.
>   6. Investigate microcomputer system options.
>   7. Determine the processor features you want.
>   8. Determine the peripheral devices you want.
>   9. "Test drive" several alternatives.
>   10. Select and buy.

C-3 FACTORS TO CONSIDER WHEN BUYING A MICRO

- *Future computing needs.* What will your computer and information-processing needs be in the future? Make sure the system you select can grow with your needs. For example, the difference between a 40-MB and 100-MB Winchester disk may be several hundred dollars. However, if you estimate your disk-storage needs to be in excess of 40 MB within a couple of years, you may be better off in the long run buying the 100-MB disk.
- *Who will use the system?* Plan not only for yourself but for others in your home or office who also will use the system. Get their input and consider their needs along with yours.
- *Availability of software.* Software is developed for one or several platforms, but not for all of them. As you might expect, a more extensive array of software is available for the more popular platforms (MS-DOS, Windows, and Apple Macintosh).
- *Service.* Computing hardware is very reliable. Even so, the possibility exists that one or several of the components eventually will malfunction and have to be repaired. Before purchasing a micro, identify a reliable source of hardware maintenance. Most retailers service what they sell. If a retailer says the hardware must be returned to the manufacturer for repair, choose another retailer or another system. If you plan on purchasing via mail order, identify a nearby computer-repair store or a computer retailer that does repair work on the system you intend to buy.

    Most retailers or vendors will offer a variety of maintenance contracts. Maintenance-contract options range from same-day, on-site repairs that cover all parts and service to a carry-in service that does not include parts. Most domestic users elect to treat their micros like their televisions and cars: When the warranty runs out, they pay for repairs as they are needed. Under normal circumstances, this strategy will prove the least expensive. Business users are sometimes willing to pay extra for the convenience of an on-site maintenance contract.

    Service extends beyond hardware maintenance. Service is also an organization's willingness to respond to your inquiries before *and* after the sale. Some retailers and vendors offer classes in programming and in the use of the hardware and software they sell.

When you purchase a computer for the home, you must consider the computing needs of the whole family.

Most hardware and software vendors offer a *technical support hotline*. The extent of the hotline service varies considerably. Some companies provide their licensed users with a toll-free 24-hour hotline—free of charge for as long as they own the product. At the other end of the spectrum, companies charge their users as much as $50 an hour for using their technical support hotlines. Typically, companies will provide hotline service for a limited period of time (six months or a year), then charge after that.

- *Hardware obsolescence.* "I'm going to buy one as soon as the price goes down a little more." If you adopt this strategy, you may never purchase a computer. If you wait another six months, you probably will be able to get a more powerful micro for less money. But what about the lost opportunity?

  There is, however, a danger in purchasing a micro that is near or at the end of its life cycle. If you are planning on using a micro frequently at school, home, or work, focus your search on micros with state-of-the-art technology. Although you may get a substantial discount on a micro with dated technology, you may be better off in the long run by choosing an up-to-date one.

- *Software obsolescence.* Software can become obsolete as well. Software vendors are continually improving their software packages. Each package is assigned a *version number*. The first *release* might be identified as 1.0 (referred to as *one-point-zero*). Subsequent updates to Version 1.0 become

Version 1.1, Version 1.2, and so on. The next major revision of the package is released as Version 2.0. Make sure you are buying the most recent release of a particular software package.

- *Product documentation (internal and external).* PC products are consumer items and are distributed with user manuals, just like automobiles and VCRs. In most cases, the person who purchases the product installs it and uses it. To install it and use it, you will need effective product documentation. Inevitably you will spend many hours with the product's documentation—make sure that it is good.

When you purchase a PC or other hardware device, you should receive one or more user manuals. Examine the hardware documentation to ensure that it is visually and conceptually clear (especially the installation procedure), contains plenty of illustrations, has a good index, has a troubleshooting guide, and lists numbers to call for help.

When you purchase a software package, you usually will receive at least one manual, the software on diskettes, and often a tutorial disk. The best software documentation contains a user manual, a reference guide, and a workbook/tutorial. Depending on the complexity of the package, this documentation can be packaged in one, two, or three manuals. The user manual contains information on the features and the procedures that you would fol-

The first-time micro user is encouraged to take a college course or an employer's in-house course to learn about micro hardware and software.

APPENDIX C Buying Microcomputers and Their Peripheral Devices

low to use these features. (The most effective user manuals present the product at two levels—overview and in detail.) The reference guide provides a technical description of the package's capabilities (often at the menu-item level). The workbook/tutorial leads you, keystroke by keystroke, through the major features of the software.

A word of warning: Manuals and tutorials tell you everything you *can* do but say very little about what you *cannot* do. That may take a bit of experimentation to learn.

- *Availability of training.* Proper documentation should contain everything you need to know about how to use a PC, an I/O device, or a software package. However, learning strictly from the product's documentation can be difficult unless you are a seasoned PC veteran. Most people will opt to learn about micros or a particular software package by taking a course of some kind, perhaps at a local college. Many companies offer in-house courses for their employees. Retail computer stores offer courses for their customers. Self-paced multimedia courses are available commercially for most of the more popular software packages.

  Before you opt for a particular PC or software program, check the availability of training.

- *Other costs.* The cost of the actual microcomputer system is the major expense, but there are many incidental expenses that can mount up and so influence your selection of a micro. If you have a spending limit, consider these costs when purchasing the hardware (the cost ranges listed are for a first-time user): software ($100–$1500); maintenance ($0–$500 a year); diskettes and tape cassettes, including holders ($50–$200); furniture ($0–$350); cables ($0–$40); insurance ($0–$40); and printer ribbons or cartridges, paper, and other supplies ($40–$400).

> **MEMORY BITS**
>
> *Factors to Consider When Buying a Micro*
> - Future computing needs
> - Who will use the system
> - Availability of software
> - Service
> - Hardware obsolescence
> - Software obsolescence
> - Product documentation
> - Availability of training
> - Other costs

C-4 PC BUYER'S WORKSHEET

After you have looked at two or three systems, their features, options, and specifications tend to blur in your mind. It is difficult to remember whether the first system had a 30-MB Winchester disk and a 40-MHz processor or a 40-MB Winchester disk and a 30-MHz processor. The best way to make an informed purchase decision is to capture pertinent information in a way that will allow an easy comparison between alternatives. The template for a PC Buyer's Worksheet in Figure C-1 is designed to help you document this information.

The two approaches to using the worksheet are:

- *Gather information on proposed systems.* Discuss your processing and I/O needs with a sales representative, then ask the representative to propose a system to meet these needs. Complete a separate worksheet for each system configuration proposed by each sales organization.
- *Document the ideal system for your needs.* Determine your own processing and I/O needs, then fill in the worksheet with a description of your ideal system. When you visit or talk with an organization's sales representative, discuss the worksheet description. You probably will not find exactly what you want, so be prepared to make minor modifications to your ideal system. Make copies of your ideal worksheet, then for each system discussed, note differences on a copy of your worksheet.

Once you have investigated the alternatives and are ready to make a decision, the information on the worksheet helps you in the decision-making process.

PC Buyer's Worksheet

Name of vendor_____
Contact person_____
Telephone number (____) _____ – _____ ext._____

                                                                                                      Cost

Processor and Memory Specifications: Make_____Model_____ $_____
       Microprocessor_____ Speed____*MHz*
       RAM____*KB/MB* Word *16/32 bits*
       Type system: *pocket\laptop\desktop\tower*
       Expansion slots: full___half___
       Ports: serial___parallel___
       Extra RAM ($____ *per MB*) $_____
       Add-ons (*included in price*)_____
       Add-ons (*not included in price*)_____ $_____
       Special features (*included in price*)_____
       Special features (*not included in price*)_____ $_____

Keyboard Specifications: Make_____Model_____ $_____
       Number of keys____   Number of function keys___
       Keypad: *yes/no*   Stand-alone cursor control: *yes/no*

Monitor Specifications: Make_____Model_____ $_____
       Display: color/monochrome
       Size of display____(*inches width*)   Resolution____X____
       Technology (*pocket and laptop only*)_____
       Port or expansion slot requirements_____

Disk Drive Specifications:
       Interchangeable disk drive A: Make_____Model_____ $_____
       Size: *3½/5¼* Capacity: *DD/HD*
       Interchangeable disk drive B: Make_____Model_____ $_____
       Size: *3½/5¼* Capacity: *DD/HD*
       Winchester disk drive B: Make_____Model_____ $_____
       Capacity____*MB*

Tape Drive Specifications: Make_____Model_____ $_____
       Capacity____*MB*

FIGURE C–1 PC Buyer's Worksheet

Printer Specifications: Make_____ Model_____ $_____
　　　　Technology_____
　　　　Speed____(*cps/ppm*)　　　Resolution____(*pins/dpi*)
　　　　Port or expansion slot requirements_____
　　　　Cable requirement (*connectors and length*)_____
　　　　Special features (*included in price*)_____
　　　　Special features (*not included in price*)_____ $_____

Mouse Specifications: Make_____ Model_____ $_____
　　　　Number of buttons: *2/3*
　　　　Port or expansion slot requirements_____

Other I/O Device Specifications:
　　　　Device_____: Make_____ Model_____ $_____
　　　　Specs:_____
　　　　Device_____: Make_____ Model_____ $_____
　　　　Specs:_____
　　　　Device_____: Make_____ Model_____ $_____
　　　　Specs:_____

Software (included with price of PC):
　　　　Name_____ Description_____
　　　　Name_____ Description_____
　　　　Name_____ Description_____

　　　　　　　　　　Total Hardware Cost $_____

Software Requirements:
　　　　Name_____ Description_____
　　　　Name_____ Description_____
　　　　Name_____ Description_____

　　　　　　　　　　Total Software Cost $_____

　　　　　　　　　　TOTAL SYSTEM COST $_____

General comments:_____
_____
_____
_____

REVIEW EXERCISES

1. Name four retail outlets within five miles of your college that sell micros and micro software. Associate each of these outlets with one of the retail categories listed and described in Section C-1.
2. What is the first step in buying a microcomputer?
3. Visit a local library and identify at least two periodicals that may be helpful to people who are planning to buy a microcomputer system. Briefly explain why these periodicals would be helpful.
4. Name two microcomputer platforms.
5. List three factors to consider when purchasing a microcomputer system.
6. Briefly describe the purpose of a vendor's technical-support hotline.
7. Seven versions of CalPAC software have been introduced over the past 10 years: versions 2.01, 1.0, 2.0, 3.0, 1.2, 1.1, and 2.1. List the versions in the order in which they were introduced.
8. What three items are included in a good software documentation package?
9. List five costs, other than those for computer hardware and software, associated with the purchase of a new microcomputer system.
10. Use the PC Buyer's Worksheet template in Figure C-1 and create a worksheet that would help you in purchasing a PC. If you already have purchased a PC, create one that would have helped you during the decision process.
11. Fill out the PC Buyer's Worksheet that you created in Exercise 10 to reflect your ideal microcomputer system.

GLOSSARY

Abacus Probably the original mechanical counting device, which can be traced back at least 5000 years. Beads are moved along parallel wires to count and perform arithmetic computations.

Absolute cell address A cell address in an electronic spreadsheet that always refers to the same cell.

Access arm The disk-drive mechanism used to position the read/write heads over the appropriate track.

Access time The time interval between the instant a computer makes a request for a transfer of data from a secondary storage device and the instant this operation is completed.

Accumulator The computer register in which the result of an arithmetic or logic operation is formed (related to *arithmetic and logic unit*).

Acoustical coupler A device on which a telephone handset is mounted for the purpose of transmitting data over telephone lines. Used with a modem.

Active window The window containing the active software application. Commands issued via the keyboard or mouse apply to the active window.

Ada A multipurpose, procedure-oriented language.

Add-on boards Circuit boards that contain the electronic circuitry for a wide variety of computer-related functions (also called *add-on cards*).

Add-on cards See *add-on boards*.

Address (1) A name, numeral, or label that designates a particular location in primary or secondary storage. (2) A location identifier for terminals in a computer network.

ALGOL [*ALGOrithmic Language*] A high-level programming language designed primarily for scientific applications.

Algorithm A procedure that can be used to solve a particular problem.

Alpha A reference to the letters of the alphabet.

Alpha test The in-house testing of a software product by the vendor prior to its release for beta testing. (Contrast with *beta test*.)

Alphanumeric Pertaining to a character set that contains letters, digits, punctuation, and special symbols (related to *alpha* and *numeric*).

Analog computer A computer that operates on data expressed as a continuously changing representation of a physical variable, such as voltage. (Contrast with *digital computer*.)

Analog-to-digital (A-D) converter A device that translates an analog signal into a digital signal. (Contrast with *digital-to-analog converter*.)

Animation The rapid repositioning of part of a screen display to create movement within the display.

ANSI [*American National Standards Institute*] An organization that coordinates the setting of standards in the United States, including certain software standards.

APL [*A Programming Language*] An interactive symbolic programming language used primarily for mathematical applications.

Application A problem or task to which the computer can be applied.

Application generator A very high-level programming language in which programmers specify, through an interactive dialog with the system, which processing tasks are to be performed (also called *code generator*).

Applications portfolio The current mix of existing and proposed information systems in an organization.

Applications programmer A programmer who writes programs for specific business applications.

Applications software Software designed and written to address a specific personal, business, or processing task.

APT [*Automatically Programmed Tools*] A special-purpose programming language used to program machine tools.

Architecture The design of a computer system.

Argument That portion of a function which identifies the data to be operated on.

Arithmetic and logic unit That portion of the computer that performs arithmetic and logic operations (related to *accumulator*).

Arithmetic operators Mathematical operators (add [+], subtract [-], multiply [*], divide [/], and exponentiation [∧ ∧]) used in electronic spreadsheet and database software for computations.

Array A programming concept that permits access to a list or table of values by the use of a single variable name.

Array processor A processor composed of several processors, all under the control of a single control unit.

Artificial intelligence (AI) The ability of a computer to reason, to learn, to strive for self-improvement, and to simulate human sensory capabilities.

ASCII [*American Standard Code for Information Interchange*] An encoding system.

ASCII file A generic text file that is stripped of program-specific control characters.

Assembler language A low-level symbolic language with an instruction set that is essentially one-to-one with machine language.

Assistant system A type of knowledge-based system that helps users make relatively straightforward decisions. (Contrast with *expert system*.)

Asynchronous transmission Data transmission at irregular

349

intervals that is synchronized with start/stop bits. (Contrast with *synchronous transmission*.)

Attribute A data element in a relational data base.

Authorization code A code or number used in conjunction with a password to permit the end user to gain access to the system.

Auto-answer A modem function that permits the automatic answering of a call from a remote computer.

Auto-dial A modem function that permits the automatic dialing of the number of a remote computer.

AUTOEXEC.BAT file A special MS-DOS batch file that is loaded to RAM and executed following the booting procedure.

Automatic teller machine (ATM) An automated deposit/withdrawal device used in banking.

Automation The automatic control and operation of machines, processes, and procedures.

Auxiliary storage See *secondary storage*.

Back-end processor A host-subordinate processor that handles administrative tasks associated with retrieval and manipulation of data (same as *data base machine*).

Background (1) That part of RAM that contains the lowest priority programs. (2) In Windows, the area of the display over which the foreground is superimposed. (Contrast with *foreground*.)

Backup Pertaining to equipment, procedures, or data bases that can be used to restart the system in the event of system failure.

Backup file Duplicate of an existing production file.

Badge reader An input device that reads data on badges and cards (related to *magnetic stripe*).

Bar code A graphic encoding technique in which vertical bars of varying widths are used to represent data.

Bar graph A graph that contains vertical bars that represent specified numeric values.

Bar menu A menu in which the options are displayed across the screen.

BASIC A popular multipurpose programming language.

Batch file A user-created disk file that contains operating system commands, executable program filenames, and/or special batch file commands. When loaded to RAM, the commands and/or programs are executed.

Batch processing A technique in which transactions and/or jobs are collected into groups (batched) and processed together.

Baud (1) A measure of the maximum number of electronic signals that can be transmitted via a communications channel. (2) Bits per second (common-use definition).

Benchmark test A test for comparing the performance of several computer systems while running the same software, or comparing the performance of several programs that are run on the same computer.

Beta test Testing a software product in a live environment prior to its release to the public. (Contrast with *alpha test*.)

Binary A base-2 numbering system.

Binary notation Using the binary (base-2) numbering system (0, 1) for internal representation of alphanumeric data.

Bit A *bi*nary digi*t* (0 or 1).

Bit-mapping Projecting an image onto a screen via binary bits.

Bits per second (bps) The number of bits that can be transmitted per second over a communications channel.

Block A group of data that is either read from or written to an I/O device in one operation.

Blocking Combining two or more records into one block.

Boilerplate Existing text in a word processing file that can in some way be customized so that it can be used in a variety of word processing applications.

Boot The procedure for loading the operating system to primary storage and readying a computer system for use.

BPI [*B*ytes *P*er *I*nch] A measure of data-recording density on secondary storage.

Bridge A protocol-independent hardware device that permits communication between devices in local area networks of the same type.

Bubble memory Nonvolatile solid-state memory.

Buffer Intermediate memory that temporarily holds data that are en route from main memory to another computer or an input/output device.

Bug A logic or syntax error in a program, a logic error in the design of a computer system, or a hardware fault. (See *debug*.)

Bulletin-board system (BBS) The electronic counterpart of a wall-mounted bulletin board that enables end users in a computer network to exchange ideas and information via a centralized data base.

Bus An electrical pathway through which the processor sends data and commands to RAM and all peripheral devices.

Bus architecture See *open architecture*.

Bus topology A computer network that permits the connection of terminals, peripheral devices, and microcomputers along an open-ended central cable.

Byte A group of adjacent bits configured to represent a character.

C A transportable programming language that can be used to develop both systems and applications software.

Cache memory High-speed solid-state memory for program instructions and data.

CAD See *computer-aided design*.

CAI See *computer-assisted instruction*.

Callback procedure A security procedure that results in a remote user being called back by the host computer system after the user password and authorization code have been verified.

CAM See *computer-aided manufacturing*.

Carrier Standard-sized pin connectors that permit chips to be attached to a circuit board.

Carrier, common [in data communications] A company that furnishes data communications services to the general public.

Cascading menu A pop-up menu displayed when a command from the active menu is chosen.

Cascading windows An on-screen arrangement in which

windows are overlapped so that all window titles are showing.

CASE [Computer-Aided Software Engineering] A collective reference to a family of software development productivity tools (also called *workbench technologies*).

Cathode ray tube See *CRT*.

CBT See *computer-based training*.

CD-ROM disk [Compact Disk Read-Only Memory disk] A type of optical laser storage media.

Cell The intersection of a particular row and column in an electronic spreadsheet.

Cell address The location—column and row—of a cell in an electronic spreadsheet.

Central processing unit (CPU) See *CPU, processor*.

Centronics connector A 36-pin connector used for the electronic interconnection of computers, modems, and other peripheral devices.

Channel The facility by which data are transmitted between locations in a computer network (e.g., workstation to host, host to printer).

Channel capacity The number of bits that can be transmitted over a communications channel per second.

Character A unit of alphanumeric datum.

Checkpoint/restart When a system fails, backup files/data bases and/or backup transaction logs are used to re-create processing from the last "checkpoint." The system is "restarted" at the last checkpoint, and normal operation is resumed.

Chief information officer (CIO) The individual responsible for all information services in a company.

CIM [Computer-Integrated Manufacturing] Using the computer at every stage of the manufacturing process, from the time a part is conceived until it is shipped.

Clip art Prepackaged electronic images that are stored on disk to be used as needed in word processing or desktop publishing documents.

Clone A hardware device or a software package that emulates a product with an established reputation and market acceptance.

Closed architecture Refers to micros with a fixed, unalterable configuration. (Contrast with *open architecture*.)

Cluster controller See *down-line processor*.

Clustered-bar graph A modified bar graph that can be used to represent a two-dimensional set of numeric data (for example, multiple product sales by region).

Coaxial cable A shielded wire used as a medium to transmit data between computers and between computers and peripheral devices.

COBOL [COmmon Business Oriented Language] A programming language used primarily for administrative information systems.

Code (1) The rules used to translate a bit configuration into alphanumeric characters. (2) The process of compiling computer instructions in the form of a computer program. (3) The actual computer program.

Code generator See *application generator*.

Cold site A backup site equipped for housing a computer system. (Contrast with *hot site*.)

Collate To combine two or more files for processing.

Column A vertical block of cells that runs the length of a spreadsheet and is labeled by a letter.

COM [Computer Output Microfilm/Microfiche] A device that produces a microform image of a computer output on microfilm or microfiche.

Command An instruction to a computer that invokes the execution of a preprogrammed sequence of instructions.

Command-driven Pertaining to software packages that respond to user directives entered as commands.

Common carrier [in data communications] See *carrier, common*.

Common system An information system that can be installed and run on computers in several locations.

Communications See *data communications*.

Communications channel The facility by which data are transmitted between locations in a computer network (same as *line* and *data link*).

Communications protocols Rules established to govern the way data are transmitted in a computer network.

Communications software Software that enables a microcomputer to emulate a terminal and to transfer files between a micro and another computer.

Compatibility (1) Pertaining to the ability of one computer to execute programs of, access the data base of, and communicate with, another computer. (2) Pertaining to the ability of a particular hardware device to interface with a particular computer.

Compile To translate a high-level programming language, such as COBOL, into machine language in preparation for execution.

Compiler Systems software that performs the compilation process. (Compare with *interpreter*.)

Computer See *processor*.

Computer competency A fundamental understanding of the technology, operation, applications, and issues surrounding computers.

Computer console The unit of a computer system that allows operator and computer to communicate.

Computer matching The procedure whereby separate data bases are examined and individual records common to both are identified.

Computer network An integration of computer systems, workstations, and communications links.

Computer system A collective reference to all interconnected computing hardware, including processors, storage devices, input/output devices, and communications equipment.

Computer virus A program written with malicious intent and loaded to the computer system of an unsuspecting victim. Ultimately, the program destroys or introduces errors into programs and data bases.

Computer-aided design (CAD) Use of computer graphics in design, drafting, and documentation in product and manufacturing engineering.

Computer-aided manufacturing (CAM) A term coined to highlight the use of computers in the manufacturing process.

Computer-assisted instruction (CAI) Use of the computer

in the educational process. (Contrast with *computer-based training*.)

Computer-based training (CBT) Using computer technologies for training and education. (Contrast with *computer-assisted instruction*.)

Computerese A slang term for the jargon associated with computers and information processing.

Concatenation The joining together of labels or fields and other character strings into a single character string in electronic spreadsheet or database software.

Concentrator See *down-line processor*.

Configuration The computer and its peripheral devices.

Connectivity Pertains to the degree to which hardware devices, software, and data bases can be functionally linked to one another.

Contention A line-control procedure in which each workstation "contends" with other workstations for service by sending requests for service to the host processor.

Context-sensitive An on-screen explanation that relates to a user's current software activity.

Contingency plan A plan that details what to do in case an event drastically disrupts the operation of a computer center (same as *disaster plan*).

Control clerk A person who accounts for all input to and output from a computer center.

Control field See *key data element*.

Control total An accumulated number that is checked against a known value for the purpose of output control.

Control unit The portion of the processor that interprets program instructions, directs internal operations, and directs the flow of input/output to or from main memory.

Conventional memory The random-access memory between Position 0 and the 1-MB limit on an IBM-PC–compatible microcomputer.

Conversion The transition process from one system (manual or computer-based) to a computer-based information system.

Cooperative computing An environment in which businesses cooperate internally and externally to take full advantage of available information and to obtain meaningful, accurate, and timely information (see also *intracompany networking*).

Coprocessor An extra processor under the control of the main processor that helps relieve it of certain tasks.

Core memory A main-memory technology that was popular in the 1950s and 1960s.

Cottage industry People who do work for profit from their homes.

Counter One or several programming instructions used to tally processing events.

CPU [*Central Processing Unit*] The main processor in a computer system (see also *host processor*).

CRT [*Cathode Ray Tube*] The video monitor component of a workstation.

Cryptography A communications crime-prevention technology that uses methods of data encryption and decryption to scramble codes sent over communications channels.

Current program The program with which the user is currently interacting.

Current window The window in which the user is currently manipulating text, data, or graphics.

Cursor, graphics Typically, an arrow or crosshair that can be moved about a monitor's screen by an input device to create a graphic image or select an item from a menu. (See also *cursor, text*.)

Cursor, text A blinking character that indicates the location of the next keyed-in character on the display screen. (See also *cursor, graphics*.)

Cursor-control keys The arrow keys on the keyboard that move the text cursor vertically a line at a time and horizontally a character at a time.

Cyberphobia The irrational fear of, and aversion to, computers.

Cylinder A disk-storage concept. A cylinder is that portion of the disk that can be read in any given position of the access arm. (Contrast with *sector*.)

Daisy-wheel printer A letter-quality serial printer. Its interchangeable character set is located on a spoked print wheel.

DASD [*Direct-Access Storage Device*] A random-access secondary storage device.

Data Representations of facts. Raw material for information. (Plural of *datum*.)

Data base (1) An organization's data resource for all computer-based information processing in which the data are integrated and related to minimize data redundancy. (2) Same as a file in the context of microcomputer usage. (Contrast with *database*.)

Data base administrator (DBA) The individual responsible for the physical and logical maintenance of the data base.

Data base machine See *back-end processor*.

Data base management system (DBMS) A systems software package for the creation, manipulation, and maintenance of the data base.

Data base record Related data that are read from, or written to, the data base as a unit.

Data bits A data communications parameter that refers to the number of bits in a message.

Data cartridge Magnetic tape storage in cassette format.

Data communications The collection and distribution of the electronic representation of information from and to remote facilities.

Data communications specialist A person who designs and implements computer networks.

Data dictionary A listing and description of all data elements in the data base.

Data diddling The unauthorized revision of data upon being entered into a system or placed in storage.

Data element The smallest logical unit of data. Examples are employee number, first name, and price; same as *field*. (Compare with *data item*.)

Data entry The transcription of source data into machine-readable format.

Data entry operator A person who uses key entry devices to transcribe data into a machine-readable format.

Data flow diagram (DFD) A design technique that permits documentation of a system or a program at several levels of generality.

Data item The value of a data element. (Compare with *data element*.)

Data link See *communications channel*.

Data management software See *database software*.

Data processing (DP) Using the computer to perform operations on data.

Database Another term for microcomputer-based data management software. (Contrast with *data base*.)

Database software Software that permits users to create and maintain a data base and to extract information from the data base (also called *data management software*).

DB2 IBM's mainframe-based relational DBMS.

Debug To eliminate bugs in a program or system. (See *bug*.)

Decimal The base-10 numbering system.

Decision support system (DSS) An interactive information system that relies on an integrated set of user-friendly hardware and software tools to produce and present information to support management decision making to solve semistructured and unstructured problems. (Contrast with *executive support system* and *management information system*.)

Decision table A graphic technique used to illustrate possible occurrences and appropriate actions within a system.

Decode To reverse the encoding process. (Contrast with *encode*.)

Decoder That portion of a processor's control unit that interprets instructions.

Default options Preset software options that are assumed valid unless specified otherwise by the user.

Density The number of bytes per linear length of track of a recording medium. Usually measured in bytes per inch (bpi) and applied to magnetic tapes and disks.

Departmental computing Any type of computing done at the departmental level.

Departmental computing system Computer systems used both as stand-alone systems in support of a particular department and as part of a network of departmental minicomputers, all linked to a large centralized computer.

Desktop computer Any computer that can be placed conveniently on the top of a desk (same as *microcomputer*, *personal computer*, *PC*). Also called *desktop PC*.

Desktop film recorders An output device that permits the reproduction of high-resolution computer-generated graphic images on 35-mm film.

Desktop page printer A small printer that uses laser technology to print near-typeset-quality text and graphics one page at a time.

Desktop PC See *desktop computer*.

Desktop publishing (DTP) Refers to the hardware and software capability of producing near-typeset-quality copy from the confines of a desktop.

Detail system design That portion of the system development process in which the target system is defined in detail.

Diagnostic The isolation and/or explanation of a program error.

Dial-up line See *switched line*.

Dialog box A window that is displayed when the user must choose parameters or enter further information before the chosen menu option can be executed.

Dictionary See *information repository*.

Digital computer A computer that operates on data expressed in a discrete format (such as an on-bit or off-bit). (Contrast with *analog computer*.)

Digital-to-analog (D-A) converter A device that translates a digital signal into an analog signal. (Contrast with *analog-to-digital converter*.)

Digitize To translate data or an image into a discrete format that can be interpreted by computers.

Digitizing tablet A pressure-sensitive tablet with the same x-y coordinates as a computer-generated screen. The outline of an image drawn on a tablet with a stylus or puck is reproduced on the display.

DIP [*Dual Inline Package*] A toggle switch typically used to designate certain computer-system configuration specifications (such as the amount of RAM).

Direct access See *random access*.

Direct conversion An approach to system conversion whereby operational support by the new system is begun when the existing system is terminated.

Direct-access file See *random file*.

Direct-access processing See *random processing*.

Direct-access storage device See *DASD*.

Director of information services The person who has responsibility for computer and information systems in an organization.

Directory A list of the names of the files stored on a particular diskette or in a named area on a hard disk.

Disaster plan See *contingency plan*.

Disk, magnetic A secondary storage medium for random-access data storage. Available as microdisk, diskette, disk cartridge, or disk pack.

Disk cartridge An environmentally sealed interchangeable disk module that contains one or more hard-disk platters.

Disk drive, magnetic A magnetic storage device that records data on flat rotating disks. (Compare with *tape drive, magnetic*.)

Disk pack An interchangeable disk module that contains several hard-disk platters mounted on a central spindle.

Diskette A thin, flexible disk for secondary random-access data storage (same as *floppy disk* and *flexible disk*).

Distributed data processing Both a technological and an organizational concept based on the premise that information systems can be made more responsive to users by moving computer hardware and personnel physically closer to the people who use them.

Distributed DBMS Software that permits the interfacing of data bases located in various places throughout a computer network.

Distributed processor The nucleus of a small computer system linked to the host computer and physically located in the functional area departments.

Documentation Permanent and continuously updated written and graphic descriptions of information systems and programs.

Domain expert An expert in a particular field who provides the factual knowledge and the heuristic rules for input to a knowledge base.

DOS [*Disk Operating System*] A generic reference to a disk-based operating system.

Download The transmission of data from a mainframe computer to a workstation.

Down-line processor A computer that collects data from a number of low-speed devices, then transmits "concentrated" data over a single communications channel (also called a *concentrator* and *cluster controller*).

Downtime The time during which a computer system is not operational.

DP Abbreviation for *data processing*.

Drag A mouse-based procedure by which an object is moved or a contiguous area on the display is marked for processing.

Draw software Software that enables users to create electronic images, which are stored as vector-graphics images.

Driver module The program module that calls other subordinate program modules to be executed as they are needed (also called a *main program*).

E-mail See *electronic mail*.

E-time See *execution time*.

Earth station An earth-based communications station that can transmit and receive data from communications satellites.

EBCDIC [*Extended Binary Coded Decimal Interchange Code*] An encoding system.

Echo A host computer's retransmission of characters back to the sending device.

EDP Abbreviation for *electronic data processing*.

Education coordinator The person who coordinates all computer-related educational activities within an organization.

EFT [*Electronic Funds Transfer*] A computer-based system allowing electronic transfer of money from one account to another.

EGA [*Enhanced Graphics Adapter*] A circuit board that enables the interfacing of high-resolution monitors to microcomputers.

EISA [*Extended Industry Standard Architecture*] An architecture for microcomputers that use the Intel 80386 or 80486 microprocessors.

Electromechanical accounting machine (EAM) A family of data processing machines that used the punched card as the basis for data storage.

Electronic bulletin board A computer-based "bulletin board" that permits external users to read and send messages to the system via data communication.

Electronic data interchange (EDI) The use of computers and data communications to transmit data electronically between companies.

Electronic data processing Same as *data processing*.

Electronic dictionary A disk-based dictionary used in conjunction with a spell-check program to verify the spelling of words in a word processing document.

Electronic funds transfer See *EFT*.

Electronic mail A computer application whereby messages are transmitted via data communications to "electronic mailboxes." Also called *E-mail*. (Contrast with *voice message switching*.)

Electronic spreadsheet See *spreadsheet, electronic*.

Encode To apply the rules of a code. (Contrast with *decode*.)

Encoding system A system that permits alphanumeric characters to be coded in terms of bits.

Encyclopedia See *information repository*.

End user The individual providing input to the computer or using computer output (same as *user*).

End user computing A computing environment in which the end users handle both the technical and functional tasks of the information systems projects.

End-of-file (EOF) marker A marker placed at the end of a sequential file.

EPROM Erasable PROM [*Programmable Read-Only Memory*]. See *PROM*.

Exception report A report that has been filtered to highlight critical information.

Execution time The elapsed time it takes to execute a computer instruction and store the results. Also called *E-time*.

Executive support system (ESS) A system designed specifically to support decision making at the strategic level. (Contrast with *decision support system* and *management information system*.)

Expanded memory Random-access memory used in conjunction with special software and an add-on expanded-memory board to expand the amount of RAM of an IBM-PC–compatible computer that can run MS-DOS programs.

Expansion slots Slots within the processing component of a microcomputer into which optional add-on circuit boards can be inserted.

Expert system An interactive knowledge-based system that responds to questions, asks for clarification, makes recommendations, and generally helps users make complex decisions. (Contrast with *assistant system*.)

Expert system shell The software that enables the development of expert systems.

Extended memory An extension of the IBM-PC–compatible's conventional random-access memory.

Facsimile (FAX) Equipment that transfers images of hard-copy documents via telephone lines to another office.

Fault-tolerant system A computer system that can operate under adverse environmental conditions.

FAX See *facsimile*.

Feasibility study A study performed to determine the economic and procedural feasibility of a proposed information system.

Feedback loop In a process control environment, the output of the process being controlled is input to the system.

Fetch instruction That part of the instruction cycle in which the control unit retrieves a program instruction from main memory and loads it to the processor.

Field See *data element*.

File (1) A collection of related records. (2) A named area on a secondary storage device that contains a program, data, or textual material.

Filtering The process of selecting and presenting only that information that is appropriate to support a particular decision.

Firmware Logic for performing certain computer functions that is built into a particular computer by the manufacturer, often in the form of ROM or PROM.

Fixed disk See *hard disk*.

Flat files A traditional file structure in which records are related to no other files.

Flat-panel monitor A monitor, thin from front to back, that uses liquid crystal and gas plasma technology.

Flexible disk See *diskette*.

Floppy disk See *diskette*.

Flops Floating point operations per second.

Flowchart A diagram that illustrates data, information, and work flow via specialized symbols which, when connected by flow lines, portray the logic of a system or program.

Font A typeface of a particular point size.

Footprint The evidence of unlawful entry or use of a computer system.

Foreground (1) That part of RAM that contains the highest priority program. (2) In Windows, the area of the display containing the active window. (Contrast with *background*.)

FORTH A programming language particularly suited for microcomputers that enables users to tailor the language's set of commands to any application.

FORTRAN [*FOR*mula *TRAN*slator] A high-level programming language designed primarily for scientific applications.

Fourth-generation language (4GL) A programming language that uses high-level Englishlike instructions to retrieve and format data for inquiries and reporting.

Frame A rectangular area in a desktop-publishing–produced document that holds the text or an image of a particular file.

Frequency division multiplexing A method of simultaneously transmitting several communications signals over a transmission medium by dividing its band width into narrower bands, each carrying a communications signal.

Front-end processor A processor used to offload certain data communications tasks from the host processor.

Frozen specifications System specifications that have been approved and are not to be changed during the system development process.

Full-duplex line A communications channel that transmits data in both directions at the same time.

Full-screen editing This word processing feature permits the user to move the cursor to any position in the document to insert or replace text.

Function A predefined operation that performs mathematical, logical, statistical, financial, and character-string operations on data in an electronic spreadsheet or a data base.

Function key A special-function key on the keyboard that can be used to instruct the computer to perform a specific operation (also called *soft key*).

Function-based information system An information system designed for the exclusive support of a specific application area, such as inventory management or accounting.

Functional specifications Specifications that describe the logic of an information system from the perspective of the user.

Functionally adjacent systems Information systems that feed each other, have functional overlap, and/or share all or part of a data base.

Gateway Software that permits computers of different architectures to communicate with one another.

Gateway computer A subordinate computer that translates communications protocols of remote computers to a protocol that is compatible with the host computer, thereby enabling the transmission of data from external sources.

General system design That portion of the system development process in which the target system is defined in general.

General-purpose computer Computer systems that are designed with the flexibility to do a variety of tasks, such as CAI, payroll processing, climate control, and so on. (Contrast with *special-purpose computer*.)

General-purpose software Software that provides the framework for a number of business and personal applications.

Geostationary orbit See *geosynchronous orbit*.

Geosynchronous orbit An orbit that permits a communications satellite to maintain a fixed position relative to the surface of the earth (also known as *geostationary orbit*).

Gigabyte (G) Referring to one billion bytes of storage.

GIGO [*Garbage In, Garbage Out*] A euphemism implying that information is only as good as the data from which it is derived.

Global memory Pertaining to random-access memory that is shared by several processors.

Graceful exit Quitting a program according to normal procedures and returning to a higher level program.

Grammar checker An add-on program to word processing software that highlights grammatical concerns and deviations from conventions in a word processing document.

Grandfather-father-son method A secondary storage back-up procedure that results in the master file having two generations of backup.

Graphical user interface (GUI) Software that permits the user to select processing options by simply positioning an arrow over a graphic representation of the desired function or program.

Graphics-conversion program A program that converts graphics files from one format to another.

Graphics cursor A symbol on a display screen which can be positioned anywhere on a display screen by a light pen, joystick, track ball, digitizing tablet and pen, or mouse to initiate action or to draw.

Graphics software Software that enables the user to create line drawings, art, and presentation graphics.

Graphics workstation A terminal with a high-resolution graphics monitor for the sophisticated user that is endowed with its own processing capability as well as the ability to interface with a mainframe.

Gray scales The number of shades of a color that can be presented on a monochrome monitor's screen or on a monochrome printer's output.

Groupware Software whose application is designed to benefit a group of people on a local area network.

Hacker A computer enthusiast who uses the computer as a source of recreation.

Half-duplex line A communications channel that transmits data in both directions, but not at the same time.

Half-size expansion board An add-on board that fits in a half an expansion slot.

Handshaking The process by which both sending and receiving devices in a computer network maintain and coordinate data communications.

Hard carriage return In word processing, a special character that is inserted in the document when the carriage return is pressed. Typically, the character denotes the end of a paragraph or of a string of contiguous text.

Hard copy A readable printed copy of computer output. (Contrast with *soft copy*.)

Hard disk A permanently installed, continuously spinning magnetic storage medium made up of one or more rigid disk platters. (Same as *fixed disk*; contrast with *interchangeable magnetic disk*.) See also *Winchester disk*.

Hard-wired Logic that is designed into chips.

Hardware The physical devices that comprise a computer system. (Contrast with *software*.)

Hashing A method of random access in which the address is arithmetically calculated from the key data element.

Head crash A disk-drive malfunction that causes the read/write head to touch the surface of the disk, thereby resulting in the loss of the disk head, the disk, and the data stored on the disk.

Header label A file identification record found at the beginning of a sequential file.

Help command A software feature that provides an on-line explanation of or instruction on how to proceed.

Help screen The display that results from initiating the help command.

Hertz One cycle per second.

Heuristic knowledge Rules of thumb that evolve from experience.

Hexadecimal A base-16 numbering system used as a programmer convenience in information processing to condense binary output and make it more easily readable.

Hierarchical data base A data base whose organization employs the tree data structure. (Contrast with *relational data base* and *network data base*.)

High-level programming language A language with instructions that combine several machine-level instructions into one instruction. (Compare with *machine language* or *low-level programming language*.)

High memory area (HMA) Extended memory between Positions 1024 KB and 1088 KB on an IBM-PC–compatible microcomputer on which MS-DOS programs can be run.

HIPO [*Hierarchical Plus Input-Processing-Output*] A design technique that encourages the top-down approach, dividing the system into easily manageable modules.

Historical reports Reports generated from data that were gathered in the past and do not reflect the current status. Reports based solely on historical data are rare in practice. (Contrast with *status reports*.)

Host computer See *host processor*.

Host processor The processor responsible for the overall control of a computer system. The host processor is the focal point of a communications-based system (also called *host computer*).

Hot key A key combination that activates a memory-resident program.

Hot site A backup site equipped with a functioning computer system. (Contrast with *cold site*.)

Hypertext Data management software that provides the ability to link portions of unstructured text-based documents via key words.

I/O [*Input/Output*] Input or output, or both.

I-time See *instruction time*.

Icons Pictographs used in place of words or phrases on screen displays.

Idea processor A software productivity tool that allows the user to organize and document thoughts and ideas (also called an *outliner*).

Identifier A name used in computer programs to recall a value, an array, a program, or a function from storage.

Image scanner A device that uses a camera to scan and digitize an image that can be stored on a disk and manipulated by a computer.

Index file Within the context of database software, a file that contains logical pointers to records in a data base.

Indexed-sequential organization A direct-access data storage scheme that uses an index to locate and access data stored on magnetic disk.

Industrial robot A robot that is used in industry (see *robot*).

Inference engine The logic embodied in the software of an expert system.

Information Data that have been collected and processed into a meaningful form.

Information center A facility in which computing resources are made available to various user groups.

Information center specialist Someone who works with users in an information center.

Information engineering A term coined to emphasize using the rigors of engineering discipline in the handling of the information resource.

Information management systems (IMS) IBM's mainframe-based hierarchical DBMS.

Information network Same as *information service*.

Information overload The circumstance that occurs when the volume of available information is so great that the decision maker cannot distinguish relevant from irrelevant information.

Information repository A central-computer–based storage facility for all system design information (also called *dictionary* and *encyclopedia*).

Information resource management (IRM) A concept advocating that information be treated as a corporate resource.

Information service An on-line commercial network that provides remote users with access to a variety of information services (same as *information network*).

Information services auditor Someone who is responsible for ensuring the integrity of operational information systems.

Information services department The organizational entity that develops and maintains computer-based information systems.

Information society A society in which the generation and dissemination of information becomes the central focus of commerce.

Information system A computer-based system that provides both data processing capability and information for managerial decision making.

Information technology A collective reference to the combined fields of computers and information systems.
Information-based decision See *nonprogrammed decision*.
Input Data to be processed by a computer system.
Input/output-bound operation The amount of work that can be performed by the computer system is limited primarily by the speeds of the I/O devices.
Inquiry An on-line request for information.
Insert mode A data entry mode in which the character entered is inserted at the cursor position.
Instruction A programming language statement that specifies a particular computer operation to be performed.
Instruction register The register that contains the instruction being executed.
Instruction time The elapsed time it takes to fetch and decode a computer instruction. Also called *I-time*.
Integer Any positive or negative whole number and zero.
Integrated circuit (IC) Thousands of electronic components that are etched into a tiny silicon chip in the form of a special-function electronic circuit.
Integrated information system An information system that services two or more functional areas, all of which share a common data base.
Integrated software Two or more of the major microcomputer productivity tools integrated into a single commercial software package.
Intelligent Pertaining to computer aided.
Intelligent terminal A terminal with a built-in microprocessor.
Intelligent workstation A workstation endowed with its own sophisticated processing capability as well as the ability to interface with a mainframe.
Interactive Pertaining to on-line and immediate communication between the end user and computer.
Interactive computer system A computer system that permits users to communicate directly with the system.
Interblock gap (IBG) A physical space between record blocks on magnetic tapes.
Interchangeable magnetic disk A magnetic disk that can be stored off-line and loaded to the magnetic disk drive as it is needed. (Contrast with *hard disk*, or *fixed disk*.)
Intercompany networking See *electronic data interchange*.
Interpreter Systems software that translates and executes each program instruction before translating and executing the next. (Compare with *compiler*.)
Interrupt A signal that causes a program or a device to stop or pause temporarily.
Intracompany networking The use of computers and data communications to transmit data electronically within a company (see also *cooperative computing*).
Invoke Execute a command or a macro.
ISO [*International Standards Organization*] An organization that coordinates the setting of international standards.

Job A unit of work for the computer system.
Job control language (JCL) A language used to tell the computer the order in which programs are to be executed.
Job stream The sequence in which programs are to be executed.
Joystick A single vertical stick that moves the cursor on a screen in the direction in which the stick is pushed.

Kb See *kilobyte*.
Kernel An independent software module that is part of a larger program.
Key data element The data element in a record that is used as an identifier for accessing, sorting, and collating records. (Same as *control field*.)
Key pad That portion of a keyboard that permits rapid numeric data entry.
Key word See *reserved word*.
Keyboard A device used for key data entry.
Keyboard templates Typically, a plastic keyboard overlay that indicates which commands are assigned to particular function keys.
Keystroke buffer An intermediate storage area for keystrokes entered in advance of processing.
Kilobit (Kb) 1024, or about 1000, bits.
Kilobyte (KB) 1024, or about 1000, bytes.
Knowledge acquisition facility That component of the expert system shell that permits the construction of the knowledge base.
Knowledge base The foundation of a knowledge-based system that contains facts, rules, inferences, and procedures.
Knowledge engineer Someone trained in the use of expert system shells and in the interview techniques needed to extract information from a domain expert.
Knowledge worker Someone whose job function revolves around the use, manipulation, and dissemination of information.
Knowledge-based system A computer-based system, often associated with artificial intelligence, that helps users make decisions by enabling them to interact with a knowledge base.

Landscape The orientation of the print on a page in which printed lines run parallel to the longer side of the page. Contrast with *portrait*.
Laptop PC Portable briefcase-size PC that can operate without an external power source.
Large-scale integration (LSI) An integrated circuit with a densely packed concentration of electronic components. (Contrast with *very large-scale integration*, or *VLSI*.)
Layout A detailed output and/or input specification that graphically illustrates exactly where information should be placed/entered on a VDT display screen or placed on a printed output.
Layout line A line on a word processing screen that graphically illustrates appropriate user settings (margins, tabs). Also called a format line.
Leased line A permanent or semipermanent communications channel leased through a common carrier.
Lexicon The dictionary of words that can be interpreted by a particular natural language.
Librarian A person who functions to catalog, monitor, and control the distribution of disks, tapes, system documentation, and computer-related literature.
Light-emitting diode (LED) A device that responds to electrical current by emitting light.

Limits check A system check that assesses whether the value of an entry is out of line with that expected.

Line See *communications channel*.

Line graph A graph in which conceptually similar points are plotted and connected so they are represented by one or several lines.

Line printer Printers that print a line at a time.

Linkage editor An operating system program that assigns a primary storage address to each byte of an object program.

Liquid crystal display (LCD) An output device that displays characters and other images as composites of actuated liquid crystal.

LISP [*LISt Processing*] A programming language particularly suited for the manipulation of words and phrases that is often used in applications of artificial intelligence.

Live data Test data that have already been processed through an existing system.

Load To transfer programs or data from secondary to primary storage.

Local area network (LAN or local net) A system of hardware, software, and communications channels that connects devices on the local premises.

Local memory Pertaining to the random-access memory associated with a particular processor or peripheral device.

Log on procedure The procedure by which a user establishes a communications link with a remote computer.

Logic bomb A Trojan horse that is executed when a certain set of conditions are met.

Logic operations Computer operations that make comparisons between numbers and between words, then perform appropriate functions, based on the result of the comparison.

Logical operators Used to combine relational expressions logically in electronic spreadsheet and database software (such as AND, OR). See also *relational operators*.

Logical record See *record*.

LOGO A programming language often used to teach children concepts in mathematics, geometry, and computer programming.

Loop A sequence of program instructions that are executed repeatedly until a particular condition is met.

Low-level programming language A language comprising the fundamental instruction set of a particular computer. (Compare with *high-level programming language*.)

Machine cycle The cycle of operations performed by the processor to process a single program instruction: fetch, decode, execute, and place result in memory.

Machine independent Pertaining to programs that can be executed on computers of different designs.

Machine language The programming language that is interpreted and executed directly by the computer.

Macro A sequence of frequently used operations or keystrokes that can be recalled and invoked to help speed user interaction with microcomputer productivity software.

Magnetic disk See *disk, magnetic*.

Magnetic disk drive See *disk drive, magnetic*.

Magnetic ink character recognition (MICR) A data entry technique used primarily in banking. Magnetic characters are imprinted on checks and deposits, then scanned to retrieve the data.

Magnetic stripe A magnetic storage medium for low-volume storage of data on badges and cards (related to *badge reader*).

Magnetic tape See *tape, magnetic*.

Magnetic tape drive See *tape drive, magnetic*.

Magneto-optical disk An optical laser disk with read and write capabilities.

Mail merge A computer application in which text generated by word processing is merged with data from a data base (e.g., a form letter with an address).

Main memory See *primary storage*.

Main menu The highest level menu in a menu tree.

Main program Same as *driver module*.

Mainframe computer A large computer that can service many users simultaneously.

Maintenance The ongoing process by which information systems (and software) are updated and enhanced to keep up with changing requirements.

Management information system (MIS) An integrated structure of data bases and information flow throughout all levels and components of an organization, whereby the collection, transfer, and presentation of information is optimized to meet the needs of the organization. (Contrast with *decision support system* and *executive support system*.)

Manipulator arm The movable part of an industrial robot to which special-function tools are attached.

MAP [*Manufacturing Automation Protocol*] A communications protocol, developed by General Motors, that enables the linking of robots, machine tools, automated carts, and other automated elements of manufacturing into an integrated network.

Master file The permanent source of data for a particular computer application area.

Maxicomputers That category of computers that falls between minicomputers and supercomputers.

MB See *megabyte*.

MCA [*Micro Channel Architecture*] The architecture of the high-end IBM PS/2 line of microcomputers.

Megabit (Mb) 1,048,576, or about 1000, bits.

Megabyte (MB) 1,048,576, or about 1000, bytes.

Megahertz See *MHz*.

Memory See *primary storage*.

Memory dump The duplication of the contents of a storage device to another storage device or to a printer.

Memory-resident program A program, other than the operating system, that remains operational while another applications program is running.

Menu A workstation display with a list of processing choices from which an end user may select.

Menu bar A bar menu that lists menus available for the active application.

Menu driven Pertaining to software packages that respond to user directives that are entered via a hierarchy of menus.

Menu tree A hierarchy of menus.

Message A series of bits sent from a workstation to a computer, or vice versa.

Metal-oxide semiconductor (MOS) A technology for cre-

GLOSSARY

ating tiny integrated circuits in layers of conducting metal that are separated by silicon dioxide insulators.

Methodology A set of standardized procedures, including technical methods, management techniques, and documentation, that provides the framework for accomplishing a particular task (e.g., system development methodology).

MHz [megahertz] One million hertz.

MICR inscriber An output device that enables the printing of characters for magnetic ink character recognition on bank checks and deposit slips.

MICR reader-sorter An input device that reads the magnetic ink character recognition data on bank documents and sorts them.

Micro/mainframe link Linking microcomputers and mainframes for the purpose of data communication.

Microchip An integrated circuit on a chip.

Microcomputer (or micro) A small computer (same as *desktop computer*, *personal computer*, *PC*).

Microcomputer specialist A specialist in the use and application of microcomputer hardware and software.

Microdisk A $3\frac{1}{2}$-inch flexible disk used for data storage.

Microfloppy Same as *microdisk*.

Microframe A high-end microcomputer.

Microprocessor A computer on a single chip. The processing component of a microcomputer.

Microsecond One millionth of a second.

Microwave radio signal A high-frequency line-of-sight electromagnetic wave that is used in communications satellites.

Milestone A significant point in the development of a system or program.

Millisecond One thousandth of a second.

Minicomputer (or mini) A midsized computer.

MIPS Millions of instructions per second.

MIS See *management information system*.

MIS planner The person in a company who has the responsibility for coordinating and preparing the MIS plans.

MIS steering committee A committee of top executives who are charged with providing long-range guidance and direction for computer and MIS activities.

Mnemonics Symbols that represent instructions in assembler languages.

Modem [*MO*dulator-*DEM*odulator] A device used to convert computer-compatible signals to signals suitable for data transmission facilities, and vice versa.

Modula-2 A general-purpose language that enables self-contained modules to be combined in a program.

Module A task within a program that is independent of other tasks.

Monitor A televisionlike display for soft-copy output in a computer system.

Motherboard A microcomputer circuit board that contains the microprocessor, electronic circuitry for handling such tasks as input/output signals from peripheral devices, and memory chips.

Mouse A small device that, when moved across a desktop a particular distance and direction, causes the same movement of the cursor on a screen.

MS-DOS [*M*icro*S*oft *D*isk *O*perating *S*ystem] A microcomputer operating system.

Multicomputer A complex of interconnected computers that share memory while operating in concert or independently.

Multidrop The connection of more than one terminal to a single communications channel.

Multifunction add-on board An add-on circuit board that performs more than one function.

Multiplexing The simultaneous transmission of multiple transmissions of data over a single communications channel.

Multiprocessing Using two or more processors in the same computer system in the simultaneous execution of two or more programs.

Multiprogramming Pertaining to the concurrent execution of two or more programs by a single computer.

Multitasking The concurrent execution of more than one program at a time.

Multiuser microcomputer A microcomputer that can serve more than one user at any given time.

Nanosecond One billionth of a second.

Natural language A programming language in which the programmer writes specifications without regard to the computer's instruction format or syntax—essentially, using everyday human language to program.

Navigation Movement within and between a software application's work areas.

Nested loop A programming situation where at least one loop is entirely within another loop.

Network, computer See *computer network*.

Network data base A data base organization that permits children in a tree data structure to have more than one parent. (Contrast with *relational data base* and *hierarchical data base*.)

Network topology The configuration of interconnection between the nodes in a communications network.

Node An endpoint in a computer network.

Nonprocedural language A programming language that can automatically generate the instructions needed to create a programmer-described end result.

Nonprogrammed decision A decision that involves an ill-defined and unstructured problem (also called *information-based decision*).

Nubus The architecture of high-end Apple Macintosh computers.

Numeric A reference to any of the digits 0–9. (Compare with *alpha* and *alphanumeric*.)

Object program A machine-level program that results from the compilation of a source program. (Compare with *source program*.)

Object-oriented language A programming language structured to enable the interaction between user-defined concepts (such as a computer screen, a list of items) that contain data and operations to be performed on the data.

OCR scanner A light-sensitive input device that bounces a beam of light off an image to determine the value of the image.

Octal A base-8 numbering system used as a programmer convenience in information processing to condense binary output and make it easier to read.

Off-line Pertaining to data that are not accessible by, or hardware devices that are not connected to, a computer system. (Contrast with *on-line*.)

Office automation (OA) Pertaining collectively to those computer-based applications associated with general office work.

Office automation specialist A person who specializes in the use and application of office automation hardware and software (see *office automation*).

On-line Pertaining to data and/or hardware devices accessible to and under the control of a computer system. (Contrast with *off-line*.)

On-line thesaurus Software that enables a user to request synonyms interactively during a word processing session.

Opcode Pertaining to that portion of a computer machine-language instruction that designates the operation to be performed. Short for *operation code*. (Related to *operand*.)

Open architecture Refers to micros that give users the flexibility to configure the system with a variety of peripheral devices. (Contrast with *closed architecture*; also called *bus architecture*.)

Open systems interconnect (OSI) A standard for data communications within a computer network established by the International Standards Organization (ISO).

Operand Pertaining to that portion of a computer machine-language instruction that designates the address of the data to be operated on. (Related to *opcode*.)

Operating environment (1) Same as *platform*. (2) A user-friendly DOS interface. (3) The conditions under which a computer system functions.

Operating system The software that controls the execution of all applications and systems software programs.

Operation code See *opcode*.

Operator The person who performs those hardware-based activities necessary to keep information systems operational.

Operator console The machine-room operator's workstation.

Optical character recognition (OCR) A data entry technique that permits original-source data entry. Coded symbols or characters are scanned to retrieve the data.

Optical fiber A data transmission medium that carries data in the form of light in very thin transparent fibers.

Optical laser disk A secondary storage medium that uses laser technology to score the surface of a disk to represent a bit.

Optical scanners Devices that provide input to computer systems by using a beam of light to interpret printed characters and various types of codes.

Orphan The first line of a paragraph that is printed as the last line on a page in a word processing document.

Outliner See *idea processor*.

Output Data transferred from primary storage to an output device.

Packaged software Software that is generalized and "packaged" to be used with little or no modification in a variety of environments. (Related to *proprietary software*.)

Packet switching A data communications process in which communications messages are divided into packets (subsets of the whole message), transmitted independent of one another in a communications network, then reassembled at the source.

Page A program segment that is loaded to primary storage only if it is needed for execution (related to *virtual memory*).

Page break In word processing, an in-line command or special character that causes the text that follows to be printed on a new page.

Page offset The distance between the left edge of the paper and the left margin in a word processing document.

Page printer Printers that print a page at a time.

Page-composition software The software component of desktop publishing software that enables users to design and make up pages.

Pagination The word processing feature that provides automatic numbering of the pages of a document.

Paint software Software that enables users to "paint" electronic images, which are stored as raster-graphics images.

Palmtop PC See *pocket PC*.

Parallel Pertaining to processing data in groups of bits versus one bit at a time. (Contrast with *serial*.)

Parallel conversion An approach to system conversion whereby the existing system and the new system operate simultaneously until the project team is confident that the new system is working properly.

Parallel host processor A redundant host processor used for backup and supplemental processing.

Parallel port A direct link with the microcomputer's bus that facilitates the parallel transmission of data, usually one byte at a time.

Parallel processing A processing procedure in which one main processor examines the programming problem and determines what portions, if any, of the problem can be solved in pieces by other subordinate processors.

Parallel processor A processor in which many, even millions, of processing elements simultaneously address parts of a processing problem.

Parallel representation The storing of bits side-by-side on a secondary storage medium.

Parameter A descriptor that can take on different values.

Parity bit A bit appended to a bit configuration (byte) that is used to check the accuracy of data transmission from one hardware device to another (related to *parity checking* and *parity error*).

Parity checking A built-in checking procedure in a computer system to help ensure that the transmission of data is complete and accurate (related to *parity bit* and *parity error*).

Parity error Occurs when a bit is dropped in the transmission of data from one hardware device to another (related to *parity bit* and *parity checking*).

Parsing A process whereby user-written natural language commands are analyzed and translated to commands that can be interpreted by the computer.

Pascal A multipurpose, procedure-oriented programming language.

Password A word or phrase known only to the end user. When entered, it permits the end user to gain access to the system.

GLOSSARY

Patch A modification of a program or an information system.

Path The logical route that an operating system would follow when searching through a series of directories and subdirectories to locate a specific file on disk storage.

PBX A computer that electronically connects computers and workstations for the purpose of data communication.

PC [*Personal Computer*] See *desktop computer* and *microcomputer*.

PC-DOS [*PC Disk Operating System*] A microcomputer operating system.

Pen plotter An output device that can generate high-quality hard-copy graphic output that is perfectly proportioned.

Performance monitoring software System software used to monitor, analyze, and report on the performance of the overall computer system and the computer system components.

Peripheral equipment Any hardware device other than the processor.

Personal computer (PC) See *desktop computer* and *microcomputer*.

Personal computing A computing environment in which individuals use microcomputers for both domestic and business applications.

Personal identification number (PIN) A unique number that is assigned to and identifies a user of a computer network.

Phased conversion An approach to system conversion whereby an information system is implemented one module at a time by either parallel or direct conversion.

Pick-and-place robot An industrial robot that physically transfers material from one place to another.

Picosecond One trillionth of a second.

Pie graph A circular graph that illustrates each "piece" of data in its proper relationship to the whole "pie."

Pilferage A special case of software piracy where a company purchases a software product without a site-usage license agreement, then copies and distributes it throughout the company.

Pilot conversion An approach to system conversion whereby the new system is implemented by parallel, direct, or phased conversion as a pilot system in only one of the several areas for which it is targeted.

Pipe Under the Unix operating system, the "connection" of two programs so that the output of one becomes the input of the other.

Pitch Horizontal spacing (characters per inch) in printed output.

Pixel An addressable point on a display screen to which light can be directed under program control.

Platform A definition of the standards followed by those who create proprietary software packages.

PL/I A multipurpose, procedure-oriented programming language.

Plotter A device that produces hard copy graphic output.

Plug-Compatible Manufacturer (PCM) A company that makes peripheral devices that can be attached directly to another manufacturer's computer.

Pocket PC Hand-held personal computers. Also called *palmtop PC*.

Point-of-sale (POS) terminal A cash-register-like terminal designed for key and/or scanner data entry.

Point-to-point connection A single communications channel linking a workstation or a microcomputer to a computer.

Pointer The highlighted area in an electronic spreadsheet display that indicates the current cell.

Polling A line-control procedure in which each workstation is "polled" in rotation to determine whether a message is ready to be sent.

Pop-out menu See *pop-up menu*.

Pop-up menu A menu that is superimposed in a window over whatever is currently being displayed on the monitor. Also called *pop-out menu*.

Port An access point in a computer system that permits communication between the computer and a peripheral device.

Portrait The orientation of the print on the page in which printed lines run parallel to the shorter side of the paper. Contrast with *landscape*.

Post-implementation evaluation A critical examination of a computer-based system after it has been put into production.

Power down To turn off the electrical power for a computer system.

Power up To turn on the electrical power for a computer system.

Presentation graphics Business graphics, such as pie graphs and bar graphs, that are used to present information in a graphic format in meetings, reports, and oral presentations.

Prespecification An approach to information systems development where users determine their information processing needs during the early stages of the project, then commit to these specifications through system implementation.

Primary storage The memory area in which all programs and data must reside before programs can be executed or data manipulated. (Same as *main memory*, *memory*, and *RAM*; compare with *secondary storage*.)

Printer A device used to prepare hard copy output.

Printer spooler A circuit board that enables data to be printed while a microcomputer user continues with other processing activities.

Private line A dedicated communications channel between any two points in a computer network.

Problem-oriented language A high-level language whose instruction set is designed to address a specific problem (such as process control of machine tools, simulation).

Procedure-oriented language A high-level language whose general-purpose instruction set can be used to produce a sequence of instructions to model scientific and business procedures.

Process control Using the computer to control an ongoing process in a continuous feedback loop.

Process control system A system that uses the computer to control an ongoing process in a continuous feedback loop.

Processor The logical component of a computer system that interprets and executes program instructions (same as *computer*).

Processor-bound operation The amount of work that can be performed by the computer system is limited primarily by the speed of the computer.

Program (1) Computer instructions structured and ordered in a manner that, when executed, cause a computer to perform a particular function. (2) The act of producing computer software (related to *software*).

Program register The register that contains the address of the next instruction to be executed.

Programmed decisions Decisions that address well-defined problems with easily identifiable solutions.

Programmer One who writes computer programs.

Programmer/analyst The title of one who performs both the programming and systems analysis function.

Programming The act of writing a computer program.

Programming language A language that programmers use to communicate instructions to a computer.

Project Evaluation and Review Technique (PERT) A network modeling technique that enables managers to show the relationships between the various activities involved in the project and to select the approach that optimizes the use of resources while meeting project deadlines (similar to *Critical Path Method*, or *CPM*).

Project leader The person in charge of organizing the efforts of a project team.

Project team A group of users and computer professionals who work together to create an information system.

Prolog A descriptive programming language often used in applications of artificial intelligence.

PROM [Programmable Read-Only Memory] ROM in which the user can load read-only programs and data. (See *EPROM*.)

Prompt A program-generated message describing what should be entered by the end user operator at a workstation.

Proportional spacing A spacing option for word processing documents in which the spacing between characters remains relatively constant for any given line of output.

Proprietary software Vendor-developed software that is marketed to the public. (Related to *packaged software*.)

Protocols Rules established to govern the way data are transmitted in a computer network.

Prototype system A model of a full-scale system.

Pseudocode Nonexecutable program code used as an aid to develop and document structured programs.

Puck A flat hand-held device with cross hairs used in conjunction with a digitizing tablet to translate an image into machine-readable format.

Pull-down menu A menu that is "pulled down" and superimposed in a window over whatever is currently being displayed on a monitor.

Punched cards A paper card storage medium, which is now obsolete, that holds data in various configurations of punched holes.

Purging The act of erasing unwanted data, files, or programs from RAM or magnetic memory.

Quality assurance An area of specialty concerned with monitoring the quality of every aspect of the design and operation of information systems, including system

Query by example (QBE) A method of data base inquiry in which the user sets conditions for the selection of records by composing one or more example relational expressions.

RAM [Random-Access Memory] See *primary storage*.

Random access Direct access to records, regardless of their physical location on the storage medium. (Contrast with *sequential access*.)

Random file A collection of records that can be processed randomly. (Same as *direct-access file*.)

Random processing Processing data and records randomly. (Same as *direct-access processing*; contrast with *sequential processing*.)

Range A cell or a rectangular group of adjacent cells in an electronic spreadsheet.

Raster graphics A method for creating and maintaining a screen image as patterns of dots.

Raster-scan monitor An electron beam forms the image by scanning the screen from left to right and from top to bottom. (Contrast with *vector-scan monitor*.)

Read The process by which a record or a portion of a record is accessed from the magnetic storage medium (tape or disk) of a secondary storage device and transferred to primary storage for processing. (Contrast with *write*.)

Read/write head That component of a disk drive or tape drive that reads from and writes to its respective magnetic storage medium.

Real-time computing The processing of events as they occur, usually in a continuous feedback loop.

Record A collection of related data elements (such as an employee record) describing an event or an item. Also called *logical record*.

Recursion Pertaining to the capability of a program to reference itself as a subroutine.

Register A small high-speed storage area in which data pertaining to the execution of a particular instruction are stored. Data stored in a specific register have a special meaning to the logic of the computer.

Relational data base A data base in which data are accessed by content rather than by address. (Contrast with *hierarchical data base* and *network data base*.)

Relational operators Used in electronic spreadsheet and database formulas to show the equality relationship between two expressions (= [equal to], < [less than], > [greater than], <= [less than or equal to], >= [greater than or equal to], <> [not equal to]). See also *logical operators*.

Relative cell address Refers to a cell's position in an electronic spreadsheet in relation to the cell containing the formula in which the address is used.

Replace mode A data entry mode in which the character entered overstrikes the character at the cursor position.

Report generator Software that produces reports automatically based on user specifications.

Request for information (RFI) See *RFI*.

Request for proposal (RFP) See *RFP*.

Reserved word A word that has a special meaning to a software package. (Also called *key word*.)

Resident font A font that is accessed directly from the printer's built-in read-only memory.

Resolution Referring to the number of addressable points on a monitor's screen. The greater the number of points, the higher the resolution.

Response time The elapsed time between when a data communications message is sent and when a response is received. (Compare with *turnaround time*.)

Reusable code Modules of programming code that can be called and used as needed.

Reverse video Characters on a video display terminal presented as black on a light background; used for highlighting.

RFI [*Request For Information*] A request to a prospective vendor for information about a particular type of product.

RFP [*Request For Proposal*] A formal request to a vendor for a proposal.

Ring topology A computer network that involves computer systems connected in a closed loop, with no one computer system the focal point of the network.

Robot A computer-controlled manipulator capable of locomotion and/or moving items through a variety of spatial motions.

Robotics The integration of computers and industrial robots.

ROM [*Read-Only Memory*] RAM that can only be read, not written to.

Root directory The directory at the highest level of a hierarchy of directories.

Row A horizontal block of cells that runs the width of a spreadsheet and is labeled by a number.

RPG A programming language in which the programmer communicates instructions interactively by entering appropriate specifications in prompting formats.

RS-232-C connector A 25-pin connector used for the electronic interconnection of computers, modems, and other peripheral devices.

Run The continuous execution of one or more logically related programs (such as printing payroll checks).

Scalable typeface An outline-based typeface from which fonts of any point size can be created.

Scheduler Someone who schedules the use of hardware resources to optimize system efficiency.

Schema A graphical representation of the logical structure of a CODASYL data base.

Screen formatter Same as *screen generator*.

Screen generator A system design tool that enables a systems analyst to produce a mockup of a display while in direct consultation with the user. (Also called a *screen formatter*.)

Screen-capture programs Memory-resident programs that enable users to transfer all or part of the current screen image to a disk file.

Screen-image projector An output device that can project a computer-generated image onto a large screen.

Scroll bar A horizontal or vertical bar that appears at the bottom or right side of a window when the entire workspace cannot be displayed in a window.

Scrolling Using the cursor keys to view parts of a word processing document or an electronic spreadsheet that extends past the bottom or top or sides of the screen.

Secondary storage Permanent data storage on magnetic disk and/or tape. (Same as *auxiliary storage*; compare with *primary storage*.)

Sector A disk storage concept: a pie-shaped portion of a disk or diskette in which records are stored and subsequently retrieved. (Contrast with *cylinder*.)

Self-booting diskette A diskette that contains both the operating system and an applications software package.

Semiconductor A crystalline substance whose properties of electrical conductivity permit the manufacture of integrated circuits.

Sequential access Accessing records in the order in which they are stored. (Contrast with *random access*.)

Sequential files Files containing records that are ordered according to a key data element.

Sequential processing Processing of files that are ordered numerically or alphabetically by a key data element. (Contrast with *direct-access processing* or *random processing*.)

Serial Pertaining to processing data one bit at a time. (Contrast with *parallel*.)

Serial port A direct link with the microcomputer's bus that facilitates the serial transmission of data, one bit at a time.

Serial printer Printers that print one character at a time.

Serial representation The storing of bits one after another on a secondary storage medium.

Serpentine A magnetic tape storage scheme in which data are recorded serially in tracks.

Service bureau A company that provides almost any kind of information processing service for a fee.

Service request A formal request from a user for some kind of computer- or MIS-related service.

Set A CODASYL data base concept that serves to define the relationship between two records.

Shareware Software that is made readily available via bulletin boards and other distribution channels. Users are ask to pay a nominal fee to register the software with its developer.

Shelfware Software that was purchased but never used or implemented.

Shell Software that provides a graphical user-interface alternative to command-driven software.

Shortcut key A key combination that initiates processing of a menu option without displaying the menu.

Shrink (1) To deactivate the current software application in a graphical user interface and reduce it to an icon. (2) To reduce the size of an object or area within a graphic image.

Simplex line A communications channel that transmits data in only one direction.

Situation assessment An MIS planning activity that results in a definition of where the information services division and the functional areas stand with respect to their use of computer and information technologies.

Skeletal code A partially complete program produced by a code generator.

Smalltalk An object-oriented language.

Smart card A card or badge with an embedded microprocessor.

Smart modems Modems that have embedded microprocessors.

SNA [*Systems Network Architecture*] IBM's scheme for networking its computers.

Soft carriage return In word processing, an invisible special character that is automatically inserted after the last full word within the right margin of entered text.

Soft copy Temporary output that can be interpreted visually, as on a workstation monitor. (Contrast with *hard copy*.)

Soft font An electronic description of a font that is retrieved from disk storage and downloaded to the printer's memory.

Soft key See *function key*.

Software The programs used to direct the functions of a computer system. (Contrast with *hardware*; related to *program*.)

Software engineering A term coined to emphasize an approach to software development that embodies the rigors of the engineering discipline. (Also called *systems engineering*.)

Software package One or more programs designed to perform a particular processing task.

Software piracy The unlawful duplication of proprietary software (related to *pilferage*.)

Sort The rearrangement of data elements or records in an ordered sequence by a key data element.

Source code See *source program*.

Source data Original data that usually involves the recording of a transaction or the documenting of an event or item.

Source data automation Entering data directly to a computer system at the source without the need for key entry transcription.

Source document The original hard copy from which data are entered.

Source program The code of the original program. (Compare with *object program*.) Also called *source code*.

Special-purpose computer Computers designed for a specific application, such as CAD, video games, robots. (Contrast with *general-purpose computer*.)

Specialized common carrier A company that provides services over and above those offered by a communications common carrier.

Speech recognition device

Speech synthesizers Devices that convert raw data into electronically produced speech.

Spelling checker An add-on program to word processing that checks the spelling of every word in a word processing document against an electronic dictionary.

Spooling The process by which output (or input) is loaded temporarily to secondary storage. It is then output (or input) as appropriate devices become available.

Spreadsheet, electronic Refers to software that permits users to work with rows and columns of data.

Stacked-bar graph A modified bar graph in which the bars are divided to highlight visually the relative contribution of the components that make up the bar.

Star topology A computer network that involves a centralized host computer connected to a number of smaller computer systems.

Statement See *instruction* (for a computer program).

Status reports Reports that reflect current status. (Contrast with *historical reports*.)

Streamer tape drive Tape drive for $\frac{1}{4}$-inch tape cartridges that stores data in a serpentine manner.

Structure chart A chart that graphically illustrates the conceptualization of an information system as a hierarchy of modules.

Structured Analysis and Design Technique (SADT) A top-down design technique in which a system is conceptualized as being composed of things and activities and the relationships between them.

Structured programming A design technique by which the logic of a program is addressed hierarchically in logical modules.

Structured Query Language (SQL) The ANSI and ISO standard data access query language for relational data bases.

Structured system design A system design technique that encourages top-down design.

Structured walkthrough A peer evaluation procedure for programs and systems under development. It is used to minimize the possibility of something being overlooked or done incorrectly.

Style checker An add-on program to word processing software that identifies deviations from effective writing style in a word processing document (for example, long, complex sentences).

Stylus A penlike device used in conjunction with a digitizing tablet to translate an image into computer format.

Subdirectory A directory that is subordinate to a higher-level directory.

Subroutine A sequence of program instructions that are called and executed as needed.

Subscripts Characters that are positioned slightly below the line of type.

Summary report A report that presents a summary of information about a particular subject.

Supercomputer The category that includes the largest and most powerful computers.

Superscripts Characters that are positioned slightly above the line of type.

Supervisor The operating system program that loads programs to primary storage as they are needed.

Switched line A telephone line used as a regular data communications channel. Also called *dial-up line*.

Synchronous transmission Transmission of data at timed intervals between terminals and/or computers. (Contrast with *asynchronous transmission*.)

Syntax The rules that govern the formulation of the instructions in a computer program.

Syntax error An invalid format for a program instruction.

Sysop [*system op*erator] The sponsor who provides the hardware and software support for an electronic bulletin board system.

System Any group of components (functions, people, activities, events, and so on) that interface with and complement one another to achieve one or more predefined goals.

System board See *motherboard*.

System check An internal verification of the operational capabilities of a computer's electronic components.

System development methodology Written standardized procedures that depict the activities in the systems development process and define individual and group responsibilities.

System integrators See *turnkey company*.

System life cycle A reference to the four stages of a computer-based information system—birth, development, production, and death.

System maintenance The process of modifying an information system to meet changing needs.

System prompt A visual prompt to the user to enter a system command.

Systems analysis The analysis, design, development, and implementation of computer-based information systems.

Systems analyst A person who does systems analysis.

Systems engineering See *software engineering*.

Systems programmer A programmer who develops and maintains systems software.

Systems software Software that is independent of any specific applications area.

Systems testing A phase of testing where all programs in a system are tested together.

Tape, magnetic A secondary storage medium for sequential data storage. Available as a reel or as a cartridge.

Tape drive, magnetic The hardware device that contains the read/write mechanism for the magnetic tape storage medium. (Compare with *disk drive, magnetic*.)

Tape reel Magnetic tape storage in reel format.

Task The basic unit of work for a processor.

Telecommunications Communication between remote devices.

Telecommuting "Commuting" via a communications link between home and office.

Teleconferencing A meeting in which people in different locations use electronic means to see and talk to each other and to share charts and other meeting materials.

Teleprocessing A term coined to represent the merging of telecommunications and data processing.

Template A model for a particular microcomputer software application.

Terminal Any device capable of sending and receiving data over a communications channel.

Terminal emulation mode The software transformation of a microcomputer so that its keyboard, monitor, and data interface emulate that of a terminal.

Terminate-and-stay-resident (TSR) A memory-resident program that can be activated instantly while running another program.

Test data Data that are created to test all facets of an information system's operational capabilities.

Test data base A data base made up of test data.

Text cursor A blinking character on a display screen that indicates the location of the next keyed-in character on the screen.

Thesaurus, on-line See *on-line thesaurus*.

Third-party provider An intermediary who facilitates electronic data interchange between trading partners with incompatible hardware and software.

Three-tier network A computer network with three layers—a host mainframe at the top, which is linked to multiple minicomputers, which are linked to multiple microcomputers.

Throughput A measure of computer system efficiency; the rate at which work can be performed by a computer system.

Throwaway system An information system developed to support information for a one-time decision, then discarded.

Tiled windows An on-screen arrangement of windows in which no window overlaps another.

Time-division multiplexing A method of concurrently transmitting several communications signals over a transmission media.

Timesharing Multiple end users sharing time on a single computer system in an on-line environment.

Toggle The action of pressing a single key on a keyboard to switch between two or more modes of operation such as insert and replace.

Top-down design An approach to system and program design that begins at the highest level of generalization; design strategies are then developed at successive levels of decreasing generalization, until the detailed specifications are achieved.

Tower PC A vertical PC designed to rest on the floor. Processing component of a desktop PC that has been placed on end.

Trace A procedure used to debug programs whereby all processing events are recorded and related to the steps in the program. The objective of a trace is to isolate program logic errors.

Track, disk That portion of a magnetic disk face surface that can be accessed in any given setting of a single read/write head. Tracks are configured in concentric circles.

Track, tape That portion of a magnetic tape that can be accessed by any one of the nine read/write heads. A track runs the length of the tape.

Track ball A ball mounted in a box that, when moved, results in a similar movement of the cursor on a display screen.

Tracks per inch (TPI) A measure of the recording density, or spacing, of tracks on a magnetic disk.

Trailer label The last record in a sequential file that contains file information.

Transaction A procedural event in a system that prompts manual or computer-based activity.

Transaction file A file containing records of data activity (transactions); used to update the master file.

Transaction-oriented processing Transactions are recorded and entered as they occur.

Transcribe To convert source data into machine-readable format.

Transfer rate The number of characters per second that can be transmitted between primary storage and a peripheral device.

Transistor An electronic switching device that can be used to vary voltage or alter the flow of current.

Transmission medium The central cable along which terminals, peripheral devices, and microcomputers are connected in a bus topology.

Transparent A reference to a procedure or activity that occurs automatically. It does not have to be considered in the use or design of a program or an information system.

Trap door A Trojan horse that permits unauthorized and undetected access to a computer system.

Trojan horse A set of unauthorized instructions hidden in a legitimate program, such as an operating system.

TSR See *terminate-and-stay-resident*.

Tuple A group of related fields (a row) in a relational data base.

Turbo Pascal A microcomputer version of the Pascal programming language.

Turnaround document A computer-produced output that is

ultimately returned to a computer system as a machine-readable input. (Compare with *response time*.)

Turnaround time Elapsed time between the submission of a job and the distribution of the results. (Compare with *response time*.)

Turnkey company A company that contracts with a client to install a complete system, both hardware and software (also called *system integrators*).

Twisted-pair wire Two twisted copper wires. The foundation of telephone services through the 1970s.

Two-tier network A computer network with two layers—a host mainframe at the top that is linked directly to multiple minicomputers and/or microcomputers.

Typeface A set of characters that are of the same type style.

Uninterruptible power source (UPS) A buffer between an external power source and a computer system that supplies clean and continuous power.

Unit testing That phase of testing in which the programs that make up an information system are tested individually.

Universal product code (UPC) A 10-digit machine-readable bar code placed on consumer products.

UNIX A multiuser operating system.

Upload The transmission of data from a workstation to the mainframe computer.

Uptime That time when the computer system is in operation.

Upward compatibility A computing environment that can be upgraded without the need for redesign and reprogramming.

User See *end user*.

User acceptance testing That stage of testing where the system is presented to the scrutiny of the user managers whose departments will ultimately use the system.

User interface A reference to the software, method, or displays that enable interaction between the user and the application or system software being used.

User liaison A person who serves as the technical interface between the information services department and the users.

User sign-off A procedure whereby the user manager is asked to "sign off," or commit, to the specifications defined by the systems development project team.

User-friendly Pertaining to an on-line system that permits a person with relatively little experience to interact successfully with the system.

Utility program An often-used service routine, such as a program to sort records.

Vaccine An antiviral program.

Value-added network (VAN) A specialized common carrier that "adds value" over and above the standard services of common carriers.

Value-added reseller (VAR) A company that integrates the hardware and software of several vendors with its own software, then sells the entire package.

Variable A primary storage location that can assume different numeric or alphanumeric values.

Variable name An identifier in a program that represents the actual value of a storage location.

VDT [*Video Display Terminal*] A terminal on which printed and graphic information are displayed on a televisionlike monitor and into which data are entered on a typewriterlike keyboard.

Vector graphics A method for creating and maintaining a screen image as patterns of lines, points, and other geometric shapes.

Vector-scan monitor An electron beam forms the image by scanning the screen from point to point. (Contrast with *raster-scan monitor*.)

Version number A number that identifies the release version of a software package.

Very large-scale integration (VLSI) An integrated circuit with a very densely packed concentration of electronic components. (Contrast with *large-scale integration*, or *LSI*.)

VGA [*Video Graphics Array*] A circuit board that enables the interfacing of very high-resolution monitors to microcomputers.

Video display terminal See *VDT*.

Videodisk A secondary storage medium that permits storage and random access to video or pictorial information.

Videotext The merging of text and graphics in an interactive communications-based information network.

Virtual machine (VM) The processing capabilities of one computer system created through software (and sometimes hardware) in a different computer system.

Virtual memory The use of secondary storage devices and primary storage to expand effectively a computer system's primary storage. (Related to *page*.)

Virus See *computer virus*.

Vision input systems A device that enables limited visual input to a computer system.

Voice data entry device A device that permits voice input to a computer system (also called a *voice recognition device*).

Voice message switching Using computers, the telephone system, and other electronic means to store and forward voice messages. (Contrast with *electronic mail*.)

Voice recognition device See *voice data entry device*.

Voice response unit A device that enables output from a computer system in the form of user-recorded words, phrases, music, alarms, or anything that might be recorded on tape.

Walkthrough, structured See *structured walkthrough*.

Widow The last line of a paragraph that is printed as the first line on a page in a word processing document.

Wildcard (character) Usually a ? or an * that is used in microcomputer software commands as a generic reference to any character or any combination of characters, respectively.

Winchester disk Permanently installed, continuously spinning magnetic storage medium that is made up of one or more rigid disk platters. (See also *hard disk*.)

Window (1) A rectangular section of a display screen that is dedicated to a specific activity or application. (2) In integrated software, a "view" of a designated area of a worksheet, such as a spreadsheet or word processing text.

Window panes Simultaneous display of subareas of a particular window.

Windows A software product of Microsoft Corporation that provides a graphical user interface and multitasking capabilities for the MS-DOS environment.

Word For a given computer, an established number of bits that are handled as a unit.

Word processing Using the computer to enter, store, manipulate, and print text.

Word wrap A word processing feature that automatically moves, or "wraps," text to the next line when that text would otherwise exceed the right margin limit.

Workbench technologies See *CASE*.

Workspace The area in a Windows window in which the software application is run.

Workstation The hardware that permits interaction with a computer system, be it a mainframe or a multiuser micro. A VDT and a microcomputer can be workstations.

Worm A program that erases data and/or programs from a computer system's memory, usually with malicious intent.

WORM [*Write-Once, Read Many disk*] An optical laser disk that can be read many times after the data are written to it, but the data cannot be changed or erased.

Write To record data on the output medium of a particular I/O device (tape, hard copy, workstation display). (Contrast with *read*.)

WYSIWYG [*What You See Is What You Get*] A word processing package in which what is displayed on the screen is very similar in appearance to what you get when the document is printed.

XMODEM A standard data communications protocol for file transfers.

XON/XOFF A standard data communications protocol.

X.12 An ANSI communications protocol that has been adopted for electronic data interchange transactions.

X.25 A standard communications protocol for networks that involves packet switching.

X.75 A standard communications protocol for networks that involves international interconnections.

Zoom An integrated software command that expands a window to fill the entire screen.

INDEX

Note: When several page references are noted for a single entry, **boldface** denotes the page(s) on which the term is defined or discussed in some depth. Page references refer to the text, photo, and figure caption material.

Absolute cell addressing, **170–71**
Accelerator, 81
Access arm, 112–15
Access time, 115
Accumulator, 73
Accuracy of computers, 26
Acoustical coupler, 207
Active drive, **284**, 289
Add-on boards, **21**, 81–82 (*see also* Add-on cards)
Add-on cards, 81–82
Address:
   data communications, 208–209
   disk, 114
   memory, 68
Alpha character, 65–66
Alphanumeric keyboard, **44**
ALT (alternate key), 47
Altair 8800, **26**, 28, 30
Alternate key (*see* ALT)
Analog signal, 205
Animation, 156
Apple Computer, Inc., 27
Apple Macintosh, 28, 30, 84
Apple II, **26–27**, 30, 84
Application window, **316**, 319
Applications of computers:
   art, 143, 149, 154
   artificial intelligence, 16
   construction/architecture, 7, 218
   data communications, 200, 203, 208, 210, 212, 217, 220, 224, 227
   education, 13, 15, 55, 108
   entertainment, 8, 14–15, 119, 266
   financial services, 12, 14–15, 17
   food and beverage, 236
   general:
      accounts payable, 236
      accounts receivable, 236
      inventory management and control, 7–8
      office automation, 10
      payroll, 23–24
      project management and control, 236
   health care, 16, 22
   insurance, 22
   legal, 8, 93
   manufacturing, 95, 102, 267
   personal computing, 7–8
   publishing, 236
   real estate, 15–16
   retail sales, 15, 75, 103, 118, 236
   science and research, 5
Applications software, 29 (*see also* Productivity software)
Architecture, 78–79 (*see also* Open architecture *and* Closed architecture)
Argument (electronic spreadsheet), 174
Arithmetic and logic unit, 67, **72**
Arithmetic operations, **170**, 172
Artificial intelligence (AI), 16–17
ASCII, **65–66**, 95, 201
ASCII file, 139
Asynchronous transmission, 222–23
Atanasoff, John, 26
AT&T, **29**, 39, 214
Attributes, 185
AUTOEXEC.BAT FILE, 303–304
Authorization codes, 259
Automated design tools, 256
Automation, effects of, 279–80

Background, 76
Backspace key, 47
Backup, 40–41, **56–57**, 109
Backup, file, **56–57**, 259, 301–302
Bar codes, 95
Bar graph, 12, **155**, 178–79
Bar menu, 50–51
BASIC, **28–29**, 30, 72, 247
Batch files, 303–307
Baud, 209
Binary numbering system, 64
Bit, **64–66**, 74, 79–80, 182–83, 225–26
Bit-mapped, 149
Bits per inch (*see* bpi, disk)
Bits per second (*see* bps)
BKSP (backspace) key, 47
Block operations (word processing), 129–30
Boilerplate, 140–41
Boldface (word processing), 133–35
Boot the system, 41–42, **69**, 288–89
bpi, disk (bits per inch), 114
bpi, tape (bytes per inch), 116
bps (bits per second), **209**, 226

Bridge, 221
Bubble memory, 67
Bug, 250
Bulletin board, **15**, 226–27, 276
Bus architecture, 79–80
Bus topology, 214–16
Buying a micro, 336–47
Byte, **65**, 74
Bytes per inch (*see* bpi, tape)

C, 247
Cables (data communications), 220
Cache memory, **69**, 116
CAD (computer-aided design), 158–59
CAL command, 304
Calendar (Windows), 330
Capacity of RAM, 73–75
Cardfile (Windows), 330
Careers, 271–72
Cascading menu (Windows), 317
Cascading windows, 323
CD (change directory), 295
CD-ROM, **118–19**, 217
Cell (spreadsheet), **11**, 167–68
Cell address, 167
Cell status line, 168
Centering (word processing), 133
Centronics connector, 80
CGA (color graphics adaptor), 101–102
Channel, **209–13**, 217, 225
Character, 182–83
Characters per second (cps), 102
Chips, 20–21
   making of, 70–71
CHKDSK (check disk), 302–303
Click, 48
Clip art, 142, **144**
Clock (Windows), 330
Clock cycle, 74
Clone, 84
Closed architecture, 78–79
CLS (DOS clear screen), 296
Cluster controller, 207
Clustered bar graph, 179
CMOS, 67
Coaxial cable, **210**, 217, 220
COBOL, 72, **247**

369

Coding programs, 247–50
Color adaptor, 81
Color/graphics adaptor (*see* CGA)
Color monitor, 100–102
Columns (spreadsheet), 167
COMMAND.COM, 40
Command levels, 49–52
Commodore-64, **28**, 30
Common carriers, 213–14
Common systems, 236
Communications, data (*see* Data communications)
Compaq Computer Corporation, **26**, 84–85
Compaq Portable Computer, **28**, 30
Computer, 22–23 (*see also* Computer system, Microcomputer, *and* Processors)
Computer careers, 271–72
Computer competency, **6–7**, 339
Computer crime, 256–59, **273–76**
Computer graphics (*see* Presentation graphics)
Computer hardware (*see* Hardware)
Computer network, 14–16, 201–203, **214–21**, 276
Computer programming (*see* Programming)
Computer retail stores, 337–38
Computer revolution, 5
Computer systems, **22–26**, 66–69, 72–85, 233–38
Computer virus (*see* Virus)
Computers in society, 266–80
CON (console keyboard), 296
Configuration (computer system), **78–82**, 92
Connectivity, **201**, 204 (*see also* Data communications)
Context sensitive, 53
Continuous-form scanners, 96
Control unit, 67, **69**
Conventional memory, 76–77
Coprocessor, 81
COPY command, 297–98
COPY CON command, 296–97
Cottage industry, 227
CP/M, 29
CPU (central processing unit), 67
Crime (*see* Computer crime)
Crosshair device, 94
Cryptography, 259
Crystal oscillator, 74
CSMA/CD (Carrier Sense Multiple Access/Collision Detection), 218
CTRL (control) key, **47**, 298–99, 301
Current cell, 168
Current program, 76
Current window, 53
Cursor, graphics, **48**, 51, 93–94, 150, 319, 329
Cursor, text, 44
Cursor-control keys, 44
Customized reports, 192–93
Cyberphobia, 6
Cylinder, 114–15

Daisy-wheel printer, 102–104
Data, 24
  hierarchy of, 182–85
Data base, 12, **182–85**
  design, 241–42
  structure, 188
Database software, **12**
  concepts, 182–93
  function, 181–82
  use, 193–94
Data bits, 225–26
Data cartridge, 116
Data communications, **200–201** (*see also* Connectivity)
  carriers, 213–14
  channels, **209–12**, 217, 225
  hardware, 204–209
  line controls, 221–23
  networks, 14–16, 201–203, **214–21**, 276
  parameters, 225–26
  protocols, 204, **221–23**
  security, 259
  server, 220
  satellites, 211–12
  software, 8–9, **12–13**, 201, 223–27
Data diddling, 275
Data encryption/decryption, 259
Data flow, 225
Data flow diagram (DFD), 240, **244–45**
Data item, 183
Data management, 165–94
Data store symbol, 244
dBASE II, 29–30
dBASE IV, 246
Decision support system (DSS), 237–38
Decode, 65
Decoder, 69
Decryption, 259
DEC VT-52, 225
DEC VT-100, 225
Default options, **41**, 51, 127
DEL (delete) command, 298
DEL (delete) key, 47
Density (secondary storage), **111**, 116
Desktop (Windows), 314–15
Desktop film recorders, **107**, 157
Desktop page printer, **105–106**, 142–43
Desktop personal computers, 21
Desktop publishing (DTP), 8, **11**, 106, 136
  concepts, 143–48
  function, 142
  use, 148
Desktop typesetters, 105
Desktop software (Windows), 330
DESQVIEW, 77
Detailed system design, 241, **243–45**
Device controller, 65
Dialog box, **318–20**, 327
Dial-up line, 214
Digital signal, 205
Digitize, 96
Digitizer tablet and pen, 94
Dimmed (Windows), 316–17
DIR (directory) command, 293–96
Direct access, 110

Direct conversion, 252–53
Direct-access processing (*see* Random processing)
Direct processing (*see* Random processing)
Directory, **284–86**
  changing, 295
  creating, 295
  removing, 295–96
  tree, 285, 326
Disk address, 114
Disk, magnetic (*see* Magnetic disk)
Disk caching, 116
Disk drive (*see* Magnetic disk drives)
Disk drive icon, 321–22
Disk organization, 113–14
DISKCOPY (copy a disk), 301–302
Diskette, 55–56, 78, **111**
  care of, 55–56
Diskette-based PC, 283
Document-composition, 146
Document-composition software, 142–43
Document-conversion programs, 139
Document file (word processing), 137
Document icon, 321
Document scanners, 96
Document window (Windows) 319–20
Documentation, 248–51
DOS (*see* MS-DOS)
Dot-matrix printer, **102–104**, 157
Dots per inch (*see* dpi)
Down-line processor, 205, **207–208**
Downloading, **14**, 216, 224
dpi (dots per inch), 105
Drag (mouse), 48–49
Draw software, 153–54
Drive specifier, 284
Drum plotter, 106
Dumb terminal, **216**, 224
Dvorak keyboard, 93
Dynamic show, 156

Echo, **226**, 304–305
EDI (electronic data interchange), **202–203**, 221
EFT (electronic funds transfer), 15
EGA (enhanced graphics adapter), **81**, 101–102
EISA (Extended Industry Standard Architecture), 85
EL (electroluminescent) technology, 100
Electroluminescent technology (*see* EL technology)
Electronic bulletin board, **15**, 226–27, 276
Electronic data interchange (*see* EDI)
Electronic dictionary, 137–38
Electronic funds transfer (*see* EFT)
Electronic mail, **15**, 226–27, 269–70
Electronic spreadsheet (*see* Spreadsheet software)
E-mail (*see* Electronic mail)
Encode, 65
Encoding systems, 65–66
Encryption, 259
END key, 46

INDEX 371

Enhanced graphics adapter (*see* EGA)
ENIAC, 70
ENTER key, 46
Entity symbol, 244
EPROM, 68–69
ERASE command, 298
ESC (escape) key, 47
Ethernet, 218
Even parity, 225–26
Execution time (E-time), 73
Expanded memory, 76–78
Expansion slot, **21**, 81–82
Expert system, **16–17**, 238
Extended Industry Standard Architecture (*see* EISA)
Extended memory, 76–78
External modem, 205–206
External DOS commands, 283, **289**, 292

Facsimile machine, 227
FAX (*see* Facsimile machine)
Field, 48, **182–84**
File, **182–84**, 284
File (desktop publishing), **144**, 146
File (MS-DOS):
   naming a, 284
   referencing a, 284
File (word processing), 136–37
File management, 40
File Manager (Windows), 318, 321, **324–28**
File menu, 327–28
File server, 220–21
File transfer, 223–24
Filtering (data base), 191
Microprocessors, 21
Fixed disk (*see* Hard disk)
Flatbed plotter, 106
Flatbed image scanner, 96–97
Flat file, 185
Flat-panel monitor, 100
Flexible disk (*see* Diskette)
Floppy disk (*see* Diskette)
Flowcharting, 240, **249–50**
Flow line symbol, 244
Fonts, 142, **144**
Footer label, 136
Footnote, 36
Footprint, 276
Foreground, 76
FORMAT (a disk), 292–93
Formatting:
   spreadsheet, 175–76
   word processing, 127
Formulas (spreadsheet), 168, **172–75**
Fourth-generation languages (4GLs), **237–38**, 247
Frame (desktop publishing), 144
Front-end processor, 205, **207–209**
Full-duplex channel, 225
Full-screen editing, 128
Functional specifications, 241
Function keys, **43–44**, 92–93, 298–301
Functions (spreadsheet), 174–75

Gang of Nine, 84–85
Gas plasma technology, 100
Gateways, 221
General system design, 241–42
Geosynchronous orbit, 211
Graceful exit, 43
Grammar checker, 138
Graphical user interface (GUI), 29–30, **38**, 54, 83, 100, 312–13
Graphics adapter, 81
Graphics-conversion program, 159
Graphics mode, **100–101**, 149
Graphics cursor, **48–49**, 150
Graphics software, 8–9, **12**, 148–59, 177–79
Grey scales, 100
Groupware, 286
GUI (*see* Graphical user interface)

Half-duplex channels, 225
Half-size expansion slots, 82
Hand-held image scanner, 96–97
Handshaking, **208–209**, 222
Hard-copy output, 9–10, 75
Hard disk, 42, 81, **110–113**, 143, 283
Hardware, 24
   data communications, 204–209
   input devices, 24, **92–99**
   output devices, 24, 92, **100–108**
Header (token ring network), 218
Header label (word processing), 136
Help (Windows), 332
Help commands, 52–53
Heuristic knowledge base, 238
Hierarchy of data organization, 182–85
High memory area (HMA), 77–78
History, microcomputer, 26–30
HOME key, 46
Host processor, 205, **207–208**
Hot key, 76
Hypertext, 193–94
Hyphenation, 136

IBM (International Business Machines), 27
   AT, 78
   compatibles, 27
   OS/2, **39**, 83
   PC (Personal Computer), **27–28**, 30, 78, 84
   PC-DOS, 39
   PS/2 (Personal System 2), **28**, 30, 79, 84
   XT, 20
Icon, 48, 78
Icon (Windows), 321–22
   application, 321
   disk drive, 321
   document, 321
   program item, 321
Idea processor, 138–39
Image processing, 125, **148–59**
Image scanners, **96–97**, 142–43
Impact printers, 102–105
Indent (word processing), 139
Industrial robots, 267

Information, **24**, 234
Information network, 14–16
Information services, **14–16**, 226–27, 270–71, 339
Information society, 4
Information systems, 234–37
   development (*see* Systems development process)
   security (*see* Security)
Ink-jet printer, 102, **105**, 157
Input, **18**, 23–25
Input devices, 24, **92–99**
INS (insert key), 47
Insert mode, 47, **127–28**
Installing hardware and software, 40–41
Instruction register, 72
Instruction time (I-time), 73
Integrated circuits, 70–71
Integrated software package, **14**, 141–42, 177–81
Intel microprocessors, **20–21**
   286, 21
   386, **21**, 74
   486, **21**, 74, 85
   686, 21
Intelligent terminal, 224
Interchangeable magnetic disk, 42, **110–16**
Internal battery powered clock/calendar, 81
Internal DOS commands, **289**, 293–98
Internal modem, 205–206
International Business Machines (*see* IBM)
Intracompany networking, 202–203
Invoke (macro), 52

Jobs, Steven, 27
Joystick, 93–94
Justification (word processing), 135

KB (*see* Kilobyte)
Kb (*see* Kilobit)
Keyboard, 24, **43–48**, 78, 92–93
Keyboard template, 44
Key field, 191
Key pad, 44
Keystroke buffer, 48
Kilobit (Kb), 74
Kilobyte (KB), 74
Knowledge base, **16–17**, 238
Knowledge engineer, **16**, 238
Knowledge worker, **4**, 268

Label (spreadsheet), 168
Label scanner, 95
LAN (local area network) **216–21**, 286
LAN Manager (Microsoft), 221
Landscape format, 105
Laptop personal computer, 21
Layout (screen or page), 241
Layout line (word processing), 127
LCD (liquid crystal display) technology, 100
Leased line, 214
Light pen, 94

Line (communications), 209–13
Line controls, 221–23
Line-draw (word processing), 136
Line graph, 12, **179**
Liquid crystal display technology (*see* LCD technology)
Local area network (*see* LAN)
Logic bomb, 274
Logical operators, 189–91
Logical record (*see* Record)
Logon, 23
Lotus 1-2-3, **29**, 246
LPT1, 304

Machine cycle, 72–73
Machine language, 72
Macintosh computer, **28**, 30, 84
Macintosh DOS, 39
Macros, 38, 49, **52**
Magnetic disk drive, 25, 78, **109–10**
Magnetic disk, **24**, 110–115
Magnetic tape, 110, **116–17**
Magnetic tape drive, **109**, 116–17
Mail merge, 139–40
Main menu, **49–50**, 151
Mainframe computers, 17–18
Management information system (*see* MIS)
Masquerading technique (computer crime), 275
Master file, 24
Mb (*see* Megabit)
MB (*see* Megabyte)
MBASIC, 28
MCA (Micro Channel Architecture), 85
MD (make directory), 295
Mean time between failure (MTBF), 26
Megabit, 74
Megabyte, 74
MegaHertz (MHz), 74
Memory (*see* RAM)
Memory-resident program, 29, **76**
Menu, 38, **43**, 45
   hierarchy, 49–52
   tree, 49–50
   types, 50
Menu bar, 318
Message (communications), **208–209**, 218–19
Message frame, 218–19
Micro Channel Architecture (*see* MCA)
Micro-mainframe link, 216
Microcomputers, 4–5, **17–22**, 143
   buying, 336–47
   care and maintenance of, 54–56
   configuring, 78–82
   defined, 19–22
   history of, 26–30
   installing, 40–41
   operating systems, 29
   popularity of, 5–6
   productivity software (*see* Productivity software)
   reliability of, 26
   speed of, 25, **73–74**

systems, **17–18**, 22–26, 233–38
Microdisk, 55–56, **111**
Microfloppy, 111
Microns, 70
Microprocessor, **19–20**, 23, 67
Microsecond, 25–26
Microsoft Corporation, **29**, 39, 82–83
Microwave radio signals, 211–12
Millisecond, 25–26
Minicomputer, 17–18
MIS (management information system), 234–35
Mnemonics, 51
MODE command (MS-DOS), 304
Modem, 81, **205–207**, 209
Monitor, 24, **100–102**
Monochrome monitor, 100
Motherboard, 20
Motion video, 82
Motorola microprocessors, 20–21
Mouse, **12**, 48, 78, 93, 143
   and Windows, 82–83
MS-DOS, **29**, 39
   and multitasking, 76–78
   and windows, 82
   commands, 283, **289–307**
   directories, 284–86, 296–98
   files, 284, 296–98
   functions, 40
   keyboard functions, 298–301
   installing, 40–41
   prompt, 283–84
   tutorial, 283–307
Multifunction add-on board, 82
Multitasking, **75–78**, 82–83
Multiuser micros, 21–22
Multiuser operating systems, 84

Nanosecond, **25–26**, 70, 74
Navigation, 52
Near-letter-quality (NLQ) printer, 104
Near-typeset-quality copy, **11**, 142
Needs analysis, 241
Negligence (computer crime), 275
NetWare (Novell), 221
Network interface card (NIC), **81–82**, 218
Network topologies, 214–16
Networks, 14–16, 201–203, **214–21**, 276
Node, 214, 218
Nonimpact printers, **102**, 105–106
Non-Windows application, 313
Notepad (Windows), 330
Nubus, 85
Numbered list (word processing), 136
Numeric characters, 65–66
Numeric entry (spreadsheet), 168–69

OCR (optical character recognition) scanners, 95
Odd parity, 225–26
Office automation, 10
Off-line, 110

On-line, 110
On-line thesaurus, 137
Op-code (*see* Operation code)
Open architecture, 78–79
Operand, 72
Operating environment (*see* Platform)
Operating system, 29, **39–40**, 76, 283 (*see also* MS-DOS, tutorial)
Operating System/2 (*see* OS/2)
Operation code (op-code), 72–73
Optical character recognition scanners (*see* OCR scanners)
Optical fiber, **210**, 217, 220
Optical laser disk, **109**, 117–20
Optical-mark scanners, 96
OS/2 (Operating System/2), **39**, 83
Outline (word processing), 136
Output, **18**, 23–25
Output devices, 24, 92, **100–108**

Page layout, 11
PageMaker, 143
Page printers, 105–106
Page scanner, 95
Pages per minute (ppm), 102
Pagination (word processing), 136
Paintbrush (Windows), 328–29
Paint software, 150–53
Palmtop PC, 21
Paradox, 246
Parallel conversion, 252–53
Parallel port, 80–81
Parallel transmission, 80
Parameters (data communications), 225–26
Parity bit, 225
Parity checking, 225–26
Parity error, 225
Pascal, 247
Password, **14**, 275
Path (directory), 285
Payroll systems (*see* Applications of computers, general)
PC-DOS, **29**, 39 (*see also* MS-DOS)
Pen plotter, 106
Peripheral devices, **20**, 91–120, 340 (*see also* Input devices, Output devices *and* Data storage, secondary)
Personal computer (PC), 5 (*see also* Microcomputer)
Personal computing, 7–17
Personal identification number (PIN), 14
Personal System/2 (*see* PS/2)
PGUP/PGDN keys, 46
Phased conversion, 252–53
Picosecond, 25–26
Picture file, 146
Pie graph, 12, **155**, 179
Pilot conversion, 252–53
Pixels, 100
Platform, **82–85**, 312–13, 339–40
Plotters, **106**, 157
Pocket personal computer, 21
Point-and-draw devices, 93–94
Pointer (spreadsheet), 168

INDEX

Pop-out menu, 50
Pop-up menu, 50
Port, 80
Portable computer, **21**, **28**, 80
Portrait format, 105
Post-implementation evaluation, 253–54
Power down, 41, **43**
Power up, 41–42
PPM (*see* Pages per minute)
Presentation graphics, **12**, 107, 154–58, 177–79 (*see also* Graphics software)
Presentation Manager, 83
Primary key field (data base), 191
Primary storage (*see* Storage, primary)
Print buffer, 81
Print file, 146
Print server, 220
Printers, **24**, 102–106
   impact, 102–105
   nonimpact, 105–106
   page, 105–106
   serial, 102–105
Printer spooler, 81
Privacy of personal information, 272–73
Private line, 214
Process symbol, 244–45
Processing, 23–25
Processors, 23, **66–69**, 72–78, 81, 205, 207–209
   internal components, 67–69, 72–73
   speed and capacity of, 73–78
Productivity software (microcomputer), **8–14**, 246–47
   communications, 8–9, **12–13**
   database, 8–9, **12**, 29, 81–94
   desktop publishing (DTP), 8, **11**, 136, 143–48
   graphics, 8–9, **12**, 148–59, 177–79
   spreadsheet, 8, **11–12**, 29, 166–81
   word processing, **8–10**, 29, 126–42, 146, 148
Program coding, 248
Program description, 248
Program documentation, 248–51
Program icon (Windows), 321
Program Manager (Windows), 323–24
Program register, 72
Programmable read-only memory (*see* PROM)
Programmer, 28
Programming, 28–29, 52, 246–51
   tools, 246–47
Programming languages, 246–47
Project team, 239–40
PROM (programmable read-only memory), 68–69
Prompt, system (DOS), 42, 283–84
PROMPT command (DOS), 289, 303–304
Protocols, communications (*see* Communications, Protocols)
Prototyping, 254–56
PS/2, **28**, 30, 79, 84
Pull-down menu, 50–51

Quattro software, 246
Query by example, 188–91
QWERTY, 92–93

RAM (random-access memory), **40**, 42, 64, 67–69, 72–81, 115 (*see also* Storage, primary)
RAM disk, 116
Random access, 110
Random-access memory (*see* RAM)
Random processing, 110–15
Range (spreadsheet), 168–69
Raster graphics, 149–50
RD (DOS remove directory), 295–96
Read-only memory (*see* ROM)
Read operation, 25
Read/write head, **112–14**, 116
Record, **24**, 162–84
Registers, 72
Relational database, 185–86
Relational operators, 189–91
Relative cell address (spreadsheet), 170–71
Reliability of computers, 26
REM (DOS remark), 304–305
Remote terminal, **14**, 224–25
REN (DOS rename file), 298
Replace feature (word processing), 132
Replace mode (*see* Typeover mode)
Reserved memory, 76–78
Resident font, 144
Resolution (screen), 100
Reverse video, 130
Ring topology, 214–15
Robots, 267
ROM (read-only memory), **42**, 68–69, 144, 218
Root directory, 285–86
Rotational delay time, 115
Rows (spreadsheet), 167
RPG, 72
RS-232C connector, 80

Salami technique (computer crime), 275
Sans serif typeface, 144–45
Satellites, 211–12
Scalable typeface, 144–45
Scanners (OCR), 95
Scanning technique (computer crime), 275
Scavenging technique (computer crime), 275
Screen capture programs, 159
Screen format (data base), 187–88
Screen image projector, **107**, 158
Scroll arrows, 319
Scroll bar, 319
Scroll box, 319
Scrolling, 44–45
Search feature (word processing), 130–32
Search string, 132
Secondary key field (data base), 191
Secondary storage (*see* Storage, secondary)
Sector organization, 113–15
Security:
   computer center (physical), 256–59
   information systems (logical), 259

Seek time (disk), 115
Sequential access, 110
Sequential processing, 110
Serial port, 80–81
Serial printer, 102–105
Serial representation, 113
Serial transmission, 80
Serif typeface, 144–45
Serpentine organization, 117
Server, 220–21
Shareware, 10
Shell, 54
SHIFT key, **47**, 298
Short slot (*see* Half-size expansion slot)
Shortcut key, 318
Shrink (Windows), 317
SideKick, 29
16-bit bus, 79–80
16-bit processor, 74
Smart modem, 207
Societal issues, 266–80
Soft-copy output, 78
Soft font, 144
Soft keys (*see* Function keys)
Software, 5
Software, history, 28–30
Sorting (data base), 191
SPACE bar, 47
Specialized common carrier, 214
Speech-recognition device, 97
Speech synthesizer, 96–97, **107–108**
Speed of computers, 25, **73–74**
Spelling checker, 137–38
Spooling, 75
Spreadsheet software, 8, **11–12**, 29
   concepts, 166–76
   database capabilities, 179, 181
   function, 166
   graphics capabilities, 177–79
   use, 176–81
Stacked-bar graph, 178–79
Stand-alone computer, 13–14
Star topology, 214–15
Start/stop bits, **222–23**, 226
Stop bits (*see* Start/stop bits)
Storage, 23–24
   primary, **64**, 67–68, 73–78, 108–109
   secondary, **64**, 108–120
Streamer tape drive, 117
Structure data base, 188
Structure chart, **243**, 248–49
Structured system design, 243
Style checker, 138
Style-sheet file, 146
Subdirectory, 285–86
Subscripts (word processing), 136
Supercomputers, 17–18
Superscripts (Word processing), 136
Super VGA (video graphics adapter), 101–102
Superzapping technique (computer crime), 275
Surge protector, 55
Switch (DOS), 293
Switched line, 214

Synchronous transmission, 222–23
Syntax error, 250–51
System board, 20
System check, 42
System conversion, 252–53
System prompt (*see* Prompt, system)
System specification review, 247
Systems analyst, 239–41
Systems design, 241–45
Systems development methodology, 239
Systems development process, 239–54
Systems prompt, 42
Systems software, 39–40

TAB key, 47
Tables (relational data base), 185–86
Tailgating technique (computer crime), 275
Tape drive (*see* Magnetic tape drive)
Tape, magnetic (*see* Magnetic tape)
Telecommunications, **201**, 275
Telecommuting, **227**, 268–69
Telephone lines, 209–10
Teleprocessing (TP), 201
Templates, 97, **166**, 176
Terminal, 12
Terminal (Windows), 328–29
Terminal-emulation mode, **216**, 222–25
Terminate-and-stay-resident (*see* TSR)
Text chart, 155
Text cursor, 44
Text entry (spreadsheet), 168–69
Text file, 146
Text mode, **100–101**, 149
Text processing, 125–48
Thermal printer, 102, **105**
Third-generation languages, 247
32-bit bus, 79–80
32-bit processor, 79–80
36-pin Centronics connector, 80
Throughput, 69
Tiled windows, 323
Title bar, 316
Toggle, **47**, 127

Token ring, 218–19
Total connectivity, 204
Tower personal computer, 21
TPI (*see* Tracks per inch)
Track ball, 93–94
Track:
   magnetic disk, 114–15
   magnetic tape, 117
Tracks per inch (TPI), 114
Transfer rate, 116
Transmission medium, 216
Transmission time, 116
Trap door technique (computer crime), 275
Tree, directory, 285
Trojan horse, 275
TSR, 76
TTY, 225
Typefaces, 142, **144**
Typeover mode, 47, **127–28**

Underline (word processing), 133–35
Uninterruptible power source (UPS), 258
UNIX, 29, **39**, 84
Uploading, **14**, 38, 216
User friendly, 52

VCR backup, 82
VDT (video display terminal), 12
Vector graphics, 149–50
Ventura Publisher, 143,
VGA (video graphics adapter), **81**, 101–102, 143, 149
Video display terminal (*see* VDT)
Video graphics adapter (*see* VGA)
Virus, 38, **275–78**
VisiCalc, 29–30
Vision-input system, 98–99
Voice data entry, 97–98
Voice response unit, 107–108

"What if" analysis, 176–77
Wildcard characters (DOS), 286–88
Winchester disk, **111–12**, 114
Window pane, 54
Windows, 38, **53**, 312
Windows software, **29–30**, 54, 77, 82–83, 312–14
   accessory applications, 328–31
   applications, 314, 323–31
   concepts, 314–23
   desktop software, 330
   File Manager, 318, 321, 324–28
   Paintbrush, 328
   Program Manager, 323–24
   Terminal, 329
   using, 331–35
   Write, 328
Word length, 73–74
Word processing, **8–10**, 29, 142, 146, 148
   concepts, 127–39
   function, 126
   use, 139–43
WordStar, 29–30
Word wrap (word processing), 128
WordPerfect software, 84, **139**, 148
Workspace (Windows), 319
Wozniak, Steve, 27
WP command, 304
Write (Windows), 328
Write operation, 25
Write-protect notch, 55
Write-protect tab, 55
WYSIWYG, 137

XENIX, 39
XMODEM, **222**, 225
XON/XOFF, **222**, 225
X.25, 221
X.12, 221
X.75, 221–22

Zoom, 53–54

PHOTO ACKNOWLEDGMENTS

CHAPTER 1 **4, 5:** courtesy of International Business Machines Corporation; **7:** Compaq Computer Corporation; **8:** photos courtesy of Hewlett-Packard Company; **12:** courtesy of International Business Machines Corporation; **13:** Control Color Corporation; **13:** courtesy of International Business Machines Corporation; **15:** Compuserve; **16, 17:** Courtesy of International Business Machines; **18:** Boeing Computer Services; **19:** photo courtesy of Hewlett-Packard Company; **20:** courtesy of International Business Machines Corporation; **21:** photo courtesy of Hewlett-Packard Company; **22:** Grid Systems Corporation; **22:** courtesy of International Business Machines Corporation; **27:** courtesy of Apple Computer, Inc.; **28:** courtesy of International Business Machines Corporation; **30:** Microsoft Corporation.

CHAPTER 2 **38, 39:** courtesy of International Business Machines Corporation; **41:** photo courtesy of Hewlett-Packard Company; **45, 48, 53, 55:** courtesy of International Business Machines Corporation.

CHAPTER 3 **64:** courtesy of International Business Machines Corporation; **70–71:** 1, 7, 8, 12—courtesy of International Business Machines Corporation, 2—Micron Technology, 3, 4—© M/A-COM, Inc., 5, 10—courtesy of Unisys Corporation, 6—AT&T Technologies, 9—National Semiconductor Corporation, 10—courtesy Intel Corporation; **75:** courtesy of International Business Machines Corporation; **76:** photo courtesy of Hewlett-Packard Company; **79, 80:** courtesy of International Business Machines Corporation; **81:** Harcom Security Systems Corporation; **83:** courtesy of Apple Computer, Inc.; **84:** Courtesy of International Business Machines Corporation.

CHAPTER 4 **92:** courtesy of International Business Machines Corporation; **93:** GRiD Systems Corporation; **94:** courtesy of International Business Machines Corporation; **95:** photo courtesy of Hewlett-Packard Company; **96:** Xerox Imaging Systems/Kurzweil, a Xerox Company; **97, 100:** courtesy of International Business Machines Corporation; **101:** Inter-ad, Inc.; **102, 103:** courtesy of International Business Machines Corporation; **105:** photo courtesy of Hewlett-Packard Company; **106, 107:** courtesy of International Business Machines Corporation; **108:** Franklin Electronic Publishers, Inc.; **109, 111:** courtesy of International Business Machines Corporation; **113:** Seagate Technology; **115:** courtesy of International Business Machines Corporation; **118:** Information Handling Services—An ITG Company; **199:** courtesy of International Business Machines Corporation.

CHAPTER 5 **126:** courtesy of International Business Machines Corporation; **129:** photo courtesy of Hewlett-Packard Company; **138:** Reference Software; **141:** NEC Home Electronics [U.S.A.] Inc.; **143:** photo courtesy of Hewlett-Packard Company; **146:** AST Research Inc.; **149, 154:** Pansophic Graphics Systems; **157:** CalComp; **158:** Calma Company.

CHAPTER 6 **167:** Funk Software; **175:** Long and Associates; **177, 182, 184:** courtesy of International Business Machines Corporation.

CHAPTER 7 **200:** EDS photo by Steve McAlister; **203:** courtesy of International Business Machines Corporation; **206:** photo courtesy of Hewlett-Packard Company; **210:** courtesy of International Business Machines Corporation; **210:** Long and Associates; **212:** NASA; **212:** TRW Inc.; **217:** Compaq Computer Corporation; **220, 224, 227:** courtesy of International Business Machines Corporation.

CHAPTER 8 **235:** courtesy of International Business Machines Corporation; **237:** photo courtesy of Hewlett-Packard Company; **240:** courtesy of International Business Machines Corporation; **242:** Cadre Technologies Inc.; **246:** KnowledgeWare, Inc., Atlanta, GA, USA; **251:** courtesy of International Business Machines Corporation; **254:** courtesy of Compaq Computer Corporation; **255:** General Motors Corporation; **258:** courtesy of International Business Machines Corporation.

CHAPTER 9 **266:** Dynatech Corporation; **267:** courtesy of International Business Machines Corporation; **268:** GRiD Systems Corporation; **269:** courtesy of Apple Computer, Inc.; **271:** courtesy of International Business Machines Corporation; **273:** TRW, Inc.; **274, 278:** courtesy of International Business Machines Corporation; **279:** NASA.

APPENDIX B **312, 315, 331:** Microsoft Corporation.

APPENDIX C **338:** Computerland; **340:** courtesy of Apple Computer, Inc.; **341, 343:** courtesy of International Business Machines Corporation; **344:** Compaq Computer Corporation.